About the Author and this Book

"One finds new insights on every page, and what is more, finds that these become more profound with each reading."
    —**Arthur Versluis**, University of Michigan

"One of the leading authorities of the Perennialist School, Titus Burckhardt brought a unique combination of gifts to the exposition of the world's great wisdom traditions. Burckhardt was at home in a variety of religious worlds and able to speak with authority on many wide-ranging subjects. His eloquently written and beautifully crafted books are an enduring treasure."
    —**James Cutsinger**, University of South Carolina, author of *Paths to the Heart: Sufism and the Christian East*

"Two words spring to mind on reading *The Essential Titus Burckhardt*: awe and gratitude. Awe because of the extraordinary perception and beauty of his writing—from his masterly analysis of Christian art and his profound and penetrating understanding of the Renaissance, to short pieces such as 'The Wooden Chest' or 'Bathing in the Ganges' in which he opens our eyes to the language of sacred symbolism as no other author has succeeded in doing. And gratitude, such tremendous gratitude that we now have at our disposal writings of such caliber to guide us through not just sacred and traditional art but through so much else besides (for example, evolution and modern psychology). With the sharp sword of Truth he sees through the illusions of modern art as few other writers have done, as well as giving us such beautiful poetic writing as in, to give one of many examples, his book on Fez.

"As a teacher of the principles of traditional art this book will be my primary sourcebook! It is a treasure and should be on the shelves of every teacher of art and every art student today."
    —**Emma Clark**, author of *Underneath Which Rivers Flow: The Symbolism of the Islamic Garden*

"Mr. Burckhardt has attended our Indian ceremonies, including the Sun Dance, and he has learned our legends and our sacred ways around the campfires. He knows and understands the spirit of the olden-day Indians."
   —**Thomas Yellowtail**, Crow Sun Dance Chief

"As a writer and thinker on a wide range of topics integral to the sacred traditions, Titus Burckhardt has an unerring ability to reach to the essential truths and to speak persuasively of their relevance and importance to the contemporary mind."
   —**Brian Keeble**, author of *Art: For Whom and For What?*

"René Guénon remarked that it is frequently easier to understand first principles than the countless intermediate degrees which lie between mankind's ultimate metaphysical Goal and our present existential awareness. Otherwise stated, cosmology can be and often is more complex than metaphysic. Nevertheless, it is in the nature of human intelligence to seek a unified and comprehensive world-view in which to situate oneself, take one's bearing, and follow a saving orientation. Titus Burckhardt, lifelong friend of Frithjof Schuon, certainly did not neglect metaphysic but his predilection was cosmology. The great merit of *The Essential Titus Burckhardt* is that it provides lucid and salutary insights into many cosmological enigmas and into moot questions of human nature which is so intimately related to cosmology. In addition, the reader will find in this book unequivocal refutations of many of the false notions intrinsic to modernity. William Stoddart, the anthologist, has made excellent choices from the extensive Burckhardt oeuvre, and the book is highly recommended for anyone who does or would like to take seriously the human vocation to transcend oneself."
   —**Alvin Moore, Jr.**, editor of *Selected Letters of Ananda K. Coomaraswamy*

"Titus Burckhardt has always been a primary inspiration to me. I had the privilege of meeting him in London in the 1970s, with S. H. Nasr. His bearing, modesty and natural reticence hid his great stature as an artist, scholar, and man of wisdom. I recommend this book to all today."
   —**Keith Critchlow**, author of *Islamic Patterns: An Analytical and Cosmological Approach*

"Titus Burckhardt was one of the most authoritative exponents of the Perennialist school. His work was centrally concerned with the interrelationships of Truth, Beauty and Goodness, with the principles informing traditional arts and sciences, and with the nexus between intellectuality and spirituality. This marvelous compilation of some of his most arresting and significant work will command the attention of anyone seriously interested in the ways of the spirit."

> **—Kenneth Oldmeadow**, La Trobe University, Bendigo,
> author of *Traditionalism: Religion in the Light of the Perennial Philosophy*

"Burckhardt's thought is clear and soberly articulated, his argumentation intuitive and profound."

> **—Victor Danner**, Indiana University

"The writings of Titus Burckhardt convey in a uniquely faithful and transparent way the truths by which he himself lived, which sustained him and which fashioned all aspects of his existence. The total sincerity and clarity of exposition of the author cannot but attract the reader to That Itself from which these truths radiate. No doubt this was what Titus Burckhardt had wished whenever he took his pen and wrote."

> **—Jean-Claude Petitpierre**, colleague of Titus Burckhardt

"For anyone who has dreamt that art and architecture is more than a fancy play of aesthetics, Burckhardt's essays set the stage for the fiat lux of the soul before the miracle of revelational art. To read him is to see form transfigured into sacred intelligence."

> **—Mark Perry**, author of *On Awakening & Remembering*

"He devoted all his life to the study and exposition of the different aspects of Wisdom and Tradition. In the age of modern science and technocracy, Titus Burckhardt was one of the most remarkable exponents of universal truth."

> **—William Stoddart**, the Editor

World Wisdom
The Library of Perennial Philosophy

The Library of Perennial Philosophy is dedicated to the exposition of the timeless Truth underlying the diverse religions. This Truth, often referred to as the *Sophia Perennis*—or Perennial Wisdom—finds its expression in the revealed Scriptures as well as the writings of the great sages and the artistic creations of the traditional worlds.

The Perennial Philosophy provides the intellectual principles capable of explaining both the formal contradictions and the transcendent unity of the great religions.

Ranging from the writings of the great sages of the past, to the perennialist authors of our time, each series of our Library has a different focus. As a whole, they express the inner unanimity, transforming radiance, and irreplaceable values of the great spiritual traditions.

The Essential Titus Burckhardt: Reflections on Sacred Art, Faiths, and Civilizations appears as one of our selections in The Perennial Philosophy series.

The Perennial Philosophy Series

In the beginning of the Twentieth Century, a school of thought arose which has focused on the enunciation and explanation of the Perennial Philosophy. Deeply rooted in the sense of the sacred, the writings of its leading exponents establish an indispensable foundation for understanding the timeless Truth and spiritual practices which live in the heart of all religions. Some of these titles are companion volumes to the Treasures of the World's Religions series, which allows a comparison of the writings of the great sages of the past with the perennialist authors of our time.

The illustrations on the front cover are: the Temple at Chidambaram,
South India; the Byodoin Temple near Kyoto, Japan; the Cathedral
at Chartres, France; and the Mosque of the Andalusians at Fez, Morocco.

The Essential
Titus Burckhardt

Reflections on Sacred Art, Faiths, and Civilizations

Edited by
William Stoddart

Foreword by
Seyyed Hossein Nasr

World Wisdom

The Essential Titus Burckhardt:
Reflections on Sacred Art, Faiths, and Civilizations
© 2003 World Wisdom, Inc.

Library of Congress Cataloging-in-Publication Data

Burckhardt, Titus.
   [Selections. English. 2003]
   The essential Titus Burckhardt : reflections on sacred art, faiths, and civilizations / edited
by William Stoddart ; foreword by Seyyed Hossein Nasr.
         p. cm. – (The perennial philosophy series)
Includes bibliographical references (p. 311) and index.
   ISBN 0-941532-36-4
   1. Religion. 2. Religious art. 3. Tradition (Philosophy) I. Stoddart, William. II. Title. III.
Series.
BL50 .B86513 2003
291–dc21

                                                                        2002156450

Printed on acid-free paper in China

For information address World Wisdom, Inc.
P.O. Box 2682, Bloomington, Indiana 47402-2682

www.worldwisdom.com

Contents

Illustrations in Color

Black-and-white illustrations in the text

Aliquid est in anima quod est increatum et increabile; si tota anima esset talis, esset increata et increabilis; et hoc est Intellectus.

There is something in the soul which is uncreated and uncreatable; if the whole soul were such, it would be uncreated and uncreatable; and this is the Intellect.

Meister Eckhart

Preface

The Swiss art historian and cultural anthropologist, Titus Burckhardt, wrote more than a dozen books in either German or French. Most of them are now available in English translation and, as a result, his writings have, over the past few years, become familiar to certain sectors of the English-speaking public.

In order to bring Burckhardt's work to the attention of a wider readership, it was felt that an anthology of some of his more important pieces was now desirable.

Making such a selection has been both easy and difficult. Easy, because almost any passage from Burckhardt's writings conveys interesting information and enlightening interpretation, and does so in his characteristic and unique style. In this sense, one can hardly go wrong. On the other hand, the task has been difficult, because picking and choosing amongst good things is always difficult. Faced with this problem, one wants, with St. Theresa of Lisieux, to say: "I choose all!"—a very good policy, no doubt, but not for an anthology.

An attempt, therefore, has been made to select a representative range of extracts which will include many of Titus Burckhardt's most original and significant contributions to those fields in which he has become an acknowledged and admired expert. We believe that these extracts cannot fail in their purpose. Nevertheless, they are, by definition, incomplete, and it is our hope that the interested reader, having been stimulated by the part, will turn to the whole. This he may do by seeking out the original publications which are listed in the bibliography.

The sub-title of this book may call for a word of explanation. T. S. Eliot stressed that each of the great world cultures—Byzantine, Medieval, Islamic, Chinese, or other—is the social and artistic expression of one of the great world religions. Each religion originates in a revelation, and this original deposit is handed down—unchanged in essence, but often increasingly elaborated in expression—by the power of tradition. It is through this social and artistic deployment that we call "tradition" that the original revelation comes to permeate, and imprint its particular stamp on, every sector of collective life. It is precisely this permeation of a society by a religion that enables us to speak of a "traditional" culture, and justifies the quasi-equation of "faiths" and "civilizations". It is with the artistic, cultural, and philosophical aspects of the various traditional civilizations of the world that Titus Burckhardt's writings are mainly concerned.

Mention should be made of a particular, and very characteristic, procedure that Burckhardt employs in his books on cities and countries, and this is what he himself calls "allowing contemporary witnesses to speak for themselves". He brings into play long extracts from the writings of chroniclers and outstanding personalities of the place and time concerned, thus conferring an unusual degree of intimacy and immediacy on his narrative. Above all, his practice of providing long quotations gives the reader a unique access to fascinating documents of the past which he would be highly unlikely to come across otherwise. A generous number of these historical quotations have been retained in this anthology.

One of the things that strikes one most forcibly about Titus Burckhardt is the vastness of his range of interests. The world was indeed his parish. He was at home in every "traditional" civilization, and of this, the present volume gives ample evidence in the shape of the extracts dealing with Medieval Christendom, Islam, Hinduism, Buddhism, Taoism, and the religion of the Sacred Pipe and the Sun Dance. He was also well acquainted with the workings of the present-day world, as his critiques of the limitations of the modern sciences (biology, psychology, and physics) show.

The headings under which the extracts are grouped are an attempt to "marshal" the vast material, and to convey to the reader the scope and nature of the subjects dealt with. The order of presentation may or may not be logical. The subject matter is variegated, and the reader will no doubt, on consulting the table of contents, go first of all to the sections most likely to be of interest to him. Burckhardt's manner of approach, and angle of vision, however, are constant throughout.

The reader approaching the writings of Titus Burckhardt for the first time will quickly discover that they call for close and sustained attention. They do not make for easy reading. But for those who fall in love with the profound and unchanging message contained in Burckhardt's expositions, they become a joy and a necessity.

Titus Burckhardt was a major figure in what later became known as the "traditionalist" or "perennialist" school of thinkers and authors. A brief account of Titus Burckhardt's life and work, and of some of the key principles of the "traditionalist" authors, is provided in the Introduction which follows.

William Stoddart

Titus Burckhardt

Titus Burckhardt (*left*) with Frithjof Schuon in Switzerland in the 1950's.

Foreword

Titus Burckhardt is without doubt one of the central figures of what has come to be known as the School of Tradition. He is at once a master of metaphysics and cosmology; an expert on the traditional arts of East and West; a pioneering expositor and translator of major Sufi texts; the keenest observer the West has produced of the traditional art, life, and thought of the Islamic Maghrib, particularly Morocco; and a master expositor of traditional patterns of social life. Burckhardt has left behind a precious legacy of works written in German and French, of which many have been translated into several European languages, especially English, as well as into Arabic, Persian, Turkish and Urdu. Burckhardt was blessed with a remarkable power of intellectual penetration combined with visual intelligence. He was both metaphysician and artist and, above all, a saintly person in whom the truth had become realized in all aspects of his being, in his thoughts and words as well as in his actions and deeds. He was not only a person who wrote of the wedding of the soul with the spirit and the turning of the lead of the soul into gold, but one in whose being that alchemical transmutation had taken place in an operative manner. His works complement in many ways those of his close friend Frithjof Schuon and, in the domain of art, those of A. K. Coomaraswamy.

Burckhardt wrote about metaphysics with the greatest clarity and produced books and articles of unparalleled depth concerning the traditional sciences, particularly alchemy, on which he wrote what is probably the most outstanding work of the 20th century. His criticisms of the modern world, following in the wake of René Guénon's pioneering works, penetrated into the most contentious questions and brought out with exceptional clarity the errors of such modern deviations as Darwinian evolution and modern psychoanalysis. It was, however, especially in the field of art that he produced a legacy of unrivaled value. Not only did he reveal the metaphysical truths of various traditional civilizations as expressed through the language of sacred art, but he also composed a number of illuminating works on Christian art, such as *Chartres and the Origin of the Cathedral,* both in relation to the total vision of Christianity and to the traditional sciences which made the production of Christian sacred art as revealed in the medieval cathedral possible.

It was particularly in the domain of Islamic art that Burckhardt was a veritable pioneer. What Coomaraswamy achieved for Hindu and Buddhist art in unveiling their symbols and expounding their inner meaning, Burckhardt accomplished for Islamic art in a number of seminal essays as well as in his masterpieces *The Art of Islam* and *Fez, City of Islam*. It was he who for the first time in the West brought out the inner meaning of Islamic art and its relation to the inner teachings of the Islamic religion.

Burckhardt was also a pioneer in unlocking the meaning of the major doctrinal works of Sufism through the translation of the central work of Islamic gnosis, the *Fusus al-Hikam* of Ibn 'Arabi, as well as *Al-Insan al-Kamil* of 'Abd al-Karim al-Jili, while in his metaphysical masterpiece, *An Introduction to Sufi Doctrine*, he expounded the quintessence of Islamic gnosis (*al-ma'rifah*) in his own words. The extensive interest in Ibn 'Arabi manifested in the West during the past half century owes much to his works.

The influence of Burckhardt has been extensive not only in the West but also in the Islamic world. In Morocco, where he played a major role in the preservation of the city of Fez and in the revival of the traditional arts and crafts, he is widely known and respected to this day, and he is still referred to by the older generation as "wonderful Sidi Ibrahim" who first came to Morocco in the 1930s, embraced Islam, learned Arabic and made Morocco his second home.

We had the great blessing of having been closely associated with Burckhardt from 1957 until his death and of having been in his company in Europe as well as in the Islamic world, in the Alps as well as by the eastern shore of the Mediterranean. In all different circumstances he displayed a keenness of vision, both intellectual and artistic, and a remarkable state of collectedness and humanity. How wonderful it was to circumambulate the Ka'bah in Mecca with him or to sit in silent meditation by his side at the tomb of Ibn 'Arabi in Damascus! All who knew Burckhardt well were deeply impressed by the combination of extraordinary intelligence and exceptional virtue that were molded together in inseparable unity in this truly exceptional being.

Although he knew English well, Burckhardt wrote primarily in his mother tongue, German, as well as in French. It is fortunate that most of his works have been rendered into English by competent translators, of whom the most important is William Stoddart, the editor of this volume. Thoroughly versed in Burckhardt's writings and also his friend of many years, Stoddart was the most qualified person to present to the English reader an anthology of the works of this great master of traditional doctrines. World Wisdom must be congratulated in having chosen Stoddart to edit the present volume, which through carefully selected pieces makes available an anthology that is exceptional in both depth and breadth. The present work reveals nearly every major aspect of the Burckhardtian *oeuvre* and, in addition, is adorned with photos of objects of sacred art which were of special concern to Burckhardt as well as including several of his own sketches that reveal his gifts as an artist. Moreover, the editor has added a very useful bibliography of the works of Burckhardt in European languages (but not including translations into Islamic languages). One therefore hopes that the anthology will not only provide a door into the mansion of the multifarious works of Burckhardt, but will also lead the reader to discover with the help of the bibliography the original works from which the selections of the anthology have been drawn.

Both World Wisdom and William Stoddart are to be congratulated for making available this most precious anthology of one of the most important and enduring bodies of writings produced in the 20th century on metaphysics, religion, the traditional arts and sciences, and the study of traditional societies, a body of work whose message is as urgently needed now as when it was first written, for it deals with perennial truths which transcend the accidents of time and space and remain always timely because they are timeless.

Seyyed Hossein Nasr
December 2002
Laylat al-qadr of Ramadan AH1423

Introduction

Titus Burckhardt and the Perennialist School

Titus Burckhardt, a German Swiss, was born in Florence in 1908 and died in Lausanne in 1984. He devoted all his life to the study and exposition of the different aspects of Wisdom and Tradition.

In the age of modern science and technocracy, Titus Burckhardt was one of the most remarkable of the exponents of universal truth, in the realm of metaphysics as well as in the realm of cosmology and of traditional art. In a world of existentialism, psychoanalysis, and sociology, he was a major voice of the *philosophia perennis*, that "wisdom uncreate" that is expressed in Platonism, Vedanta, Sufism, Taoism, and other authentic esoteric or sapiential teachings. In literary and philosophic terms, he was an eminent member of the "traditionalist" or "perennialist" school of 20th century thinkers and writers.

The two originators of the perennialist school were the Frenchman René Guénon (1886-1951) and the German Frithjof Schuon (1907-1998). It may be of interest to note in passing that two other celebrated wisdom schools had dual originators, namely, those associated with Socrates and Plato in 5th century B.C. Athens, and with Rûmî and Shams ad-Dîn Tabrîzî in 13th century Turkey. Yet another exalted example of dual collaboration was that of Hônen and Shinran, founders of the Pure Land school of Buddhism, in 12th-13th century Japan.

René Guénon traced the origin of what he called the modern deviation to the ending of the Middle Ages and the arrival of the Renaissance, that cataclysmic inrush of secularization, when nominalism vanquished realism, individualism (or humanism) replaced universalism, and empiricism banished scholasticism. An important part of Guénon's work was therefore his critique of the modern world from an implacably "Platonic" or metaphysical point of view. This was fully expounded in his two masterly volumes *The Crisis of the Modern World* and *The Reign of Quantity*. The positive side of Guénon's work was his exposition of the immutable principles of universal metaphysics and traditional orthodoxy. His main source was the Shankaran doctrine of "non-duality" (*advaita*), and his chief work in this respect is *Man and His Becoming According to the Vedanta*. However, he also turned readily to other traditional sources, since he considered all traditional forms to be various expressions of the one supra-formal Truth. Another important aspect of Guénon's work was his brilliant exposition of the intellectual content of traditional symbols, from whichever religion they might come. See in this connection his *Fundamental Symbols of Sacred Science.*

It is important to note that Guénon's writings, decisively important though they were, were purely "theoretical" in character, and made no pretense of dealing with the question of realization. In other words, they were generally concerned with intellectuality (or doctrine) and not directly with spirituality (or method).

The sun rose for the traditionalist school with the appearance of the work of Frithjof Schuon. Thirty years ago, an English Thomist wrote of him: "His work has the intrinsic authority of a contemplative intelligence."[1] More recently, a senior American academic declared: "In depth and breadth, a paragon of our time. I know of no living thinker who begins to rival him."[2] T. S. Eliot's perception was similar. Regarding Schuon's first book, he wrote in 1953: "I have met with no more impressive work in the comparative study of Oriental and Occidental religion."

Schuon wrote more than twenty philosophical books in French, and, towards the end of his life, a cycle of more than 3,000 didactic poems in his native German. His philosophical works began to appear during the latter part of Guénon's life. Until his dying day, Guénon used to refer to him (for example in the pages of *Études Traditionnelles*) as "notre éminent collaborateur". Schuon continued, in even more notable fashion, the perspicacious and irrefutable critique of the modern world, and reached unsurpassable heights in his exposition of the essential truth—illuminating and saving—that lies at the heart of every revealed form. Schuon called this supra-formal truth the *religio perennis*. This term, which does not imply a rejection of the similar terms *philosophia perennis* and *sophia perennis*, nevertheless contains a hint of an additional dimension which is unfailingly present in Schuon's writings. This is that intellectual understanding entails a spiritual responsibility, that intelligence requires to be complemented by sincerity and faith, and that "seeing" (in height) implies "believing" (in depth). In other words, the greater our perception of essential and saving truth, the greater our obligation towards an effort of inward or spiritual "realization".

---

1. Bernard Kelly, in *Dominican Studies* (London), Vol. 7, 1954.
2. Emeritus Professor Huston Smith, 1974.

Schuon's work began with a comprehensive general study, the very title of which serves to set the scene: *The Transcendent Unity of Religions*. His further works include: *Language of the Self* (on Hinduism), *Treasures of Buddhism*, *Understanding Islam*, *Castes and Races*, *Logic and Transcendence* and *Esoterism as Principle and as Way*, a wide-ranging compendium of philosophic and spiritual enlightenment. His long German poetic cycle, of which so far only fragments have been published, covers countless aspects of metaphysical doctrine, spiritual method, the role of virtue, and the function of beauty—not merely in general terms, but with uncanny intimacy, detail, and precision. They exhibit an incredible degree of sharpness, profundity, and compassion.

The work of Guénon and Schuon was soon taken up by two illustrious continuators: the Indian Ananda K. Coomaraswamy (1877-1947) who wrote in English, and the German-Swiss Titus Burckhardt, who wrote in both German and French.

Ananda Coomaraswamy, an outstanding scholar and the distinguished Keeper of the Oriental Collection at the Boston Museum of Fine Arts, was already known as an authority on the art and esthetics of both East and West when he encountered the works of Guénon. Although this occurred relatively late in his life, he was thoroughly convinced by the traditionalist viewpoint as expounded in Guénon's books. His vast erudition enabled him to demonstrate in fascinating detail the manifold flowering of the traditional civilizations to which the great revelations gave rise. Coomaraswamy's principal earlier works include *Medieval Sinhalese Art* (1908), *The Dance of Shiva* (1912), *Rajput Paintings* (1916), and *History of Indian and Indonesian Art* (1927). Amongst the more important books of his later period are *Christian and Oriental or True Philosophy of Art* (1943), *Figures of Speech or Figures of Thought* (1946) and *Am I My Brother's Keeper?* (1947).

We shall turn presently to the other continuator, Titus Burckhardt,[3] but first let us take a closer look at what is meant by the

---

3. The works of these four key figures of the perennialist school did not remain without effect. Their influence soon began to spread, and other like-minded writers quickly followed suit, including Martin Lings, Marco Pallis, Lord Northbourne, Whitall Perry, and Joseph Epes Brown, the well-known authority on the American Indians. Several distinguished Islamicists, such as Seyyed Hossein Nasr, also took the tenets of the *religio perennis* as the basis of their expositions. Already in the mid-seventies, Professor Jacob Needleman declared that, whatever one's opinion of the main themes of the perennialist school might be,

expression *religio perennis*. One of the fundamental tenets of the *religio perennis* is that, at the center of each religion, there is a core of truth (about God, man, prayer, and salvation) which is identical. In other words, in spite of the plurality of forms, there is a common essence. In addition, within each religion, there is also a means of salvation, which is essentially a way of union. This doctrine of essential or transcendent unity has its source in universal metaphysics, which (in Vedantic terms) is fundamentally discernment between the Absolute (*Âtmâ*) and the Relative (*Mâyâ*). According to this doctrine—as represented variously by Shankara (Hinduism), Plato (Greece), Eckhart (Christianity), and Ibn 'Arabî (Islam)—only the Divine Essence ("Beyond-Being") is Absolute, whereas the Creator or Personal God ("Being"), as the first self-determination of the Divine Essence ("Beyond-Being"), is already within the domain of the relative. The Creator, nevertheless, is "absolute" with regard to his creation, and in view of this may be qualified as "the relatively Absolute". The Personal God, as originator of creation, is "the prefiguration of the relative in the Absolute". Within creation itself, there is a "reflection of the Absolute in the relative", and this is the *Avatâra*; the Prophet; the Savior; it is also Truth, Beauty, and Virtue; Symbol and Sacrament. This brings us to the doctrine of the Logos, with its two faces, created and uncreated: The "prefiguration of the relative in the Absolute" (the Creator or Personal God) is the *uncreated* Logos; the "reflection of the Absolute in the relative" (the *Avatâra*; Symbol, or Sacrament) is the *created* Logos. This is already an indication of what is meant by a means of salvation: the religious adherent, by uniting himself sacramentally with the created Logos, finds therein a means of uniting himself with the Uncreated: namely, God as such.

no serious study of religion or spirituality could henceforth be undertaken without taking its insights into account. Such indeed has proved to be the case, and an increasing number of academics in the field of religious studies, who espouse the perennialist point of view, have appeared on the scene, including Professor Huston Smith, formerly of MIT and Berkeley, Professor James Cutsinger of South Carolina, Professor Patrick Laude of Georgetown, and Professor Kenneth Oldmeadow of Victoria, Australia. Also, within the realm of Christian spirituality, the renowned Trappist monk Thomas Merton was a profound admirer of Frithjof Schuon, and had a protracted correspondence with some of the leading perennialists. The English Catholic sculptor, Eric Gill, was also deeply influenced by this school, as both his sculptures and his writings bear witness.

Let us now return to Titus Burckhardt: although he first saw the light of day in Florence, Burckhardt was the scion of a patrician family of Basle. He was the great-nephew of the famous art-historian Jacob Burckhardt and the son of the sculptor Carl Burckhardt. Titus Burckhardt was Frithjof Schuon's junior by one year, and they spent their early schooldays together in Basle around the time of the First World War. This was the beginning of an intimate friendship and a deeply harmonious intellectual and spiritual relationship that was to last a lifetime.

Burckhardt's chief metaphysical exposition, beautifully complementing the work of Schuon, is *An Introduction to Sufi Doctrine*. This is an intellectual masterpiece which analyzes comprehensively and with precision the nature of esoterism as such. It begins by making clear, by a series of lucid and economical definitions, what esoterism is and what it is not, goes on to examine the doctrinal foundations of Islamic esoterism or Sufism, and ends with an inspired description of "spiritual alchemy", or the contemplative path that leads to spiritual realization. This work clearly established Burckhardt as the leading exponent, after Schuon, of intellectual doctrine and spiritual method. On the specific question of the perennialists' use of the term "Intellect" (*Intellectus* = *Spiritus*, not *mens* or *ratio*), see the quotation from Meister Eckhart on p. *x*.

Burckhardt devoted a large portion of his writings to traditional cosmology, which he saw in a sense as the "handmaid of metaphysics". He formally presented the principles at stake in a masterly and concise article "The Cosmological Perspective", first published in French in 1948 and now constituting a chapter in the present volume. Much later—in a series of articles published in both French and German in 1964—he covered the cosmological ground very fully indeed, and also made many detailed references to the main branches of modern science. All of these articles are included in the present book, in the section entitled "Traditional and Modern Science".

Not unconnected with his interest in cosmology, Burckhardt had a particular affinity with traditional art and craftsmanship and was skilled in the evaluation of traditional architecture, iconography, and other arts and crafts. In particular, he dwelt on how they had been—and could be—turned to account spiritually, both as meaningful activities which by virtue of their inherent symbolism harbor a doctrinal message, and above all as supports for spiritual realization and means of grace. *Ars sine scientiâ nihil.* Here of course it is a case of *scientia sacra* and *ars sacra*, these being the two sides of the same coin. This is the realm of the craft initiations of the various traditional civilizations, and specifically of such things, in the Middle Ages, as operative masonry and alchemy. Indeed Burckhardt's principal work in the field of cosmology was his full-length book *Alchemy: Science of the Cosmos, Science of the Soul*, a brilliant presentation of alchemy as the expression of a spiritual psychology and as an intellectual and symbolic support for contemplation and realization.

Burckhardt's main work in the field of art was his *Sacred Art in East and West*, which contains masterly chapters on the metaphysics and esthetics of Hinduism, Buddhism, Taoism, Christianity, and Islam, and ends with a useful and practical insight into the contemporary situation entitled "The Decadence and Renewal of Christian Art". Many extracts from this book are included here.

During the fifties and sixties Burckhardt was the artistic director of the Urs Graf Publishing House of Lausanne and Olten. His main activity during these years was the production and publication of a whole series of facsimiles of exquisite illuminated medieval manuscripts, especially early Celtic manuscripts of the Gospels, such as the Book of Kells and the Book of Durrow (from Trinity College, Dublin) and the Book of Lindisfarne (from the British Library, London). This was pioneer work of the highest quality and a publishing achievement which immediately received wide acclaim both from experts and the wider public.

His production of the magnificent facsimile of the Book of Kells brought him a remarkable encounter with Pope Pius XII. The Urs Graf Publishing House wished to present a copy of the edition to the saintly and princely Pope, and it was decided that there could be no better person to effect the presentation than their artistic director Burckhardt. In the eyes of the Pope, Burckhardt was ostensibly a Protestant gentleman from Basle. The Pope granted him a private audience at his summer residence at Castelgandolfo. When, in the audience chamber, the white-clad figure of the Pope suddenly appeared, he welcomingly approached his visitor and said to him in German: "Sie sind also Herr Burckhardt?" ("So you are Herr Burckhardt?"). Burckhardt bowed and, when the Pope offered him his hand bearing the Fisherman's Ring, he respectfully took it in his. As a non-Catholic, however, he kissed, not the ring (as is the custom amongst Catholics), but the Pope's fingers. "Which the Pope smilingly permitted," Burckhardt adds.

Together they talked about the Dark Ages and about the sur-passingly beautiful manuscripts of the Gospels that had been so lov-ingly and so finely produced during them. At the end of the audience the Pope gave his blessing: "From my heart I bless you, your family, your colleagues, and your friends."

It was during these years with the Urs Graf Publishing House that Burckhardt presided over an interesting series of publications with the general title of *Stätten des Geistes* ("Homesteads of the Spirit"). These were historical-cum-spiritual studies of certain man-ifestations of sacred civilization, and covered such themes as Mount Athos, Celtic Ireland, Sinai, Constantinople, and other places. Bur-ckhardt himself contributed three books in the series: *Siena, City of the Virgin, Chartres and the Birth of the Cathedral*, and *Fez, City of Islam*. *Siena* is an enlightening account of the rise and fall of a Christian city which, architecturally speaking, remains to this day something of a Gothic jewel. Most interesting of all, however, is the story of its saints. Burckhardt devotes many of his pages to St. Catherine of Siena (who, amongst other things, was a powerful influence on the Pope of her day) and to St. Bernardino of Siena (who was one of the greatest Catholic practitioners—and teachers—of the invoca-tory mode of prayer, based on the saving power of the Holy Name). *Chartres* is the story of the religious "idealism" (in the best sense of the word) which lay behind the conception and practical realization of the medieval cathedrals—the still extant monuments of an age of faith. In *Chartres*, Burckhardt expounds the intellectual and spiri-tual contents of the different architectural styles—distinguishing in this respect not merely between the Gothic and the Romanesque, but even between the different varieties of the Romanesque. It is a dazzling example of what is meant by intellectual discernment or discrimination.

One of Burckhardt's several masterpieces is undoubtedly his *Fez, City of Islam*. As a young man, in the 1930s, he spent a few years in Morocco, where he established intimate friendships with several remarkable representatives of the as yet intact spiritual heritage of the Maghrib. This was obviously a formative period in Burckhardt's life, and much of his subsequent message and style originates in these early years. Already, at the time concerned, he had committed much of his experience to writing (not immediately published), and it was only in the late 1950s that these writings and these expe-riences ripened into a definitive and masterly book. In *Fez, City of Islam*, Burckhardt relates the history of a people and its religion—a history that was often violent, often heroic, and sometimes holy. Throughout it all runs the thread of Islamic piety and civilization. These Burckhardt expounds with a sure and enlightening hand, relating many of the teachings, parables, and miracles of the saints of many centuries, and demonstrating not only the arts and crafts of Islamic civilization, but also its "Aristotelian" sciences and its administrative skills. There is indeed much to be learnt about the governance of men and nations from Burckhardt's penetrating presentation of the principles behind dynastic and tribal vicissitudes—with their failures and their successes.

Close in spirit to *Fez* is another of Burckhardt's mature works, namely *Moorish Culture in Spain*. As always, this is a book of truth and beauty, science and art, piety and traditional culture. But in this book, perhaps more than in all others, it is a question of the romance, chivalry, and poetry of pre-modern life.

During his early years in Morocco, Burckhardt immersed himself in the Arabic language and assimilated the principal classics of Sufism (Islamic mysticism) in their original form. In later years, he was to share these treasures with a wider public through his translations of Ibn 'Arabî[4] and Jîlî.[5] One of his most important works of translation was of the spiritual letters of the renowned 18th century Moroccan Shaikh Mulay al-'Arabî ad-Darqâwî.[6] These letters constitute a spiritual classic and are a precious document of practical spiritual counsel.

Burckhardt's last major work was his widely acclaimed and impressive monograph *Art of Islam*. Here the intellectual principles and the spiritual role of artistic creativity in its Islamic forms are richly and generously displayed before us. With this noble volume, the unique Burckhardtian literary corpus comes to its end.

William Stoddart

---

4. *La Sagesse des Prophètes* [Fusûs al-Hikam] (Paris: Albin Michel, 1955).
5. *De l'Homme Universel* [al-Insân al-Kâmil] (Lyons: Derain, 1953).
6. *Letters of a Sufi Master* [Rasâ'il] (Bedfont, Middlesex, England: Perennial Books, 1969).

1

Some Fundamental Doctrines and Principles

How to Approach Medieval
and Oriental Civilizations

In order to understand a culture, it is necessary to love it, and one can only do this on the basis of the universal and timeless values that it carries within it. These values are essentially the same in all true cultures, that is to say, in cultures which meet not only the physical, but also the spiritual needs of man, without which his life has no meaning.

Nothing brings us into such immediate contact with another culture as a work of art which, within that culture, represents, as it were a "center". This may be a sacred image, a temple, a cathedral, a mosque, or even a carpet with a primordial design. Such works invariably express an essential quality or factor, which neither a historical account, nor an analysis of social and economic conditions, can capture. A similarly rich insight into another culture can be found in its literature, especially in those works that deal with eternal verities. But such works are by definition profound and symbolical, and are mostly unintelligible to the modern reader without the aid of a detailed commentary. A work of art, on the other hand, can, without any mental effort on our part, convey to us immediately and "existentially" a particular intellectual truth or spiritual attitude, and thereby grant us all manner of insights into the nature of the culture concerned. Thus one can more readily understand the intellectual and ethical forms of a Buddhist culture if one is familiar with the Buddha-image that is typical of it; and one can much more easily form a picture of the religious and social life of the Middle Ages if one has first assimilated the architecture of a Romanesque abbey or a Gothic cathedral—always assuming, of course, that one is sufficiently sensitive to the forms of an authentic traditional art.

*

* *

The purpose of my book *Chartres and the Birth of the Cathedral* was to evoke, as authentically as possible, the spiritual climate in which the Gothic cathedral was born. My aim was to show how the Gothic cathedral was the final fruit to ripen on the tree of an ancient tradition.

From the standpoint of the agitated and over-cerebral age in which we live, Medieval men often seem naïve, child-like, and untouched by any psychological uncertainty, and this can mislead us into thinking that they were less reflective and more instinct-bound than ourselves. In reality, however, their actions were inspired by a vision or an idea—namely, the spiritual meaning of life—to a much greater extent than in the case of modern man. It was precisely because they lived for a timeless truth that their love and their creative joy gave rise to that undivided strength which we see and admire in their productions. As has been said, they were closer both to Heaven and to earth than are we.

In modern man, generally speaking, it is the exact opposite: his motivation consists of feelings, in the service of which a whole apparatus of mental activity, theories, and "ideologies" are brought into play; for him, individual and collective passions are the underlying factor, while mental activity is visible on the surface. To put it another way (and following an observation by Frithjof Schuon), in traditional artists, it is the element "object" that determines the work, whereas in most modern artists, it is the element "subject".

To understand modern man, it may well be appropriate to study psychology; but one can only understand Medieval man if one acquires a true notion of his loftiest aims and aspirations, and if one grasps how and to what extent his ideas symbolically express what is universally and eternally true.

(from *Moorish Culture in Spain* and
Chartres and the Birth of the Cathedral)

Knowledge and Love in Sufism

It is characteristic of Sufism that its expressions often hold the balance between love and knowledge. The language of love makes it possible to express the most profoundly esoteric truths without coming into conflict with dogmatic theology. Furthermore, the intoxication of love symbolically corresponds to states of knowledge that go beyond discursive thought.

There are also expressions which, though they do not arise from an attitude of love, nevertheless evoke it, because they reflect an inner beauty which is the seal of Unity on the soul. It is from this Unity that clarity and rhythm spring, whereas any kind of mental rigidity or vanity of speech contradicts the simplicity, and thus also the transparency, of the soul with regard to Truth.

Some Sufi writers, such as Muhyi'd-Dîn ibn 'Arabî, Ahmad ibn al 'Ârif, Suhrawardî of Aleppo, al-Junaid, and Abû'l-Hasan ash-Shâdhilî manifest an attitude that is essentially intellectual. These writers look on the Divine Reality as the universal essence of all knowledge. Others, such as Omar ibn al-Fârid, Mansûr al-Hallâj, and Jalâl ad-Dîn Rûmî, express themselves in the language of love. For them, the Divine Reality is above all the limitless object of desire. But this diversity of attitude has nothing to do with a divergence between different schools, as is believed by those who consider that the Sufis who used an intellectual language had been influenced by doctrines foreign to Islam, such as Neo-Platonism, and that only those who represent a devotional attitude are the mouthpiece of authentic Islamic mysticism.

In fact, the diversity in question derives from a diversity of vocation: different vocations naturally graft themselves onto different types of human genius, and all find their place in true Sufism. The difference between an intellectual and a devotional attitude is merely the most important and the commonest of the differences that are to be found in this domain.

Hinduism makes a clear distinction between the three spiritual ways: the Way of Knowledge (*jñâna*), the Way of love *(bhakti)*, and the Way of action *(karma)*. This distinction is in fact to be found in every complete tradition. In Sufism the distinction of these three ways corresponds to the three fundamental reasons for an aspiration towards God—knowledge or gnosis *(ma'rifa)*, love *(mahabba)*, and fear *(makhâfa)*. But Sufism tends rather to the synthesis than to the differentiation of these three ways, and in fact, in "classical" Sufism, a certain equilibrium of the intellectual and emotional attitudes is always to be found. The reason for this lies in the general structure of Islam, which is founded on the doctrine of Unity (*tauhîd*), and which thus gives an intellectual orientation to all variants of spiritual life. As for the aspect of love, this arises spontaneously whenever the Divine Reality is recognized or contemplated.

Those who maintain the view that only Sufis who manifest an attitude of love truly represent the mystical aspect of Islam, wrongly apply criteria that are valid only in relation to Christianity, in which the basic theme is Divine Love. It is for this reason that the representatives of gnosis in Christianity generally express themselves— though there are exceptions—through the symbolism of Love.

In reality, the distinction between the Way of Knowledge and the Way of Love amounts to the question of predominance of one or the other, for there is never a complete separation between these two modes of spirituality. Knowledge of God always engenders love, while love always presupposes a knowledge of the object of love, even though this knowledge may be only indirect. The object of spiritual love is the Divine Beauty, which is an aspect of Infinity and, through this object, desire becomes lucid. It is in the object, Beauty, that love virtually coincides with knowledge. In a sense, Truth and Beauty are the criteria of one another, although sentimental prejudices can distort the concept of beauty just as, from another angle, rationalism limits truth.

It is highly significant that there is hardly a single Muslim metaphysician who did not compose poetry, and whose most abstract prose is not, in some passages, transformed into a rhythmic language full of poetic images. On the other hand, the poetry of the most famous adepts of love, such as Omar ibn al-Fârid and Jalâl ad-Dîn Rûmî, is rich in intellectual perceptions.

As for the attitude of fear (*makhâfa*), which corresponds to the Way of action, this is not directly manifested in the style of expression; its role is an implicit one. It is true that fear stands, as it were, only at the threshold of contemplation, but, when it is spiritualized, it can nonetheless bring man out of the collective dream which is the "world", and bring him face to face with Eternal Reality. "The Fear of God is the beginning of Wisdom." Love is higher than fear, even as knowledge is higher than love, but this is true only of direct, immediate knowledge which outstrips reason (or discursive thought), for spiritual love embraces every individual faculty and imprints each of them with the seal of Unity.[1]

(from *Introduction to Sufi Doctrine*)

1. On the question of knowledge and love and the distinction between the spiritual ways which respectively correspond to them, see *Spiritual Perspectives and Human Facts* by Frithjof Schuon (Bedfont, Middlesex: Perennial Books, 1987).

Metaphysics and Virtue
in Sufism

Sufi doctrine possesses several branches, the two most important of which are the domain of Universal Truths *(Haqâ'iq)* and the domain relating to the human or individual stages of the spiritual way *(daqâ'iq)*; in other words, metaphysics (the science of principles, or of the Principle) and virtue (the "science of the soul"). Needless to say, these two domains are not in watertight compartments. Metaphysics by definition includes everything, but in Sufism it is always linked to spiritual realization. Cosmology, which is derived from metaphysics, applies to both macrocosm and microcosm. Thus, there is a psychology which has a cosmic application and a psychology which, by analogy, applies to the soul or the inward constitution of man.

In order to be perfectly clear, it is necessary to dwell at some length on this relationship. Apart from the two domains of *Haqâ'iq* and *daqâ'iq* just mentioned, one can also distinguish, in the realm of doctrine, three principal domains, namely, metaphysics, cosmology, and spiritual psychology. These correspond to the ternary: "God, world, and soul" (Metacosm, macrocosm, and microcosm). Cosmology can thus be conceived both as the application of metaphysical principles to the cosmos (this is the contemplation of God in the world) and, analogously, as the application of metaphysical principles to the human soul.

A complete cosmology necessarily includes the microcosmic reality of the soul; and no spiritual psychology can detach the soul from macrocosmic principles. In the fabric of the cosmos there is no radical break. In its own fashion, discontinuity does exist; it is what it is. But discontinuity is barely conceivable apart from a principle of unity that bridges the gap, and without the background of a continuity that manifests it. Thus, for example, the apparent discontinuity between individuals—the relation of their respective centers of consciousness—is only the mark of their unique Essence, which transcends "vertically" the "horizontal" plane of their common nature.

In itself cosmology is an analytical science in the original meaning of this term, for it reduces every aspect of the cosmos to the underlying principles, which, in the last analysis, are the active and the passive poles: the "informing" principle (active), and the plastic, receptive substance—or *materia prima*—(passive). The integration of these complementary principles in primal Unity belongs to the realm of metaphysics, and not to cosmology.

It has just been said that Sufi psychology does not separate the soul from either the metaphysical or the cosmic order. The link with the metaphysical order provides spiritual psychology with qualitative criteria that are wholly lacking in profane psychology, which studies only the dynamic character of psychic phenomena and their immediate causes. When modern psychology pretends to be a science of the hidden contents of the soul, it nevertheless remains restricted to an individual perspective, because it possesses no means of distinguishing psychic forms that reflect universal realities, from forms that may appear "symbolical" but are no more than the vehicles for individual impulses. The so-called "collective unconscious" has nothing to do with the true source of symbols; it is nothing but a chaotic depository of psychic residues, rather like the mud of the ocean bed which retains traces of past ages.

For profane psychology the only link between the macrocosm and the world of the soul lies in the impressions that reach the soul through the door of the senses. Sufi psychology, on the other hand, takes account of the analogy between the macrocosm and the human microcosm. To this order of ideas belong such sciences as traditional astrology, the symbolism of which has sometimes been used by some Sufi, as well as by some Christian, masters.

The Sufi path can be considered as a way towards knowledge of oneself in conformity with the saying of Mohammed: "He who knows himself (*nafsa-hu*), knows his Lord". In the last analysis, this knowledge applies to the Divine Essence, the immutable Self (*Huwîya*), and thus transcends both the cosmological and the psychological perspective. At a relative level, however, since it concerns one's individual nature, knowledge of oneself necessarily includes a science of the soul. This science is also, in a sense, a "cosmology". It is first and foremost a discernment or discrimination with regard to the elements of the soul.

To demonstrate how discrimination with regard to the soul is inspired by cosmological principles, certain very general criteria of inspiration (*wârid*) may be mentioned. But first of all, it must be made clear that inspiration is understood here, not in the sense of prophetic inspiration, but in the sense of the sudden intuition that is normally provoked by spiritual practices. This inspiration may have very different sources. It is only of value when it comes from the timeless center of the being, in other words, from the ray of Universal Intelligence that connects man with God.

"Inspiration" is deceptive when it comes from the psychic world, be this the individual psyche and its subtle ambience, or the sub-human world and its satanic pole. On the other hand, the inspiration that comes from the Universal Intelligence, and thus from God, always communicates an understanding that illumines the ego, and at the same time relativizes the latter by dissipating its illusions.

Inspiration that comes from the individual psyche is the voice of some hidden passion; it has something egocentric about it, and is accompanied by pretentiousness, direct or indirect. As regards inspirations that come from the satanic pole, these invert hierarchical relationships and deny higher realities.

Impulsions that come from the individual or collective soul invariably fix on the same object—the object of some desire—whereas a satanic influence merely makes use of a passion: what it really seeks is not the object of the passion, but the negation of spiritual reality; that is why the devil, whenever his argument is destroyed, always deflects discussion by changing the "theme". He argues only to trouble man, whereas the passional soul still possesses a certain logic, which permits its impulsions to be directed into legitimate channels by sufficiently strong arguments. Satanic impulsions, on the other hand, must be rejected *in toto*. The three tendencies in question (angelic, unregenerately human, and satanic) correspond respectively to reintegration in the Divine Essence, centrifugal dispersion, and a "fall" into infra-human chaos. These three tendencies have their analogies in the universal order. Hinduism calls them *sattva* (the upward or luminous tendency, "lightness"), *rajas* (the horizontal tendency, "expansiveness"), and *tamas* (the downward or darksome tendency, "heaviness").

It may be surprising that so many Sufi books deal with the virtues, when Knowledge (*ma'rifa*) is the goal of the spiritual way, and perpetual concentration on God is the sole condition for reaching it. If the virtues are considered essential, it is because no mode of consciousness can he regarded as being outside total Knowledge—or outside Truth—nor can any inward attitude be regarded as indifferent. The "vision of the heart" (*ru'yat al-qalb*) is knowledge of the whole being. It is impossible for the heart to open itself to Divine Truth as long as the soul retains, even unconsciously, an attitude that denies Truth; avoidance of such an attitude is always precarious, since the soul *(nafs)* is *a priori* governed by egocentric illusion, which by definition presupposes a blind spot.[2] All of this amounts to saying that the science of the virtues, which applies Divine Truth to the soul, directly concerns spiritual realization. Its criteria are exceedingly subtle; it cannot be summarized in a moral code, and its formal fixations are no more than paradigms. Its object, spiritual virtue, is so to speak a "lived symbol", the right perception of which depends on a certain inward development. This is not necessarily so in the case of doctrinal understanding.

In a certain sense the Sufi method consists in the art of keeping the soul open to the influx of the Infinite. The soul has a natural tendency to remain enclosed in itself, and this tendency can be compensated only by a contrary movement acting on the same plane; this movement is, precisely, virtue. Metaphysical Truth as such is impersonal and motionless; virtue translates it into a "personal" mode.

Spiritual virtue is not necessarily a social virtue in a direct sense, and the external manifestations of one and the same virtue may differ according to the circumstances. Thus some Sufis have shown their contempt for the world by wearing poor and tattered garments; others have affirmed the same inner attitude by wearing sumptuous raiment. In a Sufi of the latter kind, the affirmation of his person is in reality a submission to the impersonal truth that he incarnates; his humility lies in his extinction in an aspect of glory which is not his own.

Even if Sufi virtue formally coincides with religious virtue, it nonetheless differs from it in its contemplative essence. For instance, the virtue of gratitude, for the mass of believers, is founded on the memory of benefits received from God; it implies a feeling that these benefits are more real than any sufferings. In the case of the contemplative, this feeling becomes certainty: for him, the plenitude of Being, present in every fragment of existence, is infinitely more real than the limits of things, and some Sufis have gone so far as to feel joy in what, for others, would only be a painful negation of themselves.

---

2. Nevertheless, man always has a certain awareness of any falsity in his attitude, even if this has not come to him through reason. It is said in the Koran: "Verily man is conscious of himself (i.e., of his soul), even though he may offer excuses." (75:13) The man who wishes to realize Divine Knowledge while despising virtue, is like a thief who wants to become righteous without restoring his theft.

The spiritual virtues are, as it were, the human supports for Divine Truth (*Haqîqa*); they are also reflections of that Truth. Now any reflection implies a certain inversion in relation to its source: spiritual poverty (*faqr*), for example, is the inverse reflection of the Plenitude of the Spirit. Sincerity (*ikhlâs*) and veracity (*sidq*) are expressions of the independence of the mind or Intellect from tendencies of the soul, while nobility (*karam*) is the human reflection of Divine Greatness. In these "positive" virtues, the inversion lies in the mode and not in the content, which means that they are, so to speak, saturated with humility, while their prototypes are made of majesty and glory.

(from *Introduction to Sufi Doctrine*)

2

Traditional and Modern Science

The Perspective of
Traditional Cosmology

The seven "liberal arts" of the Middle Ages have as their object disciplines which modern man would not hesitate to describe as "sciences", such as mathematics, astronomy, dialectic, and geometry. This Medieval identification of science with art[1], which is wholly in conformity with the contemplative structure of the *Trivium* and *Quadrivium,*[2] clearly indicates the fundamental nature of the cosmological perspective.

When modern historians look at traditional cosmology— whether this be of the Ancient world, the Orient, or the Medieval West—they generally see in it merely childish and fumbling attempts to explain the causes of phenomena. In so doing, they are guilty of an error in their way of looking at things which is analogous to the error of those who, with a "naturalistic" prejudice, judge Medieval works of art according to the criteria of the "exact" observation of nature and of the "cleverness" of the artist. Modern incomprehension of sacred art and contemplative cosmology thus arises from one and the same error; and this is not contradicted by the fact that some scholars (often the very ones who look on Oriental and Medieval cosmology with a mixture of pity and irony) pay homage to the arts in question and allow the artist the right to "exaggerate" some features of his natural models and to suppress others, with a view to suggesting realities of a more inward nature. This "tolerance" only proves that, for modern man, artistic symbolism has no more than an individual, psychological—or even merely sentimental—import. Modern scholars are unaware that the artistic choice of forms, when it pertains to inspired and regularly transmitted principles, is capable of tangibly conveying the permanent and inexhaustible possibilities of the Spirit, and that traditional art thus implies a "logic" in the universal sense of this term.[3] On the one hand, the modern mentality is blinded by its attachment to the sentimental aspects of art forms (and frequently reacts

1. In the Middle Ages it was said that "every science is an art, and every art is a science".
2. See the diagram of the Seven Liberal Arts on p. 128.
3. See Frithjof Schuon, *The Transcendent Unity of Religions*, Chapter 4, "Concerning Forms in Art" (Bedfont, Middlesex: Perennial Books, 1984).

because of a very particular psychic heredity); on the other, its starting-point is the prejudice that artistic intuition and science belong to two radically different domains. If this were not so, one would have in all fairness to grant to cosmology what one seemingly grants to art, namely the license to express itself by means of allusions and to use sensible forms as parables.

For modern man, however, any science becomes suspect if it leaves the plane of physically verifiable facts, and it loses its plausibility if it detaches itself from the type of reasoning that is based on a sort of plastic continuity of the mental faculty—as if the whole cosmos were constructed merely on the basis of the "material" or quantitative aspects of the human imagination. Such an attitude does not reflect something inherently in man, but represents a mental limitation (resulting from an extremely unilateral and artificial activity) rather than a philosophical position, for all knowledge, however relative or provisional it may be, presupposes a necessary correspondence between the order that is spontaneously inherent in the knowing mind and the compossibility of things, without which there would be no truth of any kind.[4] Now since the structural analogy between the macrocosm and the microcosm cannot be denied, and since it everywhere affirms principial unity— a unity that is like an axis in regard to which all things are ordered— it is impossible to see why the science of "nature", in the widest possible sense of this term, should not reject the crutches of a more or less quantitative experience, and why any intellectual vision (possessed as it were of a "bird's eye view") should be immediately dismissed as a gratuitous hypothesis. But modern scientists have a veritable aversion to anything that goes beyond the allegedly down-to-earth nature of "exact science". In their eyes, to have recourse to the "poetic" quality of a doctrine, is to discredit that doctrine as science. This deep "scientistic" distrust of the greatness and the beauty of a given conception shows a total incomprehension both of the nature of primordial art and of the nature of things.

Traditional cosmology always comprises an aspect of "art", in the primordial sense of this term: when man's knowledge extends beyond the corporeal world, or when the traditional cosmologist

4. See René Guénon, *Introduction to the Study of the Hindu Doctrines* (Ghent, NY: Sophia Perennis et Universalis, 2001), part 3, chapter 9, "*Nyaya*": ". . . if the idea, to the extent that it is true and adequate, shares in the nature of the thing, it is because, conversely, the thing itself also shares in the nature of the idea."

chooses to consider those manifestations, within this world, of transcendent qualities, it becomes impossible to "record" the object of knowledge in the same way as one records the contours and details of a sensory phenomenon. We are not saying that intellection of realities higher than the corporeal world is imperfect; we are referring only to its mental and verbal "fixation". Whatever can be conveyed of these perceptions of reality is inevitably in the form of speculative keys, which are an aid to rediscovering the "synthetic" vision in question. The proper application of these "keys" to the endless multiplicity of the faces of the cosmos is dependent on what may indeed be called an art, in the sense that it presupposes a certain spiritual realization or at least a mastery of certain "conceptual dimensions".

As for modern science, not only is it restricted, in its study of nature, to only one of its planes of existence (whence its "horizontal" dispersion which is contrary to the contemplative spirit); it also dissects as far as possible the contents of nature, as if to emphasize the "autonomous materiality" of things; and this fragmentation—both theoretical and technological—of reality is radically opposed to the nature of art; for art is always a wholeness, it is nothing without fullness in unity, that is to say, without rhythm and proportion.

In other words, modern science is ugly, with an ugliness that has ended by taking possession of the very notion of "reality", and by arrogating to itself the prestige of "objectively" assessing things,[5] whence modern man's irony regarding whatever, in the traditional sciences, may display an aspect of naïve beauty. Conversely, the ugliness of modern science deprives it of any value from the point of view of the contemplative and inspired sciences, for the central object of these sciences is the "unicity" of everything that exists, a unicity that modern scientists cannot in fact deny—since everything implicitly affirms it—but which, nevertheless, by its dissecting approach, prevents one from "intuiting" or "tasting".

(from *Mirror of the Intellect*)

---

5. Whence the use, in modern esthetics, of the term "realism". For the majority of people, the signs and characteristics of modern science are complex pieces of apparatus, the constant reporting of new data, a "surgical" approach, etc.

Traditional Symbolism and
Modern Empiricism

If the ancient cosmogonies seem childish when one takes their symbolism literally—and this means not understanding them—modern theories about the origin of the world are frankly absurd. They are so, not so much in their mathematical formulations, but because of the total unawareness with which their authors set themselves up as sovereign witnesses of cosmic becoming, while at the same time claiming that the human mind itself is a product of this becoming. What connection is there between the primordial nebulae—that vortex of matter whence they wish to derive earth, life, and man—and this little mental mirror that loses itself in conjectures (since, for scientists, intelligence amounts to little more) and yet feels so sure of discovering the logic of things within itself? How can the effect make judgements regarding its own cause? And if there are constant laws of nature—those of causality, number, space, and time—and if there is something within ourselves which has the right to say "this is true and this is false", where is the guarantee of truth, either in the object or in the subject? Is the nature of our mind merely a drop of foam on the waves of the cosmic ocean, as evolutionism maintains, or, on the contrary, is there, deep within it, a timeless witness of reality?

Some protagonists of the theories in question will perhaps say that they are concerned only with the physical and objective domain, without seeking to prejudge the domain of the subjective. They can perhaps cite Descartes, who defined spirit and matter as two realities, co-ordinated by Providence, but separated in fact. In point of fact, this division of reality into watertight compartments served to prepare people's minds to leave aside everything that is not of the physical order, as if man were not himself proof of the complexity of the real.

The man of antiquity, who pictured the earth as an island surrounded by a primordial ocean and covered by the dome of heaven, and medieval man, who saw the heavens as concentric spheres extending from the earth (viewed as the center) to the limitless sphere of the Divine Spirit, were doubtless mistaken regarding the true disposition and proportions of the sensible universe. On the other hand, they were fully conscious of the fact—infinitely more important—that this corporeal world is not the whole of reality; that

26

it is, so to speak, surrounded and pervaded by a reality that is both greater and more subtle; that this, in turn, is contained in the Spirit; and that, indirectly or directly, the universe, in all its extension, disappears in the face of the Infinite.

Modern man knows that the earth is only a ball suspended in a bottomless abyss and carried along in a dizzy and complex movement, and that this movement is governed by other celestial bodies incomparably larger than this earth and situated at immense distances from it. He knows that the earth on which he lives is but a grain of sand in comparison with the sun, that the sun itself is but a grain of sand amidst other incandescent stars, and that all is in motion. An irregularity in this assemblage of sidereal movements, an interference from a star foreign to our planetary system, a deviation of the sun's trajectory, or any other cosmic accident, would suffice to make the earth unsteady in its rotation, to trouble the course of the seasons, to change the atmosphere, and to destroy mankind. Modern man also knows that the smallest atom contains forces which, if unleashed, could involve the earth in an almost instantaneous conflagration. All of this, from the "infinitely small" to the "infinitely great", presents itself, from the point of view of modern science, as a mechanism of unimaginable complexity, the functioning of which is only due to blind forces.

In spite of this, the man of our time lives and acts as if the normal and habitual operation of the rhythms of nature were something that was guaranteed to him. In actual practice, he thinks neither of the abysses of the stellar world nor of the terrible forces latent in every particle of matter. He sees the sky above him, with the sun and the stars, as any child sees it, but the remembrance of the astronomical theories prevents him from recognizing in them divine signs. The sky for him is no longer the natural expression of the Spirit that enfolds and illuminates the world. Scientific knowledge has substituted itself for this "naïve", yet profound, vision, not as a new consciousness of a vaster cosmic order, an order of which man forms part, but as an estrangement, as an irremediable disarray before abysses that no longer have any common measure with him. For nothing now reminds him that in reality this whole universe is contained within himself, not of course in his individual being, but in the spirit or intellect which is within him, and which is both greater than himself and the whole phenomenal universe.

(from *Mirror of the Intellect*)

The Theory of Evolution

The least phenomenon participates in several continuities or cosmic dimensions incommensurable in relation to each other; thus, ice is water as regards its substance—and in this respect it is indistinguishable from liquid water or water vapor—but as regards its state it belongs to the class of solid bodies. Similarly, when a thing is constituted by diverse elements, it participates in their natures while being different from them. Cinnabar, for example, is a synthesis of sulphur and mercury; it is thus in one sense the sum of these two elements, but at the same time it possesses qualities that are not to be found in either of these two substances. Quantities can be added to one another, but a quality is never merely the sum of other qualities. By mixing the colors blue and yellow, green is obtained; this third color is thus a synthesis of the other two, but it is not the product of a simple addition, for it represents at the same time a chromatic quality that is new and unique in itself.

There is here something like a "discontinuous continuity", which is even more marked in the biological order, where the qualitative unity of an organism is plainly distinguishable from its material composition. The bird that is born from the egg is made from the same elements as the egg, but it is not the egg. Likewise, the butterfly that emerges from a chrysalis is neither that chrysalis nor the caterpillar that produced it. A kinship exists between these various organisms, a genetic continuity, but they also display a qualitative discontinuity, since between the caterpillar and the butterfly there is something like a rupture of level.

At every point in the cosmic web there is thus a warp and a woof that intersect one another, and this is indicated by the traditional symbolism of weaving, according to which the threads of the warp, which hang vertically on the primitive loom, represent the permanent essences of things—and thus also the essential qualities and forms—while the woof, which binds horizontally the threads of the warp, and at the same time covers them with its alternating waves, corresponds to the substantial or "material" continuity of the world.[6]

The same law is expressed by classical hylomorphism, which distinguishes the "form" of a thing or being—the seal of its essential

---

6. René Guénon, *Symbolism of the Cross* (Ghent, NY: Sophia Perennis et Universalis, 1996), chapter 14, "The Symbolism of Weaving".

unity—from its "matter", namely the plastic substance which receives this seal and furnishes it with a concrete and limited existence. No modern theory has ever been able to replace this ancient theory, for the fact of reducing the whole plenitude of the real to one or other of its "dimensions" hardly amounts to an explanation of it. Modern science is ignorant above all of what the Ancients designated by the term "form", precisely because it is here a question of a non-quantitative aspect of things, and this ignorance is not unconnected with the fact that modern science sees no criterion in the beauty or ugliness of a phenomenon: the beauty of a thing is the sign of its internal unity, its conformity with an indivisible essence, and thus with a reality that will not let itself be counted or measured.

It is necessary to point out here that the notion of "form" necessarily includes a twofold meaning: on the one hand it means the delimitation of a thing, and this is its most usual meaning; in this connection, form is situated on the side of matter or, in a more general sense, on the side of plastic substance, which limits and separates realities.[7] On the other hand, "form" understood in the sense given to it by the Greek philosophers and, following them, the Scholastics, is the aggregate of qualities pertaining to a being or a thing, and thus the expression or the trace of its immutable essence.

The individual world is the "formal" world because it is the domain of those realities that are constituted by the conjunction of a "form" and a "matter", whether subtle or corporeal. It is only in connection with a "matter", a plastic substance, that "form" plays the role of a principle of individuation; in itself, in its ontological basis, it is not an individual reality but an archetype, and as such beyond limitations and change. Thus a species is an archetype, and if it is only manifested by the individuals that belong to it, it is nevertheless just as real, and even incomparably more real, than they. As for the rationalist objection that tries to prove the absurdity of the doctrine of archetypes by arguing that a multiplication of mental notions would imply a corresponding multiplication of archetypes—leading to the idea of the idea of the idea, and so on— it quite misses the point, since multiplicity can in no wise be transposed onto the level of the archetypal roots. The latter are

---

7. In Hindu parlance, the distinction *nâma-rupa*, "name and form", is related to this aspect of the notion under study, "name" here standing for the essence of a being or thing, and "form" for its limited and outward existence.

distinguished in a principial way, within Being and by virtue of Being; in this connection, Being can be envisaged as a unique and homogeneous crystal potentially containing all possible crystalline forms.[8] Multiplicity and quantity thus only exist at the level of the "material" reflections of the archetypes.

From what has just been said, it follows that a species is in itself an immutable "form"; it cannot evolve and be transformed into another species, although it may include variants, which are diverse "projections" of a unique essential form, from which they can never be detached, any more than the branches of a tree can be detached from the trunk.

It has been justly said[9] that the whole thesis of the evolution of species, inaugurated by Darwin, is founded on a confusion between species and simple variation. Its advocates put forward as the "bud" or the beginning of a new species what in reality is no more than a variant within the framework of a determinate specific type. This false assimilation is, however, not enough to fill the numberless gaps that occur in the paleontological succession of species; not only are related species separated by profound gaps, but there do not even exist any forms that would indicate any possible connection between different orders such as fish, reptiles, birds, and mammals. One can doubtless find some fishes that use their fins to crawl onto a bank, but one will seek in vain in these fins for the slightest beginning of that articulation which would render possible the formation of an arm or a paw. Likewise, if there are certain resemblances between reptiles and birds, their respective skeletons are nonetheless of a fundamentally different structure. Thus, for example, the very complex articulation in the jaws of a bird, and the related organization of its hearing apparatus, pertain to an entirely different plan from the one found in reptiles; it is difficult to conceive how one might have developed from the other.[10] As for the famous fossil bird *Archaeopteryx,* it is fairly and squarely a bird, despite the claws at the end of its wings, its teeth, and its long tail.[11]

---

8. It is self-evident that all the images that one can offer of the non-separative distinction of the possibilities contained in Being must remain imperfect and paradoxical.
9. Douglas Dewar, *The Transformist Illusion* (Murfreesboro, Tennessee: Dehoff Publications, 1957; Ghent, NY: Sophia Perennis et Universalis, 1995). See also Louis Bounoure, *Déterminisme et Finalité* (Collection Philosophie, Paris: Flammarion).
10. Dewar, *The Transformist Illusion.*
11. *Ibid.*

In order to explain the absence of intermediate forms, the partisans of transformism have sometimes argued that these forms must have disappeared because of their very imperfection and precariousness; but this argument is plainly in contradiction with the principle of selection that is supposed to be the operative factor in the evolution of species: the trial forms should be incomparably more numerous than the ancestors having already acquired a definitive form. Besides, if the evolution of species represents, as is declared, a gradual and continual process, all the real links in the chain—therefore all those that are destined to be followed—will be both endpoints and intermediaries, in which case it is difficult to see why the ones would be much more precarious than the others.[12]

The more conscientious among modern biologists either reject the transformist theory, or else maintain it as a "working hypothesis", being unable to conceive any genesis of species that would not be situated on the "horizontal line" of a purely physical and temporal becoming. For Jean Rostand,

> The world postulated by transformism is a fairy-like world, phantasmagoric, surrealistic. The chief point, to which one always returns, is that we have never been present, even in a small way, at one authentic phenomenon of evolution. . . . We keep the impression that nature today has nothing to offer that might be capable of reducing our embarrassment before the veritably organic metamorphoses implied in the transformist thesis. We keep the impression that, in the matter of the genesis of species as in that of the genesis of life, the forces that constructed nature are now absent from nature.[13]

Even so, this biologist sticks to the transformist theory:

> I firmly believe—because I see no means of doing otherwise—that mammals have come from lizards, and lizards from fish; but when I declare and when I think such a thing, I try not to avoid

---

12. Teilhard de Chardin (*The Human Phenomenon*, p. 129) writes on this subject: "Nothing is by nature so delicate and fugitive as a beginning. As long as a zoological group is young, its characteristics remain undecided. Its dimensions are weak. Relatively few individuals compose it, and these are rapidly changing. Both in space and duration, the peduncle (or the bud, which comes to the same thing) of a living branch corresponds to a minimum of differentiation, expansion, and resistance. How then is time going to act on this weak zone? Inevitably by destroying it in its vestiges." This reasoning, which abusively exploits the purely external and conventional analogy between a genealogical "tree" and a real plant, is an example of the "imaginative abstraction" that characterizes this author's thought.
13. *Le Figaro Littéraire,* April 20, 1957.

seeing its indigestible enormity, and I prefer to leave vague the origin of these scandalous metamorphoses rather than add to their improbability that of a ludicrous interpretation.[14]

All that paleontology proves to us is that the various animal forms, such as are shown by fossils preserved in successive earthly layers, made their appearance in a vaguely ascending order, going from relatively undifferentiated organisms—but not simple ones[15]—to ever more complex forms, without this ascension representing, however, an unequivocal and continuous line. It seems to move in jumps; in other words, whole categories of animals appear all at once, without real predecessors. What does this order mean? Simply that, on the material plane, the simple or relatively undifferentiated always precedes the complex and differentiated. All "matter" is like a mirror that reflects the activity of the essences, while also inverting it; this is why the seed comes before the tree and the bud before the flower, whereas in the principial order the perfect "forms" pre-exist. The successive appearance of animal forms according to an ascending hierarchy therefore in no wise proves their continual and cumulative genesis.[16]

On the contrary, what links the various animal forms to one another is something like a common model, which reveals itself more or less through their structures and which is more apparent in the case of animals endowed with superior consciousness such as birds and mammals. This model is expressed especially in the symmetrical disposition of the body, in the number of extremities and sensory organs, and also in the general form of the chief internal organs. It might be suggested that the design and number of certain organs, and especially those of sensation, simply correspond to the terrestrial surroundings; but this argument is reversible, because

14. *Ibid.*
15. The electron microscope has revealed the surprising complexity of the functions at work within a unicellular being.
16. The most commonly mentioned example in favor of the transformist thesis is the hypothetical genealogy of the *Equidae*. Charles Depéret criticizes it as follows: "Geological observation establishes in a formal manner that no gradual passage took place between these genera; the last *Palaeotherium* had long been extinct, without having transformed itself, when the first *Architherium* made its appearance, and the latter disappeared in turn, without modification, before being suddenly replaced by the invasion of the *Hipparion*." (*Les Transformations du Monde Animal,* p. 107.) To this it can be added that the supposed primitive forms of the horse are hardly to be observed in equine embryology, though the development of the embryo is commonly looked on as a recapitulation of the genesis of the species.

those surroundings are precisely what the sensory organs grasp and delimit. In fact, the model underlying all animal forms establishes the analogy between the microcosm and the macrocosm. Against the background of this common cosmic pattern, the differences between species and the gaps that separate them are all the more marked.

Instead of "missing links", which the partisans of transformism seek in vain, nature offers us, as if in irony, a large variety of animal forms which, without transgressing the pre-established framework of a species, imitate the appearance and habits of a species or order foreign to them. Thus, for example, whales are mammals, but they assume the appearance and behavior of fishes; hummingbirds have the appearance, iridescent colors, flight, and mode of feeding of butterflies; the armadillo is covered with scales like a reptile, although it is a mammal; and so on. Most of these animals with imitative forms are higher species that have taken on the forms of relatively lower species, a fact which *a priori* excludes an interpretation of them as intermediary links in an evolution. As for their interpretation as forms of adaptation to a given set of surroundings, this seems more than dubious, for what could be, for example, the intermediate forms between some land mammal or other and the dolphin?[17] Among these "imitative" forms, which constitute so many extreme cases, we must also include the fossil bird *Archaeopteryx* mentioned above.

Since each animal order represents an archetype that includes the archetypes of the corresponding species, one might well ask oneself whether the existence of "imitative" animal forms does not contradict the immutability of the essential forms; but this is not the case, for the existence of these forms demonstrates, on the contrary, that very immutability by a logical exhausting of all the possibilities inherent in a given type or essential form. It is as if nature, after bringing forth fishes, reptiles, birds, and mammals, with their distinctive characteristics, wished still to show that she was able to produce an animal like the dolphin which, while being a true mammal, at the same time possesses almost all the faculties of a fish, or a creature like the tortoise, which possesses a skeleton covered by flesh,

---

17. On the subject of the hypothetical transformation of a land animal into the whale, Douglas Dewar writes: "I have often challenged transformists to describe plausible ancestors situated in the intermediate phases of this supposed transformation." (*What the Animal Fossils Tell Us*, Trans. Vict. Instit, vol. LXXIV.)

yet at the same time is enclosed in an exterior carapace after the fashion of certain molluscs.[18] Thus does nature manifest her protean power, her inexhaustible capacity for generation, while remaining faithful to the essential forms, which in fact are never blurred.

Each essential form—or each archetype—includes after its fashion all the others, but without confusion; it is like a mirror reflecting other mirrors, which reflect it in their turn.[19] In its deepest meaning the mutual reflection of types is an expression of the metaphysical homogeneity of Existence, or of the unity of Being.

Some biologists, when confronted with the discontinuity in the paleontological succession of species, postulate an evolution by leaps and, in order to make this theory plausible, refer to the sudden mutations observed in some living species. But these mutations never exceed the limits of an anomaly or a decadence, as for example the sudden appearance of albinos, or of dwarfs, or of giants; even when these characteristics become hereditary, they remain as anomalies and never constitute new specific forms.[20] For this to happen, it would be necessary for the vital substance of an existing species to serve as the "plastic material" for a newly manifested specific form; in practice, this means that one or several females of this existing species would suddenly bear offspring of a new species. Now, as the hermeticist Richard the Englishman writes:

> Nothing can be produced from a thing that is not contained in it; for this reason, every species, every genus, and every natural order develops within the limits proper to it and bears fruits according to its own kind and not according to an essentially different order; everything that receives a seed must be of the same seed.[21]

Fundamentally, the evolutionist thesis is an attempt to replace, not simply the "miracle of creation", but the cosmogonic process—largely supra-sensory—of which the Biblical narrative is a Scriptural

18. It is significant that the tortoise, whose skeleton seems to indicate an extravagant adaptation to an animal "armored" state, appears all at once among the fossils, without evolution. Similarly, the spider appears simultaneously with its prey and with its faculty of weaving already developed.
19. This is the image used by the Sufi 'Abd al-Karîm al-Jîlî in his book *al-Insân al-Kâmil*, chapter on "Divine Unicity".
20. Bounoure, *Déterminisme et Finalité*.
21. Quoted in *The Golden Treatise*, Museum Hermeticum (Frankfurt, 1678).

symbol; evolutionism, by absurdly making the greater derive from the lesser, is the opposite of this process, or this "emanation". (This term has nothing to do with the emanationist heresy, since the transcendence and immutability of the ontological principle are here in no wise called in question.) In a word, evolutionism results from an incapacity—peculiar to modern science—to conceive "dimensions" of reality other than purely physical ones; to understand the "vertical" genesis of species, it is worth recalling what Guénon said about the progressive solidification of the corporeal state through the various terrestrial ages.[22] This solidification must obviously not be taken to imply that the stones of the earliest ages were soft, for this would be tantamount to saying that certain physical qualities—and in particular hardness and density—were then wanting; what has hardened and become fixed with time is the corporeal state taken as a whole, with the result that it no longer receives directly the imprint of subtle forms. Assuredly, it cannot become detached from the subtle state, which is its ontological root and which dominates it entirely, but the relationship between the two states of existence no longer has the creative character that it possessed at the origin; it is as when a fruit, having reached maturity, becomes surrounded by an ever harder husk and ceases to absorb the sap of the tree. In a cyclic phase in which corporeal existence had not yet reached this degree of solidification, a new specific form could manifest itself directly from the starting-point of its first "condensation" in the subtle or animic state;[23] this means that the different types of animals pre-existed at the level immediately superior to the corporeal world as non-spatial forms, but nevertheless clothed in a certain "matter", namely that of the subtle world. From there these forms "descended" into the corporeal state each time the latter was ready to receive them; this "descent" had the nature of a sudden coagulation and hence also the nature of a limitation and fragmentation of the original animic form. Indo-Tibetan cosmology describes this descent—which is also a fall—in the case of human

22. René Guénon, *The Reign of Quantity and the Signs of the Times* (Ghent, NY: Sophia Perennis et Universalis, 1995).
23. Concerning the creation of species in a subtle "proto-matter"—in which they still preserve an androgynous form, comparable to a sphere—and their subsequent exteriorization by "crystallization" in sensible matter (which is heavy, opaque, and mortal), see Frithjof Schuon, *Light on the Ancient Worlds* (Bloomington, Indiana: World Wisdom Books, 1984), chapter 2, "In the Wake of the Fall", and *Dimensions of Islam* (New York: Fernhill House, 1970), chapter 2, "The Five Divine Presences."

beings under the form of the mythological combat of the *devas* and *asûras*: the *devas* having created man with a body that was fluid, protean, and diaphanous—in other words, in a subtle form—the *asûras* try to destroy it by a progressive petrification; it becomes opaque, gets fixed, and its skeleton, affected by the petrification, is immobilized. Thereupon the *devas,* turning evil into good, create joints, after having fractured the bones, and they also open the pathways of the senses, by piercing the skull, which threatens to imprison the seat of the mind. In this way the process of solidification stops before it reaches its extreme limit, and certain organs in man, such as the eye, still retain something of the nature of the non-corporeal states.[24]

In this story, the pictorial description of the subtle world must not be misunderstood. However, it is certain that the process of materialization, from the supra-sensory to the sensory, had to be reflected within the material or corporeal state itself, so that one can say without risk of error, that the first generations of a new species did not leave a mark in the great book of earthly layers; it is therefore vain to seek in sensible matter the ancestors of a species, and especially that of man.

Since the transformist theory is not founded on any real proof, its corollary and conclusion, namely the theory of the infra-human origin of man, remains suspended in the void. The facts adduced in favor of this thesis are restricted to a few groups of skeletons of disparate chronology: it happens that some skeletal types deemed to be more "evolved", such as "Steinheim man", precede others, of a seemingly more primitive character, such as "Neanderthal man", even though the latter was doubtless not so apelike as tendentious reconstructions would have us believe.[25]

If, instead of always putting the questions: at what point does humankind begin, and what is the degree of evolution of such and such a type regarded as being pre-human, we were to ask ourselves: how far does the monkey go, things might well appear in a very different light; for a fragment from a skeleton, even one related to that of man, is hardly enough to establish the presence of that which constitutes man, namely reason, whereas it is possible to conceive of

24. See Krasinsky, *Tibetische Medizin-Philosophie.*
25. In general, this domain of science has been almost smothered by tendentious theories, hoaxes, and imprudently popularized discoveries. See Dewar, *The Transformist Illusion.*

a great variety of anthropoid apes whose anatomies are more or less close to that of man.

However paradoxical this may seem, the anatomical resemblance between man and the anthropoid apes is explainable precisely by the difference—not gradual, but essential—that separates man from all other animals. Since the anthropoid form is able to exist without that "central" element that characterizes man—this "central" element manifesting itself anatomically by his vertical position, amongst other things—the anthropoid form must exist; in other words, there cannot but be found, at the purely animal level, a form that realizes in its own way—that is to say, according to the laws of its own level—the very plan of the human anatomy; the ape is a prefiguration of man, not in the sense of an evolutive phase, but by virtue of the law that decrees that at every level of existence analogous possibilities will be found.

A further question arises in the case of the fossils attributed to primitive men: did some of these skeletons belong to men we can look upon as being ancestors of men presently alive, or do they bear witness to a few groups that survived the cataclysm at the end of a terrestrial age, only to disappear in their turn before the beginning of our present humanity? Instead of primitive men, it might well be a case of degenerate men, who may or may not have existed alongside our real ancestors. We know that the folklore of most peoples speaks of giants or dwarfs who lived long ago, in remote countries; now, among these skeletons, several cases of gigantism are to be found.[26] Finally, let it be recalled once more that the bodies of the most ancient men did not necessarily leave solid traces, either because their bodies were not yet at that point materialized or "solidified", or because the spiritual state of these men, along with the cosmic conditions of their time, rendered possible a resorption of the physical body into the subtle "body" at the moment of death.[27]

We must now say a few words about a thesis, much in vogue today, which claims to be something like a spiritual integration of paleontology, but which in reality is nothing but a purely mental sublimation of the crudest materialism, with all the prejudices this includes, from belief in the indefinite progress of humanity to a lev-

26. Like the Meganthrope of Java and the *Gigantopithecus* of China.
27. In some very exceptional cases—such as Enoch, Elijah, and the Virgin Mary—such a resorption took place even in the present terrestrial age.

eling and totalitarian collectivism, without forgetting the cult of the machine that is at the center of all this; it will be apparent that we are here referring to Teilhardian evolutionism.[28] According to Teilhard de Chardin, who is not given to worrying over the gaps inherent in the evolutionist system and largely relies on the climate created by the premature popularization of the transformist thesis, man himself represents only an intermediate state in an evolution that starts with unicellular organisms and ends in a sort of global cosmic entity, united to God. The craze for trying to bring everything back to a single unequivocal and uninterrupted genetic line here exceeds the material plane and launches out wildly into an irresponsible and avid "mentalization" characterized by an abstraction clothed in artificial images which their author ends up by taking literally, as if he were dealing with concrete realities. We have already mentioned the imaginary genealogical tree of species, whose supposed unity is no more than a snare, being composed of the hypothetical conjunction of many disjointed elements. Teilhard amplifies this notion to his heart's content, in a manner that is purely graphic, by completing its branches—or "scales", as he likes to call them—and by constructing a pinnacle in the direction of which humankind is supposed to be situated. By a similar sliding of thought from the abstract to the concrete, from the metaphorical to the supposedly real, he agglutinates, in one and the same pseudo-scientific outburst, the most diverse realities, such as mechanical laws, vital forces, psychic elements, and spiritual entities. Let us quote a characteristic passage:

> What explains the biological revolution caused by the appearance of Man, is an explosion of consciousness; and what, in its

28. Teilhard's materialism is revealed in all its crudity, and all its perversity, when this philosopher advocates the use of surgical means to accelerate "collective cerebralization" (*Man's Place in Nature*, [New York: Harper & Row, 1966]). Let us also quote the further highly revealing words of the same author: "It is finally on the dazzling notion of Progress and on faith in Progress that today's divided humanity can be reformed. . . . Act I is over! We have access to the heart of the atom! Now come the next steps, such as the vitalization of matter by the building of super-molecules, the modeling of the human organism by hormones, the control of heredity and of the sexes by the play of genes and chromosomes, the readjustment and liberation by direct action of the springs laid bare by psychoanalysis, the awakening and taking hold of the still dormant intellectual and emotional forces in the human mass!" (*Planète III*, 1944, p. 30.) Quite naturally, Teilhard proposes the fashioning of mankind by a universal scientific government—in short, all that is needed for the reign of the Antichrist. See also the following chapter in this book: "Contra Teilhard de Chardin".

turn, explains this explosion of consciousness, is simply the passage of a privileged radius of "corpusculization", in other words, of a zoological phylum, across the surface, hitherto impermeable, separating the zone of direct Psychism from that of reflective Psychism. Having reached, following this particular radius, a critical point of arrangement (or, as we say here, of enrolment), Life became hypercentered on itself, to the point of becoming capable of foresight and invention. . . .[29]

Thus, "corpusculization" (which is a physical process) would have as its effect that a "zoological phylum" (which is no more than a figure) should pass across the surface (purely hypothetical) separating two psychic zones. . . . But we must not be surprised at the absence of *distinguos* in Teilhard's thinking since, according to his own theory, the mind is but a metamorphosis of matter!

Without stopping to discuss the strange theology of this author, for whom God himself evolves along with matter, and without daring to define what he thinks of the prophets and sages of antiquity and other "underdeveloped" beings of this kind, we will say the following: if man, in respect of both his physical nature and his spiritual nature, were really nothing but a phase of an evolution going from the amoeba to the superman, how could he know objectively where he stands in all this? Let us suppose that this alleged evolution forms a curve, or a spiral. The man who is but a fragment thereof—and let it not be forgotten that a "fragment" of a movement is no more than a phase of that movement—can that man step out of it and say to himself: I am a fragment of a spiral which is developing in such and such a way? Now it is certain—and moreover Teilhard de Chardin himself recognizes this—that man is able to judge of his own state. Indeed he knows his own rank amongst the other earthly creatures, and he is even the only one to know objectively both himself and the world. Far from being a mere phase in an indefinite evolution, man essentially represents a central possibility, and one that is thus unique, irreplaceable, and definitive. If the human species had to evolve towards another more perfect and more "spiritual" form, man would not already now be the "point of intersection" of the Divine Spirit with the earthly plane; he would neither be capable of salvation, nor able intellectually to surmount the flux of becoming. To express these thoughts according to the perspective of the Gospels: would God have

29. *Man's Place in Nature*, pp. 62-63.

become man if the form of man were not virtually "god on earth", in other words, qualitatively central as well as definitive with regard to his own cosmic level?

As a symptom of our time, Teilhardism is comparable to one of those cracks that are due to the very solidification of the mental carapace,[30] and that do not open upward, toward the heaven of real and transcendent unity, but downward toward the realm of lower psychism. Weary of its own discontinuous vision of the world, the materialist mind lets itself slide toward a false continuity or unity, toward a pseudo-spiritual intoxication, of which this falsified and materialized faith—or this sublimated materialism—that we have just described marks a phase of particular significance.

(from *Mirror of the Intellect*)

---

30. Guénon, *The Reign of Quantity and the Signs of the Times* (Ghent, NY: Sophia Perennis et Universalis, 1945, Chap. 15 "The Illusion of 'Ordinary Life'").

Contra Teilhard de Chardin

My main objection to the evolutionary doctrine of Teilhard de Chardin is as follows: if the spiritual faculty of man—the "noetic faculty", as Teilhard de Chardin calls it—is merely a phase of a continuing biological evolution—or involution—which, seen as a whole, can be compared to a curve or a spiral, then this phase cannot step out of the whole and say: I am part of a spiral. Anything that such an evolution-bound faculty could ever grasp or express would likewise be subject to evolution, and this leads to the Marxist view that there is no truth, but only biological pragmatism and utilitarianism. It is here that Teilhard's theory breaks down completely.

The human intellect does, in fact, have the faculty of placing itself outside biological contingency, of viewing things objectively and essentially, and of making judgements. Teilhard de Chardin confuses the cerebral and the "noetic" faculties. The *Nous* (= Intellect = Spirit) is not the same as the activity of the brain; the latter considers and elaborates, whereas the former judges and knows. The truly spiritual faculty—that of discriminating between true and false, of distinguishing the relative from the absolute—is related to the biological level, metaphorically speaking, as is the vertical to the horizontal; it belongs to another ontological dimension. And precisely because this dimension exists in man, he is not an ephemeral biological appearance, but, in this physical and earthly world, and in spite of all his organic limitations, an absolute center. This is also indicated by the faculty of speech, which belongs to man alone, and which, precisely, presupposes the capacity to "objectivize" things, to place himself behind and beyond appearances.

The terrestrial absoluity of the human state and of the human form is also confirmed by the Christian doctrine of the incarnation of the Divine Word—a doctrine which, in Teilhard's system, loses all its meaning. If man fundamentally possesses the capacity of knowing God, in other words, if the fulfilling of the function, which is his by definition, is a way to God, then on the biological plane there is no occasion for a super-man. He would be a pleonasm.

The poor saints! They came a million years too soon. None of them, however, would ever have accepted the doctrine that God could be reached biologically, or again through collective scientific research.

And so I come back to my main objection: according to Teilhard's system, the "noetic" faculty of man is related to biogenesis, not as the eye is related to the other human parts, but rather as a part-process is related to a whole process—and this is something quite different. The eye can view the other limbs and organs, even if only in a mirror, but a part-process can never view the whole process of which it is a part. This has already been said by Aristotle: whoever asserts that everything is in a stream can never prove his assertion, for the simple reason that it can rest on nothing that is not itself in the stream; it is thus self-contradictory.

* * *

It is not true that "so long as a writer on religious subjects is affirming beliefs (whether his own or other people's), he is expressing the truth, but when deprecating other people's beliefs, his word is not to be trusted", for in that case the most erroneous of sects, including satanism, and the most absurd of personal beliefs would be justified; the "discerning of spirits" of which the New Testament speaks would have no meaning. But perhaps the author of this remark is thinking somehow of the principle according to which a doctrinal pronouncement—not a metaphysical one, but a dogmatic or moral one—may be perfectly valid within the framework of a given religion without necessarily being valid outside it and within the framework of another religion that is equally true in itself? Be that as it may, this principle does not apply to the case of Teilhard de Chardin, whose thesis on the genesis of man stands in opposition not only to the form and spirit of the Christian dogma, but also to all traditional wisdom. Let us simply say that his thesis is false, that it expresses no particle of transcendent truth. And how could it, seeing that it denies truth as such: according to Teilhard de Chardin, intelligence itself, including all that is deepest in it, all that is implicitly divine, is subject to change; it "evolves" together with the supposed evolution of matter, so that it could have no fixed and immutable content; the spirit of man, according to Teilhard de Chardin, is entirely "in a state of becoming". It is here, moreover, that the Teilhardian thesis contradicts itself, for if human intelligence is no more than matter which has been in a state of progressive transformation ever since the age of the first molluscs, how could modern man, "half-developed" as he is, possibly take in, with the eye of his understanding, the whole movement which is carrying him along? How is it possible for the essentially impermanent to judge the nature of impermanence? This argument should be enough to condemn the Teilhardian thesis. It remains to be seen why his thesis has had so much success.

The average modern man "believes" above all in science—the science that has produced modern surgery and modern industry— and this is almost his basic "religion". If he considers himself a Christian at the same time, the two "beliefs" stand in opposition to each other in his soul, and engender a latent crisis that calls for a solution. This solution is what Teilhard de Chardin seems to offer. He "ties the two loose ends together"; but he does so, not by making, as he should, a distinction between different planes of reality—that of empirical knowledge which is exact in its way but necessarily fragmentary and provisional, and that of faith which is bound up with timeless certainties—but by mixing them inextricably together: he endows empirical science with an absolute certainty that it does not and cannot have, and he projects the idea of indefinite progress into God Himself.

He puts forward the theory of the transformation of species as a certain fact, whereas it is no more than a hypothesis, as its most serious defenders admit; no valid proof of it has ever, in fact, been made, and if in spite of everything it keeps its hold, this is because modern minds can only conceive of a genesis which takes place in time; the "vertical" genesis of specific forms from the supra-formal and animic degrees of existence is beyond them. Nonetheless, scientific honesty demands that one should make a distinction between proof and hypothesis, and that one should not build, as Teilhard de Chardin does, a whole philosophy—indeed, a pseudo-religion—on an entirely conjectural basis. It is not for nothing that Teilhard de Chardin was the victim of the famous Piltdown hoax— the *Eoanthropos* of unhappy memory—and that he was one of the inventors of the no less fantastic "*Sinanthropos*" of Chou-Kou-Tien! But the worst and most grotesque feature of Teilhardism is the fact that it is obliged to consider the prophets and sages of ancient times as being mentally "under-developed": are they not a little nearer to the ape than modern man is? It is true that in this respect the thesis of Teilhard de Chardin is in no sense original; its novelty lies in its being a Trojan horse to introduce materialism and progressivism into the very bosom of religion.

(from *Mirror of the Intellect*)

Modern Psychology

"The object of psychology is the psychic; unfortunately it is also its subject." Thus wrote a famous psychologist of our time.[31] According to this opinion, every psychological judgement inevitably participates in the essentially subjective, not to say passionate and tendentious, nature of its object; for, according to this logic, no one understands the soul except by means of his own soul, and the latter, for the psychologist, is, precisely, purely psychic, and nothing else. Thus no psychologist, whatever be his claim to objectivity, escapes this dilemma, and the more categorical and general his affirmations in this realm are, the more they are suspect; such is the verdict that modern psychology pronounces in its own cause, when it is being sincere towards itself. But whether it be sincere or not, the relativism expressed in the words just quoted is always inherent in it. This relativism is also a kind of Prometheanism that would make of the psychic element the ultimate reality of man. It is the root of the numerous divergences within this discipline, and it dominates it to the point of contaminating everything that it touches: history, philosophy, art, and religion; all of them become psychological at its touch, and thereby also subjective, and thus devoid of objective and immutable certainties.[32]

But all *a priori* relativism is inconsequential towards itself. Despite the admitted precariousness of its point of view, modern psychology behaves like every other science: it passes judgements and believes in their validity, and in this connection it leans unwittingly, and without admitting it, on an innate certainty: indeed, if we can observe that the psychic is "subjective", in the sense of being dominated by a certain egocentric bias that imposes on it certain

---

31. C. G. Jung, *Psychology and Religion* (Yale: New Haven, 1938), p. 62.
32. "I can find no reason to be surprised at seeing psychology exchange visits with philosophy, for is not the act of thinking, the foundation of all philosophy, a psychic activity which, as such, directly concerns psychology? Must not psychology embrace the soul in its total extension, which includes philosophy, theology, and countless other things? In the face of all the richly diversified religions, there rise up, as the supreme instance perhaps of truth or error, the immutable data of the human soul." (C. C. Jung, *Modern Man in search of his soul* [London: Routledge, 1984]). This amounts to replacing truth by psychology; it is totally forgotten that there are no "immutable data" outside of that which is immutable by its own nature, namely, the Intellect. In any case, if the "act of thinking" is no more than a "psychic activity", by what right does psychology set itself up as the "supreme instance", since it too is but one "psychic activity" amongst others?

limits, or by a particular "coloring", this is because there is something in us which is not subject to these limits and tendencies, but which transcends them and in principle dominates them. This something is the intellect, and it is the intellect that normally provides us with the criteria which alone can shed light on the fluctuating and uncertain world of the psyche; this is obvious, but it nevertheless remains totally outside modern scientific and philosophical thinking.

It is important above all not to confuse intellect and reason: the latter is indeed the mental reflection of the transcendent intellect, but in practice it is only what one makes of it, by which we mean that, in the case of the modern sciences, its functioning is limited by the empirical method itself; at the level of the latter, reason is not so much a source of truth as a principle of coherence. For modern psychology it is even less than that, for if scientific rationalism lends a relatively stable framework to one's observation of the physical world, it reveals itself as entirely insufficient when it comes to describing the world of the soul; for surface psychic movements, those whose causes and aims are situated on the plane of current experience, can hardly be translated into rational terms. The whole chaos of lower—and mostly unconscious—psychic possibilities escapes both rationality and what transcends rationality, and this means that both the major part of the psychic world and the metaphysical realm will appear "irrational" according to this way of thinking. Hence the tendency, inherent in modern psychology, to relativize reason itself, a tendency that is self-contradictory, since psychology cannot dispense with rational methods. Psychology finds itself confronted with a domain which on all sides overflows the horizon of a science founded on empiricism and Cartesianism.

For this reason, the majority of modern psychologists ensconce themselves in a sort of pragmatism; it is in "committed" experience, together with a coldly clinical attitude, that they see some guarantee of "objectivity". In point of fact, the movements of the soul cannot be studied from the outside, as in the case of corporeal phenomena; to know what they mean, they have in a sense to be lived, and this involves the subject of the observer, as was justly pointed out by the psychologist at the outset. As for the mental faculty that "controls" the experiment, what is this but a more or less arbitrary "common sense", one inevitably colored by preconceived ideas? Thus the would-be objectivity of the psychic attitude changes nothing in regard to the uncertain nature of the experiment, and so, in the absence of a principle that is both inward and immutable, one returns to the dilemma of the psychic striving to grasp the psychic.

The soul, like every other domain of reality, can only be truly known by what transcends it. Moreover, this is spontaneously and implicitly admitted in people's recognition of the moral principle of justice, which demands that men should overcome their individual subjectivity. Now we could not overcome it if the intelligence, which guides our will, were itself nothing but a psychic reality; and intelligence would not transcend the psyche if, in its essence, it did not transcend the plane of phenomena, both inward and outward. This observation suffices to prove the necessity and the existence of a psychology deriving in a sense from above and not claiming *a priori* an empirical character. But although this order of things is inscribed in our very nature, it will never be recognized by modern psychology; despite its own reactions against the rationalism of yesterday, it is no closer to metaphysics than any other empirical science—indeed quite the contrary, since its perspective, which assimilates the supra-rational to the irrational, predisposes it to the worst of errors.

What modern psychology lacks entirely is criteria enabling it to situate the aspects or tendencies of the soul in their cosmic context. In traditional psychology, these criteria are provided according to two principal "dimensions": on the one hand, according to a cosmology that "situates" the soul and its modalities in the hierarchy of states of existence, and, on the other hand, according to a morality directed toward a spiritual end. The latter may provisionally espouse the individual horizon; it nonetheless keeps in view the universal principles attaching the soul to an order more vast than itself. Cosmology in a sense circumscribes the soul; spiritual morality sounds its depths. For just as a current of water reveals its force and direction only when it breaks against an object that resists it, so the soul can show its tendencies and fluctuations only in relation to an immutable principle; whoever wishes to know the nature of the psyche must resist it, and one truly resists it only when one places oneself at a point which corresponds, if not effectively then at least virtually or symbolically, to the Divine Self, or to the intellect which is like a ray that emanates from the latter.

Thus traditional psychology possesses both an impersonal and "static" dimension (namely, cosmology), and a personal and "operative" dimension (namely, morality or the science of the virtues), and it is necessarily so, because genuine knowledge of the soul results from knowledge of oneself. He who, by the eye of his essence, is able to "objectivize" his own psychic form, by that very fact knows all the possibilities of the psychic or subtle world; and this intellectual "vision" is both the outcome and, if need be, the guarantor of every sacred science of the soul.

For the majority of modern psychologists, traditional morality—which they readily confuse with a purely social or conventional morality—is nothing but a kind of psychic dam, useful on occasion but more often a hindrance or even harmful for the "normal" development of the individual. This opinion is propagated especially by Freudian psychoanalysis, which became widely applied in some countries, where it has practically usurped the function that elsewhere belongs to the sacrament of confession: the psychiatrist replaces the priest, and the bursting of complexes that had previously been repressed takes the place of absolution. In ritual confession the priest is but the impersonal representative—necessarily discreet—of the Truth that judges and pardons; the penitent, by admitting his sins, in a sense "objectivizes" the psychic tendencies that these sins manifest. By repenting, he detaches himself from them, and by receiving sacramental absolution, his soul is virtually reintegrated in its primitive equilibrium and centered on its divine essence. In the case of Freudian psychoanalysis,[33] on the other hand, man lays bare his psychic entrails, not before God, but to his fellow. He does not distance himself from the chaotic and obscure depths of his soul, which the analyst unveils or stirs up, but on the contrary, he accepts them as his own, for he must say to himself: "This is what I am like in reality." And if he does not overcome, with the help of some salutary instinct, this kind of disillusionment from below, he will retain from it something like an intimate sullying; in most cases it will be his self-abandonment to collective mediocrity that for him will play the part of absolution, for it is easier to endure one's own degradation when it is shared with others. Whatever may be the occasional or partial usefulness of such an analysis in certain cases, the state described above is its more usual result, its premises being what they are.[34]

33. The use of the adjective is to make it clear that it is indeed the method of Freud that we are discussing here, for in our own day some forms of psychoanalysis are more neutral and less pernicious, a fact which, from our point of view, is in no wise a justification.
34. René Guénon has observed that the principle whereby every psychoanalyst requires to be psychoanalyzed himself before being empowered to analyze

If the medicine of the traditional civilizations knows nothing analogous to modern psychotherapy, this is because the psychic cannot be treated by the psychic. The psyche is the realm of indefinite actions and reactions. By its own specific nature, it is essentially unstable and deceptive, so that it can be cured only by resorting to something situated "outside" or "above" it. In some cases one will act favorably upon it by re-establishing the humoral balance of the body, commonly upset by psychic affections;[35] in other cases it is only by the use of spiritual means, such as exorcism,[36] prayer, or a sojourn in holy places, that the soul can be restored to health.

Everyone is aware of the fact that modern psychology tries to explain psychologically the spiritual means just mentioned. In its eyes, the effect of a rite is one thing, and its theological or mystical interpretation is another. The effect of a rite, arbitrarily limited to the psychic and subjective domain alone, is attributed to psychic dispositions of ancestral origin, which the form of the rite is supposed to actualize. There is no hint of the timeless and superhuman meaning inherent in the rite or symbol—as if the soul could cure itself through believing in the illusory projection of its own preoccupations, whether individual or collective. There is nothing, however, in this supposition that would trouble modern psychology, since it is ready to go much further than this, when it asserts, for example, that the fundamental forms of thought, the laws of logic, merely represent a residue of ancestral habits.[37] This path is one that leads to the outright denial of intelligence and to its replacement by biological fatalities, if indeed psychology can go that far without encompassing its own ruin.

In order to be able to "situate" the soul in relation to other cosmic realities or realms, one must refer to the cosmological scheme that represents the degrees of existence in the form of con-

others, raises the troublesome question as to who occupied the first place in the line.

35. Usually a vicious circle ensues, with the psychic imbalance engendering a physical intoxication, which in its turn causes the psychic imbalance to worsen.

36. Cases of diabolical possession, such as manifestly call for the application of the rites of exorcism, seem to have become rarer nowadays, doubtless because demonic influences are no longer "compressed" by the dam of tradition, but are able to spread more or less everywhere in forms that are in a fashion "diluted".

37. They will say, for example, that logic is merely an expression of the physiological structure of our brain, and forget that, were it so, this statement would also be an expression of this same physiological fatality.

centric circles or spheres. This scheme, which makes symbolical use of the geocentric conception of the visible universe, symbolically identifies the corporeal world with our terrestrial surroundings; around this center extends the sphere—or spheres—of the subtle or psychic world, surrounded in turn by the sphere of the world of pure Spirit. This representation is naturally limited by its own spatial character, but it nevertheless expresses very well the relationship that exists between these various states. Each of the spheres, considered in itself, presents itself as a complete and perfectly homogeneous whole, whereas from the "point of view" of the sphere immediately above, it is but a content thereof. Thus the corporeal world, envisaged at its own level, does not know the subtle world, just as the latter does not know the supra-formal world, precisely because it encloses only that which has a form. Furthermore, each of these worlds is known and dominated by that which exceeds and surrounds it. It is from the immutable and formless background of the Spirit that the subtle realities become detached as forms, and it is the soul which, through its sensory faculties, knows the corporeal.

This double relationship of things, which *a priori* is hidden from our individual vision, can be grasped in all its reality when one considers the very nature of sensible perception. On the one hand, this truly reaches the corporeal world, and no philosophical artifice will be able to convince us of the contrary; on the other hand, there is no doubt that all we perceive of the world are merely those "images" of it that our mental faculty is able to keep hold of, and in this respect the whole fabric of impressions, memories, and anticipations—in short, everything that for us constitutes the sensible continuity and logical coherence of the world—is of a psychic or subtle nature. It is in vain that one will try to know what the world is "outside" this subtle continuity, since this "outside" does not exist: surrounded as it is by the subtle state, the corporeal world is but a content thereof, even though it appears, in the mirror of this state itself, as a materially autonomous order.[38]

It is obviously not the individual soul, but the entire subtle state that contains the physical world. The logical coherence of the latter presupposes the unity of the former, and this is manifested indirectly by the fact that the multiple individual visions of the sensible world, fragmentary though they be, substantially coincide and are

---

38. Nothing is more absurd than attempts to explain the perception of the material world in material terms.

integrated in one continuous whole. The individual soul partici-pates in this unity both by the structure of its cognitive faculties, which is in conformity with the cosmic order, and also by its nature as subject, containing the physical world in its own way; in other words, the physical world is a "world" only in relation to the indi-vidual subject, by virtue of the cleaving of consciousness into object and subject, a cleaving that results precisely from the "egoic" polar-ization of the soul. By this same polarization, the soul is distin-guished from the totality of the subtle state—the "total" or "universal soul" of Plotinus—without, however, being separated from it substantially. For if it were separated from it, our vision of the world would not be adequate to reality; but in fact it is so, in spite of the limitations and the relativity of all perception.

It is true that we ordinarily perceive only a fragment of the subtle world—the fragment that we "are", and that constitutes our "myself"—whereas the sensible world reveals itself to us in its macro-cosmic continuity, as a whole that seems to include us. This is because the subtle world is the very field of individuation; in reality, we are plunged in the ocean of the subtle world as fishes are in water, and like them, we do not see that which constitutes our own element.

As for the opposition between the "inward" psychic world and the "outward" corporeal world, this is actualized only in relation to, and in function of, the latter. In itself, the subtle world is neither "inward" nor "outward"; it is at most "non-outward", whereas the corporeal world is outward as such, which furthermore proves that it does not enjoy an autonomous existence.

The corporeal state and the psychic state together constitute formal existence; in its total extension, the subtle state is none other than formal existence, but one calls it "subtle" inasmuch as it escapes the laws of corporeity. According to one of the most ancient and most natural symbolisms, the subtle state may be compared to the atmosphere surrounding the earth which pervades all porous bodies and is the vehicle of life.

A phenomenon can only be truly understood through its rela-tions, both "horizontal" and "vertical", with total Reality. This truth applies particularly, and in a certain sense practically, to psychic phenomena. The same psychic "event" can simultaneously be the response to a sensory impulsion, the manifestation of a wish, the consequence of a previous action, the trace of the typical and ances-tral form of the individual, the expression of his genius, and the reflection of a supra-individual reality. It is legitimate to consider the psychic phenomenon in question under one or other of these aspects, but it would be unwarranted to seek to explain the movements and purposes of the soul by one—or even by several—of these aspects exclusively. In this connection let us quote the words of a therapist who is aware of the limitations of contemporary psychology:

> There is an ancient Hindu maxim whose truth is incontestable: "What a man thinks, that he becomes." If one steadfastly thinks of good deeds, one will end by becoming a good man; if one always thinks of weakness, one will become weak; if one thinks of how to develop one's strength (bodily or mental), one will become strong. Similarly, if for years one is engaged almost daily in stirring up Hades,[39] in explaining systematically the higher in terms of the lower, and at the same time ignoring everything in man's cultural history which, despite lamentable errors and misdeeds, has been regarded as worthwhile, one can scarcely avoid the risk of losing all discernment, of leveling down the imagination (a source of our life), and of severely reducing one's mental horizon.[40]

Ordinary consciousness illuminates only a restricted portion of the individual soul, and the latter represents only a tiny part of the psychic world. Nevertheless, the soul is not cut off from the rest of this world; its situation is not that of a body rigorously limited by its own extension and separated from other bodies. What distinguishes the soul from the rest of the vast subtle world is uniquely its own particular tendencies, which define it—if one may employ a simplified image—as a spatial direction defines the ray of light that follows it. By these very tendencies, the soul is in communion with all the cosmic possibilities of analogous tendencies or qualities; it assimilates them and is assimilated by them. For this reason, the science of cosmic tendencies—the *gunas* of Hindu cosmology—is fundamental for the knowledge of the soul. In this connection, it is not the outward context of a psychic phenomenon—the accidental occasion for its manifestation—that matters essentially, but its connection with *sattva, rajas,* or *tamas*—the "upward", "expansive", and

---

39. An allusion to the words of Virgil: *Flectere si nequeo superos, Acheronta movebo* ("If I cannot bend the Heavens, I shall stir up hell"), which Freud quoted at the beginning of his *Interpretation of Dreams*.
40. Hans Jacob, *Western Psychology and Hindu Sâdhana* (London: Allen & Unwin, 1961). The author of this work is a former disciple of Jung, who later discovered the doctrine and method—immeasurably greater—of the Hindu *sâdhana*, which enabled him to subject Western psychology to a just criticism.

"downward" tendencies—which confers on it its rank in the hierarchy of inward values.

Since the motives of the soul are perceptible only through the forms that manifest them, it is on these forms or manifestations that a psychological assessment must needs be founded. Now, the part played by the *gunas* in any form whatsoever can be measured only in a purely qualitative manner, by means of precise and decisive—but in no wise quantitative—criteria, such as are entirely lacking in the wholly profane psychology of our time.

There are some psychic "events" whose repercussions traverse all the degrees of the subtle world "vertically", since they touch on the essences; others—these are ordinary psychic movements—only obey the "horizontal" coming and going of the psyche; and finally, there are those that come from the subhuman depths. The first mentioned are not capable of being expressed entirely—they comprise an element of mystery—and yet the forms which they may from time to time evoke in the imagination are clear and precise, like those that characterize authentic sacred arts. The last mentioned, namely demonic "inspirations", are unintelligible in their very forms; they "ape" the genuinely mysterious by the nebulous, obscure, and equivocal character of their formal manifestations; examples of this are readily to be found in contemporary art.

When studying the formal manifestation of the soul, one must, however, not forget that man's psycho-physical organism can display strange caesuras or discontinuities. Thus, for instance, in the case of the somewhat "anarchical" category of contemplatives known as "fools of God", the spiritual states do not manifest themselves harmoniously and normally and do not make use of the reason; inversely, an intrinsically pathological state—and as such dominated by infrahuman and chaotic tendencies—may incidentally and by accident comprise openings onto supra-terrestrial realities; this is but saying that the human soul is of an inexhaustible complexity.

Viewed as a whole, the subtle world is incomparably vaster and more varied than the corporeal world. Dante expresses this by making the entire hierarchy of planetary spheres correspond to the subtle world, whereas he makes only the terrestrial domain correspond to the corporeal world. The subterranean position of the hells, in his system, merely indicates that the states in question are situated below the normal human state; in reality, they are also part of the subtle state, and this is why some medieval cosmologists place the hells symbolically between heaven and earth.[41]

Experience of the subtle world is subjective—except in the case of certain sciences quite unknown to the moderns—because consciousness, in identifying itself with subtle forms, is affected by their tendencies, just as a ray of light is turned from its course by the form of a wave that it happens to traverse. The subtle world is made up of forms; in other words, it comprises diversity and contrast; but these forms do not possess, in themselves or outside of their projection in the sensible imagination,[42] spatial and defined contours as in the case of corporeal forms. They are entirely active or, to be more exact, dynamic, pure activity belonging only to the essential "forms" or archetypes that are to be found in the pure Spirit. Now the ego or individual soul is itself one of the forms of the subtle world, and the consciousness that espouses this form is necessarily dynamic and exclusive; it realizes other subtle forms only insofar as these become modalities of its own egoic form.

Thus it is that in the dream state, individual consciousness, even though reabsorbed into the subtle world, nonetheless remains turned back on itself; all the forms that it experiences in this state present themselves as simple prolongations of the individual subject, or at least they appear so in retrospect and inasmuch as they verge on the waking state. For in itself, and despite this subjectivism, the consciousness of the dreamer is obviously not impermeable to influences coming from the most diverse "regions" of the subtle world, as is proved, for example, by premonitory or telepathic dreams, which many people have experienced.[43] Indeed, while the imagery of a dream is woven from the very "substance" of the subject—a "substance" that is none other than the progressive actualization of his own psychic form—it nonetheless manifests, incidentally and to different degrees, realities of a cosmic order.

The content of a dream can be considered in many different ways. If one analyzes the *materia* of which it is composed, one will find that it is constituted by all sorts of memories, and in this respect

41. In Islam, it is said that the throne of the devil is located between earth and heaven, a doctrine which also makes clear the temptations to which those who follow the "vertical" path are exposed.
42. If some masters have compared the subtle world to the imagination, it is the imaginative activity, and not the images produced by the imagination, that they had in view.
43. Empirical psychology no longer dares to deny this phenomenon.

the current psychological explanation, which makes the dream the expression of subconscious residues, is largely right. It is not, however, excluded that a dream may also comprise "matters" that in no wise proceed from the personal experience of the dreamer and that are like traces of a psychic transfusion from one individual to another. There is also the economy of the dream, and in this connection we can quote the following description by C. G. Jung, which is exact despite the radically false theses of the author:

> The dream, deriving from the activity of the unconscious, gives a representation of the contents that slumber there; not of all the contents that figure in it, but only of certain of them which, by way of association, are actualized, crystallized, and selected, in correlation with the momentary state of consciousness.[44]

As for the hermeneutics of dreams, this eludes modern psychology in spite of the latter's efforts in this direction, because one cannot validly interpret images reflected by the soul without knowing to which level of reality they refer.

The images one retains on waking from a dream generally represent only a shadow of the psychic forms experienced in the dream state itself. On passing into the waking state, a sort of decantation occurs—one can be aware of this—and something of the reality inherent in the dream evaporates more or less rapidly. There exists, nevertheless, a certain category of dreams, well-known to traditional oneirocrisy, the memory of which persists with an incisive clarity, and this can happen even if the profound content of these dreams appears to conceal itself. Such dreams, which mostly occur at dawn and continue until waking, are accompanied by an irrefutable feeling of objectivity; in other words, they comprise a more than merely mental certainty. But what characterizes them above all, and independently of their moral influence on the dreamer, is the high quality of their forms, disengaged from every turbid or chaotic residue. These are the dreams that come from the Angel; in other words, from the Essence that connects the soul to the supra-formal states of the being.

Since there are dreams of divine or angelic inspiration, their opposite must also exist, and these are dreams of satanic impulsion, containing palpable caricatures of sacred forms. The sensation accompanying them is not one of cool and serene lucidity, but of

---

44. C. G. Jung, *Modern Man in Search of His Soul.*

obsession and vertigo; it is the attraction of an abyss. The infernal influences sometimes ride the wave of a natural passion, which opens the way for them, so to speak. They are, however, distinguishable from the elementary character of passion by their prideful and negative tendency, accompanied either by bitterness or else by sadness. As Pascal said: "He who tries to play the angel will play the beast", and indeed nothing is so apt to provoke caricatures, both in dreams and out of them, as the unconsciously pretentious attitude of the man who mixes God with his own highly particularized ego—the classical cause of many of the psychoses studied by post-Freudian psychologism.[45]

It was starting from the analysis of dreams that C. G. Jung developed his famous theory about the "collective unconscious". His observation of the fact that a certain category of dream images could not be explained simply on the basis of their being residues of individual experiences led Jung to distinguish, within the unconscious domain whence dreams are fed, between a "personal" zone whose contents represent basically the other face of individual psychic life, and a "collective" zone made up of latent psychic dispositions of an impersonal character, such as never offer themselves to direct observation, but manifest themselves indirectly through "symbolic" dreams and "irrational" impulses. At first sight, this theory has nothing extravagant about it, except its use of the term "irrational" in connection with symbolism. It is easy to understand that the individual consciousness centered on the empirical ego leaves on the margin or even outside itself everything which, in the psychic order, is not effectively attached to that center, just as a light projected in a given direction decreases towards the surrounding darkness. But this is not how Jung understands the matter. For him, the non-personal zone of the soul is unconscious as such; in other words, its contents can never become the direct object of the intelligence, whatever be its modality or however great its extension.

> Just as the human body displays a common anatomy, independently of racial differences, so also the psyche possesses, beyond all cultural and mental differences, a common substratum, which I have named the collective unconscious. This unconscious psyche, which is common to all men, is not made up of contents

---

45. In a general way, contemporary psychology delves into the observation of pathological cases, and views the soul only through this clinical perspective.

capable of becoming conscious, but solely of latent dispositions giving rise to certain reactions that are always identical.[46]

And the author goes on to insinuate that it is here a question of ancestral structures that have their origin in the physical order:

> The fact that this collective unconscious exists is simply the psychic expression of the identity of cerebral structures beyond all racial differences. . . . The different lines of psychic evolution start out from one and the same trunk, whose roots plunge through all the ages. It is here that the psychic parallel with the animal is situated.[47]

One notices the plainly Darwinian turn of this thesis, the disastrous consequences of which show themselves in the following passage: "It is this that explains the analogy, indeed the identity, of mythological motives and of symbols as means of human communication in general."[48] Myths and symbols would thus be the expression of an ancestral psychic fund that brings man near to the animal! They have no intellectual or spiritual foundation, since

> from the purely psychological point of view, it is a question of common instincts of imagining and acting. All conscious imagination and action have evolved on the basis of these unconscious prototypes and remain permanently attached to them, and this is especially so when consciousness has not yet attained a very high degree of lucidity, in other words, as long as it is still, in all its functions, more dependent on instinct than on conscious will, or more affective than rational. . . .[49]

This quotation clearly indicates that, for Jung, the "collective unconscious" is situated "below", at the level of physiological instincts. It is important to bear this in mind, since the term "collective unconscious" in itself could carry a wider and in a fashion more spiritual meaning, as certain assimilations made by Jung seem to suggest, especially his use—or rather his usurpation—of the term "archetype" to signify the latent, and as such inaccessible, contents of the "collective unconscious". For though the archetypes do not belong to the psychic realm, but to the world of pure Spirit, they are nevertheless reflected at the psychic level—as virtualities of images in the first place—before becoming crystallized, according to the

---

46. C. G. Jung, *The Secret of the Golden Flower* (New York, 1931), Introduction.
47. *Ibid.*
48. *Ibid.*
49. *Ibid.*

circumstances, in images properly so-called, so that a certain psychological application of the term "archetype" could at a pinch be justified. But Jung defines the "archetype" as an "innate complex"[50] and describes its action on the soul thus: "Possession by an archetype makes of a man a purely collective personage, a kind of mask, under which human nature can no longer develop, but degenerates progressively."[51] As if an archetype, which is an immediate and supra-formal determination of Being—and non-limitative by this very fact—could in some way cast a spell on and vampirize the soul! What is really in question in the more or less pathological case envisaged by Jung? Simply a dissociation of the possibilities inherent in the subtle form of a man, a form that includes multiple aspects, each of which has something unique and irreplaceable about it. In every non-degenerate human individual there is to be found in potency a man and a woman, a father and a mother, a child and an old man, as well as various qualities or "dignities" inseparable from the original and ontological position of man, such as priestly and royal qualities, those of a creative craftsman, of a servant, and so forth. Normally all these possibilities complete one another; here there is no irrational fund of the soul, for the coexistence of these diverse possibilities or aspects of the human form is perfectly intelligible in itself and can be hidden only from the eyes of a mentality or civilization that has become one-sided and false. Any genius-like development of one of these multiple possibilities or dispositions inherent in the human soul requires, moreover, the integration of the complementary possibilities; the true man of genius is a balanced being, for where there is no balance there is no greatness either. The opposite of such a development is a barren and pathological exaggeration of one of the soul's possibilities at the expense of the others, leading to that kind of moral caricature compared by Jung to a mask; and let it be added that it is the carnivalesque mask one must think of here, and not the sacred mask which, for its part, does indeed express a true archetype and therefore a possibility that does not bewitch the soul but on the contrary liberates it.[52]

Psychic dissociation always produces a fixation as well as a tearing apart between opposing poles, and this is rendered possible only by the clouding over of that which, in the soul, corresponds to

50. See C. G. Jung, *Modern Man in Search of His Soul.*
51. See *Two Essays on Analytical Psychology* (New York: Pantheon, 1966), p. 234.
52. See *Mirror of the Intellect*, chapter 14, "The Sacred Mask".

the archetype. At the antipodes of this imbalance productive of hypertrophies, perfect virility, for example, in no wise excludes femininity, but on the contrary includes and adapts it, and the inverse is also true. Similarly, the genuine archetypes, which are not situated at the psychic level, do not mutually exclude but comprise and imply one another. According to the Platonic and hallowed meaning of the term, the archetypes are the source of being and knowledge and not, as Jung conceives them, unconscious dispositions to act and imagine. The fact that the archetypes cannot be grasped by discursive thought has no connection with the irrational and obscure character of the supposed "collective unconscious", whose contents are said to be known only indirectly through their "eruptions" on the surface. There is not only discursive thought, there is also intellectual intuition, and this attains to the archetypes from the starting-point of their symbols.

No doubt the theory according to which ancestral structures constitute the "collective unconscious" imposes itself on modern thought all the more easily in that it seems to be in agreement with the evolutionist explanation of the instinct of animals. According to this view, instinct is the expression of the heredity of a species, of an accumulation of analogous experiences down the ages. This is how they explain, for example, the fact that a flock of sheep hastily gathers together around the lambs the moment it perceives the shadow of a bird of prey, or that a kitten while playing already employs all the tricks of a hunter, or that birds know how to build their nests. In fact, it is enough to watch animals to see that their instinct has nothing of an automatism about it. The formation of such a mechanism by a purely cumulative—and consequently vague and problematical—process is highly improbable, to say the least. Instinct is a non-reflective modality of the intelligence; it is determined, not by a series of automatic reflexes, but by the "form"—the qualitative determination—of the species. This form is like a filter through which the universal intelligence is manifested. Nor must it be forgotten that the subtle form of a being is incomparably more complex than its bodily form. The same is also true for man: his intelligence too is determined by the subtle form of his species. This form, however, includes the reflective faculty, which allows of a singularization of the individual such as does not exist among the animals. Man alone is able to objectivize himself. He can say: "I am this or that." He alone possesses this two-edged faculty. Man, by virtue of his own central position in the cosmos, is able to transcend his specific norm; he can also betray it, and sink lower; *corruptio optimi pessima.* A normal animal remains true to the form and genius of its species; if its intelligence is not reflective and objectifying, but rather existential, it is nonetheless spontaneous; it is assuredly a form of the universal intelligence even if it is not recognized as such by men who, from prejudice or ignorance, identify intelligence with discursive thought exclusively.

As for Jung's thesis that certain dreams, which cannot be explained by personal reminiscences and which seem to arise from an unconscious fund common to all men, contain motives and forms that are also to be found in myths and in traditional symbolism, the thing is possible in principle; not that there is in the soul a repertory of types inherited from distant ancestors and bearing witness to a primitive vision of the world, but because true symbols are always "actual" inasmuch as they express non-temporal realities. In fact, under certain conditions, the soul is able to take on the function of a mirror that reflects, in a purely passive and imaginative manner, universal truths contained in the intellect. Nevertheless, "inspirations" of this nature remain fairly rare; they depend on circumstances that are, so to speak, providential, as in the case of dreams communicating truths or announcing future events, to which allusion has previously been made. Moreover, symbolic dreams are not clothed in just any traditional "style"; their formal language is normally determined by the tradition or religion to which the individual is effectively or virtually attached, for there is nothing arbitrary in this domain.

Now, if one examines examples of supposedly symbolical dreams quoted by Jung and other psychologists of his school, one notices that in most cases it is a matter of false symbolism, of the kind commonly met with in pseudo-spiritual circles. The soul is not only a sacred mirror; more often it is a magic mirror that deceives the one who views himself in it. Jung should have known this, since he himself speaks of the tricks of the *anima,* indicating by this term the feminine aspect of the soul; and some of his own experiences, as described in his memoirs,[53] should have told him that an investi-

---

53. The kind of introspection practiced by Jung by way of psychological investigation and of which he speaks in his memoirs, as well as certain parapsychological phenomena that he provoked by this method, takes one into a frankly spiritualistic ambience. The fact that the author proposed to study these phenomena "scientifically" changes nothing in regard to the influence they in fact had on his theory of "archetypes".

gator of the unconscious depths of the psyche exposes himself, not merely to the wiles of the egocentric soul, but also to psychic influences coming from elsewhere, from unknown beings and entities, especially when the methods of analysis used derive from hypnosis or mediumship. In this context must be placed certain designs executed by sick patients of Jung and which the latter tries to palm off as genuine *mandalas*.[54]

Over and above all this, there exists a symbolism, very general in nature and inherent in language itself, as for instance when one compares truth to light and error to darkness, or progress to an ascent or moral danger to an abyss, or when one represents fidelity by a dog or craftiness by a fox. Now, to explain the occurrence of a similar symbolism in dreams, of which the language is naturally figurative and not discursive, there is no need to refer to a "collective unconscious"; it is enough to note that rational thought is not the whole of thought and that consciousness in the waking state does not cover the whole domain of mental activity. If the figurative language of dreams is not discursive, this does not necessarily make it irrational, and it is possible, as indeed Jung has properly observed, that a dreamer may be more intelligent in his dreams than in the waking state. It would even seem that this difference of level between the two states is fairly frequent among men of our own time, doubtless because the frameworks imposed by modern life are particularly unintelligent and incapable of vehicling in any normal manner the essential contents of human life.

This has obviously nothing to do with the role of purely symbolic or sacred dreams, whether these be spontaneous or evoked through rites; we are thinking here of the example of the Indians of North America, whose whole tradition, as well as their vital ambience, favors a kind of oneiric prophetism.

So as to neglect no aspect of this question, the following should also be said: In every collectivity that has become unfaithful to its own traditional form, to the sacred framework of its life, there occurs a collapse or a sort of mummification of the symbols it had received, and this process will be reflected in the psychic life of every individual belonging to that collectivity and participating in that infidelity. To every truth there corresponds a formal trace, and every spiritual form projects a psychic shadow; when these shadows

54. See C. G. Jung, *The Secret of the Golden Flower* (New York, 1931), Introduction.

are all that remains, they do in fact take on the character of ancestral phantoms that haunt the subconscious. The most pernicious of
psychological errors is to reduce the meaning of symbolism to such
phantoms.

As for the definition of "unconscious", it must never be forgotten that this is eminently relative and provisional. Consciousness
is capable of gradation like light and is similarly refracted in contact
with the media it meets. The ego is the form of individual consciousness, not its luminous source. The latter coincides with the
source of the intelligence itself. In its universal nature, consciousness is in a sense an existential aspect of the intellect, and this
amounts to saying that basically nothing is situated outside it.[55]
Whence it follows that the "unconscious" of the psychologists is
quite simply everything which, in the soul, lies outside ordinary
consciousness—that of the empirical "I" oriented towards the corporeal world—in other words, this "unconscious" is made to
include both lower chaos and the higher states. The latter (which
the Hindus compare to the bliss of deep sleep, the state of *prâjña*)
radiate from the luminous source of the Universal Spirit; the definition of the "unconscious" thus in no wise corresponds to a particular concrete modality of the soul. Many of the errors of "depth
psychology", of which Jung is one of the chief protagonists, result
from the fact that it operates with the "unconscious" as if it were a
definite entity. One often hears it said that Jung's psychology has
"re-established the autonomous reality of the soul". In truth,
according to the perspective inherent in this psychology, the soul is
neither independent of the body nor immortal; it is merely a sort of
irrational fatality situated outside any intelligible cosmic order. If
the moral and mental behavior of man were determined behind the
scenes by some collection of ancestral "types" issuing from a fund
that is completely unconscious and completely inaccessible to the
intelligence, man would be as if suspended between two irreconcilable and divergent realities, namely that of things and that of the
soul.

For all modern psychology, the luminous point of the soul, or its
existential summit, is the consciousness of the "I", which only exists
to the extent that it can disengage itself from the darkness of the
"unconscious". Now, according to Jung, this darkness contains the

55. Let us here recall the Vedantic ternary *Sat-Chit-Ânanda* (Being, Consciousness,
    Bliss).

vital roots of the individuality: the "collective unconscious" would then be endowed with a regulatory instinct, a kind of somnambulant wisdom, no doubt of a biological nature; from this fact, the conscious emancipation of the ego would comprise the danger of a vital uprooting. According to Jung, the ideal is a balance between the two poles—the conscious and the unconscious—a balance that can be realized only by the help of a third term, a sort of center of crystallization, which he calls the "self", a term borrowed from the doctrines of Hinduism. Here is what he has written on the subject:

> With the sensation of the self as an irrational and indefinable entity, to which the "I" is neither opposed nor subordinated, but to which it adheres and round which it moves in some sort, like the earth around the sun, the aim of individuation is attained. I use this term "sensation" to express the empirical character of the relationship between the "I" and the self. In this relationship there is nothing intelligible, for one can say nothing about the contents of the self. The "I" is the only content of the self that we know. The individualized "I" feels itself to be the object of a subject unknown and superior to itself. It seems to me that psychological observation here touches its extreme limit, for the idea of a self is in itself a transcendent postulate, which one can admittedly justify psychologically, but cannot prove scientifically. The step beyond science is an absolute requirement for the psychological evolution described here, for without the postulate in question I could not sufficiently formulate the psychic processes observed from experience. Because of this, the idea of a self at least possesses the value of a hypothesis like the theories about the structure of the atom. And if it be true that here too we are prisoners of an image, it is in any case a very living image, the interpretation of which exceeds my capacities. I scarcely doubt that it is a question of an image, but it is an image that contains us.[56]

Despite a terminology too much bound up with current scientism, one might be tempted to grant full credit to the presentiments expressed in this passage and to find in it an approach to traditional metaphysical doctrines, if Jung, in a further passage, did not relativize the notion of the self by treating it this time, not as a transcendent principle, but as the outcome of a psychological process:

> One could define the self as a sort of compensation in reference to the contrast between inward and outward. Such a definition could well be applied to the self in so far as the latter possesses the character of a result, of an aim to reach, of a thing that has only

56. See C. G. Jung, *Two Essays on Analytical Psychology*, p. 240.

been produced little by little, and of which the experience has cost much travail. Thus, the self is also the aim of life, for it is the most complete expression of that combination of destiny we call an "individual", not only of man in the singular, but also of a whole group, where the one is the complement of the others with a view to a perfect image.[57]

There are some realms where dilettantism is unforgivable. It is the balance to be realized between the unconscious and the conscious, or the integration, in the empirical "personality", of certain forces or impulses emanating from the unconscious, that Jung paradoxically labels as "individuation", using a term by which was traditionally designated not some psychological process or other, but the differentiation of individuals from the starting point of the species. But what Jung understands by this term is a kind of definitive pronunciation of the individuality which is taken as an end in itself. In such a perspective, the notion of "self" plainly loses all metaphysical meaning, but this is not the only traditional notion that Jung appropriates in order to debase it to a purely psychological and even clinical level; thus he compares psychoanalysis, which he uses precisely to promote this "individuation", to an initiation in the proper and sacred meaning of the term, and he even declares that psychoanalysis represents "the only form of initiation still valid in the modern age"![58] Whence proceed a whole series of false assimilations, and intrusions into a realm where psychology is devoid of competence.[59]

---

57. *Ibid.*
58. See psychological commentary of the *Tibetan Book of the Dead*.
59. Jung's psychological interpretation of alchemy has been expressly refuted in my book *Alchemy: Science of the Cosmos, Science of the Soul.* Frithjof Schuon, after reading the present chapter, sent me the following reflections in writing: "People generally see in Jungism, as compared with Freudism, a step towards reconciliation with the traditional spiritualities, but this is in no wise the case. From this point of view, the only difference is that, whereas Freud boasted of being an irreconcilable enemy of religion, Jung sympathizes with it while emptying it of its contents, which he replaces by collective psychism, that is to say by something infra-intellectual, and therefore anti-spiritual. In this there is an immense danger for the ancient spiritualities, whose representatives, especially in the East, are too often lacking in critical sense with regard to the modern spirit, and this by reason of a complex of 'rehabilitation'; also it is not with much surprise, though with grave disquiet, that one has come across echoes of this kind from Japan, where the psychoanalyst's 'equilibrium' has been compared to the *satori* of Zen; and there is little doubt that it would be easy to meet with similar confusions in India and elsewhere. Be that as it may, the confusions in question are greatly favored by the almost universal refusal of people to see

Here it is not a case of the involuntary ignorance of some isolated seeker, for Jung carefully avoided all contact with the representatives of living tradition. During his visit to India, for example, he did not wish to see Srî Râmana Mahârshi—alleging a motive of insolent frivolity[60]—doubtless because he feared instinctively and "unconsciously" (it is a case for saying it) a contact with a reality that would give the lie to his theories. For him, metaphysics was but a speculation in the void or, to be more exact, an illusory attempt by the psychic to reach beyond itself, comparable to the senseless gesture of a man who would pull himself out of a mud-hole by his own hair. This conception is typical of modern psychologism, and this is why we mention it. To the absurd argument that metaphysics is only a production of the psyche, one can immediately object that this judgement itself is but a similar production. Man lives by truth; to accept any truth, however relative it may be, is to accept that *intellectus adequatio rei*. Merely to say "this is that" is automatically to affirm the very principle of adequation, and therefore the presence of the absolute in the relative.

Jung breached certain strictly materialistic frameworks of modern science, but this fact is of no use to anyone, to say the least—one wishes one could have rejoiced over it—because the influences that filter through this breach come from lower psychism and not from the Spirit, which alone is true and alone can save us.

(from *Mirror of the Intellect*)

the devil and to call him by his name, in other words, by a kind of tacit convention compounded of optimism to order, tolerance that in reality hates truth, and compulsory alignment with scientism and official taste, without forgetting 'culture', which swallows everything and commits one to nothing, except complicity in its neutralism; to which must be added a no less universal and quasi-official contempt for whatever is, we will not say intellectualist, but truly intellectual, and therefore tainted, in people's minds, with dogmatism, scholasticism, fanaticism, and prejudice. All this goes hand in hand with the psychologism of our time and is in large measure its result."
60. See the preface to Heinrich Zimmer's book on Shrî Râmana Mahârshi.

Islamic Science

In Moorish Spain, traditional science had reached such a peak that its influence was felt not only in the Maghrib, but also throughout Latin Christendom. Christian scholars in their writings explicitly referred to their Arab predecessors, and the Benedictine monk Adelhard of Bath, at the beginning of the 12th century, wrote as follows:

> Lest it be thought that one as ignorant as I have fashioned these thoughts for myself, I do declare that they derive from my studies of the Arabs. I do not wish—should anything I say displease certain limited minds—to be the one who displeases them, for I know full well what the truly wise must expect from the common run of men. Therefore I take care not to speak for myself; I speak only for the Arabs.

By the time the Christian kings reconquered Toledo, and later Córdoba, the highpoint of Moorish culture had already been passed. Nevertheless, the booty, in the form of books, which they appropriated, decisively influenced the formation of the medieval Schools. No less was the treasure that was taken to the already existing centers of culture in North Africa by the Moors who sought refuge there. Nevertheless, in the view of Ibn Khaldûn, who himself came from a family of scholars and diplomats that had fled from Seville to the Maghrib, and who was called by the Merinids from Tunis to Fez, the treasury of knowledge that was saved was small in comparison with what was lost.

> The principal centers of sedentary culture in the (Islamic) west were Kairuan in the Maghrib and Córdoba in Spain. When these two centers declined, the teaching of the sciences came to a halt. A portion of it remained alive in Marrakesh under the Almohads. But because of the nomadic origin of the Almohads and the brevity of their rule, sedentary culture did not develop deep roots there. . . . As a result, after the destruction of the scientific tradition in Córdoba and Kairuan, Fez and the other cities of the Maghrib remained without sound instruction. . . . (Ibn Khaldûn: *Muqaddima*, 6:7)

In contradiction to this, a scholar named Abû'l Hasan 'Alî ibn Maimûn, towards the end of the 15th century, wrote about Fez as follows:

> In my whole life, I have never seen its equal nor have I seen any other scholars who have so perfectly preserved the sacred law in word and deed (as well as the writings of its formulator, Imâm

Mâlik), and who have so perfectly mastered the other sciences, such as jurisprudence, Koranic exegesis, and expertise in *ahadîth* (plural of *hadîth*, the sayings of the Prophet). In Fez one finds masters of all branches of intellectuality, such as grammar, law of inheritance, mathematics, chronometry, geometry, metaphysics, logic, rhetoric, music, etc., and these masters know all the relevant texts by heart. Whoever does not know by heart the basic text relating to the science about which he speaks, and who cannot, on any question, quote it verbatim, will receive no attention; as a scholar, he will not be taken seriously. Since I left the city—it was in the year 901 (that is, 1495 A.D.)—I have seen nothing that can be compared with Fez and its scholars, either in the other cities of the Maghrib such as Tlemsen, Bujâya, or Tunis, or in any part of Syria or the Hejaz. (Al-Kattâni, *Salwât al-Anfâs*)

The apparent contradiction between the two opinions cited is explained by the fact that the Aristotelian philosophy and natural sciences which had flourished in the old Andalusia found virtually no continuation in the Maghrib; it was Latin Christendom that was destined to inherit these. The Maghrib on the other hand appropriated to itself the Islamic sciences and, with the instinct for the essential characteristic of the North African genius, it traced this highly ramified science back to its principal divisions, finally giving pride of place to Koranic legal science (*al-fiqh*). Thus many blossoms fell from the tree of the sciences; but its branches and its trunk, which had their roots in Koranic doctrine, remained firm. In a modern world in which science has been pulverized into thousands of specialties, each subject to hypotheses and constantly changing experiments, traditional science (the medieval *scientia*) stands out like a harmonious and perfect work of art.

People had spoken to me of Mulay 'Alî as one who possessed both "outward" and "inward" science. But no one had been willing to take me to see him, being fully aware that he shunned any contact that could give rise to public curiosity. Many regarded him as the spiritual successor of his grandfather Mulay al-'Arabî ad-Darqâwî who, at the beginning of the 19th century had revivified Islamic mysticism in its purest form, and of his father, Mulay Tayyib, who had been the grand master of the Darqâwî spiritual order. But since the French protectorate was showing all too much interest in the fate of this order, he himself had declined any office in it, and lived as a simple scholar, teaching Arabic and law at the Koranic university of Al-Qarawiyyîn.

In the spring of 1933, I made up my mind to visit him in his house in Fez. He received me without too many questions, motioned me to sit down on a low cushion in his large bare room, took up an old Arabic book, and began to read to me about the Second Coming of Christ at the end of time. Since I was not sitting directly in front of him, and since he had allowed the hood of his jellaba to slip backwards from his head, I could readily observe his noble and already aged face. It expressed a two-fold nobility: his descent from the Prophet—or at any rate from the peak of Arab aristocracy—showed itself in the clear bold line of forehead and nose and in the fine contours of his temples and cheeks which were sharply illumined by light from the inner courtyard; it made me think of the most noble of the faces in El Greco's painting "The Burial of Count Orgaz". But in addition, his features were marked by a spiritual discipline—the consciously assumed inheritance of his illustrious forefathers, which emphasized their simplicity and sobriety.

As I was marveling at the human frame, the culmination of so much venerable tradition, I had not yet fully awakened to his intellectual alertness, which every now and again would suddenly focus on me in a detached but searching manner, only to change back immediately into a simple goodness.

The text which he read aloud to me and on which he occasionally made brief comments in Moroccan dialect, was a collection of prophecies, partly symbolic and partly literal, which the Prophet and certain of his immediate successors had made with regard to the forthcoming end of the world. Mulay 'Alî had undoubtedly chosen this text in order to show me what Christ meant for him. In fact, he spoke of his Second Coming as if it were immediately imminent, and at one moment he pointed to himself and said: "If our Lord 'Isâ (Jesus) should return to earth before I die, I would immediately rise and follow him!"

Belief in Christ's Second Coming is firmly rooted in Islamic tradition: he will return to earth before the end of time to judge men "with the sword of Mohammed", to kill the antichrist (*ad-dajjâl*), and to lead the elect into a new and better world arising out of the destruction of the old one. Only true believers will be able to withstand Christ's gaze; unbelievers will perish under it. But before Christ comes, the antichrist will appear in order to lead men astray by his false promises and seeming wonders. He will call evil good, and good evil. A stream of water and a stream of fire will accompany him; whoever should drink the water will taste fire, and whoever should touch the fire, will feel cool water. According to a saying of the Prophet, the antichrist is not simply one man. A whole series of false prophets will arise, which means that one can never be sure which of the various signs prophesied apply to one or the other of them. Only those who live through these events will know exactly what, in these prophecies, is to be taken literally or symbolically.

Before the end of the world takes place, and before the antichrist as such appears, the "rightly-guided one" or *mahdî*, a descendant of Mohammed, will come to gather together the faithful and lead them into battle against the powers of darkness. When before battle, the believers are gathered together for prayer "beside the white minaret of Damascus", Christ will descend from the clouds. Under his reign a new and better age will begin, but this too will end when Gog and Magog, two hideous tribes, break through the wall which Alexander the Great, at God's command, had built against them, and overrun the earth. Christ, with the elect, will retreat to Mount Sinai, until, through his prayers and those of his faithful, the armies of darkness are destroyed, and a flood purifies the earth. Only then, on a rejuvenated earth, will the millennium begin, at the end of which a new degeneration will gradually set in, until the day of the Last Judgement arrives. "But God knows best", added Mulay 'Alî "when and how all this will happen." Then he mentioned the signs which, according to a well-known saying of the Prophet, will herald the end of the present age: "the maid-servant will give birth to her mistress, and bare-footed shepherds will vie with one another in building tall buildings." These things, he said, were already happening, for the words about the maid-servant giving birth to her mistress was a reference to the destruction of the natural social order, and the construction of high buildings "by poor shepherds" was already taking place. The Sufis (the Islamic mystics) interpreted these sayings in yet another, and more inward, sense; but the one interpretation does not exclude the other. All of a sudden Mulay 'Alî looked me straight in the face, surprising me by the severity of his regard, and said emphatically: "The antichrist is already born."

Such was my first meeting with this venerable elder who, contrary to my expectation, declared himself ready to teach me the fundaments of traditional Arab science (*scientia*).

Every morning Mulay 'Alî would walk down from the high-lying district in which he lived to the Qarawiyyîn university, carefully gath-

ering up his immaculately white garments as he made his way
through the tumult of beasts of burden trotting uphill covered with
sweat, and the swarms of porters imperiously demanding right of
way. Over his jellaba and turban he wore a wide burnous, but
without anything that might indicate his rank. And yet it often happened that some peasant from out of town, who was bringing his
wares to the market, would timidly approach him in order to kiss his
hand or the hem of his garment. At midday he made the return
journey uphill on a mule with a red saddle which a servant held
ready for him at the door of the Qarawiyyîn.

The Qarawiyyîn mosque and university consists of wide halls
supported by many pillars, ranged around a lengthy courtyard
where fountains sparkle in the sun. The light shines from the courtyard into the halls, pours onto the woven mats covering the floors,
and reaches as far as the arches joining the many pillars. Each man
of learning has the custom of sitting by one particular pillar, and, as
he leans against it, his students squat on the mats, and form a semi-
circle facing him. Men of the people and peasants from the coun-
tryside who visited the mosque would often sit down, at a respectful
distance from him, in order to hear something of the sacred science. Instruction was in the form of a conversation; one of the students would read from a classical work, and the teacher would
occasionally interrupt him, in order to give explanations. Sometimes students would put questions or make objections, to which
the master would reply. Sometimes this didactic conversation would
become rapid and lively like an altercation. In this it would
resemble what in the Middle Ages was called a *disputatio*. Nevertheless Mulay 'Alî was against any overdue haste. He did not permit an
author to be referred to hastily or without the student wishing him
God's grace, nor did he allow anyone to anticipate the proper logical development of a thought. Each brick in the edifice of a doctrine had first to be sharply cut and polished before the next one
was added to it. And although the young men who listened to him
may have been afflicted with an inner disquiet and secretly longed
for the seductions and excitements of the modern science that had
come from Europe, they nonetheless paid full attention, under his
strict surveillance, to the measured and prudent teachings of their
master.

When his listeners had departed, he would sometimes remain
for a while facing the direction of Mecca. Then he was a picture of
inwardness; his skin became as smooth and clear as wax; the con-

tours of his cheek bones turned even sharper. As if enlarged by a hidden fire, his eyes looked into the distance. He was visibly closer to the next world than to this one. He sat upright, almost motion-lessly; only a scarcely visible rapid swaying of his body seemed to sug-gest the invisible flowing of grace between him and Heaven.

From time to time Mulay 'Alî received me in a friend's orchard, in order to read Arabic texts with me. He chose these texts so that they might not only be useful to me linguistically, but would also demonstrate some aspect or other of tradition. Often, when I arrived at the orchard, which lay within the city walls encircled by high hedges of bamboo, and crossed over a narrow dyke that facili-tated the irrigation of the low-lying beds of mint and melons, he would already be sitting there, under an old fig-tree, on a red mat that he always carried with him.

According to a famous saying of the Prophet, the Islamic tradi-tion rests on three fundamental principles, namely: resignation to the Divine Will (*islâm),* faith (*imân*), and spiritual virtue (*ihsân*). The Divine Will makes itself known in the revealed religious law *(sharî'a)* and in destiny. The object of faith is the doctrine of the unity and omnipotence of God, of the divine mission of all prophets—including Jesus—up to Mohammed, and of life after death. As for spiritual virtue—or sincerity—it is by means of this that ordinary faith becomes inward certainty, and that outward con-formity to the law becomes total abandonment to the will of God. Spiritual virtue was defined by the Prophet as follows: "It is that thou shouldst worship God as if thou sawest Him; for if thou seest Him not, He nevertheless seeth thee."

The instruction that is provided in the Koranic universities relates to the first two principles just mentioned, namely to the con-tents of the faith, which are enshrined in the dogmas, and to the law which, on the one hand, determines divine worship (the rites) and, on the other hand, determines the social order. The exact knowl-edge of the third principle, spiritual virtue, exceeds the bounds of scholastic instruction, which has been called "the science of the out-ward". It is the prerogative of the contemplative sage or mystic, the Sufi, who alone has access to "the science of the inward". In the Islamic world mysticism is regarded as a science, which is handed down from master to disciple just like jurisprudence, with this dif-ference, that from the disciple a special qualification, or more exactly, an inward vocation, is required. In addition, theoretical learning must go hand in hand with spiritual practice, which alone is capable of disclosing the content of the propositions and the symbols that are taught.

Most of the students at the Qarawiyyîn are preparing themselves for the profession of advocate or judge. The law is dependent upon the Koran. Since the language of the Koran has many levels of meaning and therefore cannot be perfectly translated, a knowledge of classical Arabic is the foundation of all studies. Even more, it is the key to a whole intellectual and spiritual world. According to an Arab proverb: "Wisdom reveals herself in the dialectic of the Greeks, the craftsmanship of the Chinese, and the language of the Arabs." In fact, classical Arabic combines a rigorously logical, almost algebraic structure, with a well-nigh unlimited capacity to form words. Almost all Arabic words can be reduced to simple tri-consonantal roots, from which, by means of reduplication, sound-shifting, and addition—all according to a system of rules—a whole tree of semantically-related verbs, nouns, and adjectives can be derived. "The Arabic language," said a European philologist, "would be of an amazing intellectual transparency, if the choice of phonetic roots, from which hundreds of words derive, did not seem to be so completely arbitrary." According to Sufi tradition, however, if the meaning of these roots is not rationally explicable, it is nevertheless intuitively intelligible.

It has recently been discovered that amongst all living Semitic languages, Arabic possesses the richest and therefore the most ancient vocabulary. It is closely related to the language of Hammurabi, and therefore to the language of Abraham. That an ancient language should possess such a subtle gradation of meaning is not strange, for the younger a language is, the more its forms are simplified. What surprises scholars, however, is that a language which was first committed to writing so recently (namely in the 7th century), has preserved so much of its early inheritance. The explanation lies in the timeless manner of thinking of the nomads, and also in the fact that the nomad jealously protects and cultivates his language as his only inalienable possession. The Arabian desert also contributed to the preservation of this ancient Semitic language. And this is strong testimony to the spiritual richness of nomadism, which possesses no visible or outward sign, no image, no building, no script, and no craftsmanship.

The simplest form of the Arabic word, its root form, is the verb (*verbum*—word), and therein lies a profound meaning, an indication that every phenomenon is nothing other than a happening, a manifestation developing in time, so that language transposes everything into a phonetic happening. One day Mulay 'Alî with an other-worldly expression on his face, looked straight at me—or rather straight through me—and said: "All things other than God are ephemeral in themselves. I do not say that they are transient because one day they will no longer exist, I say that they are ephemeral now and always, and have never been anything other than ephemeral!"

According to Islamic tradition, it is the duty of every believer, to the limit of his intellectual capacity, to think out the contents of his faith to the end. "Seek ye knowledge" (*'ilm*), said the Prophet, "even if it be in China." And on another occasion he said : "One hour of reflection is worth more than two years of religious service." Thought, however, has an upper limit: "Reflect on the Divine Qualities and Acts, and not on the Divine Essence."

Islamic theology is a rational science which does not lose sight of the fact that its object, Divine Reality, cannot be grasped mentally; and this implies no contradiction: when reason recognizes its own limits, it transcends them, in a certain sense; it behaves rather like the surveyor who, from various locations, takes a sighting on a point which is inaccessible to him. This perspective makes it possible, without any illogic, on the one hand, to deny all limits, characteristics, and forms with regard to God and, on the other, to refer back to Him all the perfect aspects of existence such as beauty, goodness and power. The same also applies to apparently contradictory propositions, for example, that man possesses free choice, and that man can do nothing that God has not already foreseen and predetermined for him. That necessity and freedom are both present in God may not be graspable by the reason, but it is so by the intellect, just as is the simultaneous presence in God of past, present, and future.

The situation is similar in the case of the idea of Divine Unity (*tauhid*), which is the keystone of the whole doctrinal edifice. The highest meaning of unity cannot be exhausted mentally; it opens onto the Infinite; and yet one can understand unity at all levels of spiritual insight. That God is One is in principle apparent to all, and this is the basis of the unshakable cohesion of Islamic thought.

Islamic jurisprudence (*fiqh*) concerns on the one hand the prescriptions with regard to divine worship—profession of faith, ritual ablution, prayer, fasting, almsgiving, pilgrimage—and on the other hand the social institutions, from questions of inheritance to the regulations for buying and selling.

The two pillars of jurisprudence are tradition and the logical principles by means of which the laws mentioned in the Koran may be applied to individual cases.

What in the Koran itself is mentioned only briefly and in a general manner, is completed by the transmission, originally oral but later written, of the sayings (*ahadîth*) and the practice (*sunna*) of the Prophet. The testing of each individual tradition with regard to authenticity, bearing in mind the greater or lesser reliability of the transmitters, is a widely diversified science that makes great demands on the memory, requiring not only a knowledge of all the attested sayings of the Prophet—and there are thousands of them—but also of the chain of transmitters for each individual saying.

In Sunni Islam there are four classical schools of law, which differ from one another, firstly, as regards the extent to which they follow the Prophet's practice as it was maintained in Medina during the first Islamic centuries, and, secondly, as regards the extent to which they make use of decision by analogy (*ijtihâd*), in order to make the proper transition from a known case to an unknown one. The people of the Maghrib belong to the legal school of Mâlik ibn Anas who, more than any of the other three founders, holds fast to the practice of Medina. Since it is not possible today to find any testimonies which the founders of the four schools did not already know, any innovation can only be a deviation from the general tradition, and that is why the representatives of traditional jurisprudence defend themselves strongly against all "reforms" proposed by Arab nationalists.

For the European, whose imagination as to what a holy book is has been fashioned by the Bible or perhaps by Oriental scriptures such as the Bhagavad-Gîtâ or the Sayings of the Buddha, the Koran is at first sight disappointing. For the Koran is neither a narrative, like the Gospels, in which the Divine appears in a humanly graspable form, nor a lucidly constructed metaphysical doctrine. Its form seems to be arbitrary, and is in fact a collection of individual revelations, providing answers to the questions and needs of the first Muslim community, and exhibiting sudden changes of content, so that one can find side by side references to Divine things and to very human things. Finally, the Biblical stories which the Koran retells, are presented in an unexpected, abbreviated and dry manner that seems strange to the Christian. They are deprived of their epic character and are inserted as didactic examples of an infinitely various praise of God.

It is only when one considers individual Koranic verses and begins to be aware of their many levels of meaning, that one can assess the powerful spiritual effect which this book has been able to exert, and realize why it has become the daily nourishment of thousands of contemplatively inclined people.

For the Muslim who reads the Gospel for the first time, the disappointment and surprise are scarcely less. On one occasion I brought Mulay 'Alî, who knew Christianity only from the Islamic point of view and on the basis of those orally transmitted sayings of Christ that eventually found their way into Arabic books, a recent Arabic translation of the four Gospels. He was visibly disappointed that the Gospels, unlike the Koran, did not take the form of Divine speech, but consisted of reports on Christ's life. In the Koran, God speaks in the first person. He describes Himself and makes known His laws. The Muslim is therefore inclined to consider each individual sentence of the holy Book as a separate revelation and to experience the words themselves, and even their very sound, as a means of grace. Mulay 'Alî was put off both by the easygoing style of the translation and by the fact that the meaning lay more in the event described than in this or that verbal formula. He looked for verses that described God's qualities, His majesty, His omnipotence, and scarcely found any. I had to explain to him that the Gospels could only be completely understood against the background of the Old Testament.

What surprised him most was that God was called "Father" and Christ "Son"; for between father and son, he said, there was a similarity of nature which the incomparability of God excluded. To this I remarked that the expression "son of God" meant that Jesus had no human father, which the Koran itself teaches, and that furthermore his spirit emanated from God and was of the same essence of God, which the Koran also maintains, when it says that Christ is "Word of God and Spirit of God". Mulay 'Alî answered that this meaning was indeed acceptable, even if it touched on secrets which human language was more likely to misrepresent than to express.

Through his whole education, Mulay 'Alî was too much the Islamic man of learning—centered on the doctrinal unequivocalness of his own tradition—to come to terms with the completely different speech and symbolism of a religion that was foreign to him. Therein he differed, as I was later to learn, from many other representatives of the "science of the inward". Thus the Sufi master Ahmad ibn Mustafâ al-'Alâwî, who at that time lived in

Mostaghanem in Algeria and had many disciples from Morocco, said to a Catholic priest: "If you accept that expressions like 'God the Father' and 'Son of God' are symbols which can be interpreted metaphysically, then there is nothing that separates us from you."

"Consider the lilies of the field; they toil not, neither do they spin; and yet I say unto you that even Solomon in all his glory was not arrayed like one of these." These words of Christ have the same ring about them as the Koran, according to which everything in Heaven and earth is a "sign" from God. In order better to understand what the Koran means for the ordinary Muslim, I once observed a group of men who, early in the morning, before the sun had risen, were chanting the Koran in unison in the courtyard of the Qarawiyyîn mosque. The Arabic language is rich in sounds, from the characteristic gutterals to every abrupt or reverberating sound that it is possible for lips and palate to produce; it is as if the whole body were speaking. When all these natural drums and cymbals accommodate themselves to the inimitable rhythm of the Koran, when this rhythm is borne by a triumphant and solemn melody, and when all of this is united with the meaning of the words, there is born that unique effect that overwhelms every Arab listener.

When the chanters reached the verse: "To God belong the Heavens and the earth, and to God the journey returneth. Sawest thou not how God guideth the clouds, gathereth them together, and disposeth of them?", one of the men raised his eyes to the early morning sky as if he perceived the cloud gathering; and at the following words: "then seest thou the rain-drops fall from their midst", his eyes moved downwards from the heavens to the earth. The recitation continued: "From Heaven doth He send down mountains of hail, as a visitation on whomsoever He will"—the man looked round about him—"and which He holdeth back from whomsoever He will. The glare of His lightning almost removeth the sight from men's eyes"—the man looked as if he had been blinded. Finally his face showed repose at the words: "God suffereth the night to follow the day; verily therein dwelleth a sign for those who see."

Mulay 'Alî was of the view that in our age only very few people were capable of understanding Sufi wisdom, and that it was better to remain silent about it than to speak. If he were asked about the inward states that Sufis attain, he would decline to answer, saying: "These are fruits that grow for themselves on the tree of divine service; let us rather speak of how to care for the tree and how to water it, and not of its fruits, before they are ripe." And to a young man who had asked him to accept him as his disciple on the way of contemplation, he replied: "Dear friend, the relationship between spiritual master and spiritual disciple is something so elevated that we would be very daring if we sought to establish it. Let us rather speak of the things we should be doing." And he gave him the advice that he felt was right for him. His reticence was perhaps also caused by the *wahhâbî* influences, hostile to mysticism, which at that time had gained a certain foothold amongst the students. Nevertheless, he decided on one occasion to make Al-Ghazâlî's famous work "The Revivification of the Religious Sciences" (*Ihyâ 'ulûm ad-Dîn*) the subject of his lectures. This work was recognized by almost all the representatives of the "science of the outward", since the exoteric legitimacy of its standpoint is unassailable. At the same time, however, it contains several chapters which constitute a bridge from exoterism to esoterism or mysticism. At the end of his first lecture the students began to question Mulay 'Alî about Sufism, and one of them said: "We can readily believe that centuries ago there were great mystics who received authentic inspirations and even possessed wonderful powers; but today all those who claim to represent Sufism are nothing but charlatans. In our day and age there are no longer any Sufis." Mulay 'Alî turned to him and said, with a mildness that brooked no contradiction: "My son, how can you set a limit to the omnipotence of God?"

Islamic mysticism was not always banned from the Qarawiyyîn university. As recently as the beginning of the century, Sufi treatises were the subject of lectures, and one of the most important representatives of mysticism in the Maghrib, the Sufi Abû 'Abdallâh Ibn 'Abbâd ar-Rundî, who was born in Ronda in Andalusia in 1331, was preacher and *imâm* there. A contemporary writes of him:

> In Fez I met the saintly scholar Abû 'Abdallâh Muhammad ibn Ibrâhîm ar-Rundî, whose father before him had been a famous preacher. The son Abu 'Abdallâh is distinguished by his composure, his asceticism, and his righteousness. He is the author of the verse: "He attains no nobility who has not first weighed the clay of this earth with eternity." I met him on the Prophet's birthday in the sultan's palace, where he had been invited to hear the spiritual singing. He manifestly did not welcome this. I have never at any other time seen him at any gathering, and whoever might wish to speak with him was obliged to see him alone. Once I requested him to pray for me. He blushed and was embarrassed, but agreed nevertheless. The only luxury he permitted himself was perfumed

oils and incense. He did his own housework. He was unmarried and had no servant. At home he wore a patchwork garment, but when he went out he covered it with a green or a white robe. His disciples were all from the best and most gifted of the community. . . . Today he is imâm and preacher in the Qarawiyyîn mosque at Fez.

Al-Kattânî wrote of him:

He had something about him that won the hearts of children. They swarmed around him, as soon as they saw him, in order to kiss his hand. But kings too sought to gain his friendship. . . .

He studied in Ronda, Fez, and Tlemsen, and in Salé he was the disciple of the Andalusian master Ahmad Ibn 'Âshir. From there he traveled to Tangier where he met the Sufi Abû Marwân 'Abd al-Mâlik, who was perhaps the "unlettered man" of whom Ibn Abbâd said that he alone had been able to open his inward eye. . . .

The Shaikh Abu Mas'ûd al-Harrâs recalls: "I was reciting the Koran aloud in the courtyard of the Qarawiyyîn mosque as the muezzins were making the call for the night-prayer. Suddenly I saw Ibn 'Abbâd, in a sitting position, fly over the door of his house, across the courtyard of the mosque, and disappear into the hall that surrounds the atrium. I went to have a look, and I found him praying close to the *mihrâb.*

It is related that, as he approached death, he laid his head on the lap of one of his disciples, and began to recite the Throne Verse from the Koran. When he reached the words "the Living, the Eternal", he continued repeating "O God! O Living! O Eternal!" Thereupon one of those present addressed him by name and recited the continuation of the verse; but he went on with his invocation. Shortly before he passed on he was heard reciting the verse: "The friends are leaving me, but they will return when I leave them."

Before his death he bequeathed a sum of money which he had buried at the head of his bed. He directed that with it a piece of land should be bought, the revenue from which was to be used for the upkeep of the Qarawiyyîn mosque. When the sum of money was counted—it came to eight hundred and ten gold *mithqal*—it was discovered that it was the exact amount that he had received in salary during his twenty-five years as *imâm* and preacher.

(from *Fez, City of Islam*)

The Cosmology of the
Arab Philosophers

The Arab philosophers—and this includes all those whose works
were written in Arabic—have often been accused of having inextricably woven Platonic elements into the Aristotelian heritage which
they passed on to the Christian West, as if by so doing they were
guilty of misrepresentation. In reality, this "mingling" for which they
are censured, represents an outstanding work of adaptation, a synthesis in the true sense of the word, without which the intellectual
flowering of the Christian Middle Ages would scarcely have been
conceivable. The fertile union of intellectual discipline and contemplative spirit, for which the schools of Paris, Chartres, Oxford,
and Strasbourg—to name but a few—were renowned in the 12th
and 13th centuries, is largely the outcome of that very same "mingling" found in the works of the Arab al-Kindî, and the Persians al-
Fârâbî (Alpharabius) and Ibn Sînâ (Avicenna), and their Spanish
successors, such as Ibn Gabirol (Avicebron) and Ibn Bâjja (Avempace). All these philosophers combined the strictly methodical
thought of Aristotle, proceeding from premise to premise, with the
contemplative Platonic approach which was directed immediately
to the essence of things. Obviously the Arab scholars were sometimes mistaken about the authorship of Greek doctrines. But what
concerned the philosophers named above was not so much the
question of which writings should be attributed to Plato or to Aristotle, as from which viewpoint one master or the other reasoned.
For the Arabs were convinced that the great sages of antiquity did
not simply construct a system of ideas, but took as their starting
point a direct vision of reality, so that any contradictions were simply
like one and the same scene painted by two different artists. If we
are familiar with the subject of the painting, it is possible to reconcile the apparent discrepancies of the different renderings. It was
possible for the Arab scholars to reconcile Aristotelian philosophy
with that of Plato, because they themselves possessed a firm axis to
which they could refer all essential aspects of reality. This axis was
the doctrine of the oneness of God. Moreover, this doctrine has two
facets: on the one hand it maintains that God is unique and exalted
above the entire universe, and, on the other, it implies that everything that exists necessarily partakes of the Divine Being. There is
only *one* Being. Thus, multiplicity springs from unity and never sup-

plants it; the one Being is reflected in manifold ways and, by degrees, appears increasingly fragmented, limited, and ephemeral, while nevertheless remaining one. The Arabs took the outlines of this doctrine largely from the metaphysics of Plotinus, although in essence it is set out in the Koran.

One fundamental ingredient of this doctrine is the hierarchical structure of the universe: multiplicity in unity and unity in multiplicity—this is the law of hierarchy.

An awareness that reality embraces innumerable levels of existence was common to all the cultures of Antiquity and the Middle Ages, whether this was expressed in mythological or philosophical form. That the whole of reality should consist of the physical world which can be comprehended by our five senses is a very recent concept, and one which is basically contradicted by any knowledge of oneself. For man readily discovers that the "stuff" (so to speak) of which his soul is made is different from that of his body, and that for all its ties to the physical world, it possesses qualities that the body does not possess, such as perception, thought, and independent action. Endowed with these faculties, the soul is not, however, the only non-physical condition of human existence. For the soul, with its constant changes, is itself an object of knowledge, and this presupposes that there is something like an inner eye that sees the soul, while itself remaining constant. This is the Intellect in the medieval acceptance of this word. To try and comprehend it would be as hopeless as an attempt to see one's own faculty of vision. It transcends thought, yet it lends all possible certainty to thought. All rational evidence would be nothing without the truths that are a direct "illumination" from the Intellect. The medieval philosophers refer to the "active intellect" (*intellectus agens* in Latin, *al-'aql al-fâ'âl* in Arabic), because the Intellect consists, as it were, of the pure act of knowing, and never itself becomes the passive object of perception.

For man, the soul is his inner being, and the Intellect is the innermost part of that inner being. The physical world "outside" him is, so to speak, received and transformed into something "inward" by the sensory organs and the corresponding mental powers. Common sense, the *sensus communis*, collates the external impressions, imagination translates them into images, the intelligence sifts and presents them to the intellect, which makes the final distinction between true and false. Accordingly, the various conditions or layers of human nature can be thought of in terms of a varying number of concentric circles, with the outer circle corresponding to the physical condition, and the center to the Intellect.

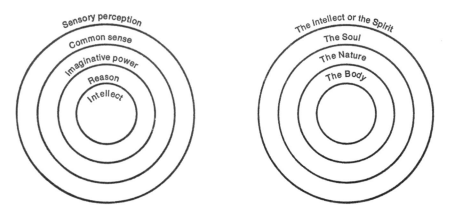

The advantage of this schema, which was well-known to medieval philosophers, and to which we shall return later, is that it illustrates the order of basic realities in the simplest way. However, its limitations, and its partial fallacy are immediately evident in that the very element representing supra-personal and universal truth—namely the Intellect—appears as the smallest thing—a mere point. The reason for this is that the entire scheme with its differentiation between "external" and "internal" is determined by an individual or "subjective" point of view. As the object of perception, the physical world appears comprehensive to subjective experience, while the Intellect, which is to the physical world what the source of light is to an illuminated room, appears as an elusive, invisible point.

But taking the different levels of reality, as revealed in man, not in their subjective role, but in their actual existence, it becomes clear that the higher must include the lower, the knower must include the known, the universal must include the individual, and the free the less free. The applied schema can thus be reversed: the Intellect then corresponds to the outer circle, because in its knowledge it encompasses everything (not in any spatial sense), just as the soul with its consciousness and its mental powers encompasses the body. This is also a manner in which the system of concentric circles—one encompassing the next one—was applied by the medieval philosophers. They saw in it not only a reflection of the essential structure of man, but of the entire universe, for the various degrees of reality existed before the individual beings that share in it. If the physical world were not essentially, and in its very nature, included in the world of the soul, there would be no perception, and the impressions that we receive of the external world would merely be so many random coincidences. And if the physical, as well as the psychical, world were not encompassed by the Intellect, there would be no universally valid knowledge that surpasses the individual. One can thus speak, not only of a physical universe, but also of a psychical and an intellectual universe, and of one encompassing the other according to the spatial symbolism which we apply metaphorically.

In this context it is appropriate to mention the Jewish philosopher, Solomon ben Gabirol, who lived in the first half of the 11th century, and appears in Spain as one of the first followers of Avicenna. In his book, *The Fountain of Life*, he makes a pupil ask his teacher why the sages often represent spiritual substances as circles or spheres, as such figures are peculiar to physical objects alone. The teacher replies that this is a symbol of the relationship between cause and effect, or of knowing and being known. He then gives the pupil the following examples—and in order to understand them it is necessary to know that the medieval philosophers considered nature as the motive power between the body and soul—:

> Observe the power of nature, and you will find that it encompasses the body, because it affects it, and because the body is subject to nature, so that it is, as it were, enveloped by nature. Consider, too, the vegetative soul, and you will find that it has an effect upon nature and dominates it, and that nature is enveloped by this soul and is subject to its action. Then consider also the rational soul and the Intellect. Both the one and the other embrace all the substances subordinate to them, by knowing, penetrating and dominating them. This applies especially to the Intellect, which is finer and more perfect than all else.
>
> Proceeding from these qualities peculiar to the individual human being, you will understand that the universal properties likewise exist within one another, in the sense that the soul contains the body, and the Intellect, the soul—for the lower quality is encompassed by the loftier one, which supports and knows it. The universal soul embraces the entire physical world; that is to say, it supports its existence within its own existence. It forms a visual image of everything within it, and sees it in much the same way that our own particular souls, each with its own corresponding body, imagine their body to be, and see all that is in them. Even more all-embracing is the universal Intellect, because of its perfection, its capacity to display itself (in everything), and because of the nobility of its nature. Hence you will also comprehend how the

first, sublime, and holy Creator (of the world) knows all things, and how they are contained in His omniscience. . . .

In these same metaphorical terms, the infinite space surrounding the outer circle on our diagram, corresponds to divine knowledge. The outermost circle is itself the universal Intellect, and the circles inscribed within it represent the universal soul and the entire physical world. In accordance with the teaching of Plotinus, universal nature is frequently inserted between the universal soul, which comprises the individual souls as the sea contains the waves, and the totality of the physical or corporeal world. It is to the purely physical condition, as is the power of movement to inert matter.

The totality of corporeal existence is represented by the all-encompassing vault of Heaven. But within this, the hierarchy of the different levels of existence is again repeated in the form of the planetary spheres, just as they can be seen from the earth. It is in this sense that Ibn Gabirol says:

> Just as corporeal existence, in its essence and form, reflects spiritual existence, so the enveloping capacity of spiritual qualities corresponds to physical envelopment, since the lower is always an imitation of the higher. . . . Thus we may say that the spiritual substance embraces the corporeal, because the latter, by its very nature, exists within it, just as all bodies exist within the One Heavenly body.

This calls to mind Dante's description of the heavenly spheres, and with reason, for in both there is the same vision of the cosmos that goes back through Avicenna to Plato, and even further. The orbits of the planets, which from the earth appear to move in ever-widening circles, offer a natural illustration of the levels of existence. The astronomic heavens do not themselves constitute these levels, but correspond to them, because physical existence, as Ibn Gabirol says, reflects spiritual existence; and Dante means the same thing, when he says:

> The physical orbits are wider or narrower, according to the measure of virtue distributed in all their parts. . . . Therefore the greatest orbit, that includes the whole great universe, corresponds to the (spiritual) cycle that loves most and knows most. (*Paradiso*, XXVIII. 64–72).

The validity of this symbol does not depend on whether or not the geocentric view of the world—the one shared by Dante and the Arab philosophers—is scientifically accurate. It is sufficient that it corresponds to general human experience. Obviously, the assumption that the earth stands still and the stars revolve around it in greater or smaller orbits is based upon an optical illusion. However, this fallacy is, to some extent, inherent in the nature of man; it merely proves that our sensory perceptions are limited, and no "exact" science, however advanced, can overcome this; something of an optical illusion will always cling. Yet the more profound meaning of the geocentric view of the world lies in its very symbolism. If the Divine Spirit envelops this world, not spatially, but by virtue of its Being, then it is no fallacy to compare it with the all-embracing, starless heaven, where even space comes to an end. And if this image is valid, then it is also true to regard the hierarchical order of the stars that appear to revolve in ever-widening orbits, as an illustration of the supra-terrestrial states of existence or consciousness. It is no coincidence that the stars are not only a source of light, but also a measure of time.

There is a profound reason why this symbol of the universe, represented by the diagram of concentric circles, can be "read" in two opposing, but complementary ways. In one sense the outer circle, or rather everything outside it, stands for Ultimate Reality; in another sense, the center of all the circles represents the Divine Origin. Both "readings" or interpretations are equally valid for, in effect, pure Being is both that which contains all, as well as being the unfathomable center of all things, even if, when expressed in spatial terms, this sounds contradictory.

*
* *

In the symbolism of the spider's web (with center, radii, and concentric circles), we can find a simple illustration of the difference between the Aristotelian and Platonic philosophies. Aristotelian philosophy looks on the different circles, or what they represent, as separate entities, and, significantly, this means that the center too is separate from the circles. Platonic philosophy, on the other hand, considers the analogies that link all levels of reality. This is symbolized by the radii that radiate out from the center and intersect all the circles. All points on the same radius, no matter which circle they intersect, are thus linked to the center. They are like traces of the same essence on different levels of existence.

83

From this, it can be seen that Aristotelian thought applies chiefly to the logical homogeneity of a given level of existence, whereas Platonic thought takes account of the symbolic character of a thing, which connects it "vertically" to the higher levels of reality. The two views can be reconciled, provided their differences are remembered.

There can be any number of concentric circles, but it is simplest to envisage three circles, which represent the inner structure of man, namely—from the center outwards—*Spiritus, anima,* and *corpus*: Spirit or Intellect, soul, and body.

Likewise, there can be any number of rays, issuing forth from the center and intersecting the circles. Understood as rays from a single light, this light is no less than the Universal Intellect (*intellectus primus* or *al-'aql al-awwal*), which, emanating from its divine source, illumines all levels of existence, and is reflected (more or less refracted) at every level.

St. Albert the Great wrote: "One cannot become an accomplished philosopher unless one knows the philosophies of both Aristotle and of Plato." Similarly, St. Bonaventura said: "Among the philosophers, Plato received the word of Wisdom, and Aristotle that of Science. The first considered principally the higher reasons, the second, the lower reasons." The Arab philosophers Avicenna (Ibn Sînâ) and Avempace (Ibn Bâjja) were of the same opinion.

(from *Moorish Culture in Spain*)

3

Sacred Art as the Expression of Religious Truth

The Universality
of Sacred Art

When historians of art apply the term "sacred" to any and every work that has a religious subject, they overlook the fact that art is essentially form. An art cannot be called sacred solely because its subjects derive from spiritual truths; its formal language must also derive from the same source. This is by no means the case with a religious art like that of the Renaissance or Baroque periods, which, as far as style is concerned, in no way differs from the fundamentally profane art of those periods; neither its subjects, which, in a wholly outward and so to speak literary manner, it takes from religion, nor the devotional feelings with which it is often permeated, nor even the nobility of soul which sometimes finds expression in it, suffice to confer on it a truly sacred character. No art merits the epithet sacred unless its very forms reflect the spiritual vision characteristic of a particular religion.

Every form "vehicles" a particular quality of being. The religious subject of a work of art can be merely superimposed on a form, in which case it lacks any relation to the formal "language" of the work, as is demonstrated by Christian art since the Renaissance. Such productions are merely profane works of art with a religious theme. On the other hand, there is no sacred art which is profane in form, for there is a rigorous analogy between form and spirit. A spiritual vision necessarily finds its expression in a particular formal language. If this language has been forgotten—with the result that a so-called sacred art draws its forms from absolutely any kind of profane art—it means that a spiritual vision of things no longer exists.

It would be meaningless to seek to excuse the protean style of a religious art, or its indefinite and ill-defined character, on the grounds of the universality of dogma or the freedom of the spirit. Granted that spirituality in itself is independent of forms, this in no way implies that it can be expressed and transmitted by any and every kind of form. Through its qualitative essence, form has a place in the sensible order analogous to that of truth in the intellectual order; this is the significance of the Greek notion of *eidos*. Just as a mental form, such as a dogma or a doctrine, can be an adequate, albeit limited, reflection of a Divine Truth, so a sensible form can retrace a truth or a reality which transcends both the plane of sensible forms and the plane of thought.

Every sacred art is therefore founded on a science of forms, or in other words, on the symbolism inherent in forms. It must be borne in mind that a sacred symbol is not merely a conventional sign; it manifests its archetype by virtue of a certain ontological law. As Ananda Coomaraswamy has observed, a sacred symbol *is*, in a sense, that which it expresses. For this very reason, traditional symbolism is never devoid of beauty. In the terms of a spiritual vision of the world, the beauty of an object is nothing other than the transparency of its existential envelopes. An art worthy of the name is beautiful because it is true.

It is neither possible nor necessary that every artist or craftsman engaged in sacred art be conscious of the Divine Law inherent in forms; he will only know certain aspects of it, or certain applications that arise within the limits of the rules of his craft. These rules will enable him to paint an icon, to fashion a sacred vessel, or to practice calligraphy in a liturgically valid manner, without it being necessary for him to know the ultimate significance of the symbols he is working with. It is tradition that transmits the sacred models and the working rules, and thereby guarantees the spiritual validity of the forms. Tradition possesses a secret power which is communicated to an entire civilization and determines even those arts and crafts whose immediate objects include nothing particularly sacred. This power creates the style of a traditional civilization. A style— something that cannot be imitated from the outside—is perpetuated without difficulty, in a quasi-organic manner, by the sole power of the spirit by which it is animated.

One of the most tenacious of modern prejudices is the one that opposes the impersonal and objective rules of an art for fear that they might stifle creative genius. In reality, there is no traditional work—one governed by immutable principles—which does not give sensible expression to creative joy in the soul; modern individualism, on the other hand, has produced, apart from a few works of genius which are nevertheless spiritually barren, all the ugliness— the endless and hopeless ugliness—of the forms that fill the "ordinary life" of our time.

One of the fundamental conditions of happiness is to know that everything one does has an eternal meaning; but who at the present time can still conceive of a civilization in which all its vital aspects are developed "in the likeness of Heaven"? In a theocentric society, the humblest activity participates in this heavenly benediction.

The ultimate objective of sacred art is not to evoke feelings or communicate impressions; it is a symbol, and as such it employs simple and primordial means. It cannot in any case be anything more than allusive, its real object being ineffable. It is of angelic origin, because its models reflect supra-formal realities. By recapitulating the creation—the "Divine art"—in parables, it demonstrates the symbolical nature of the world, and so liberates the human spirit from its attachment to crude and ephemeral "facts".

The angelic origin of art is explicitly formulated by the Hindu tradition. According to the *Aitareya Brâhmana*, every work of art in the world is achieved by imitation of the art of the *devas*, "whether it be an elephant in terracotta, a bronze object, an article of clothing, a gold ornament, or a mule-cart". The Christian legends that attribute an angelic origin to certain miraculous images, exemplify the same idea.[1]

The *devas* are nothing more nor less than particular functions of the Universal Spirit, permanent expressions of the Will of God. According to a doctrine common to all traditional civilizations, sacred art must imitate Divine Art, but it must be clearly understood that this in no way implies that the finished Divine creation, the world such as we see it, should be copied, for such would be pure pretension. A literal "naturalism" is foreign to sacred art. What must be copied is the manner in which the Divine Spirit works.[2] Its laws must be transposed into the restricted domain in which man works as man, that is to say, into craftsmanship.

*
*   *

In no traditional doctrine does the idea of the Divine Art play so fundamental a part as in Hindu doctrine. For *Mâyâ* is not only the mysterious Divine Power that causes the world to appear to exist outside of Divine Reality, and as such is the source of all duality and all illusion; but *Mâyâ*, in her positive aspect, is also the Divine Art that produces every form. In principle, *Mâyâ* is nothing other than the possibility of the Infinite to limit Itself, and so to become the object of Its own "vision", without Its infinity being thereby limited.

---

1. In the terminology of the monotheistic religions the *devas* correspond to angels, in so far as the latter represent divine aspects.
2. According to St Thomas Aquinas, "Art is the imitation of Nature in her manner of operation", *Summa Theologica*, 1.117. 1.

In this way, God both manifests, and does not manifest, Himself in the world. He both expresses Himself and remains silent.

Just as, by virtue of its *Mâyâ*, the Absolute objectivizes certain aspects of Itself, or certain possibilities contained in Itself and determines them by a distinctive vision, so the artist realizes in his work certain aspects of himself. He projects them, as it were, outside his undifferentiated being. And to the extent that his objectivization reflects the secret depths of his being, it will take on a purely symbolical character, while at the same time the artist will become more and more conscious of the abyss dividing the form, reflector of his essence, from what that essence really is in its timeless plenitude. The traditional artist knows: this form is myself, nevertheless I am infinitely more than it, for its Essence remains the pure Knower, the Witness which no form can grasp; but he also knows that it is God who expresses Himself through his work, so that the work, in its turn transcends the weak and fallible ego of the man.

Herein lies the analogy between Divine Art and human art: namely in the realization of oneself by objectivization. If this objectivization is to have spiritual significance, and not be merely a vague introversion, its means of expression must spring from an essential vision. In other words, it must not be the "ego", root of illusion and ignorance of oneself, which arbitrarily chooses those means; they must be derived from tradition, from the formal and "objective" revelation of the supreme Being, who is the "Self" of all beings.

*
* *

Likewise from the Christian point of view, God is "artist" in the most exalted sense of the word, because He created man "in His own image" (Genesis: 1,27). Moreover, since the image comprises not only a likeness to its model, but also a quasi-absolute unlikeness, it cannot but become corrupted. The divine reflection in man was troubled by the fall of Adam; the mirror was tarnished; and yet man could not be completely cast aside; for while the creature is subject to its own limitations, Divine Plenitude is not subject to limitation of any kind. This amounts to saying that the said limitations cannot in any real sense be opposed to Divine Plenitude, which manifests Itself as limitless Love, the very limitlessness of which demands that God, "pronouncing" Himself as Eternal Word, should descend into this world, and, as it were, assume the perishable outlines of the image—human nature—and so to restore to it its original beauty. In Christianity, the divine image *par excellence* is the human form of the Christ. Christian art has thus but one purpose: the transfiguration of man, and of the world that depends on man, by their participation in the Christ.

*
*   *

What the Christian view of things grasps by means of a sort of loving concentration on the Word incarnate in Jesus Christ, is transposed, in the Islamic perspective, into the universal and the impersonal. In Islam, the Divine Art—and according to the Koran God is "artist" (*musawwir*)—is in the first place the manifestation of the Divine Unity in the beauty and regularity of the cosmos. Unity is reflected in the harmony of the multiple, in order, and in equilibrium; beauty has all these aspects within itself.

To arrive at Unity from the starting-point of the beauty of the world—this is wisdom. For this reason, Islamic thought necessarily links art to wisdom; in the eyes of a Muslim, art is essentially founded on wisdom, or "science", this science being simply the formulation of wisdom in temporal terms. The purpose of art is to enable the human ambience—the world in so far as it is fashioned by man—to participate in the order that most directly manifests Divine Unity. Art clarifies the world; it helps the spirit to detach itself from the disturbing multitude of things, so that it may rise up towards Infinite Unity.

*
*   *

Transposing the notion of "Divine Art" to Buddhism—which avoids the personification of the Absolute—it applies to the miraculous, and mentally inexhaustible, beauty of the Buddha. Whereas no doctrine concerned with God can escape, in its formulation, from the illusory character of mental processes, which attribute their own limits to the limitless and their own conjectural forms to the formless, the beauty of the Buddha radiates a state of being which is not limited by any mental process. This beauty is reflected in the beauty of the lotus; it is perpetuated ritually in the painted or sculpted image of the Buddha.

91

*
* *

According to the Taoist view of things, the Divine Art is essentially the art of transformation: the whole of nature is ceaselessly being transformed, always in accordance with the laws of the cycle; its contrasts revolve around a single center which eludes apprehension. Nevertheless anyone who understands this circular movement is thereby enabled to recognize the center which is its essence. The purpose of art is to conform to this cosmic rhythm. The most simple formula states that mastery in art consists in the capacity to trace a perfect circle in a single stroke, and thereby to identify oneself implicitly with its center, without the center itself being explicitly expressed.

*
* *

All these fundamental aspects of sacred art are present, in one way or another, and in varying proportions, in each of the five great religions just mentioned, for each one essentially possesses the fullness of Divine Truth and Grace, so that each one would be capable, in principle, of manifesting every possible form of spirituality. Nevertheless, since each religion is necessarily dominated by a particular point of view which determines its spiritual "economy", its works of art—which are necessarily collective, and not individual—will reflect, in their very style, this point of view and this spiritual "economy". Moreover, form, by its very nature, is unable to express one thing without excluding another, because form limits what it expresses, and thus thereby excludes other possible expressions of its own universal archetype. This law naturally applies at every level of formal manifestation, and not to art alone; thus the various Divine Revelations, on which the different religions are founded, are also mutually exclusive when considered in terms of their formal contours, but not in their Divine Essence, which is one. Here again the analogy between "Divine Art" and human art becomes apparent.

There is no sacred art that does not depend on an aspect of metaphysics. The science of metaphysics is itself limitless, given that its object is infinite. As it is not possible to describe here all the relationships that link the different metaphysical doctrines in this domain, the reader is referred to other books which lay forth the premises on which the present essays are based. They do so by expounding, in a language accessible to the modern Western reader, the essence of the traditional doctrines of the East and of the Medieval West. We refer in particular to the writings of René Guénon[3] and Frithjof Schuon.[4]

(from *Sacred Art in East and West*)

3. See *Crisis of the Modern World* (Ghent, NY: Sophia Perennis et Universalis, 1995), *The Reign of Quantity and the Signs of Times*, and *Introduction to the Study of the Hindu Doctrines*.
4. See *The Transcendent Unity of Religions*, *Spiritual Perspectives and Human Facts*, *Castes and Races* (Bedfont, Middlesex: Perennial Books, 1982), and *Light on the Ancient Worlds*.

Hindu Art

The Hindu Temple

Among sedentary peoples, the sacred art *par excellence* is the building of a sanctuary, in which the Divine Spirit, invisibly present in the universe, will "dwell" in a direct and as it were "personal" sense. Spiritually speaking, a sanctuary is always situated at the center of the world, and it is this that makes it a *sacratum* in the true sense of the word: in such a place man is protected from the indeterminacy of space and time, since it is "here" and "now" that God is present to man. This is expressed in the design of the temple; by emphasizing the cardinal directions, it orders space in relation to its center. The design is a synthesis of the world: that which, in the universe, is in ceaseless movement, is transposed by sacred architecture into a permanent form. In the cosmos, time prevails over space: on the other hand, in the construction of the temple, time is as it were transmuted into space: the great rhythms of the visible cosmos, symbolizing the principal aspects of existence—aspects which, in the world of becoming, are disjointed and dispersed—are reassembled and fixed in the geometry of the building. Thus, through its regular and unalterable form, the temple represents the completion of the world, that is to say, its timeless aspect or final state, wherein all things repose in the equilibrium that precedes their reintegration in the undivided unity of Being. It is precisely because the sanctuary prefigures this transfiguration of the world—a transfiguration symbolized in Christianity by the "Heavenly Jerusalem"—that it is filled by the Divine Peace (*shekhina* in Hebrew, and *shânti* in Sanskrit).

This completion of the world which the temple prefigures is symbolized by its rectangular form, a form which opposes the circular form of a world subject to the cosmic movement. Whereas the spherical form of the sky is indefinite, and not accessible to any kind of measurement, the rectangular or cubical form of a sacred edifice expresses a positive and immutable law, and that is why all sacred architecture, to whatever tradition it belongs, can be seen as a development of the fundamental theme of the transformation of the circle into the square. In the genesis of the Hindu Temple, the development of this theme is particularly clear, in all the richness of its metaphysical and spiritual contents.[5]

The "crystallization" of all cosmic realities in a geometrical symbol—which is like an inverted image of the timeless—is prefigured in the Hindu tradition by the construction of the Vedic altar. Its cubical shape, represents the "body" of *Prajâpati,* the total cosmic being.[6] *Prajâpati* is the Principle in its manifested aspect; though this aspect includes the totality of the world, it appears as if fragmented by the diversity and mutability of the latter. In his Essence *Prajâpati* is none other than *Purusha,* the immutable and indivisible Essence of man and the universe; according to the *Rig-Veda* (X.90), it is *Purusha* whom the *devas* sacrificed at the beginning of the world, in order to constitute the various parts of the universe and the different kinds of living beings. This must not be understood as "pantheism", for *Purusha* is not divided in itself, nor is it "localized" in ephemeral beings; it is only its manifested and apparent form that is sacrificed, while its eternal nature remains as it ever was, so that it is both the sacrifice (the victim) and the goal of the sacrifice. Henceforth every sacrifice reproduces and in a sense compensates for the pre-temporal sacrifice of the *devas*; the unity of the total being is symbolically and spiritually reconstituted by the rite.

The art of building an altar is more ancient and more universal than sacred architecture, for altars are used by both nomads and sedentaries, whereas temples exist only amongst the latter. The primitive sanctuary is the sacred area surrounding the altar; the rites employed for consecrating and delimiting this area were later transposed to the founding of a temple—*templum* in Latin originally

---

5. Nevertheless, the relation between these two fundamental symbols—the circle and the square—bear different meanings depending on the plane of reference. If the circle is the symbol of the undivided unity of the Principle, the square signifies its first and changeless determination, the universal law or Norm; in this case the circle indicates a reality superior to that suggested by the square. The same is true if the circle is related to the heavens, whose movement it reproduces, and the square is related to the earth, whose solid and relatively inert state it recapitulates: then the circle is to the square as the active is to the passive, or as life is to the body, for it is the heavens that engender actively, while the earth conceives and gives birth passively.

6. The *devas* immolated this primordial being at the beginning of the world and its disjointed limbs, which constitute the multiple aspects or parts of the cosmos, have to be symbolically reassembled. This recalls the dismemberment of the body of Osiris in the Egyptian myth. The myth of the immolation of *Prajâpati* is analogous to the Sufi doctrine according to which God manifested the universe by virtue of His multiple Names.

meant the sacred precinct set apart for the *contemplation* of the cosmos. There are many indications to support the conclusion that these rites constitute a primordial inheritance linking the two great currents, nomads and sedentaries, whose lifestyles, in other respects, are so different.

A particularly eloquent testimony of this primordial legacy is the following description of the consecration of a fire altar by Hehaka Sapa (Black Elk), priest sage of the nomadic Sioux Indians: "Taking the ax, he (the officiant) pointed it towards the six directions, and then struck the ground to the West. Repeating the same movement, he struck the ground to the North, then in the same way to the East, and then to the South; he then raised the ax skywards and struck the ground in the center, twice for the earth, and twice for the Great Spirit. Having done this, he scratched the soil and, with a stick which he had purified in the smoke and offered to the six directions, he traced a line running from the West to the center, then from the East to the center, then from the North to the center, and finally from the South to the center; then he offered the stick to the heavens and touched the center, and then to the earth and touched the center. In this way the altar was made. In the manner described, we fixed in this place the center of the world, and this center, which in reality is everywhere, is the dwelling-place of the Great Spirit."[7]

As this example shows, the consecration of the altar consists in the evocation of the relationships that connect the principal aspects of the universe with its center. These aspects are: heaven, which in its generative activity is opposed to the earth (the passive and maternal principle), and the four directions or "winds", whose forces determine the cycle of the day and the succession of the seasons; they correspond to so many powers or aspects of the Universal Spirit.[8]

Whereas the normal shape of a temple is rectangular, the nomadic altar such as has been described is not square in outline, even though its origin is the quaternary of the celestial regions. This is explained by the "style" appropriate to the nomadic life; to nomads, buildings that are rectangular in shape express the fixation of death. Nomadic sanctuaries, made like tents or cabins of live

7. See *The Sacred Pipe: Black Elk's Account of the Rites of the Oglala Sioux*, recorded by Joseph Epes Brown (Norman: University of Oklahoma Press, 1953 and 1989).
8. See Frithjof Schuon, *The Feathered Sun* (Bloomington, Indiana: World Wisdom Books, 1990) and *Language of the Self* (Bloomington, Indiana: World Wisdom Books, 1999), the chapter "The Sacred Pipe of the Red Indians".

branches, are generally round; their model is the dome of the sky. Likewise, nomadic encampments are arranged in circular form, and the same practice is sometimes found in the cities of nomadic peoples who have become sedentary, like the Parthians. Thus it is that the cosmic polarity of the circle and the square is reflected in the contrast between nomadic and sedentary peoples. The former recognize their ideal in the dynamic and limitless nature of the circle, whereas the latter see theirs in the static character and the regularity of the square.[9] But apart from these differences of approach, the conception of the sanctuary remains the same. Whether it be built of solid materials like the temples of sedentary peoples, or whether it be no more than a *sacratum* established temporarily like the nomadic altar, it is always situated at the center of the world. Hehaka Sapa says of this center that it is the dwelling-place of the Great Spirit, and that in reality it is everywhere. That is why a symbolical point of reference is sufficient for its realization.

The basic plan of a temple is derived from the procedure of orientation, which is a rite in the proper sense of the word, for it links the form of the sanctuary with that of the universe. An orientation rite is universal; it was practiced in the most diverse civilizations. It is mentioned in ancient Chinese books, and Vitruvius tells us that the Romans established their cities in this way. There are also numerous indications that the same procedure was used in medieval Europe. The three phases of this rite correspond to three fundamental geometrical figures: the circle, image of the solar cycle; the cross formed by the cardinal axes; and the square derived from it. These are the symbols of the Chinese Great Triad, Heaven-Man-Earth, Man, in this hierarchy, being the intermediary between Heaven, the active principle, and Earth, the passive prin-

9. Sometimes the static perfection of the square or the cube is combined with the dynamic symbolism of the circle. Such is the case with the Kaaba, one of the oldest sanctuaries in the world and an ancient center of the rite of circumambulation perpetuated by Islam. The Kaaba is situated on the "axis of the world" and its four corners are oriented towards the cardinal regions of the sky. The rite of circumambulation expresses with precision the relationship existing between the sanctuary and the celestial movement; it is accomplished seven times to correspond with the number of the celestial spheres. Abraham built the Kaaba where, according to legend, the Divine Presence (*Sakîna*), in the form of a serpent, had led him; the serpent coiled itself round the building. This recalls the symbolism of the serpent, *Ananta* or *Shesha,* which moves round the precinct of the Hindu temple, itself the center of a rite of circumambulation.

ciple—just as the cross of the cardinal axes is the intermediary between the limitless cycle of the heavens and the terrestrial "square".

Chinese ideogram of the Great Triad: Heaven-Man-Earth

According to the Hindu tradition, the square obtained by the rite of orientation is the symbol of *Purusha* insofar as it is immanent in existence. *Purusha* is pictured in the shape of a man stretched out in the fundamental square, in the position of the victim in the Vedic sacrifice: his head is to the East, his feet to the West, and his two hands touch the North-East and South-East corners of the square. The fundamental diagram of the temple is thus a symbol of the Divine Presence in the world.

This symbolism is found among peoples who have no historical link with the Hindu world. The Osages, a tribe of the plains of North America, look upon the ritual arrangement of their camp as "the form and the spirit of a perfect man" who faces the East. In the Christian tradition, medieval liturgists such as Durant de Mende and Honorius d'Autun, compared the plan of the cathedral to the form of the crucified Christ: His head corresponds to the apse with its axis to the East; His outstretched arms are the transepts; His torso and legs are the nave; His heart lies at the main altar. This interpretation evokes the Hindu symbolism of *Purusha* incorporated in the plan of the temple. In both cases, the Man-God incarnated in the sacred building is the sacrifice which reconciles Heaven with earth.

Hindu Sculpture

The Hindu sculptor must know the rules of the sacred dance, which is the first of the figurative arts, since it has man himself as its means. Sculpture is thus related to two radically different arts: by its artisanal technique it is related to architecture, which is essentially static and transforms time into space, whereas the dance is essentially dynamic and transforms space into time, by absorbing the former into the continuity of rhythm. It is therefore not surprising that these two poles of Hindu art—sculpture and dancing—should

have together engendered what is perhaps the most perfect fruit of
Hindu art, the image of Shiva dancing.

The dance of Shiva expresses at once the production, conservation, and destruction of the world, considered as phases of the permanent activity of God. Shiva is the "Lord of the Dance" (*Natarâjâ*).
He himself revealed the principles of the sacred dance to the sage
Bharatamuni, who codified them in the *Bharata-Nâtya-Shâstra*.[10]

The static laws of sculpture and the rhythm of the dance are
combined to perfection in the classical statue of Shiva dancing. The
movement is conceived as a rotation around a motionless axis; by its
decomposition into four typical gestures, following one another like
phases, it reposes so to speak in its own amplitude; it is in no way
rigid, but its rhythm is continued in a static formula, like the waves
of liquid in a vessel; time is integrated in the timeless. The limbs of
the God are arranged in such a way that the worshiper who views
the statue from in front grasps all the forms at a glance: they are
inscribed in the plane of the flaming circle, symbol of *Prakriti* (Universal Substance), without their spatial polyvalence being in any way
impaired. On the contrary, from whatever side one contemplates
the statue, its static equilibrium remains perfect, like that of a tree
outspread in space. The plastic precision of the detail is combined
with the uninterrupted continuity of the gestures.

Shiva dances on the vanquished demon of chaotic matter, the
subjective equivalent of which is spiritual indifference or forgetfulness of God (*apasmâra*). In his outermost right hand he holds the
drum whose beat corresponds to the creative act. By the gesture of
his uplifted hand he announces peace, protecting what he has created. His lowered hand points to the foot which is lifted from the
ground, as a sign of deliverance. In his outermost left hand he carries the flame which will destroy the world.

Images of Shiva dancing show sometimes the attributes of a god,
sometimes those of an ascetic, or of both together, for God is
beyond all forms, and He assumes form only so that He may
become his own victim.

(from *Sacred Art in East and West*)

10. The "celestial" origin of the Hindu dance is indirectly proved by its extension
    in space and time: in a form adapted to Buddhism, it has influenced the chore-
    ographic style of Tibet and all eastern Asia including Japan; in Java it survived
    the Islamicization of the island; and through the medium of Gypsy dancing it
    seems even to have influenced Spanish dancing.

Buddhist Art

Buddhist art springs from Hindu art by way of a sort of alchemical transmutation, which "crystallizes" the subtlest element in Hindu art, namely, the quasi-spiritual quality of the human body ennobled by the sacred dance, purified by the methods of Yoga and, as it were, saturated with a consciousness not limited by the mind. It is this quality that is condensed into an incomparable formula in the sacred image of the Buddha, which absorbs all the spiritual beatitude inherent in the ancient art of India, and becomes the central theme round which all other images revolve. The body of the Buddha and the lotus; these two forms, taken from Hindu art, express the immense calm of the Spirit awakened to Itself.

The image of the Divine Man enthroned on the lotus is a Hindu theme. Within the Vedic altar is immured a conventional image of a golden man *(hirânya-purusha)*; the image rests on a disc of gold which in its turn rests on a lotus leaf. It is a symbol of *Purusha,* the Divine Essence in its aspect of the eternal essence of man, and it is also an image of *Agni,* the son of the gods, through whom *Prajâpati,* the universe, is realized in its original totality. *Purusha* has all these aspects; It manifests Itself in every degree of existence—in conformity with the inherent laws of this degree—without undergoing any change. *Agni,* the Divine, is the spiritual germ from which the nature of universal man originates; this is why he is hidden in the altar, just as he is hidden in the heart of man; he is born of the primordial waters—the virtual potentialities of the soul and of the world—hence the lotus that supports him.

Buddhist art has perpetuated the symbol of the "golden man", though it appears nevertheless to deny that which Hinduism affirms through this same symbol. The Hindu doctrine affirms above all an infinite Essence, of which all things are but a reflection—it is of *Purusha* that all things are made, says the Veda—whereas the Buddhist doctrine has nothing to say about the Being or the Essence of things; it appears to deny it. Instead of starting its exposition from a Supreme Principle, which could be likened to the apex of a pyramid made up of all states of existence—this is what the universe looks like from a theocentric point of view—it proceeds by way of negation, as if taking man and his nothingness as starting point, and building thereon an inverted pyramid which expands indefinitely upwards towards the void. But despite this inversion of perspective, the quintessence of the two Traditions remains the same. The difference between their respective points of view is as follows: Hinduism envisages divine Realities in an "objective" manner by virtue of their reflections in the mind, such a reflection being possible, outside and independently of their immediate spiritual realization, because of the universal nature of the Intellect. Buddhism, on the other hand, lays hold on the Essence of man—or the Essence of things—by a "subjective" path, that is to say, by the spiritual or inward realization of that Essence; it rejects as false or illusory every purely speculative affirmation of supra-formal Reality. This attitude is justified by the fact that the mental objectivization of Divine Reality may constitute an obstacle to its realization, because reflection involves an inversion with respect to that which it reflects—this is shown by the above-mentioned example of the pyramid narrowing towards its apex (the symbol of the principle)—and also because thought limits consciousness and, in a sense, congeals it. Furthermore, thought directed to God appears to be situated outside its object, whereas God is infinite, and nothing can truly be situated outside Him. According to this perspective, all thought about the Absolute is vitiated by a false perspective. For these reasons, the Buddha says that he teaches nothing about the origin of the world or of the soul, and is only concerned with suffering, and the deliverance from suffering.

Given this negative doctrinal position, Buddhist art could not, in principle, depict more than the human appearance of Gautama, characterized above all, by the signs of his renunciation of the world: stripped of his royal attributes, seated in the attitude of meditation, and holding in his left hand the wooden bowl of a beggar (the symbol of surrender to the Non-Ego), his right hand touches the earth, in witness of his lordship over it. This is the fundamental image of the Buddha.

In some representations of the Buddhist paradise, the lotus throne of the *Tathâgata* rises out of a pool, just as *Agni* is born from the primordial waters. Together with the human image of the Blessed One, the lotus becomes the principal theme in Buddhist art which, in a certain sense, is thereafter wholly contained within these two poles. The form of the lotus expresses in a direct, "impersonal", and synthetic manner what the human form of the Buddha manifests in a "personal" and more complex way.

In the *Mahâyâna,* the image of the Buddha acquires a non-historical and universal character. It appears, as it were, as a compensation for the absence of "theory" or doctrine, that is to say, of a theo-centric view of the world. Thus the celestial Buddhas (sometimes called *dhyâni-buddhas*) rule over the ten directions of space—the eight directions of the "wind-rose" and the upward and downward directions of the vertical (see pp. 113-114). Physical space is here the image of spiritual "space"; the ten directions symbolize the principal aspects or qualities of *Bodhi*. The center from which these directions radiate, and with which they are all in principle identified, is the Ineffable. The celestial buddhas are in fact the spiritual projections of the one Buddha Shâkyamuni, and in this connection they are sometimes represented as springing from His head. The images of the buddhas or *bodhisattvas* who rule over the different sectors of the "winds-rose" all bear an iconographic resemblance to the classical type of Shâkyamuni from which they are usually distinguished only by their respective colors and attributes; they can also be identified by their gestures (*mudrâs*), but these same gestures are characteristic of the various attitudes of the Buddha Himself. Thus the funda-mental image of the Buddha seated on a lotus and surrounded by an aureole is susceptible of infinite variation. There is no limit to the number of *bodhisattvas*; according to the *Sûtras* they are as number-less as the grains of the sands of the Ganges, and each of them pre-sides over thousands of worlds. According to a symbolical conception developed in certain speculative schools of the *Mahâyâna*, the limitless compassion of the Buddha is present in the smallest particles of the universe in the form of so many *bodhisattvas* enthroned on lotuses. The multitude of buddhas and *bodhisattvas* indicate the relativity of the human receptacle: in his manifested personality the Buddha is distinct from principial Unity—for there is nothing unique in manifestation—so that the indefinite differen-tiation of the type or model of all Buddhahood is like an inverted reflection of the non-differentiation of the Absolute.

Tradition has it that the *Tathâgata* himself bequeathed his image to posterity: according to the *Divyâvadâna*, King Rudrâyana or Udâyana sent painters to the Blessed One to take His portrait, but while they were trying in vain to capture the "likeness" of the Buddha, he told them that their (spiritual) laziness was preventing them from succeeding, and He caused a cloth to be brought, on to which He "projected" His own likeness. This story is very directly reminiscent of the Christian tradition of the *acheiropoietos* image of the Christ on the Mandilion, where it is said that Jesus gave his image, miraculously imprinted on a fabric, to the messengers of the

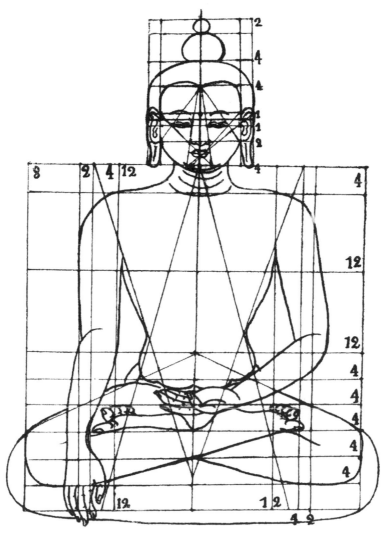

Diagram of the proportions of the "true image" of the Buddha, from a
drawing by a Tibetan artist.

King of Edessa, Abgar, who had asked him for his portrait. Another
Buddhist story is that a disciple of the *Tathâgata* tried in vain to draw
his portrait; he could not seize the right proportions, every measurement turning out to be too small; in the end the Buddha com-
manded him to trace the outline of His shadow projected on to the
ground. The important point in these two stories is that the sacred
image appears as a "projection" of the Buddha, or of the Christ; as

for the "measure" that eludes human art, it corresponds, not to any representational likeness but, like the measure of the Vedic altar, to essential "form". In this connection too there is a parallel between the Buddhist conception and a certain Christian conception: in the Middle Ages, the "true measure" of the body of Jesus was handed down, inscribed on strips of cloth or on columns.

Here a few words may be said about the apparently "non-iconic" character of early Buddhist art. On the bas-reliefs of Sânchî and Amarâvatî, which are among the earliest sculptural monuments of Buddhism, the *Tathâgata* is not represented in his human likeness. His presence in the midst of his disciples and worshipers is indicated only by emblems such as the sacred tree adorned with jewels, or the wheel of the Law (*dharmachakra*) placed on a throne. Here again, not only is there a parallel with the oldest emblems of Christ but, as we have already noted, the same symbolical iconography persisted on the tympanums of church doors up to the Romanesque period; the Christic monogram in the shape of a wheel (see p. 113), and the tree of life were used, as there was a reluctance to represent the Christ in human form. The symbol of the "throne made ready", well known in Indian art, is also found in some Byzantine icons.

In the "golden age" of Buddhism a plastic representation of the *Tathâgata* may have been superfluous; it may even have been inopportune in an environment still strongly Hindu. But in later times, when the spiritual understanding had become weaker, and when a cleavage had occurred between their thought and their will, every means of grace, including the sacred image, became indispensable.[11]

There were also reservations about figurative art in the early centuries of Christianity, which were conditioned both by the Judaic influence and by memories of ancient paganism; for as long as oral tradition was everywhere alive, and Christianity had not as yet come into the full light of day, the figuration of Christian truth in art can only have played a very occasional part.

The traditional portrait of the Buddha is founded partly on a canon of proportions and partly on a description of the distinguishing characteristics of the body of the Buddha derived from

---

11. This might be thought to contradict the doctrine of *karma*, according to which salvation is to be found only in the inward denudation (analogous to the Christian *vacare Deo*) that "arrests the wheel of births and deaths"; and according to which, when the waves of passion die out, *Bodhi* will shine forth of itself. This, however, is only one dimension of Buddhism, for Buddhism would be neither

the Scriptures (see p. 103). The image retains some of his personal characteristics, scrupulously preserved by tradition; these are superimposed on a hieratic type, the general form of which is more or less defined or fixed, and is more in the nature of a symbol than a portrait. The gestures of the hands are derived from the science of *mudrâs* inherited by Buddhism from Hinduism. Generally speaking, the symbolism of gestures is based on the fact that the right hand naturally corresponds to the active pole of the universe, whereas the left hand represents the passive or receptive pole. This is the polarity of essence and substance, of *Purusha* and *Prakriti,* of Heaven and earth, of Spirit and psyche, of will and sensibility. The "sacramental" function of the image derives from the fact that it perpetuates the bodily presence of the Buddha himself, and that it constitutes in a certain sense the indispensable complement to a doctrine based on negation. By bypassing doctrinal objectivization of the transcendent Essence, the Buddha Shâkyamuni was able to express it all the more fully by the radiant beauty of his mere existence.

In the art of the *Hînayâna*—in Ceylon, Burma and Siam—we find an almost endless repetition of the image of the earthly Buddha without the elaborate symbolism of the *Mahâyâna*. The icon of the *Hînayâna* is reduced to a formula of extreme simplicity and sobriety, often of great power, as if it were confined to a narrow region half-way between image and non-image, between iconolatry and iconoclasm, its repetitiveness recalling the serene and majestic monotony of the *Sûtras.*

There is a hidden analogy between the human image of the Buddha and the shape of the *stupa,* the shrine containing a relic. The *stupa* could be said to represent the universal body of the *Tathâgata*: its various levels or stories, square below and more or less spherical above, symbolize the multiple planes of existence. The same hierarchy is reflected on a smaller scale in the human image of the Buddha whose torso is like the cubical part of the *stupa,* while his head, crowned with the protuberance of Buddhahood, corresponds to the cupola surmounted by a pinnacle.

(from *Sacred Art in East and West*)

conceivable nor efficacious without the sacramental presence of the Buddha and his salvific grace. These two aspects of Buddhism, grace and the doctrine of *karma,* are in reality inseparable.

Taoist Art

The subject of Far Eastern landscape painting inevitably brings to mind the masterpieces of the so-called "Southern School", which are distinguished by their exquisite economy in the use of resources, and by the "spontaneous" nature of their execution. The term "Southern" has no rigorous geographical implication; it is merely a label for Taoist painting as it was perpetuated within the framework of Zen Buddhism (Sanskrit: *dhyâna*; Chinese: *ch'an*; Japanese: *zen*).

Far back in Chinese antiquity, the whole of Taoist art was summed up in the emblem of a disc perforated in the center. The disc represents the heavens or the cosmos, and the void in the center the unique and transcendent Essence. Sometimes these discs are decorated with the symbol of the two cosmic dragons, analogous to the complementary principles *Yang* and *Yin*, the "active" and the "passive"; the dragons circle round the hole in the center as if they were trying to lay hold of the ungraspable void. The point of view is the same in landscape paintings of Buddhist inspiration, in which all the elements—mountains, trees, and clouds—are there only to emphasize by contrast the void, out of which they seem to have arisen at that very instant, and from which they are detached like ephemeral islets.

In the earliest Chinese landscapes, engraved on metal mirrors, on bowls, or on funeral slabs, beings and objects seem to be subordinated to the play of the elements: wind, fire, water, and earth. To express the movement of clouds, water, and fire, various kinds of curvilinear meander are used; rocks are conceived as an ascending movement of the earth; trees are defined less by their static outlines than by their structure, which reveals the rhythm of their growth. The cosmic alternation of *Yang* and *Yin* is apparent in every form or composition. All this accords with the six maxims formulated in the 5th century A.D. by the famous painter, Hsieh Ho: (1) The creative spirit must identify itself with the rhythms of cosmic life; (2) the brush must express the intimate structure of things; (3) the likeness will be established by the outlines; (4) the particular appearances of things will be conveyed by color; (5) the groupings must be co-ordinated according to a plan; (6) tradition must be perpetuated through the models it provides. From this it can be seen that it is rhythm, and its primary expression as linear structure, that are the foundations of the work, rather than the static plan and plastic contour of things, as is the case in the traditional painting of the West.

Although Taoist-Buddhist painting does not indicate the source of light and shade, its landscapes are nonetheless filled by a light that permeates every form like a celestial ocean of pearly luster. It is the beatitude of the Void (*shûnya*) shining in the absence of all darkness. Never does a Chinese or Japanese painter represent the world in the likeness of a finished cosmos, and in this respect, his vision is as different as possible from that of the Western artist, even the traditional Western artist, whose conception of the world is always more or less "architectural". A Far Eastern painter is a contemplative, and for him the world would appear to be made of snowflakes, quickly crystallized and just as quickly dissolved. Since he is ever conscious of the non-manifested, the less solidified physical conditions are, the nearer they would seem to be, from his point of view, to the Reality underlying all phenomena; hence the subtle observation of atmosphere that we admire in Chinese paintings of ink and wash.[12]

This art, however evocative, exists in the first place for the painter himself; it is a method for actualizing contemplative intuition, and as such it was assimilated and developed by *dhyâna* Buddhism, the confluence of the two traditions being based on an identification of the Buddhist notion of universal Void (*shûnya*) with the Taoist notion of Non-Being.

The technique of painting in Indian ink, with its calligraphy made up of flowing signs that can be "crystallized" only by the workings of a superior insight, corresponds to the intellectual "style" of *dhyâna* Buddhism, which seeks with all its resources to provoke, after an inward crisis, a sudden release of illumination, the Japanese *satori*. When this sudden illumination pierces the individual con-

12. Attempts have been made to relate this style to European Impressionism, but this overlooks the fact that, despite certain accidental analogies, the points of departure of each were radically different. Impressionism seeks, not the presence of a cosmic reality higher than individual objects, but, on the contrary, a subjective "impression" as fleeting as it can be. In this case it is the ego, with its wholly passive and affective sensibility, that colors the scene. Taoist painting, on the other hand, avoids, in its method and in its intellectual orientation, the supremacy of mind and feeling, both avid for individualistic affirmation; in its eyes the instantaneity of nature is not in the first place an emotional experience; the miracle of the instant, immobilized by a sensation of eternity, unveils the primordial harmony of things, a harmony that is ordinarily hidden under the subjective continuity of the mind. When this veil is suddenly torn aside, hitherto unobserved relationships, linking together beings and things, reveal their essential unity.

sciousness, the plastic power of the soul responds spontaneously to the supra-rational action of *Prajñâ*, just as in nature all movements are apparently unconscious, while in reality they are obedient to universal Intelligence. The artist following the *dhyâna* method must therefore practice calligraphic painting until he has mastered it, and then he must forget it. Likewise, he must concentrate on his subject, and then detach himself from it. Only then will intuition take charge of his brush.[13]

It should be noted that this artistic procedure is very different from that of the other, hieratic, branch of Far Eastern Buddhist art, which derives its models from India, and concentrates on the sacred image of the Buddha. Far from postulating a sudden flash of intuition, the creation of an "icon" or a statue of the Buddha is essentially founded on the faithful transmission of a prototype, the sacred image incorporating the proportions and special signs attributed by tradition to the historical Buddha. The spiritual efficacy of this art is safeguarded by its single-minded intention, and the well-nigh immutability of its forms. The intuition of the artist may bring out certain qualities implicit in his model, but faith and adherence to tradition suffice to perpetuate the sacramental quality of his art.

In the case of landscape painting in Far Eastern art, the unalterable rules are more concerned with the artistic procedure than with the object to be represented. Before concentrating on his work, or more precisely, on his own image-free essence, the Zen disciple must prepare his instruments in a particular way, and arrange them as for a rite; the formality of his gestures precludes in advance the intrusion of any individualistic "urge". Creative spontaneity is thus actualized within a consecrated framework.

The two branches of Far Eastern art have this in common: that they both express primarily a state of being reposing in itself. In the hieratic art, this state is suggested by the attitude of the Buddha or *bodhisattva*, and by forms that are saturated with an inward beatitude, whereas the landscape painting expresses it through the "objective" content of consciousness, a contemplative vision of the world.

13. Here again an attempt has been made in recent times to suggest a similarity between Zen painting and certain so-called spontaneous and unpremeditated manifestations in contemporary art. It will be seen, however, that the spontaneity of this modern type of painting is the result of impulses from the subconscious mind, whereas Zen painting exemplifies the spontaneity of the intuitive or supra-conscious faculty of the transcendent intellect, in whose hands the artist has, by discipline and long training, learnt to place himself.

Taoist painting, Che–School, c. 1500.

The method of *dhyâna,* which finds its direct reflection in art, has given rise to many false assimilations, such as the part played in it by the "unconscious", or more precisely non-conscious, modalities of the soul. It is important not to confuse the "non-consciousness" (*Wu-nien*) or the "non-mental" (*Wu-hsin*) of *dhyâna* Buddhism with the "sub-conscious" of modern psychologists, for the state of intuitive spontaneity actualized by the *dhyâna* method is obviously not *beneath* normal individual consciousness, but, on the contrary, *above* it. The true nature of being is "non-conscious" because it is neither "conscious" in the sense of possessing a distinctive intelligence, nor "unconscious" and obscure like the inferior prolongations of the soul, which constitute the "sub-conscious".

Landscape in the eyes of the Chinese is "mountain and water". The mountain or rock represents the active or masculine principle, *Yang*, and the water corresponds to the feminine or passive principle, *Yin*. The complementary nature of the two is expressed most plainly and richly in a waterfall, the first choice of *dhyâna* painters as a subject. Sometimes it is a cascade of several stages, hugging the side of a mountain in springtime, sometimes it is a single jet dropping from the cliff edge, or a strong spate like the famous waterfall of Wang-Wei which appears from the clouds and disappears into a veil of foam in one great leap, so that the spectator soon feels that he is himself being swept into the swirl of the elements.

Like every symbol, that of the waterfall veils Reality while at the same time revealing it. The inertness of a rock is the inverse of the immutability appertaining to the celestial or divine act, and similarly the dynamism of the water veils the principal passivity of which it is the expression. Nevertheless, through an attentive contemplation of rock and waterfall, the mind or intuition eventually operates a sudden integration. In the endlessly repeated rhythm of the water, hugging the motionless rock, it recognizes both the activity of the

The Two Poles of Universal Manifestation
"Essence" and "Substance"
(*Purusha* and *Prakriti* or *Yang* and *Yin*) in their two modes

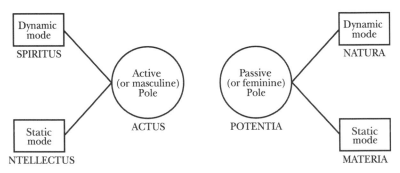

It is a question here of the union of the dynamic mode of the Passive Pole (NATURA) with the static mode of the Active Pole (INTELLECTUS). At the same time, there is a union of the dynamic mode of the Active Pole (SPIRITUS) with the static mode of the Passive Pole (MATERIA). It is the combination of the "unlikes", not of the "likes", that creates an indestructible bond. *Intellectus* stabilizes *Natura*; *Natura* vivifies *Intellectus*. *Spiritus* informs *Materia*; *Materia* captures *Spiritus* (see pp. 209–220).

immutable and the passivity of the dynamic; thereby it rises higher and, in a sudden illumination, perceives the Essence, which is both pure activity and infinite repose, which is neither motionless like rock nor changeable like water, but is ineffable in Its supra-formal reality.

*

* *

The sister art to landscape painting in the Far East is the art of siting houses, temples, and cities in the most propitious manner in a given natural ambience. Based on a science of orientation, it is a complete art in itself, directed to the conscious modification of certain elements in the landscape, with a view to actualizing its positive qualities and neutralizing evil influences arising from the chaotic aspects of nature.

This branch of the ancient Chinese tradition was assimilated by *dhyâna* Buddhism and subsequently developed to a state of perfection in Japan where interiors of an extreme sobriety are set against the natural variety of gardens and hills. When the sliding paper side-walls of a pavilion or a room are shut, there is nothing to distract the mind; on the other hand, when the side-walls are opened, attention is turned towards the surrounding nature, which is seen as if for the first time. Inside the room, where order and cleanliness prevail, every form bears witness to that objective intellectual discernment which sets things in order, while respecting the nature of each. The geometrical rigidity of the general effect is mitigated here and there by a pillar roughly hewn by an ax, or a curved beam like an untamed mountain tree; by these means poverty is allied to nobility, originality to clarity, and primordial nature to wisdom.

(from *Sacred Art in East and West*)

Christian Art

The Foundations of Christian Art

The art that springs from a genuinely Christian inspiration is derived from images of Christ and the Virgin that have a miraculous origin. It is accompanied by craft traditions which are Christian by adoption, but which are nonetheless sacred in character, in the sense that their creative methods embody a primordial wisdom that responds spontaneously to the spiritual truths of Christianity. These two currents, the traditional art of icon painting and the craft traditions, together with certain liturgical music evolved from a Pythagorean inheritance, are the only elements in Christian civilization that merit the term "sacred art".

As regards the craft tradition, with its pre-Christian roots, it is above all cosmological, for the work of the craftsman imitates quite naturally the formation of the cosmos out of chaos; its vision of the world is therefore not immediately connected with the Christian revelation, Christian language not being *a priori* cosmological. But the integration of the craft symbolism into Christianity was nevertheless a vital necessity, for the Church had need of plastic arts in order to clothe itself with visible forms, and it could not appropriate to itself the crafts without taking into account the spiritual possibilities they contain. Furthermore, the craft symbolism was a factor of equilibrium in the psychic and spiritual economy of the Christian "city"; it compensated, so to speak, the unilateral pressure of Christian morality—fundamentally ascetic—by manifesting divine truths in a relatively non-moral, and at any rate, non-volitive way. In contrast with a preaching that stresses what one must do in order to become holy, it offers a vision of the cosmos that is holy through its beauty[14]; it causes men to participate naturally, and almost involuntarily, in a world of holiness. By cleansing the craft inheritance of the artificial accretions imposed on it by Greco-Roman naturalism—drunk as it was with human glories—Christianity released

---

14. "Gnosis, by virtue of the fact that it is a 'knowing' and not a 'being', is centered on 'that which is' and not on 'that which ought to be'. It gives rise to a worldview that differs sharply from the view, more 'meritorious' perhaps but less 'true', adopted by the volitive temperament regarding the vicissitudes of existence." (Frithjof Schuon, *Gnosis, Divine Wisdom,* [Bedfont, Middlesex: Perennial Books, 1990], chapter 6, "Gnosis, Language of the Self").

the perennial elements retained in that inheritance, elements that re-enact the laws of the cosmos.[15]

The point of junction between the purely Christian tradition— in essence, theological—and pre-Christian cosmology can be clearly discerned in the Christian signs in the Catacombs, and particularly in the monogram in the form of a wheel with six or eight spokes. It is known that this monogram, the use of which dates from the earliest times, is made up of the Greek letters X and P (*Chi* and *Rho*), either alone or combined with a cross. When this sign is inscribed in a circle it clearly assumes the form of the cosmic wheel; sometimes it is replaced by a plain cross inscribed in a circle. There can be no doubt about the solar nature of the last mentioned sign: in some Christian inscriptions in the Catacombs the circle emits rays having hands, an element derived from the solar emblems of ancient Egypt. Furthermore, through the loop of the P which adorns the vertical axis like a polar star, the monogram combined with the cross shows a relationship to the looped cross, the Egyptian *ankh*.

The circle surrounding the sign is the solar orbit, which is divided by the two axes of the heavens. The eight-spoked wheel, formed by the combination of the monogram and the cross, is analogous to the wind-rose (the compass), namely the diagram of

Three different forms of the Monogram of Christ
found in the Catacombs.

15. It is noteworthy that the general form of the Christian temple does not perpetuate that of the Greco-Roman temple, but the forms of the basilica with apse and of domed buildings. These types of building do not appear in Rome until a relatively late period. The inside of the Pantheon, with its immense dome that receives light from above through a "solar eye", is not without grandeur, but this is neutralized by the anthropomorphic and banal character of the details. It may have a sort of philosophical grandeur, but it is a grandeur that has nothing to do with contemplation.

the four cardinal directions and the four intermediate directions of the heavens.

The monogram of Christ is very often placed between the letters *Alpha* and *Omega*, symbolizing the beginning and the end. The combination of the cross, the monogram, and the circle represent Christ as the spiritual synthesis of the universe. He is the all, He is the beginning, the end, and the timeless center; He is the "victorious" and "invincible" sun (*sol invictus*); His Cross rules the cosmos,[16] and judges the cosmos. Because of this, the monogram is also the sign of victory. The Emperor Constantine, whose position as supreme monarch in itself symbolized the *sol invictus*, inscribed this sign on his standard, thereby announcing that the cosmic purpose of the Roman Empire was fulfilled in Christ.

Christian architecture perpetuates the fundamental diagram of the cross inscribed in the circle. It is significant that this design is both the symbol of Christ and the synthesis of the cosmos. The circle represents the totality of space, and consequently the totality of existence, and also the celestial cycle, the natural divisions of which—indicated by the cross of the cardinal axes—are projected into the rectangular shape of the temple. The plan of a church emphasizes the form of the cross, and this corresponds not only to the specifically Christian meaning of the cross, but also to its cosmological role in pre-Christian architecture. The cross of the cardinal axes is the mediating element between the circle of the heavens and the square of the earth. The Christian perspective emphasizes above all the role of the Divine Mediator.

*
* *

The symbolism of the Christian temple is based on the analogy between the temple and the body of the Christ, in accordance with the following words from the Gospel: "Jesus answered and said unto them, Destroy this temple and in three days I will raise it up. Then said the Jews, Forty and six years was this temple in building, and

---

16. In the Orthodox feast of the Elevation of the Cross, the liturgy exalts the universal power of the Cross, which "makes to flower anew the incorruptible life, and confers deification on creatures, and brings the devil finally to the ground". In these words, the analogy of the tree of the world, changeless axis of the cosmos, can be discerned.

wilt thou rear it up in three days? But he spake of the temple of his body" (John 2:19-21).

The temple of Solomon was to be replaced by the body of the Christ:[17] when He died on the Cross, the curtain before the holy of holies in the temple was rent. The body of the Christ is also the Church in its aspect of the communion of saints: the symbol of this Church is the Christian temple.

The Church Fathers say that the sacred building represents first and foremost Christ as Divinity manifested on earth; at the same time it represents the universe constructed of substances visible and invisible, and finally, it represents man and his various "parts"[18]. According to some of the Fathers, the holy of holies is an image of the Spirit, the nave is an image of reason, and the symbol of the altar summarizes both;[19] according to others the holy of holies, that is to say the choir or the apse, represents the soul, while the nave is analogous to the body, and the altar to the heart.[20]

Some medieval liturgists, such as Durant de Mende and Honorius d'Autun, compare the plan of the cathedral to the form of the one Crucified: His head corresponds to the apse with its axis to the East, His outstretched arms are the transepts, His torso and legs are at rest in the nave, His heart lies at the main altar.

The circle of the gnomon, which was the means of finding the East-West and North-South axes, represents the directing circle from which all the measurements of the building were deduced. It is known that the proportions of a church were usually derived from the harmonious division of a large circle, that is to say, its division into five or ten. This Pythagorean method, which the Christian builders had probably inherited from the *collegia fabrorum*, was employed not only in the horizontal plane but also in a vertical plane, so that the body of the building was as it were inscribed in an

---

17. According to St. Augustine, Solomon built the temple as a "type" of the Church and of the body of the Christ (*Enarr. in Ps.*, 126). According to Theodoret, the temple of Solomon is the prototype of all the churches built in the world.
18. St. Augustine compares the temple of Solomon with the Church, the stones of which it is built being the believers, and its foundations being the prophets and the apostles. All these elements are combined in Charity or Love (*Enarr. in Ps.* 39). This symbolism was developed by Origen. St. Maxim the Confessor sees in the church built on earth the body of the Christ, as well as man and the universe.
19. Maxim the Confessor adopts this point of view.
20. This is St. Augustine's point of view. See also Simeon of Thessalonica, *De divino Templo*, Patrologia Migne.

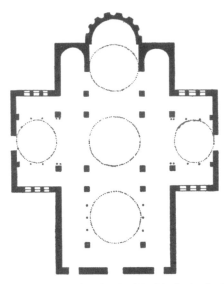

The earliest Byzantine plan for St. Mark's Cathedral at Venice.

imaginary sphere. The crystal that is the sacred building is "coagulated" out of the limitless sphere of the cosmos. This sphere is also like an image of the universal nature of the Word, whose concrete and terrestrial form is the temple.

Division into ten does not correspond to the purely geometrical nature of the circle, for the compass divides it into six and twelve; it corresponds however to the cycle, of which it indicates the successively decreasing phases, according to the formula $4 + 3 + 2 + 1 = 10$. This method of establishing the proportions of a building therefore partakes of the nature of time, so that it would be true to say that the proportions of a medieval cathedral reflect a cosmic rhythm. Proportion is in space what rhythm is in time, and in this connection it is significant that harmonious proportion is derived from the circle, which is the most direct image of the celestial cycle. In this way the natural continuity of the circle is introduced into the architectural domain, the unity of which is non-rational, and not graspable in purely quantitative terms.

The tools of the sculptor, the mallet and chisel, are thus Divine instruments, or "cosmic agents", which differentiate the *materia prima*, represented in this case by unworked stone. The complementarism of the chisel and the stone necessarily reappears elsewhere and in other forms in most traditional crafts, if not in all. The plow works the soil,[21] as the chisel works the stone, and in a similar way and in a principial sense, the pen "transforms" the paper;[22] the instrument that cuts or shapes always appears as the agent of a male principle which acts on a female *materia*. The chisel obviously corresponds to a faculty of distinction or discrimination; active with respect to the stone, it becomes passive in its turn when it is considered in connection with the mallet, to the "impulsion" of which it is subject. In its initiatic and "operative" application the chisel symbolizes distinctive knowledge and the mallet the spiritual will that "actualizes" or "stimulates" that knowledge. Here the cognitive faculty is situated below the volitive faculty, and this seems at first sight to contradict the normal hierarchy, but the apparent reversal is explained by the fact that the principial relationship, according to which knowledge has precedence over will, necessarily undergoes a metaphysical inversion in the "practical" domain. It is moreover the right hand that wields the mallet and the left that guides the chisel. Pure principial, or doctrinal, knowledge—the "discernment" in question is merely its practical or "methodic" application—does not intervene "actively", or "directly", in the work of spiritual realization, but orders it in conformity with changeless truths. This transcendent knowledge is symbolized, in the spiritual method of the stone carver, by the various measuring instruments, such as the plumb-line, the level, the square, and the compass—all images of the changeless archetypes which preside over all the phases of the work.[23]

21. The art of plowing is often viewed as having a divine origin. Physically the act of plowing has the effect of opening up the ground to the air, and thus promoting the fermentation that is indispensable for the assimilation of the soil by vegetation. Symbolically the soil is opened up to the influences of Heaven, and the plow is the active agent or generative organ. It may be noted that the replacement of the plow by machines has reduced many fertile soils to sterility and thus changed them into deserts; it is a case of the curse inherent in machines spoken of by René Guénon in his book, *The Reign of Quantity and the Signs of the Times* (Ghent, NY: Sophia Perennis et Universalis 1995).
22. The symbolism of the reed pen (*calamus*) and the book, or the pen and the tablet, plays a very important part in the Islamic tradition. According to the doctrine of the Sufis, the "supreme *calamus*" is the "Universal Intellect", and the "guarded tablet" on which the *calamus* writes the destiny of the world corresponds to the *Materia prima,* the un-created—or non-manifested—"Substance", which under the influence of the "Intellect" or the "Essence" produces everything comprised in the "creation". See the author's book *Introduction to Sufi Doctrine,* Chapter 11, "The Spirit".
23. It could equally well be said that these instruments correspond to the different "dimensions" of knowledge. See Frithjof Schuon, *The Transcendent Unity of Religions,* chapter 1 "Conceptual Dimensions".

By analogy with certain craft initiations that exist to this day in the East, it may be supposed that the rhythmic activity of the stone-carver was sometimes combined with the invocation, voiced or silent, of a Divine Name. This Name, considered as the symbol and vehicle of the creative and transforming Word, was a gift bequeathed to the craft by the Christian tradition.

*

* *

Forma and *materia* (in Greek: *eidos* and *hyle*) were familiar terms in medieval thought; they have been intentionally chosen here to designate the poles of a work of art. Aristotle, who referred the nature of every being or object to these two basic principles, used the artistic procedure for the purposes of his demonstrations, for the two principles in question are not *a priori* logical determinations, but something more. Thought does not deduce them, but presupposes them; their conception is not essentially founded on rational analysis, but on intellectual intuition, the normal support for which is not argument but symbol; the clearest symbol of this ontological complementarism is indeed the relationship between the model or the idea *(eidos* or *forma)* which pre-exists in the mind of the artist, and the material, be it wood, clay, stone, or metal, that is to receive the imprint of that idea. Without the example of plastic material, ontological *hyle* or *materia* cannot be conceived, for it is not measurable or definable; it is "amorphous", not only in the relative sense in which the material of a craft is "amorphous" or crude, but also in a radical sense, for it is without intelligibility of any kind until it is joined to an *eidos* or *forma*. Also, although *eidos* or *forma* may up to a point be conceivable in itself, it is nevertheless not imaginable apart from its union with *materia*, which determines it by lending to it an "extension", either subtle or quantitative. In short, although the two ontological principles, once they have been recognized, are intellectually evident, it is no less true that the concrete symbolism provided by the work of the artist or craftsman cannot be dispensed with for their demonstration. Moreover, since the range of the symbolism extends far beyond the domain of reason, one must conclude that Aristotle borrowed the notions of *eidos* and *hyle* (translated into Latin as *forma* and *materia)* from a real tradition, that is to say, from a method of teaching derived both from doctrine and from Divine art.

It is also worthy of note that the Greek word *hyle* literally means wood; wood is in fact the principal material used in the crafts of the archaic civilizations. In some Asiatic traditions, especially Hindu and Tibetan symbolism, wood is also regarded as a "tangible" equivalent of the *materia prima,* the universal plastic substance.

Individual existence is always woven of *forma* and *materia,* simply because the polarity they represent has its foundation in Being itself. Indeed *materia* proceeds from *materia prima,* the universal passive **substance**, while *forma* corresponds to the active pole of Being, or **essence**. When essence is referred to in connection with a particular being, it represents the archetype of that being, its permanent possibility in the Spirit or in God. It is true that Aristotle does not make this last transposition; he does not relate *forma* back to its metacosmic principle, no doubt because he consciously limits himself to the domain accessible to his method of demonstration;·this domain is characterized by the possibility of a coincidence within it of ontological and logical laws. Nevertheless, Aristotle's axioms, for example hylemorphic complementarism, presuppose a metacosmic background, which Medieval thought discerned quite naturally in the Platonic vision of things. The doctrines of Plato and of Aristotle contradict one another only on the rational plane; if one understands the myths of Plato, they encompass that aspect of reality to which Aristotle confines his attention. Those who represent the highest development of the Middle Ages were therefore right in subordinating the perspective of Aristotle to that of Plato.[24]

Whether or not one accepts the doctrine of Plato in its characteristic dialectical form, it is impossible from the Christian point of view to deny that the essential possibilities of all things are eternally contained in the Divine Word, the Logos. For "all things were made" by the Word (John 1:3), and in It alone—or through It—are all things known, since It is the "true Light, that lighteth every man that cometh into the world" (John 1:9-10). Therefore the light of the Intellect does not belong to us, it belongs to the omnipresent

---

24. St. Albert the Great wrote: "One cannot become an accomplished philosopher unless one knows the philosophies of both Aristotle and of Plato." (See E. Gilson, *La Philosophie au moyen âge,* [Paris: Payot, 1944], p. 512.) Similarly, St. Bonaventura said: "Among the philosophers, Plato received the word of Wisdom, Aristotle that of Science. The first considered principally the higher reasons, the second, the lower reasons." (See St. Bonaventura, works presented by Father Valentin—M. Breton, [Paris: Aubier, 1943], p. 66.) The Sufis were of the same opinion.

Word; and this light contains essentially the qualities of knowable things, for the innermost reality of the cognitive act is quality, and quality is "form" (*forma* or *eidos*), understood in the Aristotelian sense of the word. "The form of a thing," says Boethius, "is like a light by which that thing is known."[25] This is the eminently spiritual significance of hylemorphism: the "forms" of things, their qualitative essences, are in themselves transcendent; they can be found at all levels of existence; it is their coincidence with this or that material—or with some modality of the *materia prima*—which limits them and reduces them to their more or less ephemeral "traces".

In terms of the *quadrivium* (arithmetic, geometry, music, and astronomy), as expounded by Boethius (see diagram on p. 128), we may comment as follows: Arithmetic, geometry, and music correspond to the three existential conditions of number, space, and time. Astronomy, which is essentially a science of cosmic rhythms, comprehends all these domains.

Proportion is in space what harmony is in the realm of sound. The analogy between these two orders is demonstrated by the use of the monocord, the string of which produces sounds that vary according to the length of its vibrating part.

The qualitative unity of number is more evident in geometry than in arithmetic, for quantitative criteria are not sufficient to distinguish between two figures such as the triangle and the square, each of which has its unique and so to speak inimitable quality.

Whereas modern empirical science considers above all the quantitative aspect of things, and as far as possible detaches this from all its qualitative connotations, traditional science contemplates qualities independently of their quantitative associations. The world is like a fabric made up of a warp and a weft. The threads of the weft, normally horizontal, symbolize *materia* or, more immediately, such causal relations as are rationally controllable and quantitatively definable; the vertical threads of the warp correspond to *formae*, that is to say to the qualitative essences of things.[26] The science and art of the modern period are developed in the horizontal plane of the "material" weft; the science and art of the Middle Ages, on the other hand, are related to the vertical plane of the transcendent warp.

---

25. Cf. Anicius Manlius T. S. Boethius, *De Unitate et Uno*, Patrologie Migne.
26. See also René Guénon, *The Symbolism of the Cross*, chapter 14, "The symbolism of weaving".

*
* *

The various hieratic forms of the Cross represent different modalities of Divine radiation: the Divine Center reveals itself in the dark space that is the world. In these various forms, all of which blossomed during the early centuries of Christianity, it is sometimes the radiating aspect of the cross, and sometimes the static aspect of the square, that predominates, and these two elements combine in various ways with the circle or the disc. The Cross of Jerusalem, for example, with its branches ending in so many smaller crosses, evokes, in its multiple reflection of the Divine Center, the omnipresence of Grace, while at the same time mysteriously linking the cross with the square. In Celtic Christian art, the cross and the solar wheel are united in a synthesis rich in spiritual suggestiveness. The cross inscribed in a circle can be considered as the key-figure in sacred architecture.

First row: Romanesque, Jerusalem, and Greek crosses.
Second row: Irish, Copt, and Anglo-Saxon.
At the bottom: Irish.

121

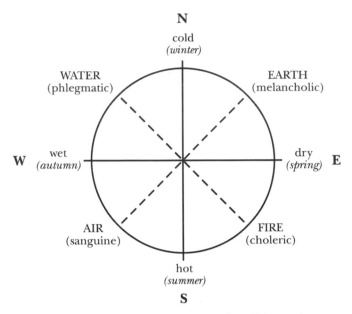

The four elements, temperaments, natural qualities, and seasons.

The essential cosmic law is an equilibrium of opposites, which either exclude each other or reciprocally complement each other, and whose relationships, referred to a center, are most easily represented in the form of a cross. The permanent characteristics or "powers" of the sensible world—the four elements (fire, air, water, earth—grouped around their quintessence ether), along with the corresponding four temperaments (choleric, sanguine, phlegmatic, and melancholic), and the four natural qualities (dry, hot, wet, and cold)—can best be represented by two crosses, one diagonal and one upright, as shown above. This manner of perceiving the cosmic attributes can also be applied to the psychological and spiritual realms. The cosmologists of Antiquity and the Middle Ages, who thought in terms of the great cosmic analogies, ordered things according to this basic ground plan of all discrimination.

(from *Chartres,* p.24)

The Royal Door of Chartres Cathedral

Between the years 1140 and 1150 the three-part doorway on the west front of Chartres cathedral was constructed. This has always been called the Royal Door, because the upright figures on the door-supports in part represent kings and queens of the Old Covenant.

The style of this door is still Romanesque in its reposeful equilibrium, and yet it is already Gothic in that the repose of its parts no longer strives earthwards, but upwards, as if these parts rose aloft like lights burning motionlessly. The forms are still austere and enclosed within themselves; they deliver themselves up as little to the uncertain light that changes constantly from morning to evening, as to the uncertain movements of the human soul. Bright and dark areas are created by smooth and rough surfaces (themselves fluted, jagged, or broken up by ornaments), with an effect rather like colors, and indeed, at one time, they were actually coated with gold and other colors. The original coating has now gone, but a still extant enamel—a mild, melodic brightness encasing the rawness of the stone—covers the surfaces and articulations.

From the point of view of their deepest meanings, the images on the three-fold Royal Door represent the most complete expression of doctrine that has ever been incorporated in the walls and supports of a doorway. Christ appears three times, each time in the middle of a tympanum: above the right-hand entrance, we see Him freshly descended to earth, sitting on the lap of His enthroned Mother; above the left-hand entrance, He ascends to Heaven, surrounded by angels; and on the central tympanum, He reveals Himself in His eternal majesty. The Nativity seems to indicate Christ's human nature, and the Ascension, His Divine nature; but the immediate reference is simply to His coming and His going, to the fact that He is the alpha and omega of earthly existence, between which two extremes His eternal majesty stands, like the present moment between yesterday and tomorrow. These are the three different meanings of the Door—the Door that is Christ Himself.

The lower portion of the whole doorway represents earth, and the upper portion Heaven. For the figures on the door pillars, though their names are unknown, are certainly representatives of the Old Covenant, and the earthly forefathers of the Divine Incarnation. Like the Incarnation, they bear the Heaven of the tympanums. Between these lower and upper domains, and interrupted only by the entrance doors themselves, runs the exquisite row of capitals, on which all the main incidents in the life of Christ are successively portrayed: it is like the demarcation line between two worlds.

That the figures on the door pillars seem so tall and narrow signifies that they themselves are the "pillars of the Church", to which St. Paul refers in the Scripture. Durand de Mende writes: "The pillars of the Church are the bishops and the learned divines who keep the Church upright. . . ." Strictly speaking, the door pillars and the figures associated with them represent a kind of ante-chamber, just as does the Old Covenant with regard to the New. In a similar doorway at Le Mans, this division into ante-chamber and main body of the church is overt: the forward wall pillars are all decorated with Old Testament personalities, while the doorposts themselves are decorated with statues of the Apostles. The latter alone belong to the "body" of the Church.

In the pictorial or sculptural decoration of a building, Medieval art—especially Romanesque and early Gothic—bases itself on the meaning that inheres in each of its constituent parts as a result of its structural role. At the beginning, on the doors of some Romanesque churches, the spiritual meaning of the supporting pillars was indicated only by flat chiseled figures; one hesitated to bestow three dimensions on a human representation, and thus to detach it from the body of the building; a free-standing statue resembled too much the ancient idols. As, however, the figures carved on the door-posts or pillars began to take on their round or multi-faceted form, they became as if round figures themselves, and finally emerged from out of the building structure, without however detaching themselves from it completely. In this way the pillar, thanks to its spiritual meaning, gave birth to the statue, just as had also occurred in ancient times.

As a sign that the sculpted Old Testament patriarchs or prophets are incorporated in the eternal edifice of the Heavenly Jerusalem, one can see over their heads—not over all of them but over those on the right- and left-hand doors—a small building crowned with a tower.

The feet of the sculpted figures rest either on a calyx of petals (which gives them an astonishing similarity to the sacred statues of the Far East) or on monsters, seen as the vanquished might of the passions and of the devil.

The unusually large number of female figures amongst these Old Testament personages—eight have been preserved—points to the redemptive role of the Virgin Mary, the Protectress of the Church. She appears herself in the right-hand tympanum with the Divine Child, whose Nativity is represented there. On the lowest panel of the tympanum are depicted the Annunciation, the Visitation, the Nativity, the Adoration of the Shepherds, and, on the middle panel, the Presentation of Jesus in the Temple. In the Nativity scene, the Virgin rests on a bed that resembles a chest; a table covers this, like the sky or the heavens. On top of this table lies the Child in a basket, and an ox and an ass (of which only traces now remain) stretch out their heads towards Him. The table is not only the crib in which the newly born Christ-child lies, but also the altar on which the body of the Savior is forever sacrificed.[27] At the same time He is present on the other altar, portrayed immediately above, on which the mother offers her Child to the priest. The resting mother in the lowest panel, the temple altar in the middle panel, and the Virgin and Child in the uppermost panel (surmounted by a baldachin) are all situated centrally; for it is the same mystery expressed three times over: the Blessed Virgin is the foundation, the altar, and the throne of the manifestation of God in human form. The way in which the artist has expressed the theological truths by the very geometry of the representation bears witness to his mastership: in the lowest panel, the horizontal, resting position of the mother, with the Child portrayed above her, represents passive resignation, by means of which the Virgin, affirming the will of God, becomes the "substantial cause" of salvation. In her pure receptivity, open to grace, she is comparable to the *materia prima* of both the world and the soul. On the middle panel, the altar rises vertically, and on it the Child stands upright as His mother offers Him to the priest of God: she offers herself in the form of her Child, just as the soul must offer itself. In the figure of the Queen of Heaven in the topmost section, two concentric circles may be inscribed: the larger one surrounds the mother, the smaller one the Child on her lap, just as the nature of the mother surrounds on all sides the nature of the Child, and just as the soul that has reached true knowledge contains in its center the Divine Light, Emmanuel.

As the lowest and the highest in creation, the Virgin appears in the manner described by Dante in the famous verses that he puts in the mouth of St. Bernard: *Vergine madre, figlia del tuo figlio, ùmile ed alta più che creatura* ("Virgin mother, daughter of thy son, lowly and exalted more than any creature").

St. Albert the Great wrote of the Virgin: "Her son is King of Kings and Lord of Lords; so she must be called Queen of Queens

27. See Émile Male, *L'Art religieux du XIIIe siècle en France* (Paris, 1931), p. 188ff.

and Lady of Ladies. . . . Her son is called God of Gods; so she must be called Goddess of Goddesses".[28] This is the meaning expressed by the representation of Mary with her Child sitting on the throne, which, taken from a Byzantine model, has an even more peaceful and inaccessible aura because of the two angels swinging censers, who, like doves beginning their flight, rush to the center represented by the figures. Their blazing deportment contrasts with that of the other two angels, on the tympanum of the left-hand door, who bear Christ aloft in a cloud and, in so doing, fall back overpowered by the Divine Light.

According to the Medieval theologians, the Virgin Mary, by virtue of the innate perfection of her soul, possessed in natural fashion all the wisdom of which man is capable. A direct reference to this wisdom is to be found in the allegories of the Seven Liberal Arts which, just outside an inner circle of adoring angels, decorate the tympanum of the Door of the Virgin. In the medieval context the seven sciences—which were classified as the *trivium* of grammar, dialectic, and rhetoric and the *quadrivium* of arithmetic, music, geometry, and astronomy—were not exclusively empirical sciences, as are those we know today. They were the expression of so many faculties of the soul, faculties demanding harmonious development. This is why they were also called arts.

Following an ancient tradition, Dante, in his *Convivio*, compares the Seven Liberal Arts to the seven planets, grammar corresponding to the moon, dialectic to Mercury, rhetoric to Venus, arithmetic to the sun, music to Mars, geometry to Jupiter, and astronomy to Saturn. The creators of the Royal Door of Chartres were certainly aware of this correspondence. It is thus doubly significant that on the tympanum of the left of the three doors the signs of the zodiac are displayed. These belong to the unchanging heaven of the fixed stars and thus represent the kingdom of the Divine Spirit, to whom this door, with its representation of the ascension of Christ, is dedicated. The seven planets, on the other hand, govern, according to the ancient viewpoint, the world of the soul. And Mary is the human soul in all its perfection.

By means of the signs of the zodiac—not all of which, incidentally, appear on the same door, *Pisces* and *Gemini* having had to be transposed, for want of room, to the Door of the Virgin—the arches

28. St. Albert the Great, Mariale, CLXII, 13-14 (Collection *Les Maitres de la Spiritualité chrétienne*, translated by Albert Carreau [Paris, 1942]).

surrounding the representation of Christ's ascension (on the left-hand door) can be seen to represent the firmament. Beside each of the twelve signs of the zodiac, the corresponding month is represented pictorially in the form of its natural activity.

These natural activities—one for each month—are the terrestrial reflections of the twelve signs of the zodiac. From them one learns to what extent the course of human existence depends upon the heavens: in seedtime and harvest, in work and leisure; for the heavens, in their cycle, bring heat after cold, dry after wet, and thus keep life in being.

This is significant for Medieval art: in two tympanums, and in the arches surrounding them, the whole cosmos is represented in its three great divisions: spiritual, psychic, and corporeal. Medieval man always kept the profounder order of things in mind.

The tympanum of the central door is wider and higher than those of the right- and left-hand doors and has only two zones, whereas the lateral doors have three. On the right-hand tympanum, the successive images of the human mother, of the sacrificial presentation in the temple, and of the Heavenly Queen are positioned one above the other; on the left-hand tympanum, where Christ ascends, a host of angels, like so many flashes of lightning from out of a storm-cloud, descend upon the disciples gathered below.

On the tympanum of the main door, the image of the eternal majesty of Christ, which has been portrayed on so many Romanesque church doors, finds its most harmonious representation. One can inscribe every geometrical figure into this tympanum; it will always be in consonance with the ordering of the five figures and with the wave of movements which go out from the central figure and return to it. Between the curve of the arch and the almond-shaped aureole surrounding Christ—these forms which separate and re-unite—a breathing or respiration goes back and forth, giving the whole image its life.

Christ is surrounded by the four creatures described by Ezechiel and John: the lion, the ox, the eagle, and the winged man. These are interpreted as the eternal prototypes of the four evangelists and their fantastical animal form serves to raise the anthropomorphic representation of the Divinity in their midst to a supra-human level.

On the innermost of the three arches, angels surround the majesty of Christ, and the twenty-four elders of the Apocalypse, who appear on the two outer arches, look up towards Him. On the lintel, the twelve apostles are present in groups of three, and to their right

The Seven Liberal Arts

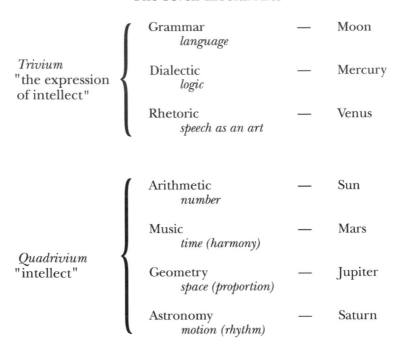

Trivium "the expression of intellect"	Grammar *language*	—	Moon
	Dialectic *logic*	—	Mercury
	Rhetoric *speech as an art*	—	Venus
Quadrivium "intellect"	Arithmetic *number*	—	Sun
	Music *time (harmony)*	—	Mars
	Geometry *space (proportion)*	—	Jupiter
	Astronomy *motion (rhythm)*	—	Saturn

and left are two prophetic witnesses, perhaps Elias and Enoch, who are to come again at the end of time.

Why is the birth of Christ portrayed over the right-hand entrance, which lies south of the main axis of the church, and the ascension of Christ over the left-hand entrance, north of the main axis, given that north and south, according to their liturgical interpretation, correspond to the Old and New Covenants respectively? Presumably the physical positioning of the doors harbors an allusion to the ancient cosmic symbol of the *januae coeli*, the two doors of the heavens, known to the later Roman period.[29] Heaven has two doors, namely the two solstices; through the "door of winter", the "new sun" enters the world, and through the "door of summer", the fullness of light leaves the world. According to an ancient view of things mentioned by Plato, the gods enter this world by the first door, and leave it through the second. The location of the winter

---

29. René Guénon, *Fundamental Symbols* (Cambridge, UK: Quinta Essentia, 1995), chapter 37, "The Solstitial Gate".

solstice, which occurs during the Christmas season, is in the southern heavens, and the location of the summer solstice in the northern; it would seem that the representational order in the west door of Chartres Cathedral is a direct reference to this: through the southern door the Divine Light descends into the world; through the northern it returns into the invisible. Between the two gates of Heaven stands the immutable axis of the world; to this the central door corresponds.

We can now return to the Seven Liberal Arts. The order in which they are listed, when properly understood, testifies to a Pythagorean view of things, and this was not without influence on Medieval art. The division of these sciences—and all their elements—into *trivium* and *quadrivium* came into Christian culture from Greek antiquity in a late and simplified form. The Medieval spirit, however, was able to reanimate the integral vision originally inherent in it.

"Philosophy has two main instruments," writes Thierry of Chartres, "namely intellect (*intellectus*) and its expression. Intellect is illumined by the *quadrivium* (arithmetic, music, geometry, and astronomy). Its expression is the concern of the *trivium* (grammar, dialectic, and rhetoric)."[30]

In fact, the *trivium* was a schooling in both language and thought. It is language that makes man, man; and that is why grammar comes at the beginning. Not without humor, the sculptor of the door of the Virgin has portrayed this art as a woman threatening with a rod two young children who are writing. The figures of the famous grammarians Donat and Priscian stand beside her. Dialectic, whose feminine representation in Chartres carries a scorpion and has Aristotle as a companion, is none other than logic. Rhetoric is the art of speaking, or rather, speaking in so far as it is an art; Cicero accompanies its allegorical figure.

The four members of the *quadrivium* are likewise represented in a feminine form in Chartres. They are: arithmetic, with a reckoning board; music, with a glockenspiel; geometry with a drawing-board; and astronomy, contemplating the heavens and accompanied by Boethius, Pythagoras, Euclid, and Ptolemy. These four arts or sciences refer to the four conditions of corporeal existence: number, time, space, and motion. Music, of course, is not only concerned with time, but also with sound; but it is in the realm of sound that

30. Thierry of Chartres, *Handbook of the Seven Liberal Arts*, quoted in *Das Königsportal von Chartres* by Wolfgang Schöne (Stuttgart: Reclam, 1961).

time manifests itself most immediately and characteristically; otherwise we can grasp it only in movement, in which it is united with space.

"Everything proceeding from the profound nature of things," writes Boethius, the great transmitter of the *quadrivium*, "shows the influence of the law of number; for this is the highest prototype contained in the mind of the Founder. From this are derived the four elements, the succession of the seasons, the movement of the stars, and the course of the heavens."[31]

It is a qualitative, and not quantitative, conception of number that lies at the basis of Medieval arithmetic. It is thus less a method of reckoning than a way of understanding the nature of number, its properties, and the uniqueness of numerical series obtained by certain constant relationships.

That each individual number does not merely represent a sum of elements, but is in itself an expression of an essential unity, appears most clearly when one transposes each number into its corresponding geometrical form: three into an equilateral triangle, four into a square, five into a regular pentagon, etc. In each of these figures innumerable relationships occur, which variously exploit and demonstrate the law inherent in the figure concerned.

The connection between arithmetic, geometry, and music can be seen from the fact that the relationship of musical notes to one another is rendered visible in the mutual relationship of the variously long strings which produce them. This can be easily demonstrated on a monochord, which has a single string and a movable bridge.

Following Greek tradition, Boethius distinguishes three kinds of proportions: the arithmetic, in which the same interval obtains between all members of the series, as, for example: 1,2,3,4,5,6 . . . ; the geometric, which progresses by means of a constant multiplication (a:c = c:b); and the harmonic, which unites the preceding two, according to the formula a:c = a-b:b-c. The harmonic is the most perfect proportion: in music it appears as harmony, and in geometry as the "golden section".

The regular relationship of different movements to one another is rhythm. The day, the year, the lunar cycle, are the great rhythms which measure all change, and in this regard, astronomy, the last member of the *quadrivium*, is the science of cosmic rhythms.

31. Ancius Manlius T. S. Boethius, *De Arithmetica libri duo.*

Number, proportion, harmony, and rhythm are clear manifestations of unity in diversity, and also clear indications of the way of return from diversity to unity. According to Boethius, the essence of things is intimately connected with unity: the more unity a thing possesses in itself, the more profoundly it participates in being.

In Medieval science, it is less a question of knowing many things, than of having a "whole" view of existence. Its method was anything but designed for the investigation of the material world and the furthering of technology. On the contrary: it possessed the means to open the spiritual eye to the beauty of mathematical proportions, and the spiritual ear to the music of the spheres.

When today we say "form", we mean only the visible and measurable aspects of a thing, especially its spatial contours. For the Medieval masters, on the other hand—for the scholars and, in a certain sense, also for the artists—"form" was the sum total of the essential properties or qualities of a thing; it was what constituted the inner unity of a manifested object. "The forms of things," writes Thierry of Chartres, "are, outside and beyond matter, contained in the Divine Spirit. There, in its simple and immutable fullness, true forms exist. But those which, in a certain and not fully explicable way, are impregnated into matter, are so to speak ephemeral and not forms in the true sense. They are only something like the reflections or representations of true forms."[32]

True form is thus neither limitable nor mutable; it is like a ray of the creative Spirit which, descending into matter, fleetingly lends it form. An analogy for this is artistic creation: just as the artist may more or less completely, depending on his humility, imprint on a material the spiritual picture that he carries within himself, so the essence of a thing may manifest itself more or less perfectly in that particular thing.

This way of looking at things is generally called Platonic, and so the men who taught in Chartres at the beginning of the twelfth century—such as Bernard, Gilbert de la Porée, William of Conques, and Thierry (who, at the very time that the Royal Door was being constructed, was chancellor of the Cathedral school)—were all Platonists. Yet it would do them an injustice simply to attribute their thought to a philosophical school; in their works there is an ele-

32. Thierry de Chartres, Librum Hunc, quoted by J. M. Parent, *La doctrine de la création dans l'École de Chartres* (Paris, 1938).

ment that transcends thinking as such, namely a genuine spiritual contemplation which, though far from being dependent upon words, nevertheless has to make use of words in order to communicate itself.

According to the Platonic point of view, all existence emanates hierarchically from the one Divine Source, which is neither diminished nor altered thereby. Can this perspective be reconciled with the creation story as related in the Bible? There is indeed a contradiction between envisaging a light which shines because it is in its nature to shine (and which one can conceive of in no other way than as shining), and envisaging a creative act which, at a given moment, calls into existence something that previously was not there. The masters of Chartres asked themselves this question and also answered it. When, with William of Conques,[33] one regards time itself as something created, the apparent contradiction disappears. Before the creation of the world, God was not in time: he was in Eternity, which lies beyond all time, in the eternal Now. One cannot say that God created the world at a given time, for time itself began with the world; from the standpoint of this world, existence (which shines or radiates forth from God) appears as if it began in time. In such a bridging of two apparently incompatible images, the more than merely mental character of spiritual contemplation can be seen.

The art of the Royal Door, in its inimitable and unsurpassed reconciliation of stellar farness and living nearness, is born of the same spirit.

(from *Chartres and the Birth of the Cathedral*)

Because of its intrinsic interest and its relevance to the other themes dealt with in the present section, we include here the following short extracts from the author's earliest book Schweizer Volkskunst (*Swiss Folk Art*).

Gargoyles

The purpose of the grotesque masks on the outside walls of Romanesque churches was undoubtedly that they should serve as a

33. William of Conques, *Philosophia mundi* (Migne, *Patrologia latina*, 172: 39-115).

means of exorcism against impure spirits. The mode of action of such exorcistic masks can be readily understood if one considers how, when a man approaches a sanctuary and seeks to direct his spirit towards the highest, all the dregs in his being, owing to a natural reaction of the soul, tend to arise and seek to enter his thoughts under a multitude of guises. If, at this moment, he espies a mask which represents, with unmistakable grossness, any hidden greed, passivity, or lust, he can look on them "objectively", and laugh at them. In this way the evil spirit is exorcized and flees the scene.

These stone masks thus contribute to a process of unmasking in the soul, but on a basis that is the exact opposite of modern psychoanalysis. For whereas in the latter the one who is plagued by dubious impulses is invited to accept his complexes as himself, the medieval man, awakened by an exorcistic device, looks on the mischievous intruder as an enemy from without, as an impulse foreign to himself which, like a disease, has sought to take root in him, and which he has only to perceive with clarity in order to be freed from it. For, according to Christian doctrine, the devil cannot tolerate the truth.

(from *Swiss Folk Art*)

The Wooden Chest

Because of its geometrical form, comprising six flat sides, which the chest (traditionally carved out of one piece of wood) has in common with the ark, the house, and the coffin, it is regarded, in the traditional lore of all peoples, as a symbol of the earth—not the earth in a geographical sense, but symbolically, as a degree of existence (the terrestrial state), which supports or contains life, just as the chest contains precious possessions, and which like the ark floats on the waters of the deep. There is an inverse relationship between the symbol of the three-dimensional or six-armed cross, which represents the world as radiating outwards from a center, and the sacred chest which, in its hexahedral, crystalline form, symbolizes the terminal stage of creation.

(from *Swiss Folk Art*)

The Decadence and the Renewal of Christian Art

A work of art, if it is to be of spiritual import, need not be a "work of genius"; the authenticity of sacred art is guaranteed by its prototypes. A certain monotony is in any case inseparable from traditional methods: amid all the gaiety and pageantry that are the privilege of art, this monotony safeguards spiritual poverty—the non-attachment of the "poor in spirit" (Matthew, 5:3)—and prevents individual genius from foundering in some sort of hybrid monomania; genius is as it were absorbed by the collective style, with its norm derived from the universal. It is by the qualitative interpretation, to whatever degree, of the sacred models that the genius of the artist shows itself in a particular art; that is to say: instead of squandering itself in "breadth", it is refined and developed in "depth". One need only think of an art such as that of ancient Egypt to see clearly how severity of style can itself lead to extreme perfection.

This allows us to understand how, at the time of the Renaissance, artistic geniuses suddenly sprang up almost everywhere, and with an overflowing vitality. The phenomenon is analogous to what happens in the soul of one who abandons a spiritual discipline. Psychic tendencies that have been kept in the background suddenly come to the fore, accompanied by a glittering riot of new sensations with the compulsive attraction of as yet unexhausted possibilities; but they lose their fascination as soon as the initial pressure on the soul is relaxed. Nevertheless, the emancipation of the "ego" being thenceforth the dominant motive, individualistic expansivity will continue to assert itself; it will conquer new planes, relatively lower than the first, the difference in psychic "levels" acting as the source of potential energy. That is the whole secret of the Promethean urge of the Renaissance.

We must add, however, that the psychic phenomenon just referred to is not in every respect parallel to a collective phenomenon such as the Renaissance, since the individual implicated in a collective "fall" of that kind is not directly responsible for it, hence his relative innocence. Genius in particular often partakes of the quasi "natural" or "cosmic" innocence of the psychic forces that are unlocked by the great crises of history; this indeed is the source of its charm. Nonetheless, its influence is not any the less pernicious, to one degree or another.

For the same reason, in every work of real genius—in the current and individualistic sense of the word—there are real values previously unperceived or neglected. It is necessarily so, since every traditional art obeys a particular spiritual economy that limits its themes and means of expression, so that an abandonment of that economy almost immediately releases new and apparently unlimited artistic possibilities. Nonetheless, such new possibilities can never henceforth be co-ordinated with respect to a single center; they will never again reflect the amplitude of the soul at rest within itself, in its "state of grace"; their tendency being centrifugal, their various modalities of vision and expression will be mutually exclusive and will succeed one another with ever-growing rapidity. Such in fact are the "stylistic periods", the dizzying succession of which is so characteristic of the European art of the last five centuries. Traditional art does not have this dynamism, but it is not for that reason "frozen": protected by the "magic circle" of sacred form, the traditional artist creates both like a child and like a sage: the models he reproduces are symbolically timeless.

In art as in everything else, man finds himself faced by the following alternative: he must seek the Infinite in a relatively simple form, keeping within the limits of that form and working through its qualitative aspect, while sacrificing some possible developments, or he must seek the Infinite in the apparent richness of diversity and change, though it must lead in the end to dispersion and exhaustion.

The economy of a traditional art can be more or less ample, it can be flexible or rigid; all depends on the power of spiritual assimilation inherent in a particular civilization, environment, or collective vocation. Racial homogeneity and historical continuity also have a part to play: millennial civilizations like those of India and China have been able, spiritually speaking, to integrate very diverse artistic possibilities—and sometimes very close to naturalism—without losing their unity. Christian art was less broadly based; the residues of a pagan art jostled it, so that it had to defend itself against their dissolving influence; but before that influence could prevail, the comprehension of traditional symbolism had first to become blurred. Nothing but an intellectual decadence, and more particularly a weakening of contemplative vision, can explain why Medieval art later came to be regarded as "barbarous", clumsy, and poor.

Among the possibilities excluded by the spiritual economy of traditional Christian art is the representation of the nude. There are many representations of Christ crucified, as well as of Adam and Eve and of souls in hell or purgatory, but their nudity is, as it were, abstract and does not engage the attention of the artist. Be that as it may, the "rediscovery" of the naked body, considered as such and in its natural beauty, provided without doubt one of the most powerful springs of action of the Renaissance. So long as Christian art conserved its hieratic forms, surrounded by a folk-lore of decoration far removed from any concern with naturalism, the absence of the nude in art passed unnoticed, so to speak; icons were made, not to reveal this or that natural beauty, but to recall theological truths and to be the vehicles of a spiritual presence. As for the beauty of nature, of mountains, forests, or human bodies, it could be admired everywhere, outside the domain of art, all the more so because prudery, which grew up only with the urban culture of the 14th century, did not obsess the soul of the Middle Ages. Thus it was only when art began to try to imitate nature that the absence of "nudism" in Medieval art came to be felt as a gap; but thereafter, the absence of any representation of the naked body could only be taken for prudery, and by the same stroke, the example of Greco-Roman statuary—not entirely unknown in the Middle Ages—became an irresistible temptation. In this connection the Renaissance appears as a cosmic retribution. It was perhaps dangerous to banish human beauty from the plastic arts—if indeed they already existed—human beauty being made in the image of God, but on the other hand one must not lose sight of the maleficent symbolism of "the flesh" in the Christian perspective and of the associations of ideas that might arise from this. Be that as it may, one can certainly not look to the Renaissance to confer afresh on physical beauty the sacred significance it held in certain ancient civilizations and still retains in India. The earliest and the most beautiful statues of the Renaissance, for example the *Fonte Gaia* of Jacopo della Quercia or the *David* of Donatello, have a tenderness that is still quite springlike, but they soon gave place to a Greco-Roman rhetoric devoid of content, and to a passionate expansivity which signifies "amplitude" only to a spirit bound to "this world". Nevertheless it sometimes happens that Renaissance sculpture is superior in qualities of nobility and intelligence to that of classical antiquity, and this can no doubt be explained by the influence of Christian experience, but it is by no means enough to confer on Renaissance art the slightest trace of traditional authenticity.

Similar considerations apply to the discovery of landscape in 14th century painting, and also, at a later period, of "open air", that is to say, the play of atmosphere and light. As subjects of artistic expression, each of these contains values precious in themselves and susceptible of becoming symbols—they function as symbols in other arts, particularly in the Far East—but Western art had discarded its sacred models, and lost its internal hierarchy, that formal principle that linked it to its traditional source. Indeed what makes the "desacralization" of art final and in a sense irreversible is not so much the choice of themes or subjects as the choice of formal language or "style".

There can be no better illustration of this law than the introduction into Renaissance painting of mathematical perspective, which is nothing but a logical expression of the individual point of view, that of the individual subject who takes himself as the center of the world. For if naturalism seems to capture the visible world as it is in its "objective" reality, it is because it has first projected the purely mental continuity of the individual subject onto the outer world. It makes that world poor and hard, and empty of all mystery, whereas traditional painting is limited to the transcription of symbols, while leaving to reality its own unfathomable depths. It is mathematical perspective, be it noted, centered on a single point that is here in question, and not a perspective of approximation, modified by occasional translocations of the optical center; such a perspective is not irreconcilable with an art having a spiritual foundation, for its purpose is not illusion but narrative coherence.

In the case of painters like Andrea Mantegna and Paolo Uccello, the science of perspective became a real mental passion, a cold passion perhaps, and one not far removed from intellectual research, but destructive of pictorial symbolism: through perspective the picture becomes an imaginary work, and at the same time the world becomes a closed system, opaque to every gleam of the supernatural. In mural painting, a mathematical perspective is properly absurd, for it not only destroys the architectural unity of the wall, but also obliges the spectator to place himself on the imaginary visual axis, on pain of subjecting all the forms to a false foreshortening. In much the same way architecture is stripped of its most subtle qualities when the purely geometrical proportions of Medieval art are replaced by arithmetical, and therefore relatively quantitative, proportions; in this respect the prescriptions of Vitruvius did much harm. It is here that one can see the pedantic character of the Renaissance: in losing its attachment to Heaven, it loses also its link with the earth, that is to say, with the people, and with true craft-tradition.

A rigorous perspective in painting inevitably involves a loss of color symbolism: by their dependence on an artificial illumination that goes hand-in-hand with spatial illusion, the colors lose their direct nature. A Medieval painting is luminous, not because it suggests a source of light situated in the world depicted, but because its colors directly manifest the qualities inherent in light; they are glimpses of the primordial light that is present in the heart. The development of *chiaroscuro*, on the contrary, reduces color into nothing more than the play of an imaginary light; the magic of lighting carries painting into a sort of intermediate world analogous to a dream, a dream sometimes grandiose, but one that envelops the spirit instead of liberating it. Baroque art carried this development to an extreme, until finally spatial forms, suggested by *chiaroscuro*, lose the almost tangible corporeity conferred on them in Renaissance painting; at this point color seems to acquire an autonomous quality, but it is color lacking in sincerity, almost feverish, with a sort of phosphorescence that ends by devouring forms like a smouldering fire. Finally the normal relationship between form and color is reversed, so that it is no longer form, the graphic outline, that gives meaning to color, but it is color which, by its gradation, produces an illusion of volume.

* * *

So far as post-medieval sculpture is concerned, its illogicality— and its consequent incapacity to express transcendent essences— resides primarily in the fact that it tries to capture instantaneous movement, while its own material is static. Traditional sculpture accepts movement only in some of its more typical phases, themselves reduced to static formulations. A traditional statue, be it Romanesque, Hindu, Egyptian, or otherwise, always affirms the motionless axis; it dominates its environment by ideally relating it to the three-dimensional cross. With the coming of the Renaissance, and still more of the Baroque, the "sense of space" becomes centrifugal; in the works of Michelangelo for instance, it is like a spiral that "devours" space; his works dominate the surrounding void, not because they relate it back to its center, or to its omnipresent axis, but because they project into it their suggestive power, their magic spell.

At this point a possible misunderstanding must be forestalled. Autonomous statuary is a product of the Renaissance, or more exactly its rediscovery is; statuary detached from the body of a building is scarcely known in Christian medieval art. Sculpture which, in the guise of an independent column, dominates an architectural ambience or a landscape fashioned according to architectural principles, is fully in the spirit of Greco-Roman art; in Christian art, any such isolation of a sculptured figure would be close to idolatry. The fact is that sculpture expresses more completely than any other plastic art the principle of individuation, for it participates directly in the separative character of space; this quality is accentuated in a statue that is free on all sides. Christian art does not allow any such autonomy except to certain objects connected with worship, such as statues of the Virgin, crucifixes, or figured reliquaries. Statues which are not liturgical objects, such as those that adorn cathedrals, are almost always incorporated into the building; for the individual human form does not realize its full meaning save through its attachment to the form, both human and universal, of the Incarnate Word, and that form is represented by the sacred edifice, itself the "mystical body" of Christ.

There is however nothing absolute about this way of looking at things, nor is it common to all traditions. In Hindu art for example, the independent statue is accepted; if one considers the principles of Yoga and the point of view it adopts towards the Divine Presence in man, it becomes clear that this must be so. Nevertheless, a close linkage between sacred sculpture and sacred architecture also exists in Hindu art, and it is in this aspect that it most closely approaches the art of the cathedrals.

The question of statuary brings us back to the subject that is fundamental to Christian art: the image of man. In the first place it is the image of God-made-man, and then that of man integrated in the Word, which is God. In the second case the individual form of man regains its original beauty by the very fact that it is reintegrated in the beauty of the Incarnate Word; this is expressed in the faces of the saints and prophets on the doors of cathedrals: the Face of the Christ contains them, they repose in Its "form".

In his masterly work *Verlust der Mitte* ("The Loss of the Center"), Hans Sedlmayr has shown how the decadence of Christian art, right up to its most recent phases, is above all a decadence of the image of man: the image of God-made-man, transmitted by Medieval art, is succeeded by the image of autonomous man, of man glorifying himself, in the art of the Renaissance. This illusory autonomy implies from the first the "loss of the center", for man is no longer truly man when he no longer has his center in God; thereafter the image of man decomposes; first it is replaced, as regards dignity, by other aspects of nature, and then it is progressively destroyed; its systematic negation and disfigurement is the goal of modern art.

Here again we can discern a sort of "cosmic retribution". Just as the Incarnation of the Word has its corollary in the supreme sacrifice, and just as the "imitation of Christ" is not conceivable without asceticism, so the representation of the Man-God demands a "humility" in the means employed, that is to say, an emphasis on their remoteness from the Divine model. There is thus no true Christian art without a certain degree of "abstraction", if indeed it be permissible to use so equivocal a term to designate that which really constitutes the "concrete" character, the "spiritual realism", of sacred art. In short, if Christian art were entirely abstract, it could not bear witness to the Incarnation of the Word; if it were naturalistic, it would belie the Divine nature of that Incarnation.

* * *

Like the bursting of a dam, the Renaissance produced a cascade of creative forces; the successive stages of this cascade are the psychic levels; towards its base it broadens out and at the same time loses unity and strength.

To a certain extent this fall can be detected even before the Renaissance properly so called, in Gothic art. The state of equilibrium is, in the West, Romanesque art and, in the Christian East, Byzantine art. Gothic art, more particularly in its later phases, represents a unilateral development, a predominance of the volitive element over the intellectual, an urge rather than a state of contemplation. The Renaissance can be looked on as a reaction, both rational and Latin, against this precarious development of the Gothic style. Nevertheless, the passage from Romanesque to Gothic art is continuous and without a break, and the methods of Gothic art remain traditional—they are founded on symbolism and on intuition—whereas in the case of the Renaissance the break is almost complete. It is true that not all branches of art run in parallel; thus, Gothic architecture remains traditional until its disappearance, whereas late Gothic sculpture and painting succumbed to naturalistic influence.

Thus the Renaissance rejects intuition, vehicled by symbolism, in favor of discursive reasoning, which obviously does not prevent it from being passional; on the contrary, because rationalism and passion go very well together. As soon as man's center, the contemplative intellect or the heart, is abandoned or obscured, his other faculties are divided among themselves, and psychological oppositions appear. Thus, Renaissance art is rationalistic—this is expressed in its use of perspective and in its architectural theory—and also passional, its passion having a global character: the affirmation of the ego in general, a thirst for what is big and without limit. Since the fundamental unity of vital forms still persists in one way or another, the opposition of the faculties continues to look like a free play; it does not yet seem to be irreducible, as it does in later times, when reason and feeling are separated by such a distance that art cannot contain them both at once. At the time of the Renaissance, the sciences were still called arts, and art still appears as a science.

Nevertheless, the cascade had been unleashed. The Baroque reacted against the rationalism of the Renaissance, the imprisonment of forms within Greco-Roman formulae, and their subsequent dissociation. But instead of overcoming these weaknesses by means of a return to the supra-rational sources of tradition, the Baroque sought to melt the congealed forms of Renaissance classicism into the dynamism of an uncontrolled imagination. It readily attaches itself to the later phases of Hellenistic art, the imagination of which is nevertheless much more controlled, more calm, and more concrete; Baroque art is animated by a psychic anxiety unknown to Antiquity.

Baroque art is sometimes worldly and sometimes "mystical", but in neither case does it penetrate beyond the world of dreams; its sensual orgies and its gruesome *memento mori* are no more than phantasmagorias. Shakespeare, who lived on the threshold of that epoch, could say that the world was of "the stuff that dreams are made on"; Calderón de la Barca, in *La vida es sueño* ("Life is a Dream"), implicitly says the same thing; but both he and Shakespeare stood far above the level on which the plastic art of their time was developed.

The protean power of imagination plays a certain part in most traditional arts, especially in Hindu art; but here it corresponds symbolically to the productive power of *Mâyâ*, the cosmic illusion. To a Hindu, the Proteism of forms is not a proof of their reality, but on the contrary, of their unreality with respect to the Absolute. This is by no means true of Baroque art, which loves illusion; the interiors of Baroque churches, such as Il Gesù and St. Ignatius in Rome, produce a hallucinatory effect; their cupolas, with their concealed bases and irrational curves, elude every intelligible standard of measurement. The eye seems to be absorbed by a false infinity, instead of reposing in a simple and perfect form; the paintings on the ceiling appear to lie open towards a sky full of sensual and mawkish angels. . . . An imperfect form can be a symbol, but illusion and lies are not symbols of anything.

The best plastic creations of the Baroque style are found outside the domain of religion, in squares and fountains. Here Baroque art is both original and unsophisticated, for it has in itself something of the nature of water, like the imagination; it is fond of conches and marine fauna.

Parallels have been drawn between the mysticism of a St. Teresa of Ávila or a St. John of the Cross and a particular contemporary style of painting, that of El Greco for example; but at best such comparisons can be justified by the psychological conditions of the period, and more particularly by the religious ambience. It is true that this style of Baroque painting, with its magical effects of light, lends itself to the description of affective states that are extreme and exceptional; but this bears no relation to contemplative states. The very language of Baroque art, its identification with the psychic world, and with all that mirage of sentiment and imagination, prevents it from grasping the qualitative content of a spiritual state.

Nevertheless, while considering examples of the Baroque style, mention should be made of the strange reality of certain miraculous Madonnas. In their "modernized" forms they have generally been transformed by the hieratic costumes conferred on them by the people, enormous triangles of stiff silk and heavy crowns; only the face still exemplifies the Renaissance or Baroque style, but in the face, realism, carried to an extreme by the tinting of features and animated by the light of flickering candles, assumes the quality of a tragic mask. Here is something much more closely connected with sacred drama than with sculpture, reconstituted instinctively by the people, and appearing side by side with the art of the period, and in spite of it.

There are those for whom Baroque art represents the last great manifestation of the Christian vision of the world. This is no doubt because the Baroque still aspires towards a synthesis; it is even the last attempt at a synthesis of Western life on a foundation of any breadth. Nonetheless, the unity it achieves proceeds from an overweening will, which melts everything into its own subjective mold, rather than from an objective co-ordination of things in view of a transcendent principle, as was the case in Medieval civilization.

In the art of the 17th century, the Baroque phantasmagoria congeals into rationally defined forms that are empty of substance; it is as if the surface of the lava of passion were coagulated into a thousand hardened shapes. All later stylistic phases oscillate between the same two poles of passional imagination and rational determinism, but the greatest oscillation is that which took place between the Renaissance and the Baroque, all those that followed being lesser. But from another point of view, it is in the Renaissance and the Baroque taken together that the reaction against the traditional inheritance was manifested with the greatest violence; because, to the extent that art becomes historically more and more removed from this critical phase, it recovers a certain calm, a certain—though very relative—disposition towards "contemplation". It can nevertheless be observed that esthetic experience is fresher, more immediate, and more authentic precisely where it is furthest from religious subjects: in a Renaissance "Crucifixion", for example, it may not be the sacred drama, but the landscape that manifests the higher artistic qualities; or in a Baroque "Entombment", it may be the play of light that is the real theme of the work—that is to say, the thing that reveals the soul of the artist—while the persons represented are secondary. This is as much to say that the hierarchy of values has collapsed.

Throughout the whole course of this decadence, the individual quality of the artist is not necessarily the point at issue; art is above all a collective phenomenon, and men of genius who stand out from the crowd can never reverse the direction of an entire movement; at the most they can only accelerate or maybe slow down certain rhythms. The judgements made here on the art of the post-Medieval centuries never take as a term of comparison the art of our times; that goes without saying. Renaissance and Baroque art had a scale of artistic and human values incomparably richer than anything that can be met with today. A proof of this, if proof be needed, is the progressive destruction of the beauty of our towns.

In every phase of the decadence inaugurated by the Renaissance, partial beauties are revealed, and virtues are manifested; but nothing of the sort can compensate for the loss of the essential.

What does all that human greatness profit us, if the nostalgia for the Infinite that is innate in us is left without response?

* * *

The succession of "styles" met with at the end of the Middle Ages can be compared to the succession of the castes that attained predominance in their respective periods. The word "caste" as used here means "human types", such as are in a sense analogous—though not parallel—to the different temperaments, and which may or may not coincide with the social rank normally occupied by each.

Romanesque art corresponds to a synthesis of the castes; it is essentially a sacerdotal art, but it comprises nonetheless a popular aspect; it satisfies the contemplative spirit, while responding to the needs of the simplest soul. Here is both serenity of intellect and the rough realism of the peasant.

Gothic art puts a growing emphasis on the spirit of chivalrous nobility, on a whole-hearted and vibrant aspiration towards an ideal. Though it has less "breadth" than Romanesque art, it still has a spiritual quality that is completely lacking in Renaissance art.

The relative equilibrium of Renaissance art is of an entirely rational and vital order; it is the congenital equilibrium of the third caste, that of merchants and craftsmen. The "temperament" of this caste is like water, which spreads horizontally, whereas nobility corresponds to fire, which surges upwards, consumes and transforms. The first caste, the sacerdotal, is like air, which is everywhere, and invisibly gives life, while the fourth caste, that of the serfs, is like the heavy and motionless earth.

It is significant that the phenomenon of the Renaissance is essentially a "bourgeois" phenomenon, and that is why Renaissance art is as much opposed to popular art, as preserved in rural communities, as it is to sacerdotal art. Chivalrous art on the other hand, which is reflected in the Gothic style, never loses its direct connection with popular art, just as the feudal lord is normally the paternal head of the peasants in his fief.

It may be noted, however, that the equations: Gothic style = noble and warrior caste, Renaissance style = mercantile and bourgeois caste, are valid only in a broad sense, and are subject to all sorts of nuances. Thus, for example, the bourgeois and city-dwelling spirit, that of the third caste—whose natural preoccupation is the conservation and increase of wealth, both in the domain of science and that of practical utility—is already manifested in certain aspects of Gothic art; the Gothic was moreover the period of the development of urbanism. Likewise, although Gothic art is strongly impregnated with the chivalrous spirit, it is nonetheless determined as a whole by the sacerdotal spirit; and this is significant as regards the normal relationship between the first two castes. The break with tradition, and the loss of understanding of symbolism, came only with the supremacy of the bourgeois caste. But even here certain reservations must be made: the beginnings of Renaissance art are without doubt characterized by a certain sense of nobility; it could even be said that they show a partial reaction against the bourgeois tendencies manifested in late Gothic art. But this was only a brief interlude; in fact, the Renaissance was promoted by nobles who had become merchants and merchants who had become princes.

The Baroque style was an aristocratic reaction in bourgeois form, hence its pompous and sometimes suffocating aspect; true nobility loves forms that are clear-cut and light, virile, and graceful, like those of a medieval coat of arms. Contrariwise, the classicism of the Napoleonic era was a bourgeois reaction in aristocratic form.

The fourth caste, that of the serfs, or more generally that of men tied to the earth, preoccupied with nothing but their physical well-being and devoid of social or intellectual genius, has no style of its own, nor even, strictly speaking, any art, if that word is used in its full sense. Under the rule of this caste, art is replaced by industry, which itself is the final creation of the mercantile and craftsman caste after it became detached from tradition.

* * *

Natura non facit saltus, but all the same, the human spirit does "make jumps". Between Medieval civilization, centered on the Divine Mysteries, and that of the Renaissance, centered on the ideal man, there is a deep cleavage, despite historical continuity. In the 19th century another cleavage appeared, perhaps even more radical. Up till then, man and the world around him still constituted an organic whole, at least in practice and in the domain of art which is here our concern; scientific discoveries, it is true, continually extended the horizon of this world, but the forms of everyday life remained within the "measure of man", that is to say, within the measure of his immediate psychic and physical needs. This is the fundamental condition under which art flourished, for art is the result of a spontaneous harmony between heart and hand. With the coming of industrial civilization, this organic unity was broken; man found himself confronted, not by maternal nature, but by lifeless matter, by a matter which, in the form of ever more autonomous machines, usurped the very laws of thought. Thus man, having turned his back on the immutable reality of the spirit—of "reason" in the ancient and Medieval sense of the word—saw his own creation rising up against him like a "reason" external to himself, a "reason" hostile to everything which, in the soul and in nature, is generous, noble, and sacred. And man has submitted to this situation: with his new science of "economics", by means of which he hopes to maintain his mastery, he merely confirms and establishes his dependence on the machine. The machine caricatures the creative act, through which a supra-formal archetype is reflected into multiple forms, analogous one to another but never the same; the machine merely produces an indefinite number of strictly uniform copies.

The result of this is that art is uprooted from the soil that fed it; it is no longer the spontaneous complement of the craftsman's labor, nor the natural expression of a truly social life, but is thrust back into a purely subjective domain. As for the artist, he is no longer what he was at the time of the Renaissance, a kind of philosopher or demiurge; he is now a solitary seeker, without principle and without aim, unless indeed he is no more than the medium, or the clown, of his public.

This crisis broke out in the second half of the 19th century; as at all historical turning-points, there was then a sudden and fleeting opening up of fundamental possibilities. With the rejection of naturalism, still connected as it was with the "homocentricity" of the Renaissance, the worth of "archaic" arts was recognized; it was understood that a picture is not an imaginary window looking out on nature, that the laws of painting are derived in the first place from geometry and chromatic harmony, and that a statue is not a figure frozen in full movement and by chance transformed into stone or bronze. The role of "stylization", the suggestive power of simple forms, and the intrinsic luminosity of colors were all discovered. At this moment a return to an art more honest, if not traditional art, seemed possible; in order to understand this, it is enough to recall some of Gauguin's pictures, or the reflections of Rodin on Gothic cathedrals and Hindu sculpture. But art no longer had either heaven or earth; it lacked not only a metaphysical foundation, but also an artisanal basis, with the result that artistic development rapidly by-passed certain half-open possibilities, and fell back into the domain of pure individual subjectivity—and did so all the more deeply, because a universal and collective language was no longer imposed on it. Thrown back on himself, the artist sought new sources of inspiration. As Heaven was henceforth closed to him, and as the sensible world was no longer an object of adoration for him, he delved in certain cases into the chaotic region of the subconscious; in so doing, he released a new force, independent of the world of experience, uncontrollable by ordinary reason, and contagiously suggestive: *flectere si nequeo superos, acheronta movebo!* ("If I cannot move the celestial beings, I will stir up hell!"—Virgil, *Aeneid*, VII:312). Whatever it is that comes to the surface of the soul from out of this subconscious darkness, it has certainly nothing to do with the symbolism of the "archaic" or traditional arts; whatever may be reflected in these lucubrations are certainly not "archetypes", but psychic residues of the lowest kind; not symbols, but specters.

Sometimes this sub-human subjectivism assumes the "impersonal" demeanor of its congeneric antithesis, which could be called "machinism". Nothing could be more grotesque and more sinister than these machine-dreams, and nothing could more clearly reveal the satanic nature of certain features that underlie modern civilization!

* * *

Let us now consider whether Christian art can be reborn, and under what conditions its renewal might be possible. First, let it be said that there is a certain chance, slight though it be, in the fact—negative in itself—that the Christian tradition and Western civilization are moving farther and farther apart. The Church, if it is not to be carried away in the chaos of the modern world, must retreat into itself. Some of its representatives are still trying to enlist the most modern and the most spurious artistic movements for the purposes of religious propaganda, but we shall soon see that anything of that kind can only accelerate the intellectual dissolution that threatens to engulf religion itself. The Church must have recourse to all those things that affirm its timeless nature; then only can Christian art return to its essential models and assume the role, not of a collective art permeating an entire civilization, but of a spiritual support; this will be all the more effective to the degree that it clearly opposes the formal chaos of the modern world. There are a few signs of a development in this direction; the interest in Byzantine and

Romanesque art now appearing in religious circles may be mentioned as one of them. But a renewal of Christian art is not conceivable without an awakening of the contemplative spirit at the heart of Christianity; in the absence of this foundation, every attempt to restore Christian art will fail; it can never be anything but a barren reconstruction.

What has been said above about the principles of sacred painting lets us see the other conditions of its renewal. It is out of the question that Christian painting can ever be "abstract", that is to say, that it can legitimately be developed from the starting-point of purely geometrical symbols. Non-figurative art has its place in the crafts, and especially in the art of building, where the symbolism is inseparable from the technical procedure itself. Contrarily to a theory that may be encountered in certain quarters, an image is not the outcome of a "gesture" made by the artist, but, on the contrary, his "gesture" proceeds from an inward image, from the mental prototype of the work. Whenever religious painting comprises a geometrical schematism, this has been superimposed on the image properly so called; the image remains the basis and substance of the art, and this is so for practical as well as for metaphysical reasons, since the image must not only be an anthropomorphic symbol, in conformity with "God become man", but also a teaching that is intelligible to the people. Painting, when considered in its technical aspects, no doubt partakes of the character of a craft, but this does not directly concern the spectator; in its subject-matter and in its relation to the religious community, Christian painting must always be figurative. Abstract composition occurs only—and in its proper place—in ornament, thus constituting as it were a bridge between conscious and quasi-theological perception on the one hand, and unconscious and instinctive perception on the other.

Some maintain that the age during which a figurative religious art was necessary has come to an end, and that it is consequently impossible to "recapitulate" Medieval Christian art; the Christianity of today, it is said, has come into contact with the non-figurative or archaic arts of so many different peoples that it could never recover an essential vision except in abstract forms, freed from all anthropomorphism. The answer to these people is that an "age" not determined by tradition has no voice in the matter, and above all that the anthropomorphism of Christian art is an integral part of Christian spiritual means, since it springs from traditional Christology; and besides, every Christian ought to know that a new "cycle" imposed from without can be nothing but that of the Antichrist.

The character of Christian painting is essentially, and not accidentally, figurative. This means that it can never dispense with the traditional prototypes that safeguard it from arbitrariness. These prototypes always leave a fairly wide margin for the exercise of creative genius, as well as for the special needs of times and places, in so far as these may be legitimate. This last reservation is of capital importance in a period when almost unlimited rights are attributed to "our time". The Middle Ages were not concerned with being "up to date", the very notion did not exist; time was still space, so to speak. The fear of being taken for a "copyist", as well as the search for originality, are very modern prejudices. In the Middle Ages, and to a certain extent even in the Renaissance and Baroque periods, ancient works, considered to be the most perfect in the period concerned, were copied; and in copying them, emphasis was quite naturally placed on those aspects that were seen as essential, and it is in this way that art is normally kept alive. In the Middle Ages especially, every painter or sculptor was in the first place a craftsman who copied consecrated models; it is precisely because he identified himself with those models, and to the extent that his identification was related to their essence, that his own art was "living". The copy was evidently not a mechanical one; it passed through the filter of memory, and was adapted to the material circumstances; likewise, if today one were to copy ancient Christian models, the very choice of those models, their transposition into a particular technique, and the stripping away from them of accessories, would in itself be an art. One would have to try to condense whatever might appear to be the essential elements in several analogous models, and to eliminate any features attributable to the incompetence of a craftsman, or to his adoption of a superficial and injurious routine. The authenticity of this new art, its intrinsic vitality, would not depend on the subjective "originality" of its formulation, but on the objectivity or intelligence with which the essence of the model had been grasped. The success of any such enterprise is dependent above all on intuitive wisdom; as for originality, charm, and freshness, these will come of their own accord.

Christian art will not be reborn unless it completely frees itself from individualistic relativism, and returns to the sources of its inspiration, which by definition are situated in the "timeless".

(from *Sacred Art in East and West*)

Islamic Art

Introduction

Although the world of Islam, which is more or less co-extensive with the ancient empire of Alexander,[34] includes many peoples with a long sedentary history, the ethnic waves which periodically renewed the life of these peoples, and imposed their domination and preferences on them, have always been of nomadic origin: Arabs, Seljuks, Turks, Berbers, and Mongols. In a general way, Islam does not jibe well with an urban and bourgeois "solidification".[35]

Wall decoration from the 'Attarîn *medersa*, Fez, Morocco.

34. It can be said that Alexander was the artisan of the world that was destined for Islam, in the same way that Caesar was the artisan of the world that was to accept Christianity.
35. One of the reasons for the decadence of Muslim countries in modern times is the progressive suppression of the nomadic element.

Characteristic Aspects

In Islam, a mosque generally comprises a courtyard with a fountain where the faithful can make their ablutions before performing their prayers. The fountain is often protected by a small cupola in the form of a baldaquin. The courtyard with a fountain in the middle, as well as the enclosed garden watered by four streams of water gushing forth from its center, are made in the likeness of Paradise, for the Koran speaks of the gardens of Beatitude, where springs of water flow and where celestial virgins dwell. It is in the nature of Paradise (*janna*) to be hidden and secret; it corresponds to the inward world, the innermost soul. It is on this heavenly pattern that the Islamic house is modeled, with its inner courtyard surrounded by walls on all four sides, and with its enclosed garden containing a well or a fountain. The house is the *sacratum* (*haram*) of the family, where woman reigns and man is but a guest. The Islamic house is shut off from the outer world—the life of the family being withdrawn from the social life of the community—it is only open upwards towards the heavens, which are reflected in the fountain below.

The spiritual style of Islam is also manifested in the art of clothing, and especially in the masculine costume of the purely Muslim peoples. This could be said to be a priestly costume that has become generalized, just as Islam "generalized" the priesthood by abolishing hierarchy and making every believer a priest, so that any Muslim can perform for himself the essential rites of his religion. The masculine costume of Islam is a synthesis of sacerdotal and monastic attire, and as such affirms masculine dignity; and the turban, called the crown or diadem of Islam is, according to the Prophet, the mark of spiritual and sacerdotal stature.

(from *Sacred Art in East and West*)

The Question of Images: Aniconism in Islamic Art

The prohibition of images in Islam applies, strictly speaking, only to the image of the Divinity; it stands, therefore, in the perspective of the decalogue, or more exactly of Abrahamic monotheism, which Islam sees itself as renewing. In its last manifestation as in its first—in the time of Mohammed as in the age of

Abraham—monotheism directly opposes idolatrous polytheism[36], so that any plastic representation of the divinity is for Islam, according to a "dialectic" that is both historical and divine, the distinctive mark of the error which "associates" the relative with the Absolute, or the created with the Uncreated, by reducing the second level to the first. To deny idols, or still better to destroy them, is like translating into concrete terms the fundamental testimony of Islam, the formula *lâ ilâha illâ 'Llâh* ("there is no divinity but God"), and, just as this testimony, in Islam, dominates everything or consumes everything in the manner of a purifying fire, so also the denial of idols, whether actual or virtual, tends to become generalized. Thus it is that portraiture of the divine messengers (*rusul*), prophets (*anbiyâ'*), and saints (*auliyâ'*) is avoided, not only because their images could become the object of idolatrous worship, but also because of the respect inspired by their inimitability. They are the vice-regents of God on earth. "God created Adam in His form" (a saying of the Prophet Mohammed), and this resemblance of man to God becomes fully manifest, in a fashion, in prophets and saints, without it being possible, nevertheless, to grasp this on the purely corporeal level. According to this perspective, the stiff, inanimate image of a divine man could not be other than an empty shell, an imposture, an idol.

In Sunni Arab circles, the representation of any living being is frowned upon, because of respect for the divine secret contained within every creature,[37] and if the prohibition of images is not observed with equal rigor in all ethnic groups, it is nevertheless strictly mandatory for everything that falls within the liturgical framework of Islam. Aniconism—which is the appropriate term here, and not iconoclasm[38]—became somehow an inseparable con-

---

36. It is not a pleonasm to speak of "idolatrous polytheism", as is shown by Hinduism, which is polytheist but in no wise idolatrous, since it recognizes the provisional and symbolic nature of idols, and also the relative nature of the "gods" (*devas*) as "aspects" of the Absolute. Esoteric Muslims, or Sufis, occasionally compare idols to Divine Names, whose significance has been forgotten by pagans.

37. According to a saying of the Prophet, artists who seek to imitate the works of the Creator will be condemned in the hereafter to give life to their creations, and their inability to do so will cause them to be cast into the worst of torments. This saying can clearly be understood in several ways; it has, in fact, never prevented the growth, in certain Muslim circles, of a figurative art, of a kind entirely free from naturalism.

38. "Aniconism" can have a spiritually positive character, whereas "iconoclasm" has only a negative sense.

comitant of the sacred; it is even one of the foundations, if not the main foundation, of the sacred art of Islam.

This may appear paradoxical, for the normal foundation of a sacred art is symbolism, and in a religion expressing itself in anthropomorphic symbols—the Koran speaks of God's "Face", His "hands", and the throne on which He sits—the rejection of images seems to strike at the very roots of a visual art dealing with things divine. But there is a whole array of subtle compensations which need to be borne in mind, and in particular the following: a sacred art is not necessarily made of images, even in the broadest sense of the term; it may be no more than the silent exteriorization, so to speak, of a contemplative state, and, in this case—or in this respect—it does not reflect ideas, but qualitatively transforms the ambience, by causing it to share in an equilibrium whose center of gravity is the Unseen. That such is the nature of Islamic art can easily be verified. Its object, above all, is man's environment—hence the dominant role of architecture—and its quality is essentially contemplative. Aniconism does not detract from this quality; quite the contrary, for, by precluding every image inviting man to fix his mind on something outside himself, and to project his soul onto an "individualizing" form, it creates a void. In this respect, the function of Islamic art is analogous to that of virgin nature, especially the desert, which is likewise favorable to contemplation, although, in another respect the order created by art opposes the chaos of desert landscape.

The proliferation of decoration in Muslim art does not contradict this quality of contemplative emptiness; on the contrary, ornamentation with abstract forms enhances it through its unbroken rhythm and its endless interweaving. Instead of ensnaring the mind and leading it into some imaginary world, it dissolves mental "fixations", just as contemplation of a running stream, a flame, or leaves quivering in the wind, can detach consciousness from its inward "idols". (From *Art of Islam, Language and Meaning*)

The Impact of the Arabic Language on Islamic Art

The extraordinary normative power of the Arabic language derives from its role as a sacred language, as well as from its archaic nature, these two factors being related. It is its archaic quality that predestined Arabic for its role as a sacred language, and it was the Koranic revelation which, as it were, actualized its primordial substance. Archaism, in the linguistic order, is not synonymous with simplicity of structure, quite the contrary. Languages generally grow poorer with the passage of time by gradually losing the richness of their vocabulary, the ease with which they can diversify various aspects of one and the same idea, and their power of synthesis, which is the ability to express many things with few words. In order to make up for this impoverishment, modern languages have become more complicated on the rhetorical level. While perhaps gaining in surface precision, they have not done so as regards content. Historians of language are astonished by the fact that Arabic was able to retain a morphology attested to by the Code of Hammurabi[39] (as early as the 19th–18th century B.C.), and to retain a phonetic system which preserves, with the exception of one single sound, the extremely rich sound-range attested to by the most ancient Semitic alphabets ever discovered,[40] although there was no "literary tradition" to bridge the gap between the far-off age of the Patriarchs and the time when the Koranic revelation was to fix the language for all time.

The explanation of this perennial quality of Arabic is to be found in the conserving role of nomadism. It is in towns that languages degenerate, by becoming worn out, like the things and institutions they designate. Nomads, who live to some extent outside time, conserve their language better; it is the only treasure they can carry around with them in their pastoral existence; the nomad is a jealous guardian of his linguistic heritage, his poetry, and his rhetorical art. On the other hand, his inheritance as regards visual art cannot be rich; architecture presupposes stability, and the same is broadly true of sculpture and painting. Nomadic art in general is limited to simple, yet striking, graphic forms, ornamental motifs, heraldic emblems, and symbols. In the situation we are studying, the existence of these forms is by no means a negligible factor, for they carry creative potentialities that blossom forth when they encounter

---

39. See Édouard Dorme, "L'Arabe littéral et la langue de Hammourabi", in *Mélanges Louis Massignon* (Damascus, 1957).

40. The most ancient Semitic alphabets have a total of twenty-nine sounds or letters, twenty-eight of which are retained by Arabic, the "missing" sound being a variant of "S". It is possible that the reduction of the alphabet to twenty-eight letters conveys a symbolic purpose, for certain Arab authors see a correspondence between these sounds and the twenty-eight stations of the moon. The phonetic cycle, progressing from gutturals to palatals, dentals, and labials, retraces the "lunar phases" of the primordial sound emanating from the sun.

the artistic techniques of the sedentary civilizations. It is true that the presence of these model forms among the pre-Islamic Arabs is not generally apparent except retrospectively, by analogy with what we find in the case of other nomads, and in the phenomenon, in the Muslim art of the early centuries, of the sudden flowering of ornamental motifs which are vastly different in their modes from anything coming from the sedentary civilizations and which, in a sense, are parallel to the figurative "devices" of the Arab language.

(from *Art of Islam, Language and Meaning*)

Arabic Compared With Other Languages

The Arabic language is such that a whole doctrine can be condensed into a short and concise formula of adamantine clarity. This means of expression is realized in all its fullness only in the Koran; yet it is part of the Arab genius nonetheless, and is reflected in Arabo-Muslim art, for this art is not only rhythmical, it is also crystalline.

The conciseness of the Arabic sentence obviously does not limit the profundity of the meaning, but neither does it facilitate synthesis on the descriptive level: an Arab will rarely assemble a number of conditions or circumstances in a single sentence; he prefers to string together a series of brief phrases. In this respect, an agglutinative language like Turkish, which belongs to the family of Mongol languages, is less austere and more flexible than Arabic; when it comes to describing a situation or a landscape, Turkish is clearly superior to Arabic, and the same applies to Persian, which is an Indo-European language close to Gothic; however, both Turkish and Persian languages borrowed not only their theological terminology, but also their philosophical and scientific terminology, from Arabic.

The extreme opposite to Arabic is Chinese, which is ruled by a static vision of things, and which groups the elements of a thought around generic images, as is indicated by the ideographic nature of the Chinese script.

The Turks, like the Arabs, were originally nomads, but their language links them to a vastly different mental type; the Arab is incisive and dynamic in his manner of thinking; the Turk, for his part, is enveloping and circumspect. In the general framework of Muslim art, the Turkish genius reveals itself by a certain power of synthesis—one might almost say, by a totalitarian spirit. The Turk has a plastic or sculptural gift which the Arab does not have; his works always proceed from a global conception; they are as if hewn from a single block.

As for Persian art, it is distinguished by its sense of hierarchical differentiations; Persian architecture is perfectly articulated, without ever being "functional" in the modern sense of the term. For the Persian, Unity manifests itself above all as harmony. Moreover, Persians are "visuals" by nature and culture, but they see, so to speak, with lyrical eyes; their artistic activity is as if animated by an inner melody. It is said proverbially in the East that "Arabic is the language of God, but Persian is the language of paradise", and this describes well the difference that exists, for example, between a distinctively Arab type of architecture, like that of the Maghrib where crystalline geometry of forms proclaims the unitary principle, and Persian architecture with its blue domes and floral decoration.

The Arab architect is not afraid of monotony; he will build pillar upon pillar and arcade upon arcade, and dominate the repetitiveness by the rhythmic alternation and qualitative perfection of each element.

(from *Art of Islam, Language and Meaning*)

The Arabic Language and the Koran

The language of the Koran is omnipresent in the world of Islam; the entire life of a Muslim is filled with Koranic formulae, prayers, litanies, and invocations in Arabic, the elements of which are drawn from the Sacred Book; innumerable inscriptions bear witness to this. It could be said that this ubiquity of the Koran works like a spiritual vibration—there is no better term to describe an influence that is both spiritual and sonorous—and this vibration necessarily determines the modes and measures of Muslim art; the plastic art of Islam is therefore, in a certain fashion, a reflection of the words of the Koran. It is nevertheless difficult to grasp the principle by which this art is linked to the text of the Koran, not on the narrative plane, which plays no part in the normal plastic art of Islam, but on the level of formal structures, since the Koran obeys no laws of composition, either in the strangely discontinuous linking together of its themes, or in its verbal presentation, which eludes all rules of meter. Its rhythm, powerful and penetrating as it is, follows no fixed measure; entirely unpredictable, it maintains at times an insistent rhyme like the beat of a drum and then suddenly changes its breadth and pace, shifting its cadences in a manner as unexpected as it is striking. To affirm that the Koran is Arabic verse, because it includes passages with a monotonous rhyme like the Bedouin *rajaz*, would be mistaken; but to deny that these monotonies and abrupt breaks correspond profoundly to the Arab soul, would be equally so. Arab art—poetry and music as well as the plastic arts—loves to repeat certain forms and to introduce sudden and unforeseen variants against this repetitive background. But the play of art always obeys easily fathomable rules, whereas the waves of sacred speech, though they sometimes exhibit regular patterns, have behind them a whole ocean without form. In the same way, the state of inner harmony engendered by the words and sonorous magic of the Koran is situated on quite another plane than the satisfaction that can be obtained, for example, in perfect poetry. The Koran does not satisfy, it gives and takes away at the same time, it expands the soul by lending it wings, and then lays it low and leaves it naked; for the believer, it is both comforting and purifying, like a rainstorm. Purely human art does not possess this virtue. That is to say, there is no such thing as a Koranic style which can simply be transposed into art; but there does exist a state of soul which is sustained by the recitation of the Koran, and which favors some formal manifestations while excluding others. The diapason of the Koran never fails to unite an intoxicating nostalgia with the greatest sobriety: it is a radiation of the divine Sun on the human desert. It is to these two poles, drunkenness and sobriety, that the fluid and flamboyant rhythm of the arabesque and the abstract and crystalline character of architecture respectively correspond.

But the most profound link between Islamic art and the Koran is of another kind: it lies not in the form of the Koran, but in its *haqîqa*, its formless essence, and more particularly in the notion of *tauhîd*, unity or union, with its contemplative implications; Islamic art—by which we mean the entirety of plastic arts of Islam—is essentially the projection into the visual order of certain aspects or dimensions of Divine Unity.

(from *Art of Islam, Language and Meaning*)

4

History, the Governance of Men and Nations, and the Modern World

The Nature of Kingship

Consciousness of the purity of their descent is a characteristic of the Bedouins. This is an aristocratic characteristic, a natural prerequisite for the founding of princely houses and dynasties.

Another law of desert life is allegiance, the cohesion of a group under a leader: "In the Bedouin tribes all discipline and direction come from the elders, the shaikhs; they usually enjoy considerable respect amongst their people. . . . The allegiance of a tribe to its leader, however, is something quite different from servility; the shaikh is obeyed because he is the head of a large family or because he is courageous and wise, and successful in his deeds. It is expected of him that, before taking important decisions, he consult with the elders of the other families of the tribe. This chivalrous conception of leadership also obtained when the Sultan, as legal head of the state, invested the shaikh with a public office, which always occurred when the ruler sought to ensure the loyalty of a tribe. The report of a French diplomat who, in 1886, as ambassador for his government, rode from Tangier to Fez, lets us see this state of affairs as clearly as if it were in a mirror:

> Towards ten o'clock in the morning we arrived at the place of Shaikh Mubârak of the Aulâd Delîm and erected our camp opposite his house, on a hill completely covered with marigolds that were fluttering in the morning breeze. In front of us rose the first hills of the Zerhûn range, where the founder of the Moroccan empire, the famous Mulay Idrîs, found his first refuge. Round about us, as far as the eye could see, there stretched out other high mountains, without trees and apparently without villages, so that their creviced ridges were completely bare. They looked like enormous waves that had suddenly frozen under the hand of Allâh. This impression was strengthened by the reflection on their flat surfaces of the bluish color of the sky. Here and there this was broken by large white cracks in the chalky ground that resembled flecks of foam in a powerful ocean. The house of Shaikh Mubârak lay in the valley at the foot of the hill on which was our camp. Compared with the size of the neighboring villages, the space occupied by his house indicated clearly that it was the abode of a lord, a citadel filled with vassals, a meeting place, and the seat of the power dominating the region. This impression was strengthened further when, in the afternoon, we went to visit the *caïd*. Firstly, we were taken to an Arab courtyard, in the middle of which a fountain played. The courtyard served as a stable; the horses of the bodyguard stood there in the open with their forelegs bound. In the

corners all sorts of baggage was heaped up. A few women washed clothes at the fountain, while others were weaving in a sort of hall. Servants ran hither and thither; there was a life and a bustle that bore witness to the presence of a large number of people. We were not to visit the whole building, however, which apart from the women's quarters contained enough apartments to lodge a hundred warriors. We were taken up to the reception room, which was composed of two long chambers linked to each other by elegant arches. One of these chambers was used by the servants; in the other, along the walls of which cushions had been placed for our use, Shaikh Mubârak sat on a low divan. The odor of fever that met us as we entered the room amply proved that it was not for lack of goodwill that the old Shaikh had not met us on horseback at the border of his land. One felt this all the more on seeing the Shaikh himself. Although aged, he was still erect, and would have been handsome if the fever had not ravaged him. His yellow skin was in stark contrast with the whiteness of his turban and his beard. His eyes shone brightly, but this was not the effect of the fever. . . . As soon as we sat down, we were brought all kinds of food on large platters, while a dignified member of the household began to prepare tea with all the well-known ceremony. But our attention was caught even more by the arrival of a group of riders who seemed to have returned from some mission. Each of them approached the Shaikh, making first of all a bow, and then bending down to kiss his knee. The Shaikh put his hand paternally on the shoulder or forehead of each of them, and spoke a few words as the one concerned remained in this inclined position. All this took place, however, without any crass servility, but rather with a simplicity that was redolent of greatness. This homage to the tribal chief had nothing demeaning about it, as one could clearly see from the free and affectionate manner in which they later spoke with the Shaikh. One after another they again stood up, went into the neighboring room, and sat down together on the carpet.

(Gabriel Charmes, *Une Ambassade au Maroc*)

By their very nature the Bedouins are opposed to absolute overlordship.

Nevertheless, when a man who has attained the rank of leader on the basis of tribal consciousness sees the way to true lordship opening up before him, he follows this way, for the goal in sight is a desirable one. It can only be reached, however, on the basis of tribal consciousness, for this alone assures him of allegiance. Thus kingship is the goal to which tribal consciousness ultimately leads.

(Ibn Khaldûn, *Muqaddima*, 2:16)

For Ibn Khaldûn, kingship is the form of government that springs from nature, and thus is willed by God. For kingly dignity is something prefigured in the essence of man. It represents, in a sense, the summit of earthly existence, since it permits the development of all the faculties and demands the exercise of all the virile virtues. If this rank is attained only by a few, its realization is nevertheless like the manifestation of a prototype which every man carries within himself, so that the subjects of a king see in him, as it were, the fulfillment of their own essence.

Ibn Khaldûn considers no form of government other than monarchy, and his judgement on this matter would undoubtedly have been the same as that of the famous Emir 'Abd al-Qâdir who, during his captivity in France, learned that King Louis-Philippe had been replaced by a "Council of the Republic" composed of five members: "But to be effective a body must have a head," he remarked to the French officer who had brought him the news. "It will not have one head, but five!" the latter replied. To which 'Abd al-Qâdir exclaimed: "I tell you: it will not have five heads, but thirty-two million, and that is a little too many!"

If the city cultures repeatedly, or periodically, succumb to the onslaught of nomads or semi-nomads from the "desert", this does not necessarily mean that the Bedouins will destroy the city culture. The Bedouin conquerors may do violence to the town-dwellers, but they let town life go on and merely assume the lordship of it as an aristocratic governing class which in fact becomes gradually absorbed by it. According to Ibn Khaldûn this process of assimilation is unavoidable:

> Within a given ruling family, leadership exhausts itself after four generations: the originator of the family's fame knows what efforts his work has cost him and therefore preserves those qualities that were the foundation of his power. The son who inherits his authority has had a personal relationship with his father and has learned from him. . . . The third generation however contents itself with an outward imitation of its predecessors and relies on custom. . . . And finally the fourth generation no longer possesses any proper idea of the effort that went into the creation of the authority. It believes that deference is due to it merely on account of its noble descent. . . .
>
> (Ibn Khaldûn, *Muqaddima*, 2:14)

And so begin both the transformation of the aristocratic stratum into a city officialdom, and the decline of the ruling house.

The weakness of the Berbers lies in their very strength, in the exclusivism of tribal consciousness that makes one tribe the enemy of another. For this reason, as Ibn Khaldûn observes, a Bedouin movement can only create a large state when the demands for supremacy springing from the various tribes are subordinated to a leadership of a higher order, and this can only be prophethood, or a function deriving from it. In this encounter between a power gushing forth naturally from the timeless sea of the desert and a Truth of supernatural origin lies the whole destiny of the Islamic peoples. The epic beginning was destined to repeat itself periodically, even if on a lesser scale: the beginning, when the disunited desert tribes, mostly nomadic and scarcely noticed by the surrounding civilized cultures, were united by the message of the Koran, became the vehicle of a spiritual mission, and suddenly conquered and transformed the whole near-eastern world from the Indus to the Pyrenees. As the power of the Arabs became absorbed by the urban cultures, other nomadic peoples, like the Turks and Mongols in the east and the Berbers in the west, assumed the role of the ethnically and spiritually renewing power that had succeeded in shattering the petrifactions of the cities.

(from *Fez, City of Islam*)

The Law of Hierarchy
and the Four Social Stations

The Law of Hierarchy

The view of life on which medieval culture rested, and which Dante outlined as if by way of a final summing-up, recognized hierarchy as the highest of laws, by virtue of which all that has existence derives by stages from Eternal Being, so that each thing that has existence has its own principle in that it is the symbol of something at a higher level. From the Christian point of view, this law derives from the doctrine of the incarnation of God's eternal and divine Word, for, if man were not the distant image of God, God would never have taken on the human form.

Hierarchy is unity that reveals itself in multiplicity, through a differentiation which, being qualitative in nature, does not divide, so that each separate element, according to the particular character and rank that belong to it, remains an expression of one all-encompassing order—just as light, though it manifests its full spectrum of colors when refracted by a prism, remains one in its internal richness.

Regarding hierarchy, St. Thomas Aquinas wrote: ". . . causing the distinction of things for the perfection of the whole, the same Divine Wisdom is also the cause of inequality. The universe would not be perfect were there but one level of goodness."

(from *Siena, City of the Virgin*)

The Four Social Stations

What the four social stations or "castes" mean for the natural equilibrium of society cannot be gauged in terms of modern sociological criteria. Originally, the social stations arise out of a naturally-occurring variegation in human dispositions or talents, something that is to be found everywhere; consequently they have absolutely nothing to do with different levels of wealth, but are based on the existence of different psychological "types", whose proper distribution within the total society—according to the activities or offices which each is competent to exercise—significantly contributes to the stability of the whole. Heredity and education guarantee the perpetuation of specific predispositions and skills within an enclosed social layer; under such conditions, any departures from the norm that occur in the process of inheritance will be much rarer than the similarities.

The priesthood is the only calling which is not inherited, at least in the Christian world. A man becomes a priest as a result of an inward "call": herein lies a superiority that arises from the freedom of conscious and personal choice, but it also contains a danger, since there is no method of testing the authenticity of the "call"; renunciation of marriage and of monetary profit have in practice to suffice as a touchstone.

The priesthood presupposes the human type for which meditation on timeless truth is the indispensable "air" of life. The nobility, on the contrary, from among whom the leaders are chosen, is based on consciously purposeful character and initiative: nobles are those to whom bold decisions and daring action come naturally. Only he who is ready to risk his life for his ideals can call himself a free and noble man: *noblesse oblige*. The third social station, consisting of merchants, craftsmen, and farmers, is focused on the preservation and increase of goods and property of every kind: it consists of active and practical men, but not men of the warrior-aristocrat type. The fourth station includes mostly those who by nature are concerned only with their bodily well-being, and who therefore can find their place in the overall structure of society only by giving service.

This social division was as self-evident in the Middle Ages as was the division of the corporeal world into the four elements "air", "fire", "water", and "earth"—a gradation which in fact has a certain correspondence with that of the four social stations or castes.

This outline of social organization in the Middle Ages would not be complete without a mention of monasticism. The monks stood apart from caste, just as they stood apart from worldly life: monasticism indeed constituted an "open door" for any who wished to escape from the rigid societal structure.

It would be a mistake to imagine that the medieval caste-differentiation caused a greater division between man and man than the difference between rich and poor in later days: indeed, the contrary was the case. Society in the Middle Ages was based on the patriarchal system, whereby the higher and the lower orders were bound together as in one large family. The priest was the father of the faithful under his care, and the high-born landowner looked upon his tenant-farmers as, in a sense, belonging to his own family, just as the city merchant had his team of helpers living in his house. In this manner, the different castes were in a constant, albeit "vertical", relationship with one another. The day of the uprootedness and isolation of the "proletarians" had not yet arrived.

The Church strove to spiritualize the particular qualities of each social station by favoring the formation of Orders of Knighthood, and by incorporating the guilds into the liturgical life, thereby providing a special consecration of craftsmanship. This arose not so much out of ecclesiastical power politics, as from a knowledge of men's differing needs. Not only does each caste possess its particular abilities which can develop into virtues, but also its particular weaknesses, and these can become dangerous once the stability of the social orders is imperiled. Thus the particular virtue of the aristocracy is their combination of courage and generosity, of the sword and love. A degenerate aristocracy, on the other hand, gives rise to immoderate pride, coupled with a destructive passion that is analogous to one of the aspects of the element "fire".

In the face of a degenerate nobility, the third order, that of the merchants, craftsmen, and farmers, has the advantage that it instinctively seeks an equilibrium, tending, like the element "water", to cover over anything projecting. The virtue of the third order is a sense of moderation: its weakness is greed for gain. This gets the upper hand when the higher orders lose their sense of responsibility towards those who are subordinate to them. When, in its turn, the middle class degenerates, it is not long before the fourth caste— whose chief virtue is patience, as of the element "earth"—rises in rebellion against the whole traditional order.

(from *Siena, City of the Virgin*)

Chess as a Symbol of Rulership

What most fascinates the man of noble and warlike caste is the relationship between will and destiny. Now it is precisely this that is so clearly illustrated by the game of chess, inasmuch as its moves always remain intelligible without being limited in their variation. Alphonsus the Wise, in his book on chess, relates how a king of India wished to know whether the world obeyed intelligence or chance. Two wise men, his advisers, gave opposing answers, and to prove their respective theses, one of them took as his example the game of chess, in which intelligence prevails over chance, while the other produced dice, the symbol of fatality.[1] Al-Mas'ûdî writes likewise that the king "Balhit", who is said to have codified the game of chess, gave it preference over *nerd*, a game of chance, because in the former intelligence always has the upper hand over ignorance.

At each stage of the game, the player is free to choose between several possibilities, but each movement will entail a series of unavoidable consequences, so that necessity increasingly limits free choice, the end of the game being seen, not as the fruit of hazard, but as the result of rigorous laws.

It is here that we see not only the relationship between will and fate but also between liberty and knowledge; except in the case of inadvertence on the part of his opponent, the player will only safeguard his liberty of action when his decisions correspond with the nature of the game, that is to say with the possibilities that the game implies. In other words, freedom of action is here in complete solidarity with foresight and knowledge of the possibilities; contrariwise, blind impulse, however free and spontaneous it may appear at first sight, is revealed in the final outcome as a non-liberty.

The "royal art" is to govern the world—outward and inward—in conformity with its own laws. This art presupposes wisdom, which is the knowledge of possibilities; now all possibilities are contained, in a synthetic manner, in the universal and divine Spirit. True wisdom is a more or less perfect identification with the Spirit (*Purusha*), this latter being symbolized by the geometrical quality of the chessboard, "seal" of the essential unity of the cosmic possibilities. The Spirit is Truth; through Truth, man is free; outside Truth, he is the

1. The *mandala* of the chessboard, on the one hand, and dice, on the other, represent two different and complementary symbols of the cosmos.

slave of fate. That is the teaching of the game of chess; the *kshatriya* who gives himself over to it does not only find in it a pastime or a means of sublimating his warlike passion and his need for adventure, but also, according to his intellectual capacity, a speculative support, and a "way" that leads from action to contemplation.

(from *Mirror of the Intellect*)

St. Catherine of Siena
and the City of the Soul

The City as the Image of the Soul

In the words of St. Catherine of Siena, the city is the image of the soul, the surrounding walls being the frontier between the outward and the inward life. The gates are the faculties or senses connecting the life of the soul with the outer world. The intelligence, according to the saint, questions each one who approaches the gates whether he be friend or foe, thus watching over the security of the city. Living springs of water rise within it; gardens lie protected by its walls, and at the center, where beats the heart, stands the Holy Sanctuary.

Because of its meaningful design, the city of Siena itself corresponds to this simile: it is indeed an image of the soul. Like the soul, the city can be filled with light: when, in the early morning, before the song of the swallows is drowned by the noise of the working day, one sees, as one climbs up from one of the terraced gardens, the first shafts of golden light strike the city standing high aloft; or again, at sunset, as one looks down on the town from San Domenico, when the light of the sinking sun steeps the houses and towers in glowing red, and the Cathedral, as if built of pearl and jasper, seems suspended in the air, illumined by the red sky. Then indeed can one see Siena as was in the mind of her founders: a holy city.

The Monastic Orders

In the construction of Siena there are two distinctly recognizable phases or stages of development: the first can be seen in the form of the old city, gathered closely around the Cathedral, which towers above it like the Citadel of Zion, or the Temple above Jerusalem; the second arises from the location of the monasteries with their monastic churches. These are at the outer limits of the city, and look rather like foothills keeping watch: San Francesco on the east and San Domenico on the west; and to the south and south-east, stand Sant'Agostino and Santa Maria dei Servi. The presence of these monastic churches on the outer limits of the city, but still within the city walls, tells of a time when the ascetic life of the monasteries, formerly completely withdrawn from the worldly life of the city, had begun actively to influence the lives of the citizens themselves. Up to the beginning of the 13th century, monastic life was devoted entirely to meditation and contemplation, and monasteries were founded and built in the wilderness (*desertum*). But in the 13th and 14th centuries, the city was invaded by friars of the begging and preaching orders, which caused a spiritual revival, a love of God that made an appeal to the inmost heart of the people. In Siena, all the monastic churches are influenced in their architecture by the ascetic sobriety of the Cistercians. Only the church of Sant'Agostino was rebuilt at a later date, namely in the 17th century.

That the inhabitants of Siena during the Middle Ages were deeply rooted in religious faith is clearly seen in the events which preceded the battle of Montaperto, when the people called down the assistance of Heaven by prayer and penance, and also in their consecration of the city to the Holy Virgin.

The preaching and charitable monastic orders began to intervene in worldly matters just when the theocratic unanimity of the citizens of Siena was weakening. Henceforth, they built their monasteries within the confines of the town, with the aim, precisely, of rebuilding the "City of the Soul".

Worldly events in the second half of the 14th century, however, had almost paralyzed the influence of the monasteries, when suddenly—as though to compensate for the threatened degeneration—all the spirituality that had previously sanctified and beautified the life of the city found a new embodiment in the form of St. Catherine. Through her deeds and words, everything that had hitherto seemed like a divine mystery-play naïvely and subconsciously experienced by the people, was suddenly given a deeper meaning, and freed from what had to some extent become custom and pageantry.

St. Catherine

Caterina Benincasa, the daughter of a simple master-dyer, had neither wealth, position, nor power, yet through the spiritual magnetism of her personality, she influenced the lives of individuals and whole communities far beyond the confines of her native city, and even eventually induced the Pope, against the will of most of his cardinals, to forsake Avignon and return to Rome. Because of her, the whole political outlook of the Sienese was transmuted into a consciousness of the unity of all Christendom; the chivalrous character of Siena resounded in the spiritual love song that sprang from her, and the object of which she became; the robust, full-toned speech of Tuscany—which to this day adorns the women of Siena, just as a dance can ennoble the body—became, on her lips, spiritual music. If Siena has produced a counterpart to the great poet of Florence, it is to be found in the writings of St. Catherine.

The Inner Light

The great soul of St. Catherine, however, is not to be explained by the laws of heredity; such greatness transcends all that can be inherited from ancestors, or is fashioned by environment and nourished by nature. The key to this greatness of soul lies in the words which Catherine, in a state of ecstasy, heard from the very mouth of Christ: "I am He who is and thou art she who is not". The "thou" has no "being" of its own when separated from its divine origin; it expresses that frail web of changing impressions and desires which man is wont to call his self. Its chief characteristic is self-love, which Catherine compares to a cloud veiling the Divine Light in our hearts. Considered from the level of our human nature, this light is our ability to distinguish between right and wrong, good and evil; on the higher plane it is the Knowledge of God, through grace. It is "the Light that lighteth every man that cometh into the world" (John 1:9). In Him alone each soul finds its own abiding reality.

In her writings, St. Catherine returns again and again to this fundamental truth. Among many such letters may be cited the following, written to one of her disciples, Ristoro Canigiani of Florence:

Epistolario

We have been endowed by God with a natural, inborn light enabling us to distinguish between good and evil, perfection and imperfection, purity and impurity, light and darkness, and between the infinite and the finite. It is a Knowledge that God has placed in our nature, and experience repeatedly shows us that we possess this ability. You will say: "If this power of discrimination is ours, how comes it that we so often cling to that which is harmful?" To which I would reply: "That comes from self-love veiling the divine Light, just as the light of the sun is veiled by a cloud." Therefore our mistakes come not from lack of light but from the cloud which darkens it. And so it happens that we blindly choose that which harms instead of that which benefits the soul. By her very nature the soul inclines towards the good and good things; but error comes from the fact that self-love, depriving the soul of light, causes her to seek good where it is not to be found. Therefore deluded people set their heart and their love on the things of this world, things as transient as the wind. O man, foolish beyond all foolishness, who seekest good where there is evil, and light where there is darkness! Where there is death, thou seekest life; where there is poverty, thou seekest riches, and thou seekest infinity among finite things. Good will elude the seeker so long as he seeks it where it cannot be found. We must seek it in God, who is the high and eternal good. If we seek it in Him, we shall assuredly find it, for Almighty God contains no evil, but only pure and perfect goodness. Just as the sun, the giver of light, could never give us darkness, so God can never give us other than that which is in His perfect Self. Thus shall we know (if we will but see by the aid of the Divine Light), that everything that God gives us, even everything troubling, painful, or fearful that He permits this life to bring us, is intended to lead us to the Highest Good, and to teach us not to look for it in this world, but in Him. For the Good is not in this world, neither in riches nor in any other condition which earthly life can offer us: for on the earth bitterness and sorrow reign. If the soul should possess the world against the will of God, it loses grace. Therefore He vouchsafes to us that which is good and perfect, namely the grace truly to seek Him, while man, blinded by his own imperfection, thinks to be bad that which is for his good. His own wrongdoing robs him of God and of God's grace; he fails to see his wrongdoing as an evil, and so he continues in his delusion.

We should therefore strengthen the natural light of perception which has been given us by avoiding evil and practicing virtue, seeking by this same light perfection where alone it can be found. Truly seeking, we shall find it in God. Only then shall we know the ineffable love that God has shown us through His Son, and know His Son who, with such a great fire of Love, shed His blood for us.

By using this natural light, which is imperfect, we shall attain, through grace, a supernatural Light which is perfect, and which will bind us to the truth, and give us steadfastness at all times, and in every condition of life, into which God may lead us. His loving-kindness will grant us this grace, for His only desire is our sanctification. The first light, as I have said, separates us from the world; the second light binds us and unites us with virtue. . . .

Caterina Benincasa was born in the Fontebranda quarter of Siena in 1347, just one year before the outbreak of the Black Death, described by Agnolo di Tura, which raged throughout the city. At the age of seventeen she entered the Dominican Third Order, living as a nun in the house of her father. In 1374, when the plague broke out once more, Catherine and a few Sisters of the Third Order whom she had gathered around her devoted themselves to the care of the sick, without considering the danger to themselves. Even before this, a group of young people of both sexes, drawn from all social circles and professions, had already rallied around her. By the time she was twenty-three years old, this group of disciples was meeting regularly for spiritual discourse in the Chapel of the Vault under the Hospice of Santa Maria della Scala—where to the present day the Brethren of St. Catherine meet for devotions. The circle of her devotees and followers gradually spread beyond Siena. With advice and exhortation, Catherine intervened in public life: she reconciled warring families, particularly the two powerful Sienese aristocratic clans of the Salimbeni and the Tolomei, exhorted to greater watchfulness the princes of the Church who had become negligent, and challenged royal princes to participate in crusades rather than wage war against each other.

Political Dissensions

At that time Siena was torn by internal party dissensions. The government of the "Nine", consisting of rich merchants, had fallen from power in 1355. There followed a series of political subversions, brought about each time by militant intervention of the deposed aristocracy. The rule of the merchants was replaced by that of the small shopkeepers, headed by a council of twelve senators. The rich merchants as well as the nobility, having both been excluded from political power, had now produced a strong counterpoise, against which the Council of twelve senators could only retain office by resorting to terror. In 1368, they were supplanted by the rule of the craftsmen who called themselves the "Reformers". These Reformers succeeded to a certain extent in preserving the balance of power by admitting, as collaborators, representatives of previous ruling parties—known as "mountains" (*monti*)—into the Council of their democratic government. So, for a while, political peace was restored, the remaining fragments of the earlier hierarchy being more or less reduced to the level of the common people, at the expense of what had previously been a multi-layered and qualified city body.

The Adventurers

The exclusion of the nobles from the governments of the Italian city-states had brought bitter retribution: robbed of the military element on their councils, the towns were not capable of defending themselves against the many adventurers willing, as mercenaries, to carry on war for some princely employer: these soldiers of fortune, when their services were no longer required, roamed the land terrorizing and blackmailing the cities. Among these gangs, which were mostly led by German or English *condottieri,* were to be found a number of deposed and degenerate nobles. In the years 1364, 1365, and 1366, the Sienese territory was periodically ravaged by one of these bands led by Sir John Hawkwood—named "Aguto" by the Italians. In vain did the Republic—at the cost of considerable payments of money—exact promises from this *condottiere* that Siena should in future be spared; he accepted the monies and then broke his promises. St. Catherine sent Father Raimondo of Capua to Sir John Hawkwood, exhorting him to give up his raids and to take part instead in a crusade, but her intervention was unsuccessful.

The result of depriving the council of the rich merchants was that commerce dwindled, riches decreased, and a city such as Siena suffered the gradual loss of her far-flung commercial connections.

Confusion ruled not only in Siena but in the whole of Italy. The Emperor was powerless. Charles IV was overruled and humiliated by the Sienese when, while staying in the city in 1368, he offered his support to the aristocracy and the ruling "Twelve" to raise an insurrection against the democratic government of the "Reformers".

The Pope

Since 1309, the Pope had resided in Avignon, thereby losing the support and the confidence of the Italian people.

St. Catherine recognized that the root of this evil lay not only within the framework of city politics or in the spiritual decline of the clergy, but more particularly in the fact that the head of the Church no longer lived in the holy city of long and consecrated tradition, but in exile under foreign protection and influence. She therefore concentrated the power of her prayer and exhortation on achieving the return of the Pope to Rome. She was successful in restoring peace between the cities of Tuscany and in reconciling them with the Pope. The following is an excerpt from a letter of St. Catherine to Pope Gregory XI:

Epistolario

Ambassadors from Siena are on their way to see Your Holiness. If there are any people in the world who can be won over by love, it is they. Therefore I beg of you that you try to win them over in this way. Be a little lenient towards their excuses for the fault they have committed; for they are sorry for it. It seems to them that they have gone so far that now they know not what they should do. May it please Your Holiness, that, if you should see any way in which they could act towards Your Holiness which would be acceptable to you, and whereby they might no longer remain in the war on the side of those to whom they have allied themselves, I beg you to tell it to them. Uphold them for the love of Christ crucified. I believe that, if you do this, it will be of great benefit for Holy Church and reduce the occasion for evil.

The Saint was not afraid either of reproaching the Pope with the depravity of the clergy or of imputing half-heartedness to him personally:

Epistolario

In the Name of Jesus Christ crucified and of gentle Mary.

To you, most reverend and beloved father in Christ Jesus, your unworthy, poor, miserable daughter Catherine, servant and slave of the servants of Jesus Christ, writes in His precious Blood: with the desire to see you a fruitful tree, full of mellow fruits, and planted in fruitful earth—for if the tree be removed from the earth it would dry up and bear no fruit—I speak here of the "earth" that is true knowledge of yourself. For the soul that knows itself becomes humble, because it sees nothing of which it can be proud; it nourishes itself on the sweet fruit of love, recognizing within itself the limitless goodness of God. When it becomes aware that it is not, it attributes all its being to Him who Is. Whence the soul is constrained to love what God loves and to hate what He hates.

Oh, sweet and true knowledge, which, as the knife of self-hatred, thou carriest with thee, and which, out the hand of holy desire, thou drawest forth in order to kill the worm of self-love—a worm that spoils and gnaws the root of our tree, so that it cannot bear any fruit of life, but dries up, and loses its verdure! For if a man loves himself, perverse pride (head and source of every ill) lives within him, whatever his rank, prelate or layman, may be. If he is a lover of himself alone—that is, if he loves himself for his

own sake and not for God—he cannot do other than ill, and all
virtue is dead in him. Such a one is like a woman who brings forth
her sons dead. And so it really is; for he has not the life of love
within him, and seeks only for praise and self-glory, and not the
Name of God. I say therefore: even if he is a prelate, he does ill, for
through his self-love and self-indulgence (arising from his wish to
avoid the disfavor of creatures), holy justice dies within him. He
sees his subjects commit faults and sins, and pretends not to see
them and fails to correct them; or if he does correct them, he does
it with such lukewarmness that he accomplishes nothing, but
whitewashes the vice; he is always afraid of giving displeasure or of
getting into a quarrel. All this is because he loves himself. Sometimes he tries to do everything in peace. This, however, is the very
worst of cruelties; for if a wound is not cauterized when necessary,
or cut out with steel, but simply covered with ointment, not only
does it fail to heal, but it infects everything, and many a time death
will result.

In 1376 St. Catherine traveled to Avignon as mediatrix between
Florence and Pope Gregory XI. While there, she wrote a letter to
the eight "War Lords", the Magistrature chosen by the Commons, in
Florence. The most important section of this letter is as follows:

Epistolario

I complain strongly regarding you, if what is said in these parts
is true, namely, that you have imposed a tax upon the clergy. If this
is so, it is a very great evil for two reasons. The first is that you are
wronging God, for you cannot do it with a good conscience. But it
seems to me that you are losing your conscience and everything
good; it seems as if you cared for nothing but the transitory things
of senses, that disappear like the wind. Do you not see that we are
mortal, and must die, and know not when? Therefore, it is great
folly to throw away the life of grace, and to bring death on one's
own self. I do not wish you to do so any more, for if you did you
would be turning back, and you know that it is not he who begins
who deserves glory, but he who perseveres to the end. So I tell you
that you would never reach an effective peace, unless by persever-
ance in humility, no longer insulting or offending the ministers
and priests of Holy Church.

This is the other thing that I was telling you was harmful and
bad. For besides the evil that comes from wronging God, I tell you
that such action is ruinous to your peace. For the Holy Father, if he
knew it, would conceive greater indignation against you.

This is what some of the cardinals have said, who eagerly seek
and desire peace. But on hearing this report, they say: "It doesn't
seem that the Florentines want to make peace; for if it were true,
they would avoid the least action that was against the will of the

Holy Father and the customs of Holy Church." I believe that Christ himself on earth would say these and like words, and he would have excellent reason to say them.

I tell you, dearest fathers, and I beg you, not to choose to hinder the grace of the Holy Spirit, which by no merits of yours He by His clemency is disposed to give you. You would bring great shame and reproach upon me. For nothing but shame and confusion could result if I told the Holy Father one thing and you did another. I beg you that it may no longer be so. Nay, do you exert yourselves to show in word and deed that you wish peace and not war.

I have talked to the Holy Father. He heard me graciously, by God's goodness and his own, showing that he had a warm love of peace; like a good father, who does not consider so much the wrong the son has done, as whether he has become humble, so that he may show him full mercy. How much he would rejoice, my tongue cannot tell. Having discussed with him a good length of time, at the end of our talk he said that if your case were as I presented it to him, he was ready to receive you as sons, and to do what I considered just. I say no more here. No other answer ought to be given to the Holy Father until your ambassadors arrive. I marvel that they are not here yet. When they arrive, I shall talk to them, and then to the Holy Father, and I will write you as to what the situation is. But you, with your taxes and frivolities, are spoiling all that is sown. Do so no more, for the love of Christ crucified and for your own profit. I say no more. Remain in the holy and sweet grace of God.

(Given in Avignon, the 28th day of June 1376)

Persuading the Pope to return to Rome was St. Catherine's chief object, and in convincing Gregory XI himself of the need to return she was successful. But the French cardinals had, from the beginning, done all in their power to pour ridicule on St. Catherine's efforts and to vilify her character; they now multiplied their efforts, producing every conceivable obstacle to prevent the departure of the Pope from Avignon. Catherine, who had preceded the Pope to Rome, now wrote him the following letter:

Epistolario

In the name of Jesus Christ Crucified and of gentle Mary.

Most holy Father, your unworthy and miserable daughter Catherine commends herself to you in His precious blood, with the desire to see you as a firmly planted rock, fortified in good and holy resolve; so that however many and contrary be the winds that batter you, whether from men holding office in the world or from deception or devilish malice, they may not harm you. For they only want to hinder all the good that may come about from your departure from Avignon. I understood from the letter you sent me that the cardinals claim that Pope Clement IV, when there was anything he had to do, would never do it without the advice of his brother cardinals; even if it often seemed to him that his own view was the more useful, nevertheless he would follow theirs. Alas, most holy Father, they adduce the example of Pope Clement IV, but not that of Pope Urban V, who, when he was in doubt about something, whether or not it were better to do it, would take advice; but on the matters about which he was sure and certain, as you are about the need for departure, he did not depend on the advice of others, but followed his own counsel and took no heed even if all were against him. It seems to me that the advice of good men has regard only to the honor of God, the health of souls, and the reformation of the Holy Church, and not to their own self-interest. I say that the advice of such men is to be followed, but not that of those who care only for their own lives and for honors, rewards, and pleasures; for their counsel turns on where their own preference lies. I beg of you in the name of Christ crucified that it may please Your Holiness to make haste. Employ a pious deception: give the appearance of readiness to stay on, and then act quickly and soon, since the sooner you act the less will you stay among these embarrassments and troubles. It also seems to me that they are giving you to learn from the example of wild animals, who, when once they escape from a snare, never return to it. Till now you have evaded the snare of their counsels, after they had once caused you to fall into it when you delayed your coming; and it was the devil that caused that snare to be laid, so that all the harm and evil might befall which in fact befell. You, being wise and inspired by the Holy Spirit, will not fall into that snare again. So let us go quickly, sweet my Father, and without fear. If God is with you, no one will be against you. Go quickly to your Bride (the Church) who awaits you with blanched cheeks until you bring the color back to them. I will not burden you with further words, though there is much more that I might say. Abide in the sweet and blessed favor of God. Forgive me my presumption. Humbly I ask your blessing.

Finally, in January 1377, Pope Gregory XI entered Rome where, a few months later, he died. To the day of his death, St. Catherine remained his adviser. To her great sorrow, after the death of Gregory, she lived to see the schism which befell the Church over the question of Pope Urban VI (elected in Rome) and the anti-pope Clement VII (elected in Avignon), whom the French cardinals had supported. She fought hard for the recognition of Urban VI as the rightful successor. In 1380, St. Catherine passed away, suffering and exhausted by the bitter dissension among Christians. In the very same year St. Bernardino of Siena was born.[2]

(from *Siena, City of the Virgin*)

2. See "St. Bernardino of Siena and the Sacred Monogram" later in this book.

What is Conservatism?

In these days mention is often made of "conservatism", but its philosophical basis is seldom explored. Undoubtedly, one of the most profound writers on conservatism was Edmund Burke (1729–1797) and, in our own time, T. S. Eliot sought to describe its essential features in his insightful essay "The Literature of Politics". In the following article, which is not political in intention, Titus Burckhardt traces the origin and development of conservatism in the history of Europe of the last few centuries, and explains the underlying philosophy that gives it its meaning and its strength.

Leaving aside any political overtones which the word may have, the conservative is someone who seeks to conserve. In order to say whether he is right or wrong, it should be enough to consider what it is he wishes to conserve. If the social forms he stands for—for it is always a case of social forms—are in conformity with man's highest goal and correspond to man's deepest needs, why shouldn't they be as good as, or better than, anything novel that the passage of time may bring forth? To think in this way would be normal. But the man of today no longer thinks normally. Even when he does not automatically despise the past and look to technical progress for humanity's every good, he usually has a prejudice against any conservative attitude, because, consciously or unconsciously, he is influenced by the materialistic thesis that all "conserving" is inimical to constantly changing life and so leads to stagnation.

The state of need in which, today, every community that has not kept up with "progress" finds itself, seems to confirm this thesis; but it is overlooked that this is not so much an explanation as a stimulus for even further development. That all must change is a modern dogma that seeks to make man subject to itself; and it is eagerly proclaimed, even by people who consider themselves to be believing Christians, that man himself is in the grip of change; that not only such feeling and thinking as may be influenced by our surroundings are subject to change, but also man's very being. Man is said to be in the course of developing mentally and spiritually into a superman, and consequently, 20th century man is looked on as being a different creature from the man of earlier times. In all of this, one overlooks the truth, proclaimed by every religion, that man is man, and not merely an animal, because he has within him a spiritual center which is not subject to the flux of things. Without this center, which is the source of man's capacity to make judgements—and so may be called the spiritual organ that vehicles the sense of truth—we could not even recognize change in the surrounding world, for, as Aristotle said, those who declare everything, including truth, to be in a state of flux, contradict themselves: for, if everything is in flux, on what basis can they formulate a valid statement?

Is it necessary to say that the spiritual center of man is more than the psyche, subject as this is to instincts and impressions, and also more than rational thought? There is something in man that links him to the Eternal, and this is to be found precisely at the point where "the Light which lighteth every man that cometh into the world" (John 1:9) touches the level of the psycho-physical faculties.

If this immutable kernel in man cannot be directly grasped—anymore than can the dimensionless center of a circle—the approaches to it can nevertheless be known: they are like the radii which run towards the center of a circle. These approaches constitute the permanent element in every spiritual tradition and, as guidelines both for action and for those social forms that are directed towards the center, they constitute the real basis of every truly conservative attitude. For the wish to conserve certain social forms only has meaning—and the forms themselves can only last—if they depend on the timeless center of the human condition.

In a culture which, from its very foundations (thanks to its sacred origin), is directed towards the spiritual center and thereby towards the eternal, the question of the value, or otherwise of the conservative attitude, does not arise; the very word for it is lacking. In a Christian society, one is Christian, more or less consciously and deliberately, in an Islamic society one is Muslim, in a Buddhist society Buddhist, and so on; otherwise, one does not belong to the respective community and is not a part of it, but stands outside it or is secretly inimical to it.

Such a culture lives from a spiritual strength that puts its stamp on all forms from the highest downwards, and in doing this, it is truly creative; at the same time it has need of conservational forces, without which the forms would soon disappear. It suffices that such a society be more or less integral and homogeneous, for faith, loyalty to tradition, and a conserving or conservative attitude mirror one another like concentric circles.

The conservative attitude only becomes problematical when the order of society, as in the modern West, is no longer determined by the eternal; the question then arises, in any given case, which fragments or echoes of the erstwhile all-inclusive order are worth preserving. In each condition of society (one condition now following the other in ever more rapid succession) the original prototypes are reflected in some way or other. Even if the earlier structure is destroyed, individual elements of it are still effective; a new equilibrium—however dislocated and uncertain—is established after every break with the past. Certain central values are irretrievably lost; others, more peripheral to the original plan, come to the fore. In order that these may not also be lost, it may be better to preserve the existing equilibrium than to risk all in an uncertain attempt to renew the whole.

As soon as this choice presents itself, the word "conservative" makes its appearance—in Europe, it first received currency at the time of the Napoleonic wars—and the term remains saddled with the dilemma inherent in the choice itself. Every conservative is immediately suspected of seeking only to preserve his social privileges, however small these may be. And in this process, the question as to whether the object to be preserved is worth preserving goes by default. But why shouldn't the personal advantage of this or that group coincide with what is right? And why shouldn't particular social structures and duties be conducive to a certain intelligence?

That man seldom develops intelligence when the corresponding outward stimuli are lacking, is proved by the thinking of the average man of today: only very few—generally only those who in their youth experienced a fragment of the "old order", or who chanced to visit a still traditional Oriental culture—can imagine how much happiness and inward peace a social order that is stratified according to natural vocations and spiritual functions can bring, not only to the ruling, but also to the laboring classes.

In no human society, however just it may be as a whole, are things perfect for every individual; but there is a sure proof as to whether an existing order does or does not offer happiness to the majority: this proof inheres in all those things which are made, not for some physical purpose, but with joy and devotion. A culture in which the arts are the exclusive preserve of a specially educated class—so that there is no longer any popular art or any universally understood artistic language—fails completely in this respect. The outward reward of a profession is the profit which its practice may secure; but its inner reward is that it should remind man of what, by nature and from God, he is, and in this respect it is not always the most successful occupations that are the happiest. To till the earth, to pray for rain, to create something meaningful from raw material, to compensate the lack of some with the surplus of others, to rule, while being ready to sacrifice one's life for the ruled, to teach for the sake of truth—these, amongst others, are the inwardly privileged occupations. It may be asked whether, as a result of "progress", they have been increased or diminished.

Many today will say that man has been brought to his proper measure, when, as a worker, he stands in front of a machine. But the true measure of man is that he should pray and bless, struggle and rule, build and create, sow and reap, serve and obey—all these things pertain to man.

When certain urban elements today demand that the priest should divest himself of the signs of his office and live as far as possible like other men, this merely proves that these groups no longer know what man fundamentally is; to perceive man in the priest means to recognize that priestly dignity corresponds infinitely more to original human nature than does the role of the "ordinary" man. Every theocentric culture knows a more or less explicit hierarchy of social classes or "castes". This does not mean that it regards man as a mere part which finds its fulfillment only in the people as a whole; on the contrary, it means that human nature as such is far too rich for everyone at every moment to be able to realize all its various aspects. The perfect man is not the sum total, but the kernel or essence of all the various functions. If hierarchically structured societies were able to maintain themselves for millennia, this was not because of the passivity of men or the might of the rulers, but because such a social order corresponded to human nature.

There is a widespread error to the effect that the naturally conservative class is the bourgeoisie, which originally was identified with the culture of the cities, in which all the revolutions of the last five hundred years originated. Admittedly the bourgeoisie, especially in the aftermath of the French revolution, has played a conservative role, and has occasionally assumed some aristocratic ideals—not, however, without exploiting them and gradually falsifying them. There have always been, amongst the bourgeoisie, conservatives on the basis of intelligence, but from the start they have been in the minority.

The peasant is generally conservative; he is so, as it were, from experience, for he knows—but how many still know it?—that the life of nature depends on the constant self-renewal of an equilibrium of innumerable mutually interconnected forces, and that one cannot alter any element of this equilibrium without dragging the whole along with it. Alter the course of a stream, and the flora of a whole area will be changed; eliminate an animal species, and another will be given immediate and overwhelming increase. The peasant does not believe that it will ever be possible to produce rain or shine at will.

It would be wrong to conclude from this that the conservative viewpoint is above all linked with sedentarism and man's attachment to the soil, since it has been demonstrated that no human collectivity is more conservative than the nomads. In all his constant wandering, the nomad is intent on preserving his heritage of language and custom; he consciously resists the erosion of time, for to be conservative means not to be passive.

This is a fundamentally aristocratic characteristic; in this the nomad resembles the noble, or, more exactly, the nobility of warrior-caste origin necessarily has much in common with the nomad. At the same time, however, the experience of a nobility that has not been spoiled by court and city life, but is still close to the land, resembles that of the peasant, with the difference that it comprises much wider territorial and human relationships. When the nobility, by heredity and education, is aware of the essential oneness of the powers of nature and the powers of the soul, it possesses a superiority that can hardly be acquired in any other way; and whoever is aware of a genuine superiority has the right to insist upon it, just as the master of any art has the right to prefer his own judgement to that of the unskilled.

It must be understood that the ascendancy of the aristocracy depends on both a natural and an ethical condition: the natural condition is that, within the same tribe or family, one can, in general terms, depend on the transmission by inheritance of certain qualities and capabilities; the ethical condition is expressed in the saying *noblesse oblige*: the higher the social rank—and its corresponding privilege—the greater the responsibility and the burden of duties; the lower the rank, the smaller the power and the fewer the duties, right down to the ethically unconcerned existence of passive people. If things are not always perfect, this is not principally because of the natural condition of heredity, for this is sufficient to guarantee indefinitely the homogeneous nature of a "caste"; what is much more uncertain is the accomplishment of the ethical law that demands a just combination of freedom and duty. There is no social system that excludes the misuse of power; and if there were, it would not be human, since man can only be man if he simultaneously fulfills a natural and a spiritual law. The misuse of hereditary power therefore proves nothing against the law of nobility. On the contrary, the example alone of those few people, who, when deprived of hereditary privilege, did not therefore renounce their inherited responsibility, proves the ethical calling of the aristocracy.

When, in many countries, the aristocracy fell because of its own autocracy, this was not so much because it was autocratic towards the lower orders, but rather because it was autocratic towards the higher law of religion, which alone provided the aristocracy with its ethical basis, and moderated by mercy the right of the strong.

Since the fall, not merely of the hierarchic nature of society, but of almost all traditional forms, the consciously conservative man stands as it were in a vacuum. He stands alone in a world which, in its all opaque enslavement, boasts of being free, and, in all its crushing uniformity, boasts of being rich. It is screamed in his ears that humanity is continually developing upwards, that human nature, after developing for so and so many millions of years, has now undergone a decisive mutation, which will lead to its final victory over matter. The consciously conservative man stands alone amongst manifest drunks, is alone awake amongst sleep-walkers who take their dreams for reality. From understanding and experience he knows that man, with all his passion for novelty, has remained fundamentally the same, for good or ill; the fundamental questions in human life have always remained the same; the answers to them have always been known, and, to the extent that they can be expressed in words, have been handed down from one generation to the next. The consciously conservative man is concerned with this inheritance.

Since nearly all traditional forms in life are now destroyed, it is seldom vouchsafed to him to engage in a wholly useful and meaningful activity. But every loss spells gain: the disappearance of forms calls for a trial and a discernment; and the confusion in the surrounding world is a summons to turn, by-passing all accidents, to the essential.

(previously published in *Avaloka*, vol. 5, nos. 1 & 2, Winter 1990, and in *Sacred Web*, no. 3, Summer 1999)

Râdhâ and Krishna in the Sacred Grove
(Kangra Valley, India, c. 1785 A.D.)

The Mughal Emperor Akbar (barefooted and alone, except for his
musician) visiting the Hindu ascetic Haridas
(A painting from Kishangarh, 1760 A.D.)

I

Amida Buddha "rising from behind the mountains
like a Sun of compassion"
(Japanese, 13th century)

II

Buddhist

Avalokiteshvara, the Bodhisattva of Mercy
(Bihar, India, 10th century)

III

Buddhist

Sanskrit Buddhist text in Nepalese script,
Prajñâ-Pâramitâ, with Green Târâ in the center
(11th century)

The Wat Phra Singh temple
(Chiang Mai, Siam, 14th century)

IV

Buddhist

Tibetan thangka of the Bodhisattva Manjusri
"With his sword, he severs the bonds of ignorance"

Red Indian

Red Indian painted "buffalo" skin

Crow Sun Dance attended by Titus Burckhardt in 1979
(for diagram of the Sun Dance Lodge, see page 289)

Red Indian

Head of a Red Indian
(sculpted by Titus Burckhardt)

"The Creator measuring the world"
(13th century manuscript)

VIII

"Man as microcosm, world as macrocosm"
(manuscript of St. Hildegard of Bingen, 12th century)

Christian

Christ Pantocrator
(Catalan Romanesque fresco)

The Virgin of the Sign
(Russian, 17th century)

Christian

Page from the Lindisfarne Gospel
(698 A.D.)

Romanesque Abbey of Marialaach, Germany

Christian

Resurrection Church-on-the-Debre
(Kostroma, Russia)

Tympanum above the Royal Door of Chartres Cathedral

Islamic

Page from Andalusian Koran
(Sura 26, "The Poets", verses 59-63)

'Attarîn Medersa
(Fez, Morocco)

Islamic

Door of Ince Minara Mosque
(Seljuk period, Konya, Turkey)

Taj Mahal
(Agra, India)

XV

Islamic

Hall of Prayer, the Great Mosque of Córdoba
(Spain, 9th century)

The Darasha Mirador, The Alhambra, Granada
(Spain, 14th century)

"Riding the Tiger"

In his book *Calvacare la Tigre*,[3] Julius Evola seeks to show how the "naturally traditional" man, the man who is aware of an inner reality transcending the plane of individual experiences, may not only survive in the anti-traditional ambience of the modern world, but may even use it for his own spiritual ends, according to the well-known Chinese metaphor of the man riding a tiger: if he does not let himself be unseated, he will end by gaining the upper hand of it.

The tiger, in the sense envisaged by Evola, is the dissolving and destructive force that comes into play towards the end of every cosmic cycle. In the face of this, the author says, it would be vain to maintain the forms and structure of a civilization that is already played out; the only thing to be done is to carry the negation beyond its dead point, so that, by a conscious transposition, it may end up, not in nothingness, but in a "new empty space, which may perhaps be the premiss of a new formative activity".

The world that is to be negated because it is doomed to destruction, is above all the "materialistic and bourgeois civilization" which in itself already represents the negation of an earlier and superior world. On this point, we are in agreement with the author, but we note immediately that he does not distinguish between the forms pertaining to this "bourgeois civilization" and the sacred heritage which survives within it and despite it. Likewise, he seems to include in the fate of this civilization everything that remains of the Oriental civilizations, and here too he makes no distinction between their social structures and their spiritual kernel. We shall return to this later.

Let us first refer to another aspect of this book, with which we can agree almost without reservation. This is the author's critique, often masterly, of the various currents of modern thought. Evola does not place himself on the ground of philosophical discussion, for the modern philosophy in question is no longer a "science of the true"—it does not even claim to be so. He considers it as a symptom, as the mental reflection of a vital and existential situation, essentially dominated by despair: since the dimension of transcendence has been denied, there can henceforth only be impasses; there is no longer any exit from the vicious circle of the mind left

3. Julius Evola, *Calvacare la Tigre* (Milan: Scheiwiller, 1961).

to its own devices; all that remains is a description of one's own defeat. As the starting-point of this analysis, the author chooses the "philosophy" of Nietzsche, in which he detects a presentiment of transcendent realities and, as it were, an attempt to go beyond the purely mental order, an attempt foredoomed to failure by the absence of a spiritual doctrine and discipline.

With the same acuity, the author analyzes the foundations of modern science. From this chapter, we will quote the following passage, which replies pertinently to the pseudo-spiritual illusions of some scientific circles:

> From this latter point of view, the most recent science offers no advantage over the materialistic science of yesterday. With the help of atoms and the mechanical conception of the universe, one could still imagine something (albeit in a very crude way); the entities of the latest physico-mathematical science, on the contrary, are absolutely unimaginable; they amount to nothing more than the holes in a network constructed and perfected, not in order to know in the concrete, intuitive, and living sense of the term—in other words, according to the only mode that has any value for a still undegenerate humanity—but solely in order to exert a control, ever greater but always outward, over nature which, in its essence, remains closed to man and more mysterious than ever. For its mysteries have in fact merely been "covered over"; our gaze has been diverted from them by the spectacular achievements of technology and industry onto a plane where it is no longer a question of knowing the world, but only of transforming it for the ends of a humanity that has become exclusively worldly. . . .
>
> Let us repeat that it is a hoax to speak of the spiritual value of recent science because in it one now speaks of energy instead of matter, because it peers inside the mass of coagulated irradiations, or because it envisages a space of more than three dimensions. These are notions which, when they have been substituted for those of earlier physics, can in no wise alter the experience which the man of today can have of the world. . . . When people say that there is no matter, only energy, that we do not live in a Euclidean space of three dimensions, but in a "curved" space of four or more dimensions, and so on, things remain as they were before; my real experience changes in nothing, the ultimate meaning of what I see—light, sun, fire, sea, sky, plants that flower and beings that die—the ultimate meaning of every process and phenomenon has in no way become more transparent for me. There is no justification for speaking of a knowledge that goes beyond appearances, or that knows in depth, in the spiritual and truly intellectual meaning of the term. . . .

No less pertinent are the author's remarks on the social structures and the arts of the contemporary world. We must nevertheless express a reservation regarding the thesis of the "enslavement of the negative force", as he applies it to certain aspects of modern life. Let us quote a typical passage:

> The positive possibilities (of the reign of the machine) can only concern a tiny minority, namely those beings in whom the dimension of transcendence pre-exists, or in whom it can be awakened. . . . They alone can give a completely different value to the "soulless world" of machines, technologies, modern cities, in short, of everything that is pure reality and objectivity, which appears cold, inhuman, menacing, devoid of intimacy, depersonalizing, "barbarous". It is precisely by accepting this reality and these processes that the differentiated man will be able to realize his essence and form himself according to a valid personal equation. . . .
>
> In this connection the machine itself and everything, in certain sectors of modern life, that has been formed in terms of pure functionality (especially architecture) can become symbol. As a symbol, the machine represents a form born of an exact and objective adequation of a means to an end, excluding everything that is superfluous, arbitrary, dispersive, and subjective; it is a form that realizes with precision an idea (that of the end to which it is destined). On its level, it thus in a certain way reflects the value which, in the classical world, pure geometric form (the number as essence) possessed, and also the Doric principle of nothing too much.

Here the author overlooks that the symbol is not a form that is "objectively" adequate to just any kind of end, but a form that is adequate to a spiritual end or to an intellectual essence; if there is a coincidence, in some traditional arts, between conformity to a practical end and conformity to a spiritual end, this is because the first does not contradict the second, something that cannot be said of the machine, which is inconceivable outside the context of a desacralized world. In fact, the form of the machine expresses exactly what it is, namely a sort of challenge offered to the cosmic and divine order; it may well be composed of "objective" geometric elements such as circles and squares, but in its relationship—or rather non-relationship—with the cosmic ambience, it translates, not a "Platonic idea", but a "mental coagulation", or indeed an agitation or a trick. There are certainly some border-line cases, like that of a machine that is still close to a tool, or like that of a modern ship whose shape espouses to a certain degree the movements of water and wind, but this is no more than a fragmentary conformity and does not contradict what we have just said. As for "functional" architecture, including modern urbanism, it can only be called "objective" if one accepts that its purpose is objective, which is obviously not the case: all architecture is co-ordinated to a certain conception of life and of man; now Evola himself condemns the social program underlying modern architecture. In reality, the apparent "objectivity" of modern architecture is merely a mysticism in reverse, a congealed sentimentality disguised as objectivity; moreover one has seen often enough just how quickly this attitude is converted, in its protagonists, into the most changeable and arbitrary of subjectivisms.

It is true that there is no form that is totally cut off from its eternal archetype; but this entirely general law cannot be invoked here, for the following reason: for a form to be a symbol, it is necessary that it be situated in a certain hierarchical order in relation to man. In order to be as precise as possible, let us distinguish three aspects of the symbolism inherent in things: the first is simply the very existence of the form concerned, and in this sense, each thing manifests its celestial origin; the second aspect is the meaning of a form, its intellectual interpretation, either within a given system or in itself, by virtue of its more or less essential or prototypical nature; the third aspect is the spiritual efficacy of the symbol, which presupposes, in the man who uses it, both a psychic and a ritual conformity to a given tradition.

We have emphasized this point, because Julius Evola fails to recognize the crucial importance of a traditional attachment, while admitting the possibility of a spontaneous and irregular spiritual development, guided by a sort of inborn instinct that could have been actualized by accepting the crisis of the contemporary world as a liberating catharsis. For Evola, this is almost the only perspective remaining open for the "differentiated man" of our time, for adherence to a religion, in Evola's view, amounts to integration in a more or less decadent collective milieu, and the possibility of a regular initiation is to be dismissed.

> We conclude that in our day, this possibility must be practically excluded, as a result of the almost complete non-existence of the respective organizations. If organizations of this kind have always had a more or less underground character in the West—because of the nature of the religion which succeeded in gaining dominance there and its repressive and persecuting activities—they have completely disappeared in latter times. As regards other parts of the globe, especially the Orient, these organizations have

become more and more rare and inaccessible, even if the forces of which they were the vehicles had not withdrawn from them, in parallel with the general process of degeneration and modernization, which has finished by invading even these regions. In our day, even the Orient is no longer capable of supplying anything but remnants or residues; one is already forced to admit this when one considers the spiritual level of those Asians who have begun to export Eastern wisdom and to divulge it amongst us.

The last argument is completely inconclusive: if the Asians in question were true representatives of Eastern traditions, would they divulge them? But, even if Evola were right in his judgement of the traditional organizations as human groups, his way of seeing things nonetheless involves a serious error, for as long as a tradition preserves its essential forms intact, it continues to be the guarantor of a spiritual influence—or of a divine grace—whose action, if not always apparent, immeasurably transcends anything that is in the power of man. We know full well that there exist methods or ways, such as Zen, which are founded on the "power of one's self" (*jíriki*), and which thereby distinguish themselves from other ways that are founded on the "power of the Other" (*táriki*), the latter making an appeal to Grace; but neither the ones nor the others are situated outside the formal framework of a given tradition. For example, Zen, which perhaps offers the most striking example of a non-formal spirituality, is completely, and even especially, aware of the value of sacred forms. One transcends forms, not by rejecting them in advance, but by integrating them in their supra-formal essences.

Moreover, Evola himself defines the mediating function of form when he speaks of the role of the spiritual "type", which he opposes to the individual or the "personality" in the profane and modern sense of the term:

> The type (*la tipicità*) represents the point of contact between the individual and the supra-individual, the demarcation line between the two corresponding to a perfect form. The type de-individualizes, in the sense that the person then essentially incarnates an idea, a law, a function. . . .

The author says rightly that the spiritual type is normally situated within the framework of a tradition, but apparently this does not lead him to believe in the "typical"—or supra-individual—nature of all sacred forms, doubtless because he does not take into account what the monotheistic religions call revelation. Now it is illogical to accept the "transcendent dimension" of the being—in other words the effective participation of the human intellect in the Universal Intellect—without also accepting revelation, that is to say the manifestation of this Intellect or Spirit in objective forms. There is a rigorous relationship between the supra-formal, free, and undetermined nature of the Spirit and its spontaneous—and thus "Heaven-inspired"—expression, in forms necessarily determined and immutable. In their origin, which is unlimited and inexhaustible, the sacred forms (although limited and "arrested") are the vehicles of spiritual influences, and thus of virtualities of the infinite, and in this regard it is completely improper to speak of a tradition of which only the form remains—the spirit having withdrawn from it like the soul from a dead body: the death of a tradition always starts with the corruption of its essential forms.

According to all the prophecies, the sacred deposit of the integral Tradition will remain until the end of the cycle; this means that there will always be somewhere an open door. For men capable of transcending outward shells, and animated by a sincere will, neither the decadence of the surrounding world, nor belonging to a given people or milieu, constitute absolute obstacles.

Quaerite et invenietis[4]

Let us return for a moment to the title of Evola's book: the adage that one must "ride the tiger", if one does not want to be torn to pieces by it, obviously contains a tantric meaning. The tiger is then the image of the passional force that one must tame. One may well wonder whether this metaphor really corresponds to the spiritual man's attitude regarding the destructive tendencies of the modern world: let us note first of all that not just anything is a "tiger"; behind the tendencies and forms that Julius Evola envisages, we shall find no natural and organic force, no *shakti* dispensing power and beauty; now, the spiritual man can use *rajas,* but he must reject *tamas;* finally, there are forms and attitudes that are incompatible with the intimate nature of the spiritual man and with the rhythms of every form of spirituality. In reality, it is not the particular, artificial, and hybrid characteristics of the modern world that can serve as spiritual supports, but that which, within this world, is of all time.

(from *Mirror of the Intellect*)

4. "Seek and ye shall find."

The Irruption of the Modern World
as it Affected Morocco

In Medieval Spain, Muslims, Christians, and Jews lived side by side in peace, apart from occasions when there might be political tensions between them. For the Moorish rulers this situation was a natural one, as toleration of Jews and Christians has its root in Islamic law; however the Christian kings, for whom this law did not operate, also frequently granted their Muslim and Jewish subjects the same right. This was in no wise the result of religious indifferentism, for in those days faith took precedence over all else. It seems that it was experience which led to this mutual respect, to the presentiment that behind the strange appearances of another religious form the same divine Truth was to be found, and a willingness to leave judgement on this matter to God. Moreover, in spite of the three dogmatic systems which distinguished the communities from one another, the spiritual world in which they lived was virtually the same: life and death, heaven and earth, knowledge and crafts, had for each of them the same meaning and value. It is significant that the spiritual exchange between the Islamic and Christian worlds broke off suddenly with the rationalism of the Renaissance, and that at the same time the intolerance of the absolute Spanish monarchy began: the Jews were forcibly converted or persecuted, and the Moors expelled.

From then on the Islamic West shut itself off from Christian Europe, and when, much later, in the 19th century, it was compelled to enter again into relations with European states, they no longer confronted it as Christian nations, but as something quite different and wholly foreign to the Muslim way of thinking.

What the Moroccans, who at that time made the acquaintance of Europe, thought of modern civilization can be gleaned from a conversation quoted by the author Edmondo de Amicis in his report on the journey of an Italian ambassador to Fez in 1879:

> Today I had a lively discussion with a merchant in Fez with a view to finding out what the Moors think of European civilization. . . . He was a fine man, about forty years old, with an honest and serious face, who had made business visits to the most important cities in Western Europe and had lived for a long time in Tangier, where he learnt Spanish. . . . I asked him therefore what kind of impression the large cities of Europe had made on him. . . .

He looked hard at me and answered coldly: "Large streets, fine shops, beautiful palaces, good workshops, everything clean." He gave the impression that with these words, he had mentioned everything in our countries that was worthy of praise. "Have you not found anything else in Europe that is beautiful and good?" I asked. He looked at me questioningly. "Is it possible," I went on, "that an intelligent man like you, who has visited several countries so marvelously superior to your own can speak about them without astonishment, or at least without the emotion of a country boy who has seen the pasha's palace? What can you possibly admire in the world? What sort of people are you? Who can possibly understand you?" "*Perdone Usted*", he answered coldly, "it is for me to say that I cannot understand you. I have told you all the things which I consider to be better in Europe. What more can I say? Have I to say something that I do not believe to be true? I repeat that your streets are larger than ours, your shops finer, that you have workshops such as we do not have, and also rich palaces. That is all. I can only add one more thing: that you know more than we do, because you have many books, and read more." I became impatient. "Do not lose patience, *Caballero*," he said, "let us speak together calmly. Is not a man's first duty honesty? Is it not honesty more than anything else that makes a man worthy of respect, and one country superior to another? Very well, then. As far as honesty is concerned, your countries are certainly not better than ours. That much I can say right away." "Gently, gently!" I said, "Tell me first what you mean by honesty!" "Honesty in business, *Caballero*. The Moors, for example, sometimes cheat the Europeans in trade, but you Europeans cheat the Moors much more often." "There must be a few cases," I replied, in order to say something. "*Casos raros?*" he exclaimed angrily. "It happens every day! Proof: I go to Marseilles. I buy cotton. I choose a particular thread, give the exact reference number and brand-name, as well as the amount required. I ask for it to be sent, I pay, and I return home. Back in Morocco, I receive the cotton. I open the consignment, and take a look. I find the same number, the same brand-name, and a thread that is of one third the thickness! This is anything but good, and I lose thousands of francs! I rush to the consulate, but in vain. Another case: A merchant from Fez places an order in Europe for blue cloth, so many pieces, of such and such a length and breadth. He pays for it when the bargain is made. In due course he receives the cloth, opens the package, and checks the measurements. The first pieces are all right, those underneath are shorter, and those lowest down are half a meter too short! The cloth cannot be used for cloaks, and the merchant is ruined. . . . And so on and so on!" He raised his eyes upwards, and turned to me and said: "So you are more honest than we are?" I repeated that it could only be a matter of individual cases. He said nothing, and then suddenly exclaimed: "Are you more pious than we are? No! One needs only to have visited your 'mosques' once. . . . "Tell me," he continued, since I remained silent, "are there in your country fewer murders?" I could not bring myself to answer. How could I have admitted that in Italy alone there are three thousand murders a year, and that there are nineteen thousand people in prison, convicted and not yet convicted. "I do not think there are," he said, reading the answer in my eyes.

As I could feel no confidence in this area, I turned to him with the customary objection about polygamy. He jumped up as if stung. "So it's that again", he exclaimed, blushing to the roots of his hair. "As if you Europeans only had one woman! Don't try to make us believe that! One is indeed your own, but then there are those *de los otros* and those *de todos* y *nadie*. Paris! London! The coffee-houses, the streets, the theaters are full of them. *Vergüenza!* And you criticize the Moors!" As he spoke, he fingered his rosary with a trembling hand, and sometimes turned to me with a smile, as if to say that his indignation was not directed at me personally but at Europe. Since my question had obviously embarrassed him, I changed the subject, and referred to the comforts of European civilization. . . . "That is true," he replied. "A bit of sun? A sunshade! Rain? An umbrella! Dust? A pair of gloves! Walking? A walking-stick! Looking around? Eye glasses. An excursion? A coach! Sitting down? A chair! Eating? Knives and forks! A scratch? A doctor! Death? A statue! You want for nothing! Are you really men? *Por Dios*, you are infants!" He even made fun of our architecture, when I spoke to him about the comfort of our houses. "What? Three hundred of you live in a single building, all on top of one another! You have to climb, climb, climb. . . . There is no air, no light, and no garden!"

I now spoke to him about our laws, our governments, and similar things, and since he was an intelligent man, I thought I would at last manage to give him a glimpse of the immense difference between my country and his. Since in this sector he could not hold his own, he changed the subject of the conversation, and suddenly said with a smile, looking me up and down from head to foot! "*Mal vestidos* (badly dressed)." I replied that dress was of no importance, but added that in this domain too he would surely acknowledge our superiority, for instead of idly sitting cross-legged for hours, we employed our time in thousands of useful or entertaining pursuits. To this he gave a more subtle answer than I had expected: it did not seem a good sign to him, he said, that we felt the need to do so many things in order to pass the time. Life itself must be torture for us, if we were totally unable to sit still for a single hour, without being killed by boredom and having to seek relief in some distraction or conversation. Were we afraid of ourselves? What was it that tormented us?

I now spoke of the European industries, the railways, the telegraph, and all the great public works. He let me speak without interruption, and even nodded his head from time to time. But when I finished, he sighed and said: "All very well, but what use are these things when we all must die?" "In brief," I said, "you would not exchange your situation for ours?" He thought a little and then replied: "No, for you do not live longer than we do, you are not healthier, nor better, nor more pious, nor happier. Leave us then in peace. Do not wish that everyone should live as you do and be happy according to your lights. Let us both live in the milieu in which God has placed us. It is not for nothing that God has put a sea between North Africa and Europe. Let us respect His ordinance!" "So you believe," I said, "that you will always remain as you are, that we shall not gradually succeed in compelling you to change?" "I do not know," he replied: "you have the power; you will do what you will. But everything that has to happen is already written by God. And whatever it is that must happen, God will not forsake those who remain faithful to Him." With these words, he took my right hand, pressed it to his heart, and walked away majestically. . . .

(Edmondo de Amicis, *Marocco*)

The European intervention in Morocco took place more or less suddenly. At the beginning, it had for the Moroccans a purely military character, which they could understand, and which was not completely devoid of heroic aspects. Completely other, however, was the administrative subjugation of Morocco. Lyautey, who was appointed as French Resident-General in Morocco, wrote in 1912 about the meaning of the state treaty, by means of which France's protectorate over Morocco was recognized: "A country under protectorate status retains its own institutions. It rules itself through its own organs, and is simply supervised by the European power, which takes its place in external relations, in its political dealings with other states." For Morocco, this meant that its theocratic form of government and the traditional structure of its society should remain the same, at least internally. But, in the same report, Lyautey continues: "The protecting power takes over in general responsibility for the army and the finances of the country under protection, and guides it as regards its economic development." And this opened the door to interference in every domain of native life. General Lyautey's own intention was that, as far as possible, Morocco should be governed through its own élite. He repeatedly declared: "The relationship in question (the protectorate) means supervision, and not direct administration." Unfortunately his aristocratic conception of what a protectorate implied was vastly different both from that of the French officials, who as citizens of a secular state looked on the traditional institutions of Morocco with mistrust and distaste, and from that of the European settlers who wished to acquire land. This is why Lyautey declared at Lyons in 1916:

> Morocco is not like Algeria. There we found only loose sand and no organic structure. The only power was that of the Turkish Dey, and this crumbled when we arrived. In Morocco, on the other hand, we are faced with a historic and independent empire, jealous in the extreme of its independence, and resistant to any form of servitude. Until a year or two ago it was a properly constituted state, with a hierarchy of officials, with diplomatic representation abroad, and with its own social institutions, most of which still exist, in spite of the recent collapse of central authority. Do not forget that there are still, in Morocco, a goodly number of personages who until six years ago were the ambassadors of their country at St. Petersburg, London, Berlin, Madrid, and Paris, accompanied by secretaries and attachés, all men of general culture who were perfectly capable of dealing on an equal footing with European statesmen. . . .
>
> Alongside this political establishment there also exists a religious establishment, which is anything but negligible. The Sultan's present Minister of Justice was a distinguished professor successively at the Universities of al-Azhar (Cairo), Istanbul, Bursa, and Damascus, and is in correspondence with *'ulamâ* (Islamic jurists) as far afield as India, and he is by no means the only one who maintains relations with the Islamic élite in the East.
>
> Finally, there is a first class economic team, composed of the leading merchants, who have branches in Manchester and Marseilles, and who in most instances have been to these branches in person.
>
> We are therefore confronted with three élites: political, religious, and economic. It would be madness to ignore them and to fail to seek their aid; for if we make them our allies, they can powerfully help us in the task we have to accomplish. Let us remember—and those of you who have been to Morocco know it full well—that the people there are industrious, conscientious, and open to progress and the more we respect what is sacred to them, the more we shall receive in return. This country, then, offers us the most favorable circumstances for accomplishing a great work, in cooperation with the native inhabitants, on condition that we completely abandon all the prejudices and maladroitness that have so gravely harmed us elsewhere, and that we shun like the plague the contemptible state of mind that is summed up in the phrase *sale bicot,* applied indiscriminately to all natives, an expression not

only shocking but dangerous, and in its contempt and its menace, only too well understood by those to whom it is addressed, giving rise in them to a bitterness which nothing will efface, as I have so often, alas, had occasion to observe.

No other country is better suited to this concept of protectorate, a concept which is definitive and not transitory. . . . Annexation or "colonization" would immediately and automatically involve the imposition of French law. Overnight the French administration with its inflexible structure, its power to drag its feet, and its heaviness, would come crashing down on the unfortunate country. . . . Nothing, I assure you, less resembles the suburbs of Guingamp or Trévoux than Fez or Marrakesh.

(Maréchal Lyautey, *Paroles d'Action*)

Lyautey's conception of the role of the French in Morocco presupposed a certain understanding of traditional Islamic culture which very few officials had, apart from himself, and for which the ordinary education of the Europeans who came to Morocco was scarcely a preparation. Lyautey recalls an experience of his own:

At the Fez Fair in 1916, which coincided with the Prophet's birthday, and at which the Sultan himself was present, a highly placed French official, not familiar with Morocco, said to me: "Well, I think I have understood your policy. I can see how useful it is to conserve intact this form of government, all these archaic and out-of-date things, as long as we are at war. That is very wise. But it is obvious, is it not, to you as well as to me, that as soon as peace comes, all that must be swept away, to make room for good direct administration, on the model of the Metropolis, and more and more resembling a French *département*." My reply was perhaps a trifle summary, and I shall repeat it here even more briefly: "The Sultan, his officials, and all the traditional institutions of Morocco are no mere façade. . . . None of these things must be 'swept away', because it cannot be done and may not be done. . . . If the bi-lateral pact binds us to the Sultan, it also binds us to the people. . . . In my whole soul, and on the basis of my experience, I am convinced that in this country one serves France best by winning the heart of the people for it. . . . That is the quintessence of this policy of 'protectorate'. . . . Out of love for my own country, I express the wish that my successors shall also remain true to this policy. . . ."

That he was disappointed in this hope can clearly be seen from his admonitory proclamation of 1920:

In Morocco we are in no way faced with a primitive, barbaric, or passive population. . . . Nothing could be more dangerous than that the European settlers in this country should commit imprudences, for which one will later have to pay dearly; nothing is more dangerous than causing the germs of discontent and disquiet, already present in this people, to grow. . . . The Moroccans are desirous of knowledge and very adaptable. There is a youth amongst them that is keen to live and to achieve, and that has a taste for knowledge and trade. In the absence of opportunity and scope, which our administration offers them only so grudgingly and at the lowest level, they will seek other outlets; they will attach themselves to whatever European societies they come in contact with . . . or they will turn to foreign Islamic societies, and in the end they will unite together in order to achieve their demands for themselves. . . . I am fully aware where the practical problems lie.

   Above all, all of us, whether we be officials from France or officers from Algeria, have "direct rule" in our blood. And in everything relating to the administration, all of us, to a greater or lesser degree, have the tendency to look on the "natives" as inferior and as a negligible factor.

(Maréchal Lyautey, *Paroles d'Action*)

In 1921, the revolt led by 'Abd al-Krim broke out in the Rif Mountains in the Spanish Moroccan protectorate. It spread to the French protectorate and was suppressed only after a war of several years waged by France and Spain together. In 1924 or 1925, there was even, for a while, the danger that the warring Rif Kabyles might succeed in establishing contact with the unsubdued Berber tribes in the south, and so bring about an encirclement of central Morocco, including Fez. When the French army in Morocco finally "pacified" the Kabyles in the North and the insubordinate tribes in the Atlas, the protectorate authorities, in 1930, issued an official decree, according to which the Berbers were no longer subject to the canonical and basically Koranic jurisdiction, but were to receive their own system of justice based on tribal custom. The French government, who had planned the move, were of the opinion that the majority of the Berbers had embraced Islam only superficially and as a result of Arab pressure. By freeing them from canon law, and thereby also from the need to learn Arabic, it was hoped that they could be detached from the oriental and traditional culture of Islam and won over to the European civilization of France. But the "Berber Decree" (*dahir berbère*), of 1930 provoked an indignant resistance from both Arabs and Berbers. The Berbers clearly saw in it an attempt to separate them from the community of Islam, and the Arab or Arabized population saw the decree as a betrayal of the Protectorate Agreement of 1912, according to which the French had the right to subdue the warring Berbers, not on their own behalf, but in the name of the Sultan, and for his jurisdiction.

The indignation of the Berber population led to the creation of a committee which, in 1934, demanded the honest implementation of the Protectorate Agreement with France. When the French government refused to meet this demand in any way, a political resistance movement was set up, the goal of which was complete independence for Morocco. It was formed largely by the youth of the cities, who were already more or less influenced by modern political ideology. Whether this ideology came via Turkey and Egypt, or arose because of French education, it was in any case of European origin, so that in the last analysis it was Europe itself that undermined its own domination in North Africa. The older generation were in general mistrustful with regard to this movement. They knew only too well that political independence for Morocco could not come about without its transformation into a modern state, equipped with technical means; and this meant the loss of all traditional forms of life.

*

* *

The acquisition of political independence, however, did not halt the spiritual decline in Morocco, but on the contrary speeded it up. A state cannot be independent today without possessing the technical means which were invented in Europe. The adoption of these means involves an alteration in all the forms of the civilization in question; and if traditional forms are altered, they no longer retain the spiritual content which they previously possessed. In a genuine culture, which has its origin in a revealed religion, there is virtually no outward form, the loss of which would be without significance; all traditional forms, from law and morality to the art of the craftsman, are of such a nature that they can lead, from outward to inward, to the eternal meaning of life. The one who knows this meaning most profoundly—the saint or the sage—can dispense with outward forms; the collectivity cannot. Only the individual has it in him fully to realize a spiritual prototype, because inwardly he is free; on the other hand, a collectivity—like every multiplicity—can never escape certain constraints; the best that can happen is a more or less long-lasting balance of forces, within which the individual can follow his own goal: the salvation of his soul. To strive after a perfect happiness for all on the earthly plane, as if it were possible to establish peace and well-being permanently, can only lead to the gravest deception, and consequently to damage to the soul, for the individual as for the collectivity.

The breakdown of the traditional forms of civilization in present-day Morocco is much more devastating than it ever was in Europe, because it has occurred so suddenly, and because the new has no relation whatsoever to the old, coming on the contrary from a foreign world.

The destruction, for instance, of the most outward forms sometimes has the most far-reaching results. A cultured Moroccan said to me: "According to a French proverb, it is not the cloth that makes the monk, but one could just as rightly say that it *is* the cloth that makes the monk!" Indeed in most cases the disappearance of native Moroccan dress is the sign of a changed mental outlook. The pretext that European dress is more practical is only half true, and the wide Moroccan robes which freely envelop the limbs were much more suited to the North African climate with its considerable variability between hot and cold. At the same time, in their ascetical simplicity and virile patriarchal dignity, they express a certain spiritual bearing. The turban especially is like a sign of spiritual dignity, an expression, so to say, of the priestly role which was man's in the beginning; the Islamic tradition has ascribed this significance to it from remote times. It is the first thing to disappear, and is hotly opposed by modernists as the sign of backwardness.

European dress is fundamentally out of keeping with the postures and gestures of Islamic worship; it hinders bows and prostrations, renders the prescribed ablutions more difficult, and takes away the dignity of the effortless sitting together on the flat ground; whoever wears European clothes is either a "gentleman" or a mere worker or "proletarian". Whereas previously men were differentiated only by their culture, the community is all of a sudden split into economically determined classes and, with the cheap products of the factory, a poverty without beauty invades the homes; ugly, senseless, and comfortless poverty is the most widespread of all modern achievements.

Ibn Khaldûn says that the vanquished always tend to adopt the customs and practices of the victors, and so the triumphal march of Europe—not of France alone, or of any other European country as such, still less Western Christian culture, but of impersonal, technically omnipotent Europe—continues without a halt.

Islamic Moorish art, with the craftsmanship which is basic to it, recedes before the machine; the town community is destroyed by the political press, and the cohesion of the nomadic tribes, as well as all genuine thinking, is menaced by the radio. This irruption of the modern world does not resemble any historical change of earlier times; its incision cuts through everything. Only the vigilant consciousness of an inexpressible spiritual heritage can oppose it; and such a consciousness is, in the nature of things, rare.

I recently walked through the modern part of Fez with an elderly Moroccan friend, and wondered aloud about the warehouses which had been built there, and about the numerous machines which were on show. "It is all inevitable," said my friend, "what must be, must be. And yet we had no need of any of it. For thirteen centuries we lived without all that, and we did not live badly. True, there were famines and wars, and sometimes also plagues; but we never had the worst of all plagues: unemployment." "And yet the young people admire all the novelties," I said, "and your young people who have been to Europe and studied there immediately renounce all that has been handed down to them." "That is because," he replied, "in your schools and universities the spiritual sciences have been displaced in favor of worldly 'sciences'." "And what happens when the 'golden chain' (of tradition) is broken?" I asked. "It will never be completely broken," he said simply, "but will continue in secret. There are times when the Spirit reveals itself, and times when it is veiled. But whatever happens, it will not happen without the will of God!"

(from *Fez, City of Islam*)

5

Alchemy

Insight into Alchemy

"To make of the body a spirit and of the spirit a body": this adage sums up the whole of alchemy. Gold itself, which outwardly represents the fruit of the work, appears as an opaque body that has become luminous, or as a light that has become solid. Transposed to the human and spiritual order, gold is bodily consciousness transmuted into spirit, or spirit fixated in the body.

For the base metal which represents the immediate material of the work is none other than consciousness bound to the body and as if submerged in it. This is the "metallic body" from which must be extracted the "soul" and the "spirit", which are respectively Mercury and Sulphur. If the "body" were not an inward reality, it could not serve as the material for the spiritual work.

In the ordinary man, "to know" and "to be" are, as it were, polarized into thought and bodily consciousness; the first represents an intelligence separated from the being of its objects, whereas the second is a passive state of being that is as if bereft of intelligence. This dichotomy is noticeable even in the dream state, in which the psychic form of the body is more or less detached from its sensory form. The return to the center, to the heart considered as "seat" of the spirit, is both an integration and, as it were, an inversion, of the two poles: bodily consciousness in its fashion becomes intelligent: it is transmuted into a passive state of knowledge. At the same time, thought—or the mental element—becomes crystallized under the lightning-like action of the spirit.

This transmutation of spirit into body and of body into spirit is to be found in a more or less direct and obvious manner in every method of spiritual realization; alchemy, however, has made of it its principal theme, in conformity with the metallurgical symbolism based on the possibility of changing a body's "state of aggregation".

At the beginning of the work, bodily consciousness is chaotic and obscure. It is then compared to lead, and the "régime" corresponding to this state of "matter" is attributed to Saturn. This planet represents the principle of condensation, and this is what explains its seemingly contradictory assignation to the metal lead (among corporeal substances), and to reason (among the faculties of the soul): in relation to the existential dimension of the other faculties, reason is like a point without extension. The polarity of thought and bodily consciousness—the opposition "spirit"-"body"—is thus to be found in the nature of Saturn, and this corroborates the hostile, impeding, and even sinister character which this planet assumes in divinatory astrology.

On the plane of method, Saturnine condensation becomes concentration; the intelligence withdraws from the outward to the inward; having become a single point, it descends into the inward night of the body.

According to alchemical doctrine, every metal is constituted by the more or less perfect union of the two principles known as Sulphur (*Spiritus*) and Mercury (*anima*). Likewise, bodily consciousness, assimilated to the metal to be transformed, is woven from these two principles or subtle forces, which are both opposite and complementary: Sulphur, which is male, and Mercury, which is female, are combined in the chaotic bodily consciousness—or in the base metal—in such a way that they neutralize or impede one another.

Basilius Valentinus[1] writes: "Wherever metallic soul, spirit, and form are to be found, there too are metallic quicksilver, sulphur, and salt. . . ."[2] He thus likens Mercury to the soul and Sulphur to the spirit, and it is thus that the two principles should be understood, always bearing in mind that alchemy considers them primarily as powers or forces co-operating on the same plane, namely that of "nature". If it happens that the same author, or other alchemists, should sometimes call Mercury "spirit", this is because its "volatile" nature is here being opposed to that of inert and solid bodies, and in this sense both Sulphur and Mercury are "spirits". Furthermore, Mercury, as "substance" of the inner or psychic form of the body, corresponds to the vital spirit, which is intermediary between soul and body.

(from *Mirror of the Intellect*)

---

1. A German alchemist of the 15th century.
2. See *De la grande pierre des Anciens Sages,* published together with *Les douze Clefs de la Philosophie,* translated by Eugene Canseliet (Paris, 1956).

The Witness of an African Goldsmith

The following report, from the autobiography of a Senegalese,[3] shows how, in certain African tribes, the working of gold has continued to be regarded as a sacred art right up to the present day.

... On a sign from my father, the two apprentices started working the sheepskin bellows, which were situated on either side of the forge and connected to it by means of clay pipes. ... The flames in the forge shot up and seemed to come to life—an animated and evil genius.

My father then grasped the smelting-pot with his long tongs and placed it on the flames.

All of a sudden all other work in the smithy was stilled, for during the time that gold is being smelted, and while it cools, it is forbidden to work either copper or aluminum in its proximity, in case even a particle of these base metals should enter the smelting-pot. Only steel may continue to be worked. But even those engaged on a task with steel would usually finish it quickly or lay it aside, in order to join the apprentices gathered round the forge. ...

When my father felt that his movements were being impeded by the apprentices crowding round, he would silently motion them to stand back. Neither he nor anyone else would utter a word. No one dared speak, and even the minstrel was silent. The stillness was broken only by the wheezing of the bellows and the low hissing of the gold. But though my father said not a word, I knew that he spoke inwardly; I could see that from his lips which moved silently as he stirred the gold and the charcoal with a stick—which, as it caught fire, he had to keep replacing.

What could he be saying inwardly? I cannot say for sure, as he never told me. Yet what could it be but an invocation? Did he not invoke the spirit of the fire and of the gold, of the fire, and of the wind—the wind which blew through the bellows—of the fire that was born of the wind, and of the gold that was wedded to the fire? Assuredly he summoned their help and entreated their friendship and communion; assuredly he invoked these spirits which are amongst the most important, and whose aid indeed is necessary for smelting.

The process which took place before my eyes was only outwardly the smelting of gold. It was something more besides: a magical process which the spirits could favor or hinder. That is why stillness reigned around my father.

3. Camara Laye, *L'Enfant noir* (Paris, 1953).

Was it not remarkable that at such a moment the little black snake always lay hidden under the sheepskin? For it was not always there. It did not come and visit my father every day, yet it never failed to appear when gold was being worked. This did not really surprise me. Ever since, one evening, my father told me of the spirit of our tribe, I had found it quite natural that the snake should be there, for the snake knew the future. . . .

The artisan who works the gold must first of all purify himself, must wash himself from head to foot, and, during the time of the work, must abstain from sexual intercourse. . . .

(from *Alchemy: Science of the Cosmos, Science of the Soul*)

"Nature Can Overcome Nature"

In the world of forms, Nature's "mode of operation" consists of a continuous rhythm of "dissolutions" and "coagulations", or of disintegrations and formations, so that the dissolution of any formal entity is but the preparation for a new conjunction between a *forma* and its *materia*. Nature acts like Penelope who, to rid herself of unworthy suitors, unwound at night the wedding garment which she had woven during the day.

In this way too the alchemist works. Following the adage *solve et coagula,* he dissolves the imperfect coagulations of the soul, reduces the latter to its *materia,* and crystallizes it anew in a nobler form. But he can accomplish this work only in unison with Nature, by means of a natural vibration of the soul which awakes during the course of the work and links the human and cosmic domains. Then of her own accord, Nature comes to the aid of art, according to the alchemical adage: "The progress of the work pleases nature greatly" (*operis processio multum naturae placet*).

The two phases of Nature—dissolution and coagulation—which seem opposed from a superficial point of view but which in reality are mutually complementary, can in a certain sense be related to the two poles, essence and substance, though these of course are not present within Nature as a pure opposition of Activity and Passivity, but merely as relative reflections of the latter. Within Nature it is alchemical Sulphur which corresponds to the active pole, and alchemical Quicksilver which corresponds to the passive pole. Sulphur is relatively active; it is Sulphur which confers form. Quicksilver resembles passive *materia* and is thus more immediately linked with Nature herself and her feminine character. Since Sulphur represents the essential pole in its natural refraction, it can be said to be active in passive mode, while Quicksilver, in view of the dynamic character of Nature, can be said to be passive in active mode. The relation of the two primordial forces to each other is thus similar to that of man and woman in sexual union. (See diagram on p. 110.)

The best symbol for the couple Sulphur-Mercury is the Chinese device of *yin-yang,* with the black pole in the white vortex and the white pole in the black vortex, as an indication that the passive is present in the active, and the active in the passive, just as man contains the nature of woman, and woman the nature of man.[4]

4. This has not merely a psychological, but also and above all an ontological, basis.

In the soul Sulphur represents the essence or spirit, whereas Quicksilver corresponds to the soul itself in its receptive and passive role.

According to Muhyi 'd-Dîn ibn 'Arabî, who always has the highest interpretations in mind, Sulphur corresponds to the "Divine Command", that is to say, to the *fiat lux* by means of which the world became a cosmos out of chaos, while Quicksilver represents Universal Nature, the passive counterpart of the former.[5] Thus, even although within the specific realm of alchemy the two poles appear as more or less conditioned forces, it is highly useful to remember their unconditioned prototypes, as only by so doing can one understand, for example, in what respect Sulphur corresponds to the spiritual will, and Quicksilver to the "plastic" capacity of the soul. In an immediate sense, and in its general psychological interpretation, the spiritual will proceeds from an ideal and endeavors to form the soul in accordance with this. In its original essence, however, which reveals itself only within the framework of a traditional spiritual art, the spiritual will is a vibration coming from the center of the being, a spiritual act which breaks through thought and which on the plane of the soul effects two things: a broadening and a deepening of the "sense of being", and a clarification and a stabilization of the essential contents of consciousness. In accordance with this, the "plastic" capacity of the soul, which responds to the original Act of the Spirit, is not merely the passive imagination that takes on and develops forms, but a capacity which gradually extends beyond the confines of the individual consciousness bound to the body.

*
* *

5. Muhyi 'd-Dîn ibn 'Arabî, *Futuhât al-Makkîya.*

Sulphur, the original masculine power, and Quicksilver, the original feminine power, both strive towards the wholeness of their one and eternal prototype. The latter is at the same time the reason for their opposition and of their mutual attraction—just as the masculine and feminine natures long for the integrality of the human state, and as a result of this seek both to separate from one another, and to unite with one another. By means of their physical union both try to re-establish the image of their common eternal prototype. This is the marriage of man and woman, sulphur and quicksilver, Spirit and soul.

In the mineral domain, it is gold that is born of the perfect union of the two generative principles. Gold is the true product of metallic generation. Every other metal is either a premature birth or an abortion, an imperfect gold, and, in this way of looking at things, the alchemical work is nothing other than a midwife or helper, which art offers nature, so that the latter can perfectly ripen the fruit whose maturation was being hindered by certain temporal circumstances.[6] This can be understood both in the mineral and in the microcosmic sense. Muhyi 'd-Dîn ibn 'Arabî regards gold as the symbol of the original and uncorrupted state (*fitra*) of the soul, the form in which the human soul was created at the beginning. According to the Islamic conception, the soul of every child unconsciously approaches this Adamic state, before being led away from it again by the errors imposed on it by adults.[7] The uncorrupted state possesses an inward equilibrium of forces. This is expressed by the stability of gold.

According to a widely held cosmological view—already mentioned by Aristotle—Nature is characterized by four properties, which are manifested on the sensory level by heat, cold, humidity, and dryness. Heat and dryness are associated with Quicksilver. The first two properties thus have a masculine and predominantly active character, whereas the last two have a feminine and more passive character. What this means can be seen more clearly when one relates heat to expansion, cold to contraction, humidity to dissolution, and dryness to coagulation.

---

6. The most recent discoveries in the realm of nuclear fission seem to confirm that the qualitatively lowest metals are the most unstable. Uranium closely resembles lead.

7. This doctrine is not to be confused with the opinion of J.-J. Rousseau that man is good in himself. The unconscious recapitulation of the primordial state in the child does not exclude negative tendencies or hereditary defects.

The heat, or power of expansion, proper to Sulphur, causes the growth of a given form from its essential center, and this force of Nature is closely connected with life. The dryness of Sulphur coagulates or "fixes" a *forma* on the level of its *materia*, so that it imitates the immutability of its prototype in a passive and material way. In other words, Sulphur's power of expansion is the dynamic—and therefore relatively passive—aspect of the essential Act, and coagulation is the inverse or lower aspect of the immutability of Essence. Pure Act is motionless and True Essence is active. The coldness, or power of contraction, of Quicksilver opposes the coagulating power of Sulphur, in that it surrounds forms from the outside, as it were, and holds them fast, like a cosmic womb.[8] The moist and dissolving character of Quicksilver, however, resembles feminine receptivity, which, like water, can take on all forms, without thereby being altered.

The four natural properties or "modes of operation", which are related in pairs to Sulphur and Quicksilver, can, in their successive coagulations and dissolutions, enter into a variety of combinations with one another. Generation only takes place when the properties of Sulphur and Quicksilver mutually penetrate each other. When sulphurous dryness joins one-sidedly with mercurial coldness, so that coagulation and contraction come together (without the action thereon of the expansive heat of Sulphur or the dissolving humidity of Quicksilver), a complete *rigor* of soul and body ensues. In terms of life, this is the torpor of old age, and on the ethical level, avarice. More generally and more profoundly, it is the wrapping up of the ego-consciousness in itself, a mortal condition of the soul which has lost its original receptivity and vitality, both spiritually and sensually. The other way round, a one-sided conjunction of heat and humidity (i.e., expansion and dissolution) results in a volatilization of powers. It resembles the condition of consuming passion, vice, and dissipation of spirit. Characteristically, the two types of disequilibrium are usually to be found together. One begets the other. The numbing of the powers of the soul leads to dissipation, and the fire of a passion lived out regardlessly brings inward death. The soul which is avaricious with itself and closes itself to the Spirit, is carried away in the vortex of dissolving impressions. Creative equilibrium is only

---

8. On the contracting power of Quicksilver, see René Guénon, *The Great Triad* (Cambridge, UK: Quinta Essentia, 1991), chapter 12, "Sulphur, Mercury, Salt".

produced when the expansive power of Sulphur and the contractive power of Quicksilver hold the balance, and when, at the same time, the masculine coagulating power enters into a fruitful union with the feminine dissolving capacity. This is the true marriage of the two poles of being, which are represented *inter alia* by the intersecting triangles of the Seal of Solomon—the sign which also symbolizes the synthesis of the four elements. The applications of this law are quite unlimited; only a few psychological and "vital" consequences have been mentioned here. It might also be added that traditional medicine is founded on the same principles, the four elements then corresponding to the four humors.[9]

The soul, in her entire breadth, as unfolded in the course of the alchemical work, is governed by the two fundamental forces Sulphur and Quicksilver which slumber, in the "chaotic" state of the unawakened soul, like the fire in flint and the water in ice. When they awake, they first of all manifest their opposition in a certain outward tension. From this tension they continue to grow, the one on the other, and, to the extent that they become free, they embrace one another, in that they are related to one another as man and woman. To these two phases of their development are related the first two clauses of the Hermetic formula: "Nature takes delight in Nature; Nature contains Nature, and Nature can overcome Nature". The last clause means that the two powers, when they have so grown that one can embrace the other, reunite on a higher plane, so that their opposition, which previously had bound the soul, now becomes a fruitful complementarism, by means of which the soul achieves dominion over the entire world of psychic forms and currents. Thus, Nature as a liberating force overcomes Nature as tyranny and entanglement.

When the immutable Divine Act which governs the cosmos, is symbolically represented by a motionless vertical axis, the "course" of Nature, in relation to it, is like a spiral, which winds itself around this axis, so that with each encirclement it realizes a new plane or degree of existence. This is the primordial symbol of the serpent or dragon,

---

9. To air corresponds the red constituent of blood, to fire yellow bile, to water phlegm, and to earth black bile. All four humors are contained in the blood. See diagram on p. 122.

which winds itself round the axis of the tree of the world.[10] Almost all the symbols of Nature proceed from the spiral or the circle. The rhythm of the successive "unrollings" and "rollings" of Nature, of the alchemical *solve et coagula* is represented by the double spiral:

whose form also lies at the basis of the zoomorphic representations of the *Shakti*. Also related to this is the representation of two serpents or dragons winding themselves in contrary directions round a staff or tree. These correspond to the two complementary phases of nature or the two fundamental forces.[11] This is the ancient heritage of images of nature on which both alchemy and certain traditions of the East (especially tantrism) draw.

It should also be noted here that the use of a serpent or dragon as the image of a cosmic power is to be found in all parts of the world. It is especially characteristic of those traditional arts, such as alchemy, which are concerned with the subtle world. A reptile moves without legs and by means of an uninterrupted rhythm of its body, so that it is the incorporation, so to say, of a subtle oscillation. Furthermore, its essence is both fiery and cold, conscious and elemental. The resemblance in question is so real that most, if not all, traditional cultures have regarded serpents as the occasional carriers of subtle or psychic powers. One need only think of the serpent as the guardian of tombs in Western and Far-Eastern antiquity.

In *laya-yoga*, a spiritual method belonging to the realm of tantrism, whose name signifies union (*yoga*) achieved through solution (*laya*), the awakening of the *Shakti* within the human microcosm is compared with the awakening of a serpent (*kundalinî*), which until then had remained coiled up in the subtle center known as *mûlâdhâra*. According to a certain correspondence between the subtle and corporeal orders, this center is located at the lower end of the vertebral column. *Kundalinî* is awakened by certain exercises in spiritual concentration, by means of which it gradually ascends, in spiral fashion, the spiritual axis of man, bringing into play ever wider and higher states of consciousness, until it finally restores the plenitude of consciousness in the supra-formal Spirit.[12] In this representa-

10. See René Guénon, *The Symbolism of the Cross* (Ghent, NY: Sophia Perennis at Universalis, 1995).
11. See René Guénon, op. cit.
12. See Arthur Avalon, *The Serpent Power* (Madras, 1931).

tion, which must not be conceived literally, but as a symbolical—though logical and consequential—description of inward processes, one will again recognize the image of Nature or *Shakti* twining round the world-axis. That the developing power should come "from below" is in keeping with the fact that potency (*potentia*)—like *materia prima*—in its passivity represents the "base" of the cosmos, and not the summit.

In the Hermetic tradition, Universal Nature in her latent condition is likewise represented as a coiled up reptile. This is the dragon Uroboros which, curling into a circle, bites its own tail.

Nature in her dynamic phase, on the other hand, is portrayed by means of the two serpents or dragons, which, in the form of the well-known model of the staff of Hermes or caduceus, wind them-

The seven *chakras* or power-centers in the subtle body of man, with the two power-streams *Ida* and *Pingala*, which wind round the central axis. Tantric representation from *The Serpent Power* by Arthur Avalon. The leaf design on the head represents the highest *chakra*: "the lotus with the thousand petals".

selves round an axis—that of the world or of man—in opposing directions. This duplication of the primordial serpent has also its counterpart in *laya-yoga,* for *Kundalinî* is likewise divided into two subtle forces, *Ida* and *Pingala,* which in opposite directions wind themselves round *Merudanda,* the microcosmic prolongation of the world-axis. At the beginning of the spiritual work, the *Shakti* is present in this divided form, and only after the two forces are activated alternately by means of a form of concentration based on breathing, does *Kundalinî* awake from its sleep and start to ascend. As soon as it has reached the highest threshold of ego-consciousness, the two opposing forces become completely dissolved in it. For alchemy, the two forces represented as serpents or dragons are Sulphur and Quicksilver. Their macrocosmic prototype is the two phases—increasing and decreasing—of the sun's annual course, separated from one another by the winter and summer solstices.[13] The connection between the tantric and alchemical symbolisms is obvious: of the two forces *Pingala* and *Ida,* which wind themselves round the *Merudanda,* the first is described as being hot and dry, characterized by the color red, and, like alchemical Sulphur, compared with the sun. The second force, *Ida,* is regarded as being cold and humid, and in its silvery pallor is associated with the moon.

In his book *On the Hieroglyphic Figures,* Nicolas Flamel writes of the mutual relationship of Sulphur and Quicksilver:

> ... these are the two serpents which are fixed around the caduceus, or Staff of Mercury, and by means of which Mercury wields his great power and transforms himself as he wills. Whoever kills one, says Haly,[14] also kills the other, for each one of them can only die along with her sister [by means of their death both pass over into a new state].... After both have been placed in the "vessel" of the grave [that is to say, the inward, "hermetically sealed" vessel], they begin to bite one another savagely, and, on account of their great poison and raging fury, do not let go of each other—unless the cold should deter them—until both, as a result of their dripping poison and deadly wounding, are drenched in blood. So long as Nature remains "untamed", the opposition of the two forces is manifested in destructive or "poisonous" mode, so that they finally kill one another and drown in their own poison, which, after their death, will transmute them into living and perpetual water reunited on a higher level, after they have lost, with

13. See Julius Schwabe, *Archetyp und Tierkreis* (Basle, 1961).
14. Probably the Arab name 'Ali.

their downfall and decomposition, their first, natural forms, in order to acquire a single, new, nobler, and better form.[15]

The staff of Hermes, or caduceus,
from a drawing by Hans Holbein the Younger.

This fable supplements the Hermetic myth of the staff of Hermes. Hermes, or Mercury, struck with his staff a pair of serpents in combat with one another. The blow tamed the serpents, which wound themselves round his staff and conferred on him the theurgic power of "binding" and "loosing". This means the transmutation of chaos into cosmos, of conflict into order, through the power of a spiritual act, which both discriminates and unites.

Pair of dragons from an Arab talisman.

15. The unformed, or amorphous, is the opposite of the formless, or supra-formal. The latter does not lack form, it possesses it essentially, without being limited by it. For this reason the supra-formal—that is, the pure Spirit—can only be realized by means of a perfect form.

In the Jewish tradition, as a counterpart to the staff of Hermes and the Hindu symbol of *Brahma-danda*,[16] we find Moses' rod, which indeed turns itself into a serpent. In Islamic mysticism, Moses' rod, which "on God's command" turned into a serpent, and on being "grasped" by Moses turned back into a rod, is compared with the passional soul (*nafs*), which through the influence of the Divine Spirit can be turned into a wonder-working power. Because it incorporates a spiritual power, Moses' rod, turned into serpent, can vanquish the serpents engendered by the Egyptian sorcerers and made of magic—and therefore psychic power; for the Spirit prevails over the soul and its domain.[17] This interpretation of the story of Moses' rod, mentioned in the Koran, recalls the Hindu distinction between *vidyâ-mâyâ* (Universal Nature in her "enlightening" aspect) and *avidyâ-mâyâ* (Universal Nature as the power of illusion). In this distinction, moreover, is also to be found the deepest sense of the Hermetic proverb: "Nature can overcome Nature." From the alchemical point of view, the changing of Moses' rod into a serpent and its subsequent re-solidification corresponds exactly to the *solve et coagula* of the great work.

Pair of dragons from the Romanesque choir of Basle Cathedral.

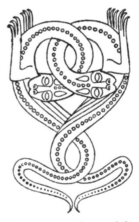

Romanesque form of the caduceus on the door of St. Michael's Church in Pavia.

In medieval Christian art, there is a representation of the staff of Hermes which Flamel's fable brings vividly to mind. The image of a pair of serpents or dragons entwined together and biting one

16. See René Guénon, op. cit.
17. See my translation of the *Fusûs al-Hikam*, chapter on Moses.

another was already common in early Irish-Anglo-Saxon art. In Romanesque sculpture it occurs so commonly and plays such a striking role in the decoration of sacred buildings,[18] that one might readily conclude that it was a kind of "signature" of certain Christian-Hermetic schools. Moreover, the same motif is connected with the symbol of the knot, whose cosmological meaning lies in the fact that the harder one pulls on the knot, the more firmly its two constituents hold together.

Birds from an alchemical manuscript of 1550 in Basle University Library.

This illustrates *inter alia* the mutual paralysis of the two forces when in a state of "chaos".[19] Sometimes one of the two reptiles representing Sulphur and Quicksilver is winged, whereas the other is without wings. Or, instead of two reptiles, there are a lion and a dragon in combat. The absence of wings always refers to the "firm" nature of Sulphur, whereas the winged animal, be it a dragon, a griffin, or an eagle, represents "volatile" Quicksilver.[20] The lion, which conquers the dragon, corresponds to Sulphur, which "fixes" Quicksilver. A winged lion, or leo-griffin, can represent the union of the two natures, and has the same meaning as the image of the male-female androgyne.

18. In fact, this motif is to be found in almost all Romanesque churches.
19. This explains the role of knots in magic.
20. See Senior Zadith, *Turba Philosophorum. Bibl. des phil. chim.*

Finally, the dragon alone can represent all phases of the work, depending on whether it is provided with feet, fins, or wings, or is without any limbs whatsoever. It can be considered as able to live either in water, air, or on the earth, and, as a salamander, even in fire. The alchemical symbol of the dragon thus closely resembles that of the Far-Eastern world-dragon, which first lives as a fish in water, and then, as a winged creature, soars into the heavens. It also recalls the Aztec myth of Quetzalcoatl, the plumed serpent, which successively moves under the earth, on the earth, and in the heavens.

All these correspondences with the animal images of alchemy have been mentioned in order to show how a cosmological wisdom of the most general bearing is reflected in alchemy, in a particular way and within specific limits.

(from *Alchemy: Science of the Cosmos, Science of the Soul*)

The Story of Nicolas Flamel
and his Wife Perrenelle

By way of illustrating what has already been said, and as a preparation for what still remains to be said, a translation—with brief commentary—of the famous story of Nicolas Flamel and his wife Perrenelle is reproduced below. This story constitutes the first part of Flamel's own book *On the Hieroglyphic Figures which he had depicted in the Cemetery of the Holy Innocents in Paris.*[21]

Records and documents have been conserved concerning Flamel's life. He was born in Pontoise in 1330 and worked in Paris as a writer and notary public. His office was at first situated beside the charnel house of the Cemetery of the Holy Innocents and later near the Church of Saint Jacques-la-Boucherie, where he himself was buried in 1417. His tomb is preserved in the Cluny museum.

Flamel's account is concerned principally with the *primus agens* of the alchemical work, about which Synesios says: "Concerning the *primus agens* the philosophers have always spoken only in parables and symbols, so that their science might not be accessible to fools; for if that were to happen, all would be lost. It should be available only to patient souls and refined spirits, who have withdrawn themselves from the corruption of the world and have purified themselves from the slimy filth of avarice. . . ."

Nicolas Flamel's own story begins as follows:

> During the time when, after the death of my parents, I earned my living by our art of writing—making inventories, preparing accounts, and calculating the expenses of guardians and their wards—I acquired for two florins a very old, large, and finely gilded book. It was neither of paper nor of parchment as are other books, but seemed to me to be made of the smoothed-out bark of young trees. Its binding was of beaten copper and it was engraved with strange letters and figures—I think they were Greek letters or letters of some similar ancient language. At any rate I could not read them, but I know they were not Latin or Gallic letters, for I understand something of these. Inside, the pages of bark had been engraved very skillfully with an iron stylus and bore very beautiful and clear Latin letters which had been finely colored. The book contained thrice-seven pages, for they were fastened together (in sections) in this way, and the seventh page was always without

21. *Bibl. des phil. chim.*

writing. On the first seventh page, instead of writing, there was a picture of a staff around which two serpents were entwined. On the second seventh page there was a cross, on which was nailed a serpent. On the last seventh page was represented a desert, in the middle of which several beautiful fountains played, out of which serpents sprang in all directions. . . .

The thrice-seven pages of the book recall the three principal phases of the work—blackening, whitening, and reddening—and the seven planets or metals.

The staff around which two serpents are entwined is the staff of Hermes, with the two forces—Sulphur and Quicksilver—which govern the spiritual axis.

The crucified snake is the symbol of the fixation of volatile Quicksilver—the first "incorporation" of the spirit. The fixation of Quicksilver corresponds to the subjugation of the ever-restless vital force, which dissipates itself in wishing and imagining. At the same time it represents the transmutation of time-dominated thought into a motionless and timeless consciousness. The cross on which the serpent is nailed signifies the body, not as flesh and sensuality, but as image of the cosmic law, of the motionless cosmic axis.

The fountains springing forth in the middle of a desert or wilderness, from which serpents emerge, represent the state of regained spiritual originality. All three pictures are variants of the serpent symbol, which always represents the same power of the soul (or cosmic power): "Nature" or *Shakti*.

> On the first page of the book was written in large golden capitals: ABRAHAM THE JEW, PRINCE, PRIEST, LEVITE, ASTROLOGER AND PHILOSOPHER. TO THE JEWISH PEOPLE, DISPERSED THROUGH GOD'S ANGER INTO GAUL, GREETINGS. D.I. The rest of the page was filled with terrible curses (in which the word MARANATHA frequently occurred) against anyone who might read this book, unless he be sacrificial priest or doctor of the Holy Law.
>
> The man who had sold me this book did not know its value—any more than I did when I acquired it. I think it must have been taken from the poor Jews, or perhaps it had been found somewhere in one of their erstwhile dwellings. . . .

Flamel is perhaps referring here to one of the expulsions of the Jews, which occurred several times at that epoch. That the book should be of Jewish origin is significant, in that the Jews were the natural link between the Christian and Islamic worlds. It is known that the renascence of alchemy in Europe in the later Middle Ages arose from the influence of Islamic culture.

On the second page the author consoled his people and counseled them to eschew all vice, especially idolatry, and to wait with meek patience until the Messiah should come and conquer all kings on earth and with his people rule eternally in majesty. Without doubt this was written by a very learned man.

On the third and following pages he taught, in simple language, the transmutation of metals, in order to help his captive people to pay their taxes to the Roman emperor and to do other things that I will not mention. Alongside, he provided illustrations of the vessels, and gave details of the colors, and other matters, excepting always the *primus agens* of which he did not speak. Instead, he painted this, with great skill, over the whole surface of the fourth and fifth pages; and though it was very clearly delineated and depicted, no one would have understood it who was not familiar with their tradition and had not studied thoroughly the books of the philosophers. The fourth and fifth pages were thus without writing, being completely filled with beautiful and skillfully executed miniatures.

On the fourth page there was portrayed first of all a youth with wings on his heels and a staff in his hand—a caduceus entwined by two serpents—with which he touched the helmet on his head. It seemed to me he represented the pagan god Mercury. Toward him ran and flew a powerful old man, on whose head was an hourglass, and who carried a sickle in his hands—like Death—with which, full of rage and fury, he tried to cut off the feet of Mercury. . . .

That Mercury or Quicksilver can be robbed of its volatility by Saturn-Chronos or time, as Flamel himself says later on, can have two different, and, in a certain sense, contrary interpretations, depending on whether time is actively used or merely endured, and whether the fixation of Quicksilver is seen as a slow death of its effective power, or as a taming of the latter. The hourglass on Saturn's head, however, seems to suggest that time is to be mastered actively, by means of a rhythm which will transmute it into an eternal now.

On the other side of the fourth page was portrayed a beautiful flower growing on the top of a high mountain and shaken violently by the north wind. It had a blue stalk, white and red flowers, and leaves shining like the finest gold. Round about it the northern dragons and griffins nested. . . .

The colors of the flower represent the three main phases of the work and its two fruits, namely silver and gold. Here blue takes the place of black, in keeping with the nature of a flower, but with the same sense of darkness and night. The flower grows on the lonely mountain of essential Being, which is one with the world-mountain, round which the heavens circle, through which the polar axis runs, and round which glide the dragons of the cosmic powers.

> On the fifth page was a rose-bush in flower, in the middle of a beautiful garden and leaning on a hollow oak. At the foot of the rose-bush gushed forth a spring of very white water, which fell away in cascades into the distance, after passing through the hands of countless peoples, who dug in the earth to find the spring, but did not find it, since they were blind, with the exception of one alone, who weighed the water. . . .

The spring of Quicksilver gushes forth from the "earth" of *materia prima*, at the roots of the flowering tree of the soul, which is protected by the hollow oak trunk of the body. The water of life flows everywhere, yet no one finds it but the sage, who weighs it. One might have expected that he would taste it, but the weighing of the water has here the same meaning as the capture of Mercury by the measure of time.

The alchemists also teach how to unite the individual elements or the various natural properties with one another, according to a definite relationship of their "weights". Jâbir ibn Hayyân calls this the art of the balance. And yet it may seem absurd to weigh elements, or even properties, such as hot, cold, moist, and dry. What is meant by alchemical "weighing" can only be understood if one first transposes the outward, quantitative measure of weight into the inward, qualitative measure of time (i.e., rhythm). Alchemical weighing, which appears to refer to physical mass, is thus none other than the mastery of rhythm, by means of which the powers of the soul can be influenced. Rhythm plays an important role in all spiritual arts. In Arabic, the rhythm of a verse is known as its "weight" (*wazn*).

> On the other side of the fifth page was a king with a large knife, who, by means of soldiers standing round him, caused a large number of young children to be killed, whose mothers wept at the feet of the merciless armed men, while the flowing blood was gathered by other soldiers and put in a large vessel in which the sun and moon from heaven came to bathe. It was because this illustration recalled the story of the innocent children killed by Herod, and because it was from this book that I learned the greater part of the art, that I had the hieroglyphic symbols of these secret sci-

ences depicted in the Cemetery of the Holy Innocents. This is what appeared on the first five pages. . . .

As Flamel himself writes in the following pages, the blood of the sacrificed innocents signifies "the mineral spirit contained in all metals, and especially in gold, silver, and quicksilver". This is none other than the "philosophic Quicksilver" which is the first manifestation of *materia prima*. Blood is the fundamental stuff of life. The holy innocents are like undefiled stirrings or out-breathings of the vital spirit which, before they can develop into ego-conscious wills, are sacrified by the king, in order to fill the vessel of the heart with their blood, so that sun and moon, spirit and soul, may bathe, be dissolved, and then united in it, and, having lost their old form, emerge from it rejuvenated.

I shall not relate what is written in beautiful and clear Latin on all the other pages, for God would punish me for this, as I would be doing something worse than did he, of whom it is told, that he wished that all men on earth had a single head, so that he might cut it off with one stroke.

As I now had this beautiful book by me, I did nothing else during day and night but study it. I thus understood very well all the processes which it described, but I did not know what was the material I must work on. This made me feel very sad and lonely and caused me to sigh incessantly. My wife Perrenelle, whom I loved like myself and whom I had married only recently, was greatly concerned about this, and asked me continually if she might not be able to release me from the concern which obviously weighed upon me. I could hide nothing from her, and told her everything, showing her the beautiful book, with which she fell in love just as much as I had done. Her greatest pleasure was to gaze on its beautiful covers, engravings, pictures, and representations, of which, however, she understood as little as did I. Nevertheless it was for me a great consolation to be able to speak to her about it, and to discuss what might be done in order to find the explanation of the signs.

Finally I had all the figures on the fourth and fifth pages copied in my house as faithfully as possible, and I showed them to various scholars, who understood them no better than myself. I even explained to them that these figures had been taken from a book that taught the production of the philosophers' stone; but most of them made fun of me and the holy stone, with the exception of a certain Master Anselm, a licentiate in medicine, who studied this art diligently. He was very eager to see my book, and did everything he could to get a sight of it. I assured him, however, that I did not possess it, but I described to him fully what it contained. He told me that the first picture represented time, which devours all things, and that, following the number of pages in the book, it would require six years in order to perfect the stone. After this period, he asserted, one would have to turn over the hourglass, and boil no more. When I said to him that this picture was meant to represent only the *primus agens* (as was written in the book itself), he replied that each six-year boiling was like a *secundus agens*. The *primus agens*, he said, whose picture was before us, was without doubt none other than that white and heavy water—namely quicksilver—which could not be grasped, and whose feet could not be cut off, that is to say, whose volatility could not be removed except by long boiling in the pure blood of young children. In this blood, quicksilver, uniting with gold and silver, would first of all be transmuted into a plant just like the one shown in the picture. Thereafter, through putrefaction, it would be changed into serpents, which, having been completely dried and cooked in the fire, would disintegrate into golden powder—and this was the philosophers' stone.

It was the fault of this counselor that, for the long period of twenty-one years, I committed thousands of mistakes, without, however, using blood, which would have been cruel and villainous. For I had discovered from my book that what the philosophers called blood was none other than the mineral spirit contained in metals, principally in the sun, moon, and Mercury, which I continually strove to combine. The above-mentioned interpretations, however, were more ingenious than exact. Since, in all my activities, I never perceived the signs which, according to the book, should appear at a definite time, I had always to start again at the beginning. Finally, when I had lost all hope of ever understanding these figures, I made a vow to God and St James of Galicia, and decided to seek the explanation from some Jewish priest or other in one of the synagogues of Spain. . . .

St. James the Elder, whose shrine is at Compostela, was the patron of alchemists, and also of all cosmological arts and sciences. It is certainly no coincidence that the pilgrim's staff (*bourdon*) of St James—a staff criss-crossed by two ribbons and crowned with a round knob, as can be seen in the saint's hand in the Romanesque statue at Compostela—bears a remarkable similarity to the staff of Hermes.

I set forth, therefore, with the agreement of my wife Perrenelle, bearing on me a copy of these figures, in pilgrim's dress and with a pilgrim's staff, as I can be seen on the outside of the chapel in the cemetery where I had the hieroglyphic figures painted, and where also, on both side walls, I had a procession depicted, in which all colors of the stone are to be seen in order, appearing and disappearing, along with the French inscription: *Moult plaist à Dieu Procession, s'elle est faite en dévotion* ("A procession pleases God greatly, when it is accomplished with devotion"). This inscription repeats almost literally the beginning of the book of King Hercules,[22] which deals with the colors of the stone and bears the title *Iris: operis processio multum naturae placet,* etc. I chose these words deliberately, knowing that the wise would understand the allusion.

In pilgrim's dress, then, I made my way, arriving finally at Montjoye, whence I proceeded to St. James of Compostela, where with great devotion I discharged my vow. Having done this, I departed and met on the way, in León, a merchant from Boulogne who introduced me to a doctor of Jewish origin but of Christian faith—called Master Canches—who lived there and was renowned for his learning. When I showed him the figures copied from my book, he was overcome with astonishment and joy, and asked me at once whether I knew anything of the whereabouts of the book from which they were taken. I answered in Latin (in which language he had questioned me) and told him that, should someone solve these riddles for me, I hoped to obtain exact information concerning the book. At this he immediately began, with great zeal and joy, to explain the beginning to me. In short, he was happy to hear where the book was, and I to hear him speak about it. He must already have heard a lot about the book, but, as he told me, it had been thought to be completely lost. We decided, therefore, to set out together. From León we traveled to Oviedo, and from there to Sanson where we boarded a ship for France. Our journey proceeded happily, and well before we reached the latter kingdom, he had truly explained to me most of my figures, revealing even in mere points great secrets (which I found most wonderful). But when we arrived at Orléans, the learned man became very ill, developing the most severe vomiting which did not stop from the moment it began at sea. He was very afraid that I might leave him, which was quite understandable. Although I never left his side, he called for me unceasingly. Finally he died, at the end of the seventh day of his illness, which filled me with sadness. I had him buried, as well as I could, in the church of the Holy Cross in Orléans, where he rests to this day. God keep his soul, for he died a good Christian. If death does not prevent me, I will settle on that Church a small rent, so that every day a few masses may be said for his soul.

Whoever would see how I arrived home and how Perrenelle rejoiced, let him look at us both in this city of Paris on the door of the chapel of Saint-Jacques de la Boucherie, on the side, and near my house. We are depicted there offering prayers of thanksgiving, I at the feet of St. James of Compostela, and Perrenelle at the feet of St. John, whom she had so often invoked. Thus, through God's grace and the intercession of the Blessed Virgin and Saints James and John, I had learned what I had wished to, namely, the first principles, though not their initial preparation, which is harder

22. Herakleios I, Emperor of Byzantium (610–641).

than anything in the world. This, however, I finally learned after making many mistakes over a period of about five years, during which I continually studied and worked—as one may see me on the outer wall of the chapel (on whose pillars I had the processions painted) at the feet of Saints James and John, ceaselessly praying to God, with my rosary in my hand, reading attentively in a book, meditating on the words of the philosophers, and thereafter accomplishing the various operations which I had divined from their words.

Finally I found what I had longed for, and I recognized it at once by its strong smell; and when I had it, I accomplished the work (*magistère*). Having learned the preparation of the first powers (*agens*), I had only to follow my book word for word, and could not have gone wrong even had I wanted to. The first time I made the projection, I applied it to quicksilver, and transmuted about one and a half pounds of it into pure silver, which was better than that from the mine—a fact which I tested and had tested several times. This took place on the 17th January 1382, a Monday, towards midday, in my house, in the presence of Perrenelle alone. Later, following my book word for word, I accomplished the work with the red stone on a similar quantity of quicksilver, again in the sole company of Perrenelle, in the same house, on the 25th day of April of the same year, at five o'clock in the evening, when I truly transmuted the quicksilver into almost the same amount of gold, which was clearly better than ordinary gold, in that it was softer and more malleable. This I can say in truth. In this way I accomplished the work three times with the help of Perrenelle, who understood it just as well as I did myself, as she helped me in carrying out the instructions; and had she wished to accomplish it entirely on her own, she would certainly have reached the goal. I possessed more than enough, after I had accomplished it once, but I found a very great joy in seeing and beholding the wonderful works of nature in the vessels. . . .

Man and woman, who in natural fashion incarnate the two poles of the alchemical work (Sulphur and Quicksilver), can by their mutual love—when this is spiritually heightened and interiorized—develop that cosmic power, or power of the soul, which operates the alchemical dissolution and coagulation (*solve et coagula*).

(from *Alchemy: Science of the Cosmos, Science of the Soul*)

6

Aspects of the Spiritual Life

The Bronze Head from the Naples Museum.

The Spiritual Life: Christian

Because Dante is Right

The incomparable greatness of the *Divine Comedy* shows itself not least in the fact that, in spite of the exceptionally wide range and variety of its influence—it even shaped the language of a nation—its full meaning has seldom been understood. Already in Dante's own lifetime those who ventured out upon the ocean of the spirit in the wake of his ship (*Paradiso,* II, 1ff) were to remain a relatively small company. They more or less disappeared with the Renaissance; the individualistic mode of thought of this period, tossed to and fro between passion and calculating reason, was already far removed from Dante's inward-looking spirit. Even Michelangelo, though he revered his fellow-Florentine to the highest degree, could no longer understand him.[1] At the time of the Renaissance, however, people did at least still debate as to whether Dante had actually seen Heaven and hell or not. At a later date, concern with the *Divine Comedy* dropped to the level of a purely scientific interest that busied itself with historical connections, or of an esthetic appreciation that no longer bothered about the spiritual sense of the work at all. Admittedly, it was known that the verses of the *Divine Comedy* contained more than just the superficial meaning of the narrative; Dante himself pointed this out in several places in his work and also in his *Convivio* (II, I), where he talks about the multiple meanings of holy scripture, and quite undisguisedly makes the same remarks apply to his own poem; the symbolical nature of the work, therefore, could not be overlooked. However, excuses were made for the poet, and his artistic mastery was even credited with enabling him to bridge over poetically "this scholastic sophistry" about multiple meanings. Thus, people fundamentally misunderstood the source upon which the poet drew for his work of creation, since the multiplicity of meaning in it is not the result of a preconceived mental construction grafted onto the actual poem; it arises directly and spontaneously out of a supra-

---

1. How greatly Michelangelo revered Dante can be seen from certain of his own sonnets. That he was not really capable of understanding him is apparent from the titanism of his sculpture: if Michelangelo had known the law of symbolism according to which higher realities are reflected in lower ones, his creations, in all their corporeality, would not have attempted to take heaven by storm.

mental inspiration, which at one and the same time penetrates and shines through every level of the soul—the reason, as well as the imagination and the inward ear. It is not "in spite of his philosophy" that Dante is a great poet; he is so thanks to his spiritual vision, and because through his art, however caught up in time it may be as regards its details, there shines forth a timeless truth, at once blissful and terrifying—in short, it is because Dante is right.

The most profound passages of the *Divine Comedy* are not simply those where a theological or philosophical explanation is placed in the mouth of one of the characters, nor those which possess an obviously allegorical nature; it is above all the most highly imaged and the most "concrete" expressions that are most highly charged with meaning.

How a spiritual truth, without the slightest degree of mental involvement, can congeal into an image, can be seen most easily in the metaphors that Dante uses in his description of hell, as, for example, the metaphor of the wood composed of dried-up, barren thorn bushes, in which the souls of those who took their own lives are shut up (*Inferno*, XIII): it depicts a situation devoid of all freedom and all pleasure, an existence bordering on the nothingness that corresponds to the inner contradiction implied by suicide, namely a will that denies the very existence that is its own basis and substance. As the ego itself cannot cast itself into nothingness, it falls as a consequence of its destructive act into the seeming nothingness that the desolate thorn bush represents, but even there it still remains "I", riveted to itself more than ever in its impotent suffering.

Everything that Dante says about the infernal wood serves to emphasize this truth: how the tree from which he unsuspectingly breaks off a branch, cries out at the wound and scolds him mercilessly; how, pursued by dogs, the souls of the dissolute—they, too, despisers of their God-given existence—break through the thorn wood, making it bleed; and how the tree, bereft of its branches, implores the poet to gather the broken pieces together at the foot of the trunk, as if the powerless ego imprisoned within still felt itself united with these dead and severed fragments. Here, as in other places in the description of hell, everything in the representation possesses an uncanny sharpness, never in the slightest degree arbitrary.

Dante's images of hell are so veridical precisely because they are fashioned from the same "stuff" as that out of which the passional human soul is made. In the description of the mount of Purgatory, a different and less immediately graspable dimension is introduced: the soul's reality now opens out on a cosmic scale, embracing the starry heavens, day and night, and all the fragrance of things: at the sight of the earthly paradise on the summit of the mount of Purgatory, Dante conjures up in a few verses the whole miracle of spring; the earthly spring turns directly into the spring of the soul, it becomes the symbol of the original and holy state of the human soul.

In representing the purely spiritual states belonging to the celestial spheres, Dante is often obliged to make use of circumlocutions, as for example when he explains how the human spirit, by penetrating more and more deeply into the Divine Wisdom, becomes gradually transformed into it: Dante looks at Beatrice, who herself keeps her eyes fixed on the "eternal wheels", and as he becomes more deeply absorbed in his vision of her, he experiences something like what befell Glaucus, who was turned into one of the sea-gods through consuming a miraculous herb:

Trasumanar significar per verba
Non si porìa; però l'esempio basti
A cui esperienza grazia serba.

To pass beyond the human state is not to be described in words; wherefore let the example satisfy him for whom grace has reserved the experience (*Paradiso*, I, 70–I)

If in this way the language of the cantos of the *Paradiso* sometimes becomes more abstract, in their turn the images that Dante uses here are even richer in meaning: they possess an inscrutable magic, which shows that Dante has seen in spirit what he seeks to express in words, and that he is to an equal degree poet and spiritual visionary, as for example when he compares the uninterrupted ascension of blessed souls, moving in response to the power of the Divine attraction, to snowflakes that are floating upwards instead of downwards (*Paradiso*, XXVII, 67-72).

The simpler an image is, the less restricted is its content; for it is the symbol's prerogative, thanks to its concrete and yet open character, to be capable of expressing truths that cannot be enclosed in rationalized concepts; which, however, in no way implies that symbols have an irrational and permanently "unconscious" background. A symbol's meaning is completely knowable, even though it does transcend reason as such; it comes from the Spirit, and opens itself to the spirit or intellect, which Dante speaks of as the highest and innermost faculty of knowledge, a faculty that is fundamentally independent of any form, either sensory or mental, and is capable of penetrating to the imperishable essence of things:

> Nel ciel che più della sua luce prende,
> Fu' io; e vidi cose che ridire
> Nè sa nè può quai di lassù discende:
> Perchè, appressando sè al suo disire,
> Nostro intelletto si profonda tanto
> Che retro la memoria non può ire.

> *In that heaven which most receiveth of His light, have I been; and have seen things which whoso descendeth from up there, hath neither faculty nor power to re-tell; because, as it draweth nigh to its desire, our intellect sinketh so deep, that memory cannot go back upon the track (Paradiso, I, 4-9).*[2]

True symbolism lies in the things themselves, in their essential qualities, which belong more to being than to becoming. This explains how Dante, in his description of the hierarchical degrees of the spiritual world, was able to relate it to the structure of the visible universe, as it appears from the earthly standpoint. This cosmic comparison was just as convincing to the medieval reader as it is unconvincing to the reader of today. How is it possible, the latter asks, to base a genuine vision of the spiritual worlds on a scientifically incorrect view of things? In answer to this it must be said that every picture of the universe that man makes for himself can only possess a conditional and provisional accuracy; it always remains in one way or another attached to sensory experience and imagination, and hence will never be entirely free from "naïve" prejudice; it is, however, scientific to the extent that it is able to provide logically satisfying answers to the questions that man has always asked. The Ptolemaic representation of the world, which Dante used as the scaffolding for his work, was in this sense completely scientific. But at the same time it was perceptible to the eye and not so remote from sensory experience as the modern, purely mathematical explanation of the universe, and it is precisely in this clarity—a clarity that still corresponds to "naïve" perceptions—that its capacity to be a symbol resides. Because it comprehends the world

---

2. See Dante's own commentary on these verses in his letter to Can Grande della Scala: "*Intellectus humanus in hac vita propter connaturalitatem et affinitatem quam habet ad substantiam separatam, quando elevatur, in tantum elevatur, ut memoriam post reditum deficiat propter transcendisse humanum modum.*"

order in relationship to man, it demonstrates the inner unity joining man to the universe and the universe to God:

> . . . Le cose tutte quante
> Hann' ordine tra loro: e questo è forma
> Che l'universo a Dio fa simigliante.

> *. . . All things whatsoever observe a mutual order; and this is the form that maketh the universe like unto God (Paradiso, I, 103).*

Dante interpreted the quantitative difference between the planetary heavens that surround one another concentrically, as a qualitative gradation in accordance with the basic notion that the higher is reflected in the lower:

> Li cerchi corporai sono ampii ed arti
> Secondo il più e il men della virtute
> Che si distende per tutte lor parti . . .
> Dunque costui che tutto quanto rape
> L'alto universo seco, corrisponde
> Al cerchio che più ama e che più sape.

> *The corporeal circles are wider or narrower according to the greater or lesser amount of virtue that spreads through all their parts . . . Therefore the one [the highest heaven], that sweepeth with it all the rest of the universe, corresponds to the circle that most loveth and most knoweth. (Paradiso, XXVIII, 64–66; 70–72)*

The geocentric—and therefore homocentric—arrangement of the planetary spheres is seen as the inverse image of the theocentric hierarchy of the angels, while hell's pit, with its circles, is its negative reflection, to which the mount of Purgatory, thrown up in the center of the earth through Lucifer's fall, provides the compensating counter-balance.[3]

Even more than by the "antiquated" world-picture that forms the framework of the *Divine Comedy*, most present-day readers—and not only "freethinkers" among them—find themselves repelled by Dante's sharp and apparently presumptuously drawn distinction between the damned, those undergoing purgation, and the blessed. To this one can reply that Dante, as a man living in the 13th century, could not have watered down psychologically the traditional

---

3. The significance of Dante's cosmography is fully discussed the earlier in this book, in the section "Cosmologia perennis" in the author's *Mirror of the Intellect* and also in his *Alchemy: Science of the Cosmos, Science of the Soul.*

teaching about salvation and damnation, nor could he have regarded the historical examples he mentions as anything but typical. But that is not the decisive factor: Dante is completely imbued with and overwhelmed by his perception of man's original dignity, measured against which the traces of hell in this world appear as they really are. He perceives the ray of Divine Light in man, and hence is bound also to recognize as such the darkness of soul that is refractory to that light.

For Dante, man's original dignity consists essentially in the gift of the "Intellect", by which is meant not merely reason or the thinking faculty, but rather that ray of light that connects the reason, and indeed the whole soul, with the Divine source of all knowledge. This is why Dante says of the damned that they have lost the gift of the intellect (*Inferno*, III, 18), which is not to imply that they cannot think, since he allows of their arguing among themselves: what they lack, and what for them has been forever cast out, is the capacity to recognize God and to understand themselves and the world in relation to Him. This capacity has its seat, as it were, in the heart, in the being's center, where love and knowledge coincide, for which reason Dante describes true love as a kind of knowledge[4], and the spirit or intellect as loving: both have fundamentally one goal, which is infinite.

In the true man, all other faculties of the soul are referred to the being's center: "I am like the center of the circle upon which every part of the circumference depends equally", Dante makes Amor-Intellectus say in his *Vita Nuova*, "but thou art not so" (*Ego tanquam centrum circuli, cui simili modo se habent circumferentie partes, tu autem non sic* [XII, 4]). To the extent that desire and will tend away from this center, even so is the soul prevented from opening spiritually onto the Eternal: *L'affetto l'intelletto lega*—"passion fetters the spirit" (*Paradiso*, XIII, 20). When Dante says of the damned that they have lost the gift of the Intellect, this means that in their case the will has become completely alienated from the center of their being. With them, the God-denying of the will has become the ruling impulse: they go to hell because basically hell is what they want: "Those who die in the wrath of God cross over Acheron quickly, since Divine justice spurs them on, so that fear is turned into desire" (*Inferno*, III, 121-126). It is different for the souls who have to endure the pun-

---

4. See "Intelletto d'Amore" by Pierre Ponsoye (*Études Traditionnelles*, Paris, May-June 1962).

ishments of Purgatory: their will has not repudiated the Divine in man, but has simply looked for it in the wrong place; in their longing for the Infinite, they have allowed themselves to be deceived: "I clearly see," says Beatrice to Dante, in one place in the *Paradiso,* "how in thy spirit already is reflected the Eternal Light, which, no sooner seen, ever enkindles love; and if aught else seduce thy love, it is naught but some vestige of that light, ill understood, that shineth through therein" (V, 7–12). When at death the object of passion, and its illusion regarding the Divine good, fall away, these souls experience their passion as it really is, namely as a burning up of oneself on an appearance that only causes pain. By coming up against the limits of the enjoyment they sought, they learn to know, negatively and indirectly, what Divine Reality is, and this knowledge is their contrition. Because of this, their falsely-directed impulse is gradually exhausted; it continues to work within them—but now without the consent of their hearts—until the denial of their denial turns into the affirmation of the original, Godward-directed freedom:

> Della mondizia il sol voler far prova,
> Che, tutto libero a mutar convento,
> L'alma sorprende, ed il voler le giova.
> Prima vuol ben, ma non lascia il talento
> Che divina giustizia contra voglia
> Come fu al peccar, pone al tormento.

> *The will alone proves the state of cleansing that has been reached; the will, now fully free, invades the soul, which now is capable of what she will. She wills well before, but that urge permits it not, which, just as it once inclined towards sin, is now directed by divine justice towards punishment, against her own will* (Purgatorio, XXI, 61–66).

Here we are touching upon one of the main themes of the *Divine Comedy,* which we must investigate more closely, even if to do so should divert us somewhat from our opening subjects; it is the question of the reciprocal relationship between knowledge and will, on which Dante, throughout his work, throws light from all sides. Knowledge of the eternal truths is potentially present in the human spirit or intellect, but its unfolding is directly conditioned by the will, negatively when the soul falls into sin, and positively when this fall is overcome. The different punishments in Purgatory that Dante describes can be regarded, not only as posthumous states, but also as stages in ascesis, that lead to the integral and primordial condition, in which knowledge and will—or, more precisely, knowledge of man's eternal goal and his striving after pleasure—are no longer separated from one another. At the moment when Dante sets foot in the earthly paradise, at the summit of the mount of Purgatory, Virgil says to him:

Non aspettar mio dir più nè mio cenno:
Libero, dritto, sano è tuo arbitrio,
E fallo fora non fare a suo senno:
Perch'io te sopra te corono e mitrio.

No longer expect my counsel nor my sign: for free, upright, and whole is thy judgement, and it were a fault not to act according to its promptings; wherefore I crown and miter thee over thyself (*Purgatorio*, XXVII, 139–142).

The earthly paradise is as it were the cosmic "place" where the ray of the Divine Spirit, which pierces through all the Heavens, touches the human state, since from here on Dante is raised up to God by Beatrice. That this place should be the summit of a mountain overtopping the whole earthly region corresponds quite simply to the nature of the earthly paradise itself.

A question arises here: what is the meaning of the fact that Dante himself scales the mount of Purgatory without suffering a single one of the punishments through which others atone for their faults? Only at the last stage does he have to walk quickly through the fire so as to reach the earthly paradise (*Purgatorio*, XXVII, 1 off). Stage by stage the angels of the gates erase the marks of sin from his forehead: on reaching the summit, Virgil acknowledges his sanctity, and yet shortly thereafter Beatrice meets him with burning reproaches that move him to agonizing repentance (*Purgatorio*, XXX, 55ff). The meaning of all this can only be that the way taken by Dante, thanks to a special grace, is not a path of merit, but a path of knowledge. When Virgil says that for him there is no other way to Beatrice, to Divine Wisdom, except by passing directly through hell, this shows that knowledge of God is to be attained along the path of self-knowledge: self-knowledge implies taking the measure of the abysses contained in human nature and consciously shedding every self-deception that has its roots in the passional soul: there exists no greater self-denial than this, and hence also no greater atonement. Properly understood, what Beatrice reproaches Dante for is not some actual sin, but simply that he has lingered too long in contemplation of her reflected earthly radiance, instead of following her into the realm of the invisible. In repenting of this, Dante throws off the last fetter binding him to this world. Much could be said here about the meaning of the two rivers of Paradise, Lethe and Eunoe, the first of which washes away the memory of sin, while the other restores the memory of good deeds; but we must return to our consideration of the will-knowledge theme.

Whereas, in those who sin, the will conditions the degree of their knowledge, in the elect the will flows from the knowledge of the divine order that they possess. This means that their will is the spontaneous expression of their vision of God, and for that reason the rank of their position in Heaven implies no constraint at all, as the soul of Piccarda Donati explains to the poet in the moon-heaven, in answer to his question whether the blessed in one sphere might not desire to occupy some higher sphere "in order to behold more and be more deeply loved?"

> Frate, la nostra volontà quieta
> Virtù di carità che fa volerne
> Sol quel ch'avemo, e d'altro non ci asseta.
> Se disiassimo esser più superne,
> Foran discordi li nostri disiri
> Dal voler di Colui che qui ci cerne;
> Che vedrai non capere in questi giri
> S'essere in caritate è qui necesse.
> E la sua natura ben rimiri:
> Anzi è formale a questo beato esse
> Tenersi dentro alla divina voglia,
> Perch' una fansi nostre voglie stesse:
> Sì che come noi siam di soglia in soglia
> Per questo regno, a tutto il regno piace,
> Com' allo Re che in suo voler ne invoglia:
> In la sua volontade è nostra pace:
> Ella è quel mare al qual tutto si muove
> Ciò ch'ella cria o che natura face.

> *Brother, the quality of love stilleth our will, and maketh us long only for what we have, and giveth us no other thirst. Did we desire to be more highly placed, our longings were discordant from His will who assigns us to this place. But that, as thou wilt see, cannot happen in these circles, since here of necessity love rules. And when thou dost rightly consider its nature, so wilt thou understand how it is of the essence of beatitude to exist in harmony with the divine will, so that our own wills themselves become one. Our being thus, from threshold to threshold throughout the realm, is joy to all the realm as to the king, who draweth our wills to what He willeth: in His will is our peace; it is that sea to which all moves that it createth and that nature maketh (Paradiso, III, 70–87).*

Submission to the Divine will is not lack of freedom: on the contrary, the will that revolts against God falls under compulsion on that very account,[5] for which reason those who die "in the wrath of God" are quick to reach hell, "since divine justice spurs them on" (*Inferno*, III, 121–6), and the seeming freedom of passion turns into dependence upon the urge which, "just as it once inclined towards sin, is now directed by divine justice towards punishment against her (the soul's) own will" (*Purgatorio*, XXX, 61–6), whereas the will of him who knows God springs from the source of freedom itself. Thus, real freedom of the will depends upon its relationship with the truth, which forms the content of essential knowledge. Conversely, the highest vision of God, of which Dante speaks in his work, is in accord with the spontaneous fulfillment of the divine will. Here knowledge has become one with divine truth and will has become one with divine love; both qualities reveal themselves as aspects of Divine Being, the one static and the other dynamic. This is the ultimate message of the *Divine Comedy,* and also the answer to Dante's effort to comprehend the human being's eternal origin in the Divinity:

> Ma non eran da ciò le proprie penne;
> Se non che la mia mente fu percossa
> Da un fulgore, in che sua voglia venne.
> All'alta fantasia qui mancò possa;
> Ma già volgeva il mio disiro e velle,
> Si come ruota ch'egualmente è mossa,
> L'amor che muove il sole e l'altre stelle.

> *But not for this did my own wings suffice; yet was my spirit smitten suddenly with a flash, whereupon its will found fulfillment. Here the power of high fantasy failed; but already my desire and my will were as a wheel that turned regularly, driven by the Love which moves the sun and the other stars* (*Paradiso*, XXXIII, 139–145).

Some scholars take the view that Beatrice never lived, and that everything that Dante says about her refers only to Divine Wisdom (*Sophia*). This opinion illustrates the confusion between genuine symbolism and allegory, taking the latter term in the sense attributed to it since the Renaissance: taken in that sense, an allegory is

---

5. The justification for the forcible defending and diffusion of a religion rests precisely on the thought that truth alone liberates while error enslaves. If man is free to choose between truth and error, then he deprives himself of freedom the moment he decides in favor of the latter.

more or less a mental invention, an artificial clothing for general ideas, whereas genuine symbolism, as we have said, lies in the very essence of things. That Dante should have bestowed upon Divine Wisdom the image and name of a beautiful and noble woman is in accordance with a compelling law, not merely because Divine Wisdom, in so far as it is the object of knowledge, includes an aspect which precisely is feminine, in the highest sense, but also because the presence of the divine *Sophia* manifested itself first and foremost to him in the appearance of the beloved woman. Herein, a key is provided that enables us to understand, at least in principle, the spiritual alchemy whereby the poet is able to transpose sensory appearances into supra-sensory essences: when love encompasses the entire will and causes it to flow towards the center of the being, it can become knowledge of God. The operative means between love and knowledge is beauty: when experienced in its inexhaustible essence—which confers release from all constraints—an aspect of Divine Wisdom is already within it, so that even sexual attraction may lead to knowledge of the Divine, to the extent that passion is absorbed and consumed by love, and passion likewise transformed by the experience of beauty.

The fire that Dante has to pass through at the last stage before entering the Earthly Paradise (*Purgatorio*, XXVII) is the same as the fire in which the lustful are purged of their sin. "This wall alone stands between thee and Beatrice," says Virgil to Dante, as the latter shrinks from stepping through the flames (*ibid*, 36). "While I was in them," Dante says, "I could have wished to throw myself into molten glass to cool myself" (*ibid*, 49-50).

The immortal Beatrice greets Dante sternly at first (*Purgatorio*, XXX, 103ff), but then with fervent love, and as she leads him upwards through the heavenly spheres she unveils her beauty to him more and more, which his regard can scarcely bear. It is significant that here Dante no longer stresses the moral beauty of Beatrice—her goodness, innocence, and humility—as he did in his *Vita Nuova*, but speaks quite simply of her visible beauty; what is most outward has here become the image of what is most inward, sensory observation the expression of spiritual vision. At the beginning, Dante is not yet capable of looking directly at the Divine Light, but sees it mirrored in Beatrice's eyes (*Paradiso*, XVIII, 82–4).

> Giustizia mosse il mio alto fattore:
> Fecemi la divina potestate
> La somma sapienza e il primo amore.

Dinanzi a me non fur cose create
Se non eterne, ed io eterno duro:
Lasciate ogni speranza, voi ch'entrate.

Justice moved my exalted Maker: Divine Power made me, Wisdom supreme and primal Love. Before me were no things created, except the eternal, and eternal I endure: abandon all hope, ye that enter. (Inferno, III, 1–9)

Faced with these famous words, which stand inscribed upon the gate of hell, many a present-day reader is inclined to say: *Maestro, il senso lor m'è duro*—"Master, their meaning is hard for me to understand" *(ibid,* 12), because it is difficult for him to reconcile the idea of eternal damnation with the idea of divine love—*il primo amore.* But for Dante, divine love is the origin, pure and simple, of creation: it is the overflowing of the eternal which endows the world, created "out of nothing", with existence, and thus permits its participation in Divine Being. In so far as the world is different from God, it has, as it were, its roots in nothingness; it necessarily includes a God-denying element, and the boundless extent of divine love is revealed precisely in the fact that it even permits this denying of God and grants it existence. Thus the existence of the infernal possibilities depends upon divine love, while at the same time these possibilities are judged through divine justice as the negation that indeed they are. "Before me was nothing created, except the eternal, and I endure eternally": the Semitic languages distinguish between eternity, which pertains to God alone and is an eternal now, and the endless duration which pertains to the posthumous states: the Latin language does not make this distinction, and thus Dante likewise cannot express it in words. Yet who knew better than Dante that the duration of the beyond is not the same thing as God's eternity, just as the timeless existence of the angelic worlds is not the same thing as the duration of hell, which is like a congealed time. For if the state of the damned, viewed in itself, has no end, nevertheless in God's sight it can only be finite.

"Abandon all hope, ye who enter": it could also be said, conversely: whoever still hopes in God will not need to pass through this gate. The condition of the damned is precisely hopelessness, since hope is the hand held out for the reception of grace.

To the modern reader, it seems strange that Virgil, the wise and good, who was able to lead Dante to the summit of the mount of Purgatory, should have to reside like all the other sages and noble heroes of antiquity in limbo, the ante-chamber of hell. But Dante could not transfer the unbaptized Virgil into any of the Heavens attainable through grace. If, however, we look a little more closely, we become aware of a remarkable rift in Dante's work, which seems to hint at a dimension that was not developed further: in general, limbo is described as a gloomy place, without light and without sky, but as soon as Dante, together with Virgil, has entered the "noble castle" where the sages of old walk upon "emerald lawns", he speaks of an "open, luminous, and high place" (*Inferno*, IV, 115ff), as though he no longer found himself in the underworld covered by the earth. Men there are "of slow and deep gaze, of great dignity in their behavior, and speak seldom, with mild voices" (*ibid*, 112-114). All this no longer has anything to do with hell, but neither does it lie directly within range of Christian grace.

In this connection, the question arises: did Dante adopt an exclusively negative attitude towards non-Christian religions? In a passage in the *Paradiso*, where he numbers the Trojan prince Ripheus among the elect, he speaks of the unfathomable nature of divine grace and warns us not to be precipitate in our judgement (XX, 67ff). What else could Ripheus be for Dante, other than some distant, innocent example of an extra-ecclesiastical saint? We do not say "extra-Christian", because for Dante every revelation of God in man is Christ.

And this leads to yet another question: did Dante, in creating the *Divine Comedy*, draw consciously upon certain Islamic mystical works, which show various analogies with it? The type of epic poem describing the path of the knower of God in symbolical form is not rare in the Islamic world. It may be surmised that certain of these works were translated into the Provençal language,[6] and we know that the community of the "Fedeli d'Amore" to which Dante belonged, was in communication with the Order of the Temple, which was established in the East and open to the intellectual world of Islam.[7] The argument can be carried a long way, and one can find a prototype in Islamic esoteric writings for almost every important

6. There exists a medieval Provençal translation of the *Mirâj*, the story of the Prophet's ascent to Heaven (*Eschiele Mahomet*, published by Múñoz Sendino and Enrico Cerulli). But this is more of a popular treatment of a theme which elsewhere provides the basis for important metaphysical and contemplative considerations.
7. See the works of Luigi Valli, especially *Il linguaggio segreto di Dante e dei Fedeli d'Amore* (Rome: Optima, 1928).

element in the *Divine Comedy*—for the interpretation of the planetary spheres as stages in spiritual knowledge, for the divisions of
hell, for the figure and role of Beatrice, and much else besides.
However, in view of certain passages in Dante's *Inferno* (XXVIII, 22),
it is scarcely credible that he can have known Islam and recognized
it as a true religion. A more likely explanation is that he drew on
writings that were not themselves Islamic, but were directly influenced by Islamic doctrines,[8] and it is probable that what actually
reached Dante through these channels amounted to much less than
comparative research[9] would have us suppose. Spiritual truths are
what they are, and minds can encounter one another at a certain
level of insight without ever having heard of one another on an
earthly plane. What matters is not so much what Dante was influenced by, as the fact that he was right: the teachings contained in
his *Divine Comedy* are all valid, those in the foreground in the sense
of the general Christian belief, and the more hidden ones—for
example, the teaching on the mutual relationship between will and
knowledge discussed above—in terms of gnosis in the Christian
sense of the word. It is significant in this connection that Dante was
not self-deceived about his own person, and that he could observe
himself from an impersonal point of view: he assessed himself cor-
rectly when he counted himself amongst the six greatest poets of all
ages (*Inferno*, IV, 100-102), and he rightly allows Virgil to say of him:
Alma sdegnosa, benedetta colei che in te s'incinse!—"Soul disdainful (of
all that is vulgar), blessed be she that bore thee!" (*Inferno*, VIII, 44-
45) He was equally unmistaken when he condemned the Papal
policy of his time, since it led to the secular explosion of the Renaissance and the Lutheran secession. His chief spiritual legacy, however, lies in the symbols and imagery of his poem, which neither
profane philosophical research nor any "psychology" will ever
exhaust. They bear the seal of an inspiration independent of all
temporal and spatial circumstances, and the spiritual nourishment
they offer is reserved for those who, as Dante says, "in the temporal

---

8. Important in this respect is MS. Latin 3236A in the Bibliothèque Nationale in
Paris, first published by M. T. D'Alverny in *Archives d'Histoire doctrinale et littéraire
du Moyen-Âge*, 1940 (42). It was also referred to in the author's book on
alchemy. It is related to the *Divine Comedy* in many ways, and all the more
remarkably in that it expressly names the founders of the three monotheistic
religions, Moses, Christ, and Mohammed, as the true teachers of the way to
God through knowledge.
9. See the studies of P. Asín Palacios.

world already stretch out their necks for the bread of the angels, by which one lives here, but is never sated" (*Paradiso,* II, 10).

(from *Mirror of the Intellect*)

St. Bernardino of Siena and the Sacred Monogram

St. Bernardino of Siena

St. Bernardino preached in Siena during the years 1425–1427. The square where he preached was always full of listeners. Moved by his words, deadly enemies were reconciled, political differences were overcome, and the town Council issued decrees against slander and usury. Furthermore, the Sacred Monogram painted on a board which St. Bernardino was wont to hold before him while preaching, was carved, by order of the Council, on the façade of the Town Hall, where it stands to this day.

Bernardino degli Albizzeschi, a descendant of an aristocratic family in the town of Massa Maríttima in Sienese territory, was brought up in the city of Siena, where, while still very young, he studied philosophy and civil and canon law before entering into the strict observance of the Franciscan Order of friars. When the Black Death once more broke out in Siena, although then only seventeen years old, he devoted himself to nursing the sick in the hospital of Santa Maria della Scala, inciting other young men to follow his example, in the same way as St. Catherine had done during the first outbreak of the plague. In later years, he traveled throughout Italy preaching and exhorting large crowds in Milan, Venice, Brescia, Ferrara, Bologna, and Florence, leaving everywhere a deep and lasting impression. In 1425, he preached Lenten sermons in Florence, whence he received the call of the Sienese Council to come to that city.

At a time when reverence for Christian tradition seemed to be on the wane, he restored to his hearers veneration for the order of the priesthood, the dignity of whose calling does not depend simply on the human perfection of the priest himself. The sermons of St. Bernardino also revived reverence for the sacrament of marriage, as well as belief in the immortality of the soul and respect for God's Name.

He used the familiar idiom of the people so that all might follow his words, lashing out fiercely against the sins prevalent at that time, giving free rein to a certain cutting humor of his own, and often appealing to the common sense and good judgment of the intellectuals, while from his own rich store of knowledge, in unexpected flashes of intuition, he threw light upon words from the Scriptures by means of countless similes and parables.

On marriage

". . . There are two extremes: It is highly profitable to preach on the subject of wedlock, for no other theme in the world is so much discussed, yet people in general are strangely ignorant about everything appertaining thereto. On the other hand people say it would be disgraceful to preach openly on the subject or to offer advice about it. In the confessional it is mentioned with hesitation for fear it should be said that the father confessor teaches evil ways; and from the pulpit wedlock is seldom spoken of for two reasons: lest ignorant people mock the preacher, or lest he, feeling some embarrassment, should become confused in his discourse.

"The fact that wedlock is discussed neither in the confessional nor from the pulpit has given rise to the prevailing ignorance of its true nature; therefore you follow your natural bent with all its mischievous practices, living as the animals do, without reverence for the high sacrament of marriage, that God established in the earthly paradise. It was the first and greatest of His gifts and you have desecrated it. You have come to believe that wedlock consists only in bodily union, whereas it consists in the trust that the woman places in the man, and the man in the woman.

"These are the two extremes: one person will say: 'Speak as frankly and openly about it, as one would about any dishonorable action.' But another will cry: 'Do not do so: it would be immoral. You will lay yourself open to evil-speakers.'

"So what will you do now, Brother Bernardino? If you remain silent for fear of incurring mockery, or from a personal feeling of embarrassment in discussing the subject, or if you should be moved by any other consideration and refrain from speaking about wedlock, you are heading for damnation. You have been instructed to preach, to remonstrate with evil-doers and to hold up their misdeeds before them, to lead them back into the way of salvation. Therefore take this burden upon you: say what must be said and let people talk as they will . . .

"In his epistle the apostle Peter writes: 'Which vessel is the weaker?' Surely the woman is the weaker: therefore be mindful of her, and treasure her, as if you possessed a frail and precious crystal vase . . .

". . . Should a woman complain and regret being a woman, being small, or being dark complexioned, or hirsute, or crooked, she will never attain to salvation until she is content with the nature God has given her . . .

". . . Of itself the soul does not incline to unnatural practices or to any action definitely opposed to the natural order. Think of the misery of the wife of a libertine drawn by her husband into all manner of dissoluteness! It were better for your daughters to have their throats cut than to marry them to such reprobates; for, were their life taken, at least their soul might have been saved, whereas when delivered into the hand of reprobates both body and soul are lost . . .

"Wisdom and discernment: one may well be in doubt—and what then is to be done? Not all circumstances are the same, or even similar, so no general rule can be laid down, just as one cannot insist that everybody eat two loaves a day, for there are some who eat their three loaves while others eat only one, and again others who hardly touch bread at all.

"Three things are to be considered:

    (1) bodily nature;

    (2) spiritual nature;

    (3) the particular state of grace.

"Firstly I will speak about the bodily considerations: I am young and she is young; or I am old and she is young; or I am young and she is old.

"Never marry your daughter to an old man, for she will only have grief and worry and will be liable to become a prey to countless sins. Nor should you, you older woman, ever marry a younger man, for when he has despoiled your treasure, he will turn against you. Look at your man from every viewpoint: is he strong? is he weak? healthy or ailing? Let not the strings of your lute be tuned to such a tension that they will snap! Be wise enough not to comply with his desire if it smacks of bestiality. . . .

"Then there are spiritual questions: Should you be in danger of losing God's grace and the state of grace of your own soul, let yourself go only as far as is meet and seemly, so that grace may quit you not. However, since there are few with spiritual natures, I will not say much on the subject. But I will give an example: Supposing a woman is richly endowed with the grace of God and wishes to live continently if she be able; but she finds it not easy to decide which mode of life is the better one. Let her first seek advice from Lady Wisdom, then from Lady Conscience, and lastly let her seek the counsel of Lady Compassion—from all three noble women: but also let her turn to the love of God, to her own soul and to her love for her husband; she will then surely be well advised . . ."

On pleasure

The sermons of St. Bernardino were always full of imagery. During Lent in 1425, he preached a sermon in Florence on pleasure.

". . . Now the subject of worldly pleasure: Of pleasure it has been said: *mane floruit, et transeat*: it blossoms at morn, but is doomed to wilt away. It is as in the month of May. See the flowering fields!"

The Sacred Monogram

The custom of having a coat-of-arms had become usual even amongst commoners. Every party, every guild, every clan and family aspired to the possession of a coat-of-arms. All these aspirants to worldly honor were now confronted with the Sacred Monogram (the divine "coat-of-arms"), held up before them by St. Bernardino. This was the visible Name of Jesus, represented by the letters IHS, (*iota, epsilon, sigma*), the first three letters of the Greek name *Iesous*. This sign was situated at the center of outwardly-radiating flames of fire and rays of light. Men were to honor this sign, and seek refuge in it. In Gothic lettering, the three letters of this Monogram were later reinterpreted as representing the initial letters of the words *Jesus Hominum Salvator* ("Jesus, Savior of Men"); and also of the words *In hoc Signo* ("In this Sign").

There is more significance to this Monogram than may at first meet the eye. By propagating this symbol, St. Bernardino made devotion to the Name of Jesus accessible in an, as it were, "concrete" manner. The devotion consisted in concentrating on the inwardly spoken Divine Name, a practice which, from the origins, had been one of the chief means of spiritual assimilation. The worship of the divine-human Name of Jesus runs like a scarlet thread throughout Christian mysticism, from the time of the Fathers in the Theban Desert to the Spanish mystics of the 16th century, and continues up to the present day. Indeed, not only in Christianity but also in the mysticisms of all religions, this concentration on a divine, or divine-human Name, sometimes presented in visible form, plays a significant part. By "objectivizing" the practice through the visible Monogram, the Sienese saint made one of the most inward treasures of the contemplative tradition outward and popular, with the object that, through its compelling power, it might, in its turn, again become inward for many souls.

The Monogram of the Name of Jesus
as propagated by St. Bernardino of Siena.

St. Bernardino said: "Put the Name of Jesus in your houses, in your rooms, and keep it in your hearts. . . . The best inscription of the Name of Jesus is the one that is in the heart, then the one that is spoken, and then the one that is painted, engraved, or sculpted. . . . Everything that God has created for the salvation of the world is contained in this Name of Jesus. . . . It is origin and without origin . . . It is worthy of praise like God Himself."

"When the Name of Jesus lives in your heart of hearts, your desire also to gaze upon it will be all the greater . . . If your heart is empty of the Name, the best way to achieve its possession is to place it visibly before your eyes. . . ."

From a sermon on the Name of Jesus

The following is an excerpt from a sermon on the virtues of the Name of Jesus given by St. Bernardino both in Florence and in Siena, in the year 1424.

"Today let us speak of the shining countenance of the Seraphim. St. Paul says : 'Before the Name of Jesus every knee shall bow, whether in Heaven, on earth, or in hell. . . .' Believe me, whosoever is not of the devil will this day tell of the wonder of the Name of Jesus. Yet how shall I adequately express the virtues of the Name?

Whether I speak or cry out, my words are but as silence; I can with my words uplift His Name, yet it is a degradation of it. I can affirm and negate a thousand times in order to explain Him, and yet leave Him unexplained. . . . What I want to convey to you is that the virtues of the Name of Jesus are so great that the more I say, the less I reveal. If all the grains of sand in the sea, all the leaves on the trees, and all the stars in the heavens were tongues praising and glorifying the Name of Jesus, all of them together could not say more than a hundred-thousand-thousandth part of what one single tongue could tell. The reason for this is that the Name of Jesus is Origin without origin: that before the creation of the sun and until the burning-out thereof, the Name was pre-ordained, from everlasting to everlasting, until the end of time and thereafter. The Name of Jesus is as worthy of praise as God Himself. The prophet David said: 'As Thou art praiseworthy, Lord, so is Thy Name (Jesus).' If all the angels of Paradise, from the lowest choir to the highest, and all men on earth who are, who were, and who ever will be, were to give themselves up to praising the Name of Jesus, it would still not suffice for a Name of which it is written at the beginning of the Book: 'My Name is the foundation of those who are saved.' In this Name of Jesus all are saved. Through faith in His Name the Holy Fathers were saved. . . .

"Everything that God has done for the salvation of the world lies hidden in the Name of Jesus.

"Read the Scriptures, the Acts of the Apostles, the letters of St. Paul and other apostles, the Apocalypse, indeed the whole Bible, and if you can point to a single sinner, sick in soul or body, who called for help in the Name of Jesus and was spurned, I will breathe my last breath! Look at the story in St. Luke's Gospel of the blind man who begged, crying: *Jesu, fili David, miserere mei*! Jesus called the man to him and spoke, saying: 'What wilt thou that I do unto thee?' The blind man answered: 'That I may see.' Take note, he meant it spiritually, he meant the Son of God. The blind man said: 'Lord, that I may see', for therein alone lies our entire happiness, namely that we may see the very Countenance of the Lord Jesus; and from this you can see how truly He is the refuge of the contrite heart. . . .

"Devils flee before the Name of Jesus and are rendered powerless by it. God first gave His Name to the Apostles, and afterwards to us all, wherewith to combat devils. This means that you can guard yourself against the devil himself, and not only against those who are bedeviled. In the last chapter of St. Mark's Gospel Jesus says: 'In my Name shalt thou cast out devils . . .'

"One day, as St. Bernard walked in the streets of Milan, a woman possessed of an evil spirit was brought before him. At once, recognizing the woman's sickness, the saint, filled with pity, kneeled down beside her to release her. Thereupon, through the mouth of the sick woman, the devil spoke, saying: 'You can do nothing against me.' St. Bernard answered: 'Not I, but the Name of Jesus will exorcize you', and so it happened. So holy and fearful is the Name of Jesus! It is holy to men who are holy and good, and terrifying to the devil, to the wicked, and to the possessed. All the more is it to be revered by merchants and craftsmen, and under the superscription of His Name should all their books and manuscripts begin. Let everything that we aspire to do be begun in the Name of Jesus. . . . For the usurer and the libertine the Name instills fear; for Jesus is humble, mild, full of earnestness and every sort of truth. . . . From the sweet-scented flower of the vine, snakes slink away: in like manner the devil flees before the fragrance of the Name of Jesus . . .

"In Padua, while listening to a sermon on the Name of Jesus, a maniac was restored to sanity. Likewise in Alessandria della Puglia, a woman was instantaneously healed of her soul's sickness when a boy touched her with the monogram of the Name of Jesus. . . .

"You, merchant trading overseas, carry it with you! You, soldier at the wars, and you, traveler, take it with you everywhere, and have faith that the Name of Jesus will protect you from every harm . . .

"Take the Name of Jesus into your homes, into your rooms, into your hearts. . . .

"In the words of Solomon: 'A strong tower is the Name of the Lord.' Thousands of experiences have shown, and continue to show every day, that with the Name of Jesus in one's hand one is safe from robbers and highwaymen, and so one says the words: *autem transiens per medio illorum ibat,* or simply: 'Jesus, Jesus, Jesus'; for whosoever turneth to the Name of Jesus will find protection. . . .

"Consider the body, that is, the flesh: there is no human disposition, be it ever so wrathful, uncontrolled, proud, lustful, mean, greedy, covetous, or otherwise filled with vice, which, if the man concerned accept the Name of Jesus with faith and love, will not immediately be released from every temptation. . . .

"Christ said: 'If you lay hands upon the sick in my Name, they shall be healed.' But make it a rule to remember what I mentioned earlier, namely, that, should you not receive the grace you pray for, it is either because your faith was weak, or else the grace was withheld for the good of your soul. . . .

"God says: 'My Word today is no less strong than it was in the early days of the Church.' All the miracles wrought by the Apostles, and by others who were not apostles, were performed in the Name of Jesus. Indeed, once the Apostles said to Jesus: 'See yonder Pharisees, who are not Thy disciples, yet they cast out devils in Thy Name.' What more proof can one have of the power of the Name of Jesus?

"When great difficulties face you, cry aloud: 'Jesus, have mercy on me!' and no harm will come to you. Carry Him with you, so that you may lay Him next to your heart; soon you will turn to Him out of very habit. In every trouble, cry: 'Jesus, Jesus', and your heart will become humble, be it as hard as diamond . . .

"In every sorrow and anxiety, He is a Comforter. . . . To those who endure in patience, He is their Refuge. He will bring you joy. In the midst of torture, the Apostles were full of trust. Take heed, Brother Bernardino! Unless you are ready to rejoice in persecution for the Name of Jesus, you will go to the cursed house. 'Be of good cheer, rejoice and be exceeding glad,' said Jesus to His Apostles, 'for great is your reward in Heaven when you are persecuted for my Name's sake.'

"Once, as St. Peter was entering the Temple, a lame man begged of him alms. St. Peter said to him: 'Gold and silver have I none, but that which I have I give thee. In the Name of Jesus rise up and walk.' The man arose and ran rejoicing into the Temple. In like manner, in whatsoever trouble your soul may be, it will arise rejoicing at the Name of Jesus. . . .

"The best inscription of the Name of Jesus is the one that is found in the inmost heart: the next best is in words, and finally it is the visible Name, be it written or carved. If the bodily eye be constantly confronted with it, it will soon become visible to the eye of the heart, that inward spiritual eye of the soul. Often you will speak His Name aloud with reverence, love, and faith, until it becomes a habit with you, a habit which will imprint itself ineradicably upon your soul in whatsoever difficulty life brings to you. 'Jesus, Jesus' are the words you will have in your heart and find yourself repeating, like the holy Bishop Ignatius who was martyred for Jesus' sake: at each blow he received, he said the word 'Jesus' aloud and no other word passed his lips. Accordingly, when they had killed him, having marveled at his patience, they cut him open and on his heart was found the Name of Jesus in golden letters. On dividing the heart into two parts they found the Name of Jesus on both sides; and however small the pieces into which his heart was cut, on each smallest part stood the Name of Jesus, proving that indeed he carried the Name in his heart. . . .

"Hear the words of St. John in his Gospel: 'Whatsoever ye shall ask of the Father in my Name, it shall be given unto you.' "

Concerning the pictorial representation of the Name

"It is surrounded by twelve broad rays denoting the twelve Apostles, or the twelve clauses of the Creed: between them are eight, ten, or twelve thinner rays standing for the doctrine of Holy Church, or the perfection of the Apostolic life. Its rightful place is on the escutcheon of Holy Church.

"When the Antichrist enters this world he will appropriate for himself all the names of the Almighty; but of the Name of Jesus he will not presume to take possession.

"The background of the Monogram is blue, the sign of faith, love, and hope. St. Paul says: 'Take the Name of Jesus for your shield and buckler.' A wondrous weapon it will be when raised aloft against the hosts of the Antichrist.

"About the three initials: To him who carries the Monogram they denote the Trinity, to be imprinted on his inmost heart: to him who thus dedicates his soul, it is not only a sign, it is a miracle of Grace . . .

"Let us now consider the place of the Holy Monogram: it is in the sun, whose rays illumine the soul. Twelve is the number of the ecstasies of unswerving faith. The main blessings vouchsafed correspond to the larger rays, the remainder denote the *gratia gratis data*. The whole is framed in a square, signifying the four cardinal virtues.

"Domine Dominus, quam admirabile nomen tuum in universa terra!

"I will describe the monogram with a simile: either you carry the Name of Jesus in your heart, or you do not. But he who does so will all the more long to have it visible before his eyes. A lover bearing the picture of his lady in his heart's eye sees her likeness in a thousand outward things. The more one's heart is possessed by it, the more pleasing is it in visible form. And so it is with the Name of Jesus; he who possesses it inwardly longs for it outwardly. The Apostle Paul was filled with the Name both within and without. Should your heart be empty of Him, the means to attain Him is by placing Him before you and confessing Him openly.

"The great Constantine carried His Name emblazoned on his banner, whereby he was victor in every battle. In Verona I saw an old book in the Sacristy, a Gospel, the pages of which were colored in purple as the garments of Christ. All the lettering was in silver except where the Name of Jesus occurred, and this was written in gold so as to show that the Name of Jesus is above all other names, as gold is above all other precious metals. . . ."

The wave of religious fervor which followed this sermon on the Name of Jesus, and which swept over the Sienese people, is something beyond our present-day powers of conception to grasp. It shows that the rationalism of the Renaissance had not yet undermined the capacity of men's souls to sense the imponderables of spiritual reality which a simple symbol is able to convey.

The Council of the city decided that the Monogram of the Name of Jesus, such as St. Bernardino was wont to hold before him as he preached, was to find a permanent place on the façade of the Town Hall in the form of a large colored relief. Many citizens placed the same sign, either painted or carved, over the entrance to their homes, so that it became almost a second coat-of-arms of the city. Also, in other Italian cities which the saint at one time or other had visited, one finds the same sign on buildings and in homes.

(from *Siena, City of the Virgin*)

The Alchemy of Prayer

In so far as alchemy contains a science of Nature—the latter comprising both gross or corporeal and subtle or psychic manifestation—its laws and concepts can be freely transposed to the domains of the other traditional sciences, for example, to humoral medicine, and also to the corresponding science of the soul and its related therapeutics (*see diagram of the four humors or temperaments on p. 122*). More important to us in the present connection is the transposition of alchemical perspectives to spirituality or mysticism, for it offers a parallel to what was said earlier regarding the "chemical marriage". Here, only brief mention of this particular transposition will be made, by way of indication and amplification, without attempting to pursue all its ramifications.

Within the framework of spirituality, alchemy is above all the alchemy of prayer. By the word prayer is to be understood not so much an individual petition, but rather the inward—and sometimes also outward—pronouncing of a formula or name directed to God and evoking God, thus especially the so-called "ejaculatory prayer". The pre-excellence of this kind of prayer rests on the fact that the word or phrase repeated as a means of concentration is not one which has been selected by some human being or other, but either derives wholly from revelation or contains a Divine Name, if indeed it does not consist exclusively of this Name. Thus the word pronounced by the person praying is, thanks to its divine origin, a symbol of the eternal Word and, in the last analysis, in view of its content and power of benediction, is one with the latter: "The foundation of this mystery (that is, the invocation of a Divine Name) is, on the one hand, that 'God and his Name are one' (Ramakrishna), and on the other, that God Himself pronounces His Name in Himself, hence in eternity and outside of all creation, so that his unique and uncreated word is the prototype of ejaculatory prayer, and even, in a less direct sense, of all prayer." (See: the chapter "Modes of Prayer" in *Stations of Wisdom* by Frithjof Schuon.)

Thus, fundamentally, the Divine Name or the sacred formula of ejaculatory prayer is related to the passive soul, as is the Divine Word, the *fiat lux,* to the passive nature or *materia prima* of the universe. This brings us back to the correspondence (mentioned by Muhyi 'd-Dîn ibn 'Arabî) that exists between, on the one hand, the Divine Command (*al-amr*) and Nature (*tabi'a*), and, on the other, Sulphur and Quicksilver, the two fundamental powers which in the soul are (respectively) relatively active and relatively passive. In its immediate sense, and from the point of view of "method", Sulphur is the will, which unites itself with the content of the word pronounced in the prayer, and acts in a formative manner upon the Quicksilver of the receptive soul. In the last analysis, however, Sulphur is the penetrating spiritual light contained in the sacred words, like the fire in flint, and whose appearance effects the real transmutation of the soul.

This transmutation goes through the same phases as are determined by the alchemical work, for the soul initially, on turning away from the outward world, becomes congealed, then dissolves as a result of inner warmth, and finally, having been a changing, volatile stream of impressions, becomes a motionless crystal filled with light. This is indeed the simplest expression to which this inward process can be reduced. If it were to be described in greater detail, it would be necessary to repeat almost everything that has been said about the alchemical work, and to relate it to the inward action of prayer and within the framework of corresponding spiritual contemplation. (See Frithjof Schuon, *op. cit.*)

It will suffice here to mention that the alchemy of prayer is treated particularly fully in the writings of the Islamic mystics.[10] Here it stands in close relation to the method of *dhikr*, an Arabic expression which can be translated as "remembrance", "recollection", and "mention", and also as "ejaculatory prayer". "Remembrance" is intended here in the sense of the Platonic *anamnesis*: "The sufficient reason for the invocation of the (Divine) Name lies in its being the 'remembering' of God; and this, in the last analysis, is consciousness of the Absolute. The Name actualizes this consciousness and, in the end, perpetuates it in the soul and fixes it in the heart, so that it penetrates the whole being and at the same time transmutes and absorbs it." (Frithjof Schuon, *op. cit.*)

The basic law of this kind of inward alchemy is to be found in the Christian formula of the *Ave Maria*, the "angelical salutation". *Maria* corresponds both to *materia prima* and to the soul in its state of pure receptivity, whereas the words of the angel are like a prolongation of the divine *fiat lux*. The "fruit of the Virgin's womb" corresponds to the miraculous elixir, the Philosophers' Stone, which is the goal of the inward work.

According to the medieval interpretation, the angel greets the Virgin *mutans Evae nomen* (reversing the name of Eve): *Ave* is indeed the reverse of *Eva*. This indicates the transmutation of the chaotic soul into the pure mirror of the Divine Word. To the objection that the angel did not speak Latin, and that *Eva* in Hebrew is *Khawwa*, it must be answered that in the domain of the sacred there is no chance, and also that things which seem mere coincidences are in reality preordained. This explains why in the Middle Ages the smallest details of Scripture, even the very names, were studied and variously interpreted according to their symbolism—and with an inspiration which rebuffs every reproach of artificiality.

The male-female androgyne symbolizes the completion of the alchemical work, with the signs of the seven planets in such an order that the three solar signs correspond to the masculine side of the androgyne, and the three lunar signs to the feminine side, while

---

10. See my *Introduction to Sufi Doctrine*, pp. 101 et seq.

the androgynous sign of Mercury represents the "keystone" between the two series. This gives rise to the schema below, in which the stages of the "lesser" and "greater" works will be recognized.

In a certain respect (and quite apart from the astrological meanings of the same sign), the signs on the right may be called active, and those on the left passive, since the "lesser work" completes the readiness of the soul, and the "greater work" completes the spiritual revelation.

The individual signs correspond to one another in pairs. One depends on the ascent of the Moon, and the other on the descent of the Sun (these two movements occurring in the course of the work). When, on the contrary, both movements are viewed as occurring in parallel, the signs are ordered as shown in the schema.

From this, it can be seen that for every active aspect, there is a corresponding passive aspect. Saturn represents a passive "abasement", and Mars an active descent. The first sign represents the extinction of the ego-bound soul, the second the victory of the spirit.

On the next level, the third sign, Jupiter, corresponds to the receptivity of soul, while the fourth sign, Venus, corresponds to the rising of the inward sun.

The Moon (the fifth sign) and the Sun (the sixth sign) respectively embody the active and passive poles in their pure state, while Mercury bears both principles within itself.

Planetary and metallurgical correspondences

Mercury ☿
(quicksilver)

1 Saturn ♄ (lead)	2 Mars ♂ (iron)
3 Jupiter ♃ (tin)	4 Venus ♀ (copper)
5 Moon ☽ (silver)	6 Sun ☉ (gold)

To see how these six stages constantly recur as fundamental themes in all spiritual realization, one should consult the above-mentioned chapter "Stations of Wisdom" in the book of the same name by Frithjof Schuon.

(from *Alchemy: Science of the Cosmos, Science of the Soul*)

The Spiritual Life: Islamic

Islamic Mysticism

The spiritual high-points of Maghribi culture are to be found in the realm of Islamic mysticism, which in Arabic is known as *tasawwuf*. Possessing as it does the dual aspects of wisdom and the love of God, it finds expression not only in metaphysical doctrines, but also in poetry and the visual arts, and, as its essence is communicated most directly in symbols and parables, it can speak without hindrance not only to learned believers, but also to the simple man of the people: the craftsman and the Bedouin; in fact, it may often be more readily accessible to the unlearned than to the learned.

Though Islamic mysticism, as it persists in Morocco down to the present day, may be compared in many respects with Christian mysticism—and in other respects with Hindu and Far-Eastern mysticism—it is nevertheless founded entirely on the religious form specific to Islam. Its point of departure is *tauhid,* the doctrine of Divine Unity. If Islamic law demands, as the first duty of every believer, that he "testify" to the unity of God, Islamic mysticism requires that this attestation (*shahâda*), should not be merely with the lips, nor even merely with the mind, but that, beyond all reflections and sentiments, it should be a total and immediate act of testimony or witness (*shahâda*); this means nothing other than the Knowledge of God.

God can only be known, however, when the human ego, which instinctively regards itself as a self-sufficient center—a kind of "divinity" in addition to the Divinity—is extinguished before the infinitude of God, in accordance with the words: "There is no divinity but God". This does not mean that the immortal essence of the soul has to be annihilated; what must be dissolved is the web-like psychic substance, made up of egoistic passions and imaginings, which restricts consciousness to the level of ephemeral appearances. When this "veil" of selfishness is lifted from the underlying Spirit or Intellect—the supra-individual faculty of direct knowledge—things are seen as they really are. God is seen in His all-embracing Presence, and the creature as pure possibility, contained within the Divine Being. "The Sufi," said the medieval spiritual master Abû'l-Hasan ash-Shâdhilî, "sees his own existence as particles of dust made visible by a ray of sunlight: neither real nor unreal."

Of this same spiritual vision the celebrated saint Abû Madyan says in a poem:

> Everything outside of God is unreal, everything taken
>   individually or collectively, when thou truly knowest it.
> Know that without Him, the whole creation, including thee,
>   would disappear, and come to naught.
> Whatever does not have its roots in His Being, can in no wise
>   be real.
> The knowers of God are as if extinguished.
> What else can they look upon, but Him, the Transcendent,
>   the Glorious?
> Everything they see outside of Him, has truly been destined
>   for destruction, in the past, in the future, and in the
>   present moment.
>   (al-Madanî, *The Holy Lights of the Shâdhilî Tarîqa*)

I once asked Mulay 'Alî ad-Darqâwî about the state of the mystic who had realized this degree of contemplation. " It is an uncovering of the Divine Unity," he answered, "but the servant (creature) remains a servant, and no illusion can arise."

The organ by means of which man can take cognizance of the presence of God is, according to Sufi teaching, not the brain but the heart. As with the Church Fathers, the heart is seen not as the seat of the sentiments, but as the seat of the Intellect or Spirit (*Rûh*), which is independent of mental forms, and capable of direct knowledge.

Deflected from its true center, which has its roots in the Eternal, the consciousness of the average man is as if imprisoned in a kind of dream or state of forgetfulness (*ghafla*). This is why man must be "reminded" (of That which he has "forgotten"), and this is the reason for what is known as *dhikr*, which the Sufi must practice in a large variety of ways, and which may be translated as "remembrance", "mention", or "invocation". *Dhikr* is closely related to the "prayer of the heart" of the Hesychasts of Eastern Christianity.

Since the goal of the mystical path is the transcending of the ego, it cannot be embarked upon without grace (*taufîq*); nor can it be followed without the help of a spiritual master (*shaikh* or *murshid*), who has himself traversed it, and without the spiritual influence or benediction which he confers on the disciple.

Islamic mysticism therefore rests on an unbroken spiritual succession or tradition which goes back, from master to master, to its origin in the Prophet Mohammed. This esoteric tradition runs in parallel to the exoteric or law-giving tradition destined for the collectivity as a whole. At its origins are to be found those counsels given by the Prophet to only some of his companions; for the mystical way presupposes extraordinary gifts and also a vocation, which are not given to everyone.

(from *Fez, City of Islam*)

The "Golden Chain" of Sufi Saints

This spiritual succession or tradition is often represented as a tree, whose roots are in revelation and whose twigs, leaves, and flowers correspond to the spiritual methods or "paths" (*turuq*), founded by the great spiritual masters. The branches of the tree represent the principal lines of succession, and are sometimes to be interpreted historically, sometimes only symbolically. On the root of the tree one can read the name *Allâh*; above it, on the trunk, is the name of the Archangel Gabriel (Jibrîl), who, in the Islamic perspective is the divine instrument of revelation, and above this is the name of Mohammed. At that point the trunk divides into two branches, which bear the names respectively of the first and fourth caliphs (Abû Bakr and 'Alî) since they were the first two mediators and masters of the Sufi tradition. These two branches divide into many twigs, which bear the names of the earliest Sufis such as Hasan al-Basrî, Habîb al-'Ajamî, and Sarî as-Saqatî. Following these come the names of the greatest spiritual masters of the first Islamic centuries such as Junaid, the great teacher of Sufi metaphysics, Dhû'n-Nûn al-Misrî, the lover, and Abû Yazîd al-Bistâmî, the absorbed in God. All of these masters lived in the Islamic east, although Sufi mysticism appeared as the "inner dimension" of Islam wherever Islam prevailed. From about the fourth Islamic century onwards (the 9th century A.D.), the blossoms of mysticism also appeared in the Far West, firstly in Spain and immediately thereafter in the Maghrib, where the name Abû Madyan stands at the origin of a whole segment of new twigs and leaves. This name appears at the top of the tree at about the same level as other famous names from which henceforth almost all subsequent spiritual orders spring. For it was at that time—the 12th century A.D.—that there appeared 'Abd al-Qâdir al-Jîlânî in the Near East (his influence was to sweep across the whole Islamic world), Mu'în ad-dîn Chishtî in North India and, a little later, Jalâl ad-Dîn Rumi in Asia Minor. From this time onwards, the Sufi tradition became organized in the form of

"The Indication of the Paths (or Brotherhoods)"

At the foot of the trunk is the Name *Allâh*. Above this are the names of Gabriel and Mohammed. The four large leaves at the top of the trunk bear the names of the first four Caliphs (Abû Bakr, Omar, Othman, 'Alî). The names of the different brotherhoods or *tarîqas* are inscribed on the leaves of the tree, but not in any particular order. Each *tarîqa* or brotherhood is named after its founding saint, through whom, by a chain (*silsila*) of previous saints, it can trace its spiritual descent back either to Abû Bakr or 'Alî, and thence to Mohammed.

On the five-pointed star, symbol of the five pillars of Islam (faith, prayer, almsgiving, fasting, pilgrimage), are the words "The Book [of God] and the Wont [of Mohammed]." (*Al Kitâb wa's-Sunna*).

spiritual orders or brotherhoods that took the name of their founders.

Abu Madyan Shu'aib was born in Seville of Arab parents in 1126. He was orphaned at a tender age, and was apprenticed to learn the weaver's craft. He fled from his brother's house, however, with a view to quenching his thirst for knowledge. After much wandering, he finally reached Fez, where he took instruction from several of the masters of "outward" and "inward" science, while he made a living from weaving.

Thanks to the scholar Abû'l-Hasan ibn Harzihim (Harazem in Moroccan dialect), Abû Madyan became acquainted not only with al-Ghazâlî's book *The Revivification of the Religious Sciences,* but also with the works of al-Muhâsibî and other Sufi masters.

Abû Madyan's beginnings on the spiritual path carry the seal of a vocation that is as inimitable as the beauty of virgin nature.

> At the beginning of my spiritual journey, (Abû Madyan himself relates), I attended the lectures of several spiritual masters. When I heard the explanation of a Koranic verse or a saying of the Prophet, I used to immerse myself in it completely. I would flee to an uninhabited place (on Mount Zalâgh) and apply myself to the exercises to which God had inspired me following my absorption in what I had heard. While I thus passed my time in solitude, a gazelle came to me and made friends with me. And when I encountered dogs in an out-lying village that belonged to Fez, they would crowd around me wagging their tails. One day, however, I met in Fez a man whom I had known in Andalusia and he greeted me warmly. I felt that I owed him hospitality and went to get a piece of cloth in which I had wrapped eight dirhams. I looked for the man in order to give him the money, but I could no longer find him and so I took the bundle with me to the lonely place to which it was my custom to withdraw. As I walked past the village, the dogs refused to come near me, and indeed prevented my passage through the village until someone came and called them off. When I reached my place of refuge, the gazelle ran past as usual, but when it scented me, it fled and seemed no longer to know me. I understood that it was all because of the money I was carrying, and I threw it away from me. The gazelle immediately became calm and was friendly with me as before. When I returned to Fez, I took the money with me, and gave it to the Andalusian as soon as I saw him. Then I again went past the village, on the way to my refuge, and the dogs ran up to me wagging their tails as before. Finally the gazelle appeared again, smelt my scent from head to foot, and nestled against me. And thus I lived for a certain time.
>
> ('Abd al-Hamîd Hamidû, *As-Sa'âdat al-abdîya li-Abî Madyan Shu'aib*)

Having returned from a pilgrimage to Mecca, Abû Madyan settled in Bujâya (Bougie) and soon became the center of a vast group of disciples. He was the living model of spiritual poverty (*faqr*), the meaning of which is expressed in the Koranic verse: "Ye are the poor (*fuqarâ*) in relation to God, and God is the Rich, to whom all praises are due." The expression *faqîr* (plural *fuqarâ*), which corresponds to the Persian expression *dervîsh,* became the term that was applied to those who followed the Sufi path. The following few words of Abû Madyan characterize his spiritual attitude:

> Trust in God until the remembrance of Him (*dhikr*) hath completely overpowered thee; for creatures are of no use to thee . . . Every spiritual truth (*haqîqa*) that extinguisheth not the traces of the creature, is no (real) truth. . . . Spiritual poverty is a pointer to the Divine Unity and a proof of detachment (*tafrîd*) from multiplicity. The meaning of poverty is simply this: that thou takest cognizance of nothing but Him.

Abû Madyan died in 1198. Two of Abû Madyan's indirect disciples were to have a lasting influence throughout the spiritual world of Islam. The first was the Arab Muhyi'd-Dîn ibn 'Arabî who was born in 1165 in Murcia, in Spain, and migrated via Fez, Bujâya, and Tunis to the Islamic east. Because of his unsurpassed metaphysical expositions, he was called "the greatest master" (*ash-Shaikh al-akbar*). The other was Abu'l-Hasan ash-Shâdhilî, the founder of the spiritual order (*tarîqa*) bearing his name.

Muhyi'd-Dîn ibn 'Arabî grew up in Seville, when Abû Madyan, as an old man, still lived in Bujaya. Ibn 'Arabi wrote as follows:

> Our master and imâm Abû Ya'qûb ben Yakhlaf al-Qûmî al-'Abbâsî—may God be pleased with him—had been a companion of Abû Madyan and had met several of the men of God in his country. He lived for a time in Egypt and married in Alexandria. . . . He was offered the governorship of Fez, but declined it. He possessed such a sure knowledge of the spiritual way that Abû Madyan, who was the founder and expounder of this way in the Maghrib, said of him: "Abu Ya'qûb is like a safe harbor for a ship." He was generous, much given to *dhikr* (the remembrance of God), and gave alms in secret. He honored the poor and humbled the rich.
>
> I was obedient to him and was educated by him—and what an education it was! He had a powerful spiritual will and for the most part followed the way of the *malâmatîya* (those who intentionally attract people's blame). Seldom was he seen without an expression of total concentration on his face. But whenever he saw a poor man, his face would light up with joy. . . .
>
> Whenever I sat before him, or before any other spiritual master, I would tremble like a leaf in the wind, my voice would desert me, and I would be unable to move my limbs. People would notice this. And if the master were indulgent to me, and sought to put me at my ease, it only increased my awe and reverence for him. This master had love for me, but concealed it by showing favor to others, and by displaying a distant manner towards me, com-

mending what others had to say while taking me to task. He went so far in this, that my companions who studied with me under his charge, began to think little of my spiritual gifts. And yet I alone of the whole group, as the master later said, reached the goal.

Of my many experiences with Abû Ya'qûb, the following is worthy of mention. I must first explain that at the time concerned I did not yet know the *Epistle* of al-Qushairî (a fundamental work of Islamic mysticism). I was unaware that anyone had written about this spiritual way, and did not even know what the expression *tasawwuf* (mysticism) meant.

One day the master mounted his horse, and bade me and one of my companions follow him to Muntabâr, a mountain that was about an hour's ride from Seville. As soon as the city gate was opened, my companion and I set out on foot. My companion carried in his hand a copy of Al-Qushairî's *Epistle*, of which as I have said, I knew nothing. We climbed the mountain and at the top we found our master, who, with a servant, had gone ahead of us. He tethered his horse, and we entered a mosque at the top of the mountain in order to pray. After the prayer, we sat with our backs towards the prayer-niche (*mihrâb*). The master handed me Qushairî's *Epistle* and told me to read from it. I was unable, however, to utter a single word. My awe of him was so great that the book even fell from my hands. Then he told my companion to read it, and he expounded on what was read until it was time for the afternoon prayer, which we said. Then the master said: "Let us now return to town." He mounted his horse, and I ran alongside him, holding on to his stirrup. Along the way he talked to me of the virtues and miracles of Abû Madyan. I was all ears, and forgot myself entirely, keeping my eyes fixed on his face the whole time. Suddenly he looked at me and smiled and, spurring his horse, made me run even more quickly in order to keep up with him. I succeeded in doing so. Finally, he stopped, and said to me: "Look and see what thou hast left behind thee." I looked back and saw that the way along which we had come was full of thorn bushes that reached as high as my tunic, and that the ground was also covered with thorns. He said: "Look at thy feet!" I looked at them and saw on them no trace of the thorns. "Look at thy garments!" On them too I found no trace. Then he said: "That comes from the grace engendered by our talking about Abû Madyan—may God be pleased with him—so persevere, my son, on the spiritual path!" Thereupon he spurred his horse and left me behind.

(Ibn 'Arabî, *Rûh al-Quds*, "The Epistle of Sanctity".)

At the beginning of the 13th century A.D., about twenty years after Muhyi'd-Dîn ibn 'Arabî had left Fez for the east, the Moroccan Abu'l-Hasan 'Alî ibn 'Abdallâh, a scion of the Hasanid branch of the Fatimids, who later achieved fame under the name of Abû'l-Hasan ash-Shâdhilî, also migrated to the east in order to seek the spiritual pole of his time. In Baghdad, a Sufi informed him that this pole was to be found in his own homeland, on Mount al-'Alam in the Rif mountains. He therefore returned home, and found in the place described a disciple of Abû Madyan, namely the spiritual master 'Abd as-Salâm ibn Mashîsh:

> As I approached his place of refuge, which was a cave near the top of the mountain, I made a halt at a spring which gushed forth a little beneath it. I washed myself with the intention of casting off all my previous knowledge and actions, then, as one completely poor, I made my way up to the cave. He came out towards me, and when he saw me, he said: "Welcome, 'Alî, son of Abdallâh, son of 'Abd al-Jabbâr . . ." and he named all my ancestors right back to the Prophet, whom God bless and greet. Then he said: "O, 'Alî, thou comest up to me here as one poor in knowing and doing in order to seek from me the riches of this world and the next." I was smitten with fear out of awe for him. Then I remained with him for a number of days, until God opened my inward eye and I beheld wonders and things that far exceeded the ordinary realm, and I experienced the goodness of God's grace. . . . One day, as I sat by my master, I said inwardly to myself: "Who knows, perhaps my master knows the Supreme Name of God." At that moment the young son of the master spoke from the depths of the cave: "O Abû'l-Hasan, it is not a question of knowing the Supreme Name of God, it is a question of being the Supreme Name." Thereupon the Shaikh said: "My young son has seen through thee and recognized thee!"

(Al-Madanî, The Holy Lights of the Shâdhilî Tarîqa)

'Abd as-Salâm ibn Mashîsh died in 1228. His tomb on Mount al-'Alam is a place of pilgrimage to this day. Only one text has come down to us from Ibn Mashîsh, a metaphysical paraphrase of a widely known prayer, in which the believer calls on God to bless the Prophet as if to thank him for having received Islam through him. Ibn Mashîsh sees in the historical Mohammed an expression of the one Spirit, from which all revelation comes, and which is the eternal mediator between the ungraspable Godhead and the world. This is the Logos, the first manifestation of God and, as such, His universal symbol as well as His highest veil. By the very fact that in this way the Absolute reveals itself in a relative and multiple fashion, it also conceals itself. This eternal mediator is called the "Mohammedan Spirit" (*ar-Rûh al-Muhammadî*), not because it is embodied only in Mohammed—for all God's messengers and prophets manifest it— but because in the Islamic perspective Mohammed is its most immediate expression. Divine Truth, according to the Sufis, is in itself unlimited and inexhaustible, so that every religious form in which it deigns to clothe itself for the salvation of men can be no more than one possible form amongst others.

Sufi mysticism is predominantly founded on gnosis, and this finds expression in the saying of Abû'l-Hasan ash-Shâdhilî: "Know, and be as thou wilt", he once said, and meant by this that the man who has realized what he is before God can do nothing else but act rightly.

He taught his disciples to look on the world with the eye of eternity: "Attribute the actions of creatures to God as Agent; this will bring no harm to thee; whereas it will bring harm to thee if thou regardest creatures as the authors of their actions." The spiritual attitude corresponding to this angle of vision is that of *vacare Deo*, unconditional self-abandonment to God:

> The servant will not attain to God as long as he harbors any desire or ulterior motive. If thou wouldst please God, renounce thyself and thine environment and thy power over it. But this abandonment is not mere inaction: each moment is a sword, if thou cuttest not with it, it will cut thee (i.e. cause that moment to be lost for the remembrance of God).
>
> (Al-Madanî, *The Holy Lights of the Shâdhilî Tarîqa*)

Abû'l-Hasan ash-Shâdhilî inaugurated a spiritual method for the acquiring of spiritual poverty and for the practicing of it in the midst of worldly cares. Amongst the disciples that came to him during his lifelong peregrination from the Islamic West to the Islamic East, there were rich and poor, educated and uneducated, government ministers and day laborers.

His first successor was Abû'l-'Abbâs al-Mursî, who lived in Egypt, and the one after that was the famous Ahmad ibn 'Atâ'illâh of Alexandria, whose "Spiritual Aphorisms" (*Hikam*) became the breviary of almost everyone who followed the Sufi path, whether in the Far West (Morocco) or the Far East (Java and Sumatra). Ibn 'Atâ'illâh died in 1309.

In addition to the Shâdhilî line of spiritual masters who—like Ahmad az-Zarrûq al-Barnûssî, born in Fez in 1441 and died in Tripoli in 1493—expounded Sufi doctrine with logical precision, there were always spiritual personalities who broke every rational framework, as if they incorporated some secret essence of the doctrine which transcended ordinary reason. One such was the master 'Alî as-Sanhâjî, who lived in Fez in the first half of the 16th century.

The Shaikh 'Alî as-Sanhâjî was known as "the roamer", which can be understood in either a physical or a spiritual sense. For the people of Fez, his holiness was as manifest as the morning star. He was a Fool of God in the style of the *Malâmatîyya* (those who intentionally draw people's criticism on themselves) and was constantly in the state of Divine attraction. He possessed neither home nor family. With his capacity for revealing what is hidden he could entirely see through those whom he met. He cared for neither praise nor blame. Thus he sometimes entered the houses of the Merinids, where women and children would crowd around him and kiss his hands and feet, without paying attention to anyone. They heaped on him costly clothes and jewelry, and the Sultan himself gave him garments of distinction. But he would go out and give away everything that he had received, and, in his fine garments, he would brush past the shops of oil merchants, so that they would become spotted with oil. During his constant roaming he increasingly invoked the name Allâh. No one knew where he lived. When he died, people swarmed to his funeral, and divided amongst themselves the planks from his bier, his prayer mat, and his clothes. He died in the year of the Hijra 950 (1542-43 A.D.) and was buried outside the Futûh gate. Even the Sultan and the scholars were present at his burial.

On one occasion, a Fez merchant, as he was entering the Qarawiyyîn mosque for the morning prayer, saw 'Ali as-Sanhâjî sitting on the threshold of the mosque eating cucumbers. It was market day (Thursday) and, as he said his prayer, the merchant considered how much he would offer for a donkey that he wished to buy. When he came out of the mosque, he saw 'Ali as-Sanhâjî still sitting on the threshold eating cucumbers. The merchant thought to himself: "He would do better if, instead of eating cucumbers, he would say the morning prayer," whereupon the Shaikh cried out to him: "Better a cucumber-breakfast than a donkey-prayer!"

(al-Kattânî, *Salwât al-Anfâs*)

Every great master who has formulated the traditional Sufi path in a particular way thereby originated a spiritual "path" or *tarîqa* for a particular category of human beings. A Sufi proverb says: "The ways to God are as numerous as the souls of men." Nevertheless there are particular categories of spiritual temperament and it is to these that the various "paths" correspond.

Towards the end of the 15th century and beginning of the 16th, Muhammad Abû 'Abdallâh al-Jazûlî, a man from the far south of Morocco, founded a branch of the Shâdhilî order. Al-Jazûlî is famous throughout Morocco to this day for his work "The Proofs of Goodness" (*Dalâ'il al-khairât*), a collection of blessings on the Prophet in the form of a litany in which Mohammed, the receptacle

The Divine Name (*Allâh*) surrounded by verses from the Koran.

of revelation, appears as the summation of all the positive—and God-reflecting—aspects of creation.

From the spiritual posterity of al-Jazûlî, several spiritual orders emerged which exist in Morocco to this day. The most popular is undoubtedly the one founded in Meknes towards the end of the 16th century by the Muhammad ibn 'Isâ al-Mukhtârî. It is related of this *sharîf* (descendant of the Prophet Mohammed) that he used his inherited wealth to recruit poor people who, for a daily wage, would invoke and praise God to the beating of drums. The Sultan, who found he was running short of laborers, forbade the unusual saint to continue this practice; but the saint simply moved with his followers to a cemetery and let it be said to the Sultan: "Thou art the ruler of the living, but not of the dead; over them thou hast no authority."

The link with the Islamic east was maintained by the pilgrims who traveled to Mecca. And thus it occurred that eastern spiritual orders like the Qadirîya, the Khalwatîya, and the Naqshbandîya spread to the Maghrib. In the middle of the 18th century, a Fez man, from the noble family of the Saqallî, brought the Naqshbandî spiritual method from Egypt to Fez.

Towards the end of the 18th century, Mulay Ahmad at-Tîjânî, who had studied in Fez and then lived for a long time in the east where he had contacts with the Khalwatîya, founded a new order which henceforth was to bear his name. His doctrine and his method held the balance between the Sufi tradition and the generally accepted theology. For this reason his order always lived on the best terms with the ruling house. The principal center of the order is 'Ayn Mâdî in the south of Algeria, but the sepulchral mosque of the founder is in Fez, in the al-Blida district, where it is easily recognizable by its richly decorated doorway. Inside, it is completely covered with blue and green arabesque mosaics. For a long time the order dominated the caravan routes through southern Algeria to the Sudan. It is well represented in Black Africa, and one can often meet Sudanese Muslims who have come to Fez to visit the tomb of the founder of the order.

The pure Shâdhilî tradition, which is representative of the earliest form of Sufism, was revivified at the end of the 18th century and the beginning of the 19th century by Mulay al-'Arabî ad-Darqâwî. His spiritual radiance extended well beyond the Maghrib. He was descended from a Hasanid family that lived amongst the Banû Zerwâl, in the hills to the north-east of Fez. As a young man he studied in Fez, and it was here too that he met his spiritual master, the Idrisid 'Alî al-Jamal, who roughly rebuffed him several times before accepting him as his disciple. In one of his letters, Mulay al-'Arabî tells how his master tested him by ordering him, a young scholar of noble lineage, to carry a load of fresh fruit through the town:

> The first lesson that my master gave me was as follows: he ordered me to carry two baskets full of fresh fruit through the town. I carried them in my hands, and did not wish, as the others told me, to put them on my shoulders, for that was unwelcome to me, and constricted my soul, so that it became agitated and fearful, and grieved beyond measure, till I almost began to weep. And, by God, I still had to weep for all the shame, humiliation, and scorn that I had to undergo as a result! Never before had my soul had to suffer such a thing, so I was not conscious of its pride and cowardice. I had not known whether it was proud or not, since no professor, amongst all those that I had frequented, had ever taught me about my soul. While I was in this state, my master, who perceived my pride and my inner distress, came up to me, took the two baskets from my hands, and placed them on my shoulders with the

words: "Distinguish thus between good and evil." Thereby he opened the door for me and led me on the right way, for I learned to discriminate between the proud and the humble, the good and the bad, the wise and the foolish, the orthodox and the heretical, between those who know and translate their knowledge into deeds, and those who do not. From that moment no orthodox person ever overpowered me with his orthodoxy, no heretic with his heresy, no scholar with his knowledge, no pious man with his piety, and no fasting man with his asceticism. For my master, may God have mercy on him, had taught me to distinguish truth from vanity, and wheat from chaff.

(Mulay ad-Darqâwî, *Rasâ'il,* "Letters")

Later his master, 'Alî al-Jamal, entrusted Mulay al-'Arabî ad-Darqâwî with the task of teaching and revivifying the Shâdhilî spiritual method, which had become almost completely forgotten. The following is an extract from his celebrated Letters of Spiritual Counsel (See *Letters of a Sufi Master,* translated by Titus Burckhardt.):

The extraordinary Shâdhilî way, on which our master journeyed—may God be pleased with him—is what you have deviated from. Whether he bequeathed this way to you or not, what does it matter? For you now follow another way. And if you should ask me, how is this so? Then I would answer: his way consisted in climbing down and not in climbing up, but your way consists in climbing up and not in climbing down. His way was outwardly humiliation and inwardly ascension, whereas your way is outwardly ascension and inwardly descent. One can also say that his way was outwardly a way of rigor and discipline, and inwardly a way of grace and beauty, whereas your way, like that of most people, is beautiful on the outside and servitude on the inside. And may God forbid that the way of the elect be like that of the multitude! It is likewise not the business of those who are spiritually aware to content themselves with the recitation of litanies, and you do nothing else but that. Moreover, one should have one sole spiritual master and not several, as you do. That is what I have perceived of your situation, and I therefore suspect that your little barque has no wind in its sails. . . .

(Mulay ad-Darqâwî, *Rasâ'il,* "Letters")

His instruction went straight to the heart of the matter, and in this way illumined both learned and unlearned, scholars and Bedouins. The following are further extracts from his letters, which his disciples collected and later, towards the beginning of the 19th century, published in a lithographed edition in Fez.

The *fuqarâ* of ancient times sought only for what could kill their souls (*nufûs* plural of *nafs*) and bring life to their hearts, whereas we do just the opposite. We seek after that which kills our hearts and enlivens our souls. They strove only to become free of their passions and dethrone their ego; but, for us, what we long for is the satisfaction of our sensual desires and the glorification of our ego, and thus we have turned our backs to the door and our faces to the wall. I say this to you only because I have seen the favors which God lavishes on him who kills his soul and enlivens his heart. Most certainly we are satisfied with less, but only the ignorant are satisfied with not arriving at the end of the journey.

I asked myself whether there could be something else, apart from our passions and our egoism, which cuts us off from the divine gifts, and as a third hindrance I found the lack of spiritual longing. For intuition is generally given only to him whose heart is pierced by an intense longing and a strong desire to contemplate the Essence of his Lord. Intuitions of the Divine Essence flow into such a man until he is extinguished in that Essence and thus freed from the illusion of any reality other that It, for this is the direction in which the Divine Essence leads those whose gaze is continually fixed upon It. On the contrary, he who aspires exclusively to theoretical knowledge, or to outward action, does not receive intuition upon intuition; he would not rejoice in it if he did, since his wish is aimed at something other than the Divine Essence, and God (may He be exalted) favors each one according to the measure of his aspiration. Certainly, every man participates in the Spirit, just as the ocean has waves, but sensual experience entirely takes possession of most men; it seizes hold of their hearts and limbs and does not allow them to open to the Spirit, because sensuality is the opposite of spirituality and opposites do not meet.

We see, besides, that the spiritual aim is reached neither by many works, nor by few, but by Grace alone. As the saint Ibn 'Atâ'illâh says in his Aphorisms (*Hikam*): "If you were destined to reach Him only after the destruction of your faults and the abandonment of all your claims, you would never reach Him. But when He wishes to bring you back towards Him, He absorbs your quality into His and your attributes into His and thus brings you back by means of what comes to you from Him, not by means of what comes to Him from you."

One of the effects of Divine Bounty, Grace, and Generosity is that one finds the master who can grant spiritual education; without Divine Grace no one would find or recognize him, since, according to the saying of the saint Abû'l-'Abbâs al-Mursî (may God be pleased with him): "It is more difficult to know a saint than to know God." Again, in the *Hikam* of Ibn 'Atâ'illâh, it is said: "Exalted be He who makes His saints known only in order to make Himself known and who leads towards them those whom He wishes to lead towards Himself."

The heart of man cannot attach itself to the Divine Essence unless his ego has been effaced, extinguished, destroyed, annihilated. . . . As the saint Abû Madyan has said: "Whoever does not die, does not see God." All the masters of our way have taught the same. And take care that you do not think that it is the things of the body and the soul that veil God from us. By God, what veils Him is nothing other than illusion, and illusion is vain. As the saint Ibn 'Ata'illâh has said: "God did not veil Himself from thee by some reality coexisting with Him, since there is no reality other than He. What veils Him from thee is naught but the illusion that something outside Him could possess any reality."

Know that the *faqîr* can only kill his soul when he has been able to see its form, and he will only see its form when he has separated himself from the world, from his companions, from his friends, and from his habits.

One *faqîr* said to me: "My wife has got the better of me," to which I replied: "It is not she, but your own soul that has got the better of you; we have no other enemy; if thou couldst dominate thy soul, thou wouldst dominate the whole world—not merely your wife."

The soul is something immense; it is the whole cosmos since it is a copy of it. Everything that is in the cosmos is in the soul and everything that is in the soul is in the cosmos. Therefore, whoever masters his soul masters the world, and whoever is mastered by his soul is mastered by the world.

Spiritual intuition is very subtle. It can only be fixed spatially by concrete symbols and temporally by interior prayer (*dhikr*), holy company, and the breaking of habits. . . .

All things are hidden in their opposites—gain in loss, gift in refusal, honor in humiliation, wealth in poverty, strength in weakness, abundance in restriction, rising up in falling down, life in death, victory in defeat, power in powerlessness, and so on. Therefore, if a man wish to find, let him be content to lose; if he wish a gift, let him be content with refusal; he who desires honor must accept humiliation, and he who desires wealth must be satisfied with poverty; let him who wishes to be strong be content to be weak; let him who wishes abundance be resigned to restriction; he who wishes to be raised up must allow himself to be cast down; he who desires life must accept death; he who wishes to conquer must be content with impotence.

(Mulay ad-Darqâwî, *Rasâ'il, Letters*)

Mulay al-'Arabî ad-Darqâwî had a large number of disciples in Fez, but he finally left the city, and founded a hermitage at Bu Berih, a remote spot in the Banû Zerwâl hills, between Fez and the Rif mountains. There he died in 1823, when several of his disciples were already active as masters in different parts of the Maghrib.

A great Shâdhilî master in the first part of the 20th century was the Algerian Shaikh Ahmad ibn Mustafâ al-'Alawî, who had many disciples in Morocco, as well as in the Near East, Southern Arabia, India, and Java.

Many true masters withdrew entirely from public life. Thus Mulay 'Alî remained silent, and Mulay as-Siddîq, hid himself under the mask of a fool. Another important master of that time, Muhammad at-Tâdilî, who lived at Magazan but often came to Fez, refrained from founding a *zawiya,* but frequented circles of *fuqarâ* here and there in order to counteract the spiritual laziness that had already become apparent.

Muhammad at-Tâdilî used to scold the members of the Sufi orders in Fez: "You imagine", he would say to them, "that you have attained something on the spiritual way, because you perform many exercises. But as long as you cannot speak about spiritual truths spontaneously and with a full heart, you have tasted nothing." And on another occasion he said: "Most of these people spend their lives in mosques and *zawiyas* sitting beside the Divine bride (the Truth, *al-haqîqa*), but alas they sit with her back to back!"

Once, when he was staying in the house of a Fez merchant, where I was also a guest, someone asked him what was the meaning of the Koranic verse: "He created the two seas that meet together, and between them is an isthmus which they do not overpass." He immediately interpreted the verse as an image of the relationship between two degrees of reality: of one of the two seas, the Koran says that it is sweet and pleasant to taste, and of the other, that it is salty and bitter. The purity and sweetness indicate a higher level of reality, while the bitterness indicates a relatively lower level, one more strongly mixed with "nothingness". The isthmus (*barzakh*) between the two seas or degrees of reality separates them, but at the same time unites them, like the narrow neck of an hourglass or like a lens that concentrates the sun's rays and then transmits them again, but inverted. Whenever two domains of reality meet there is an isthmus of this kind. Applied to man, the sweet sea means the pure Intellect or Spirit (*Rûh*), which in itself is undivided and capable of direct knowledge; while the bitter sea is the psyche (*nafs*), which is troubled and dissipated by passions. The isthmus is the Heart (*Qalb*). The psyche cannot "overpass" the threshold of the Heart. Bound as it is to imaginings and tendencies, the psyche cannot lay hold on the Spirit that transcends all forms, and in this sense the isthmus divides the two seas. But the Spirit or Intellect is able, not to remove the isthmus, but, through the Heart, to act upon the psyche. It confers its light on the psyche, just as the physical heart confers life on the body. The heart opens itself to this all-radiant light by means of the remembrance of God. Without this, the spiritual pulse becomes weak and the soul sinks into opaqueness. . . . Taking this interpretation as his starting-point, Shaikh Tâdilî expounded the whole ladder of existence up to the "isthmus" between the created and the Uncreated, and then down again to the various isthmuses between individual faculties of the soul and the external world.

When he began, it was already late evening; the light of morning was visible when he concluded his discourse—which had frequently been interspersed by long silences. His listeners, however, had the impression that it had only lasted for a moment.

Once a year, on Mulay al-'Arabî's birthday, members of his order make a pilgrimage to his grave, and that of his son and successor, Mulay at-Tayyib, in the hills to the north of Fez. On one such occasion, I joined a group of pilgrims who made their way on foot northwards up the inhospitable hillside over-grown with dark bushes, past creviced slopes from which sand constantly slid down to the depths below. They walked in single file along the crest of the hills, with staffs in their hands and their white burnouses thrown back over their shoulders. As they came closer to their destination, they could see on other hills similar white-clad groups making their way upwards in single file and could hear their half-plaintive, half-jubilant song, consisting of the words of the attestation of faith: "There is no divinity other than God!"

The pilgrims continued their way through the timeless landscape, as if they already walked on the other side of death, or along the partition separating the two worlds, and their song rose, harsh and clear, like a song of victory over death.

At the head of the procession went a few old men with wrinkled and weathered features. With their turbans and white face-veils, they looked as if they were wrapped up like mummies. As I looked up at the white-clad, half-bent figures climbing the red hill ahead of me, they made me think of souls ascending the mount of Purgatory.

Towards evening, a wide valley opened up in front of us, where, in a clearing in the oak forest, we could see a few bright houses of whitewashed mud, surrounded by fields of wheat. This was the hermitage of Mulay at-Tayyib, which had now grown into a village. Opposite, on a hillock between two oaks, rose the grey-white cupola that covered the tomb of the master. As with countless other saints' tombs in Islam, the hemispherical dome, slightly raised at the top, rested on a simple square room. Square and circle, cube and sphere—here they were so perfectly matched, that they reconciled heaven and earth and, by their harmony, charmed and blessed surrounding nature.

As we came nearer, the dome of the saint's tomb rose like a full moon over the dark oaks and against the green-gold evening sky. Swallows darted and twittered around the starkly plain building, on which the lime was crumbling with age. The heavy cedar door was open. The inside was empty except for a black oak shrine above the grave. A few inscriptions were carved in the wood, including the Koranic verses: "Think not that those who have been killed in the way of God are dead; no, they are alive. . . . Those who believe, and whose hearts are at rest in the remembrance of God. Verily in the remembrance of God do hearts find rest. . . . No fear oppresses them and no care."

The dervishes, who themselves were disciples of disciples of the master buried here, walked into the wooden shrine, touched it with their hands, and prayed softly. Amongst them were townsmen and countrymen, Arabs and Berbers, men and women. Led by an elderly woman, a group of Berber women from the mountains, unveiled and carrying large wooden rosaries, approached the tomb. They were enshrouded in woollen blankets with colored fringes, and with their yellowish faces, they reminded me of American Indians. The faces of all the pilgrims, whether young or old, sophisticated townsmen or simple country people, displayed the same gentle radiance.

In the house in which Mulay at-Tayyib had once lived, his son Mulay 'Alî awaited us. Inside the long rooms made of sun-dried brick and arranged in a semi-circle which constituted the farmyard, we were encompassed in that simple clarity that had often enchanted me in Moroccan peasant houses: the whitewashed and slightly curved walls, the floors of flattened earth, the light structure of the ceiling; rafters of knotty wood forming a long gable that ran above our heads like the upturned hull of a boat. One felt that one had found refuge, as if in a boat for living in, and that one was surrounded by peace. There was nothing in the room that could distract one's mind; it had almost no furniture, only a mat, an amphora with drinking water which stood in a recess in the floor, a candlestick, and a leather hassock. In surroundings such as these, human gestures became meaningful and full of dignity.

"A house for the wild men of the mountains," said Mulay 'Alî laughing,

> but it is all one needs. This water comes from a pure spring that my father dug out a little down the hillside. On the few slopes that you see around us, and in another valley that we made arable, we grew our bread. Everything else is either pasture for goats, or wilderness. When my father constructed this room, in order to live with his family in solitude, the place was still completely surrounded by woods. At night the wild boar and the lynx would rub against the walls. Then, as more and more disciples and followers continued to arrive, the clearing, the village, and the arable land slowly began to develop. The influence of my forefathers continued to grow. Lower in the valley more villages were founded, and the whole tribe of mountain-dwellers from all around followed the instruction that emanated from here.

In the morning of the next day the dervishes gathered in a clearing in the woods near the tomb. The clearing was on a piece of raised ground, and on it one was at the level of the surrounding tree-tops. There must have been a thousand men there, and, holding hands, they formed several concentric circles. In the middle, a space the size of a threshing floor contained a group of singers. The men in the circles intoned the name of God, in an increasingly rapid rhythm, while their bodies moved up and down. The enunciation of the Divine Name slowly changed into a deep breathing, and finally into a kind of death-rattle.

The singers, with voices as bright as flutes, sang an elegy to divine knowledge, personified as a woman, Lailâ, that was written by Shaikh Muhammad al-Harrâq, a disciple of Mulay al-'Arabî:

> Thou seekest Lailâ. Yet she manifesteth herself within thee.
> Thou deemest her to be elsewhere, but elsewhere existeth not.
> That is a madness, well-known to lovers.
> So be on your guard, for otherness is the epitome of separation.
> Seest thou not, how her beauty enfoldeth thee.
> She disappeareth only if thou refusest part of thee.
> Come close to me, thou sayst to her, to her who is thine All.
> And when she loveth thee, she leadeth thee to thyself.
> Bliss ineffable is the meeting with her.
> No one reacheth her, who knoweth not essence without form.
> I have dissimulated about her,
> After I had truly displayed her through my veil.
> I hid her from myself, with the garment of mine own existence,
> And, out of jealousy, I hid her from the envier.
> Dazzling beauty! Should the light of thy countenance
> Touch the eyes of a blind man, he would see each particle of dust.

She is adorned with every grace pertaining unto beauty.
And wherever she appeareth, she is desired by those who love.
(Muhammad al-Harrâq, *Diwân*)

The dancers' eyes were closed, their bodies weightless. Their faces seemed to be turned inwards, like the faces of the dying. Their souls seemed already to have departed from their bodies. Indeed it seemed as if their bodies had been grasped by their souls, and lifted powerfully upwards. The breathing of all present was like one single breath, and became more and more rapid, so that finally air, earth, and surrounding trees all seemed to join in the same rhythm. The space between heaven and earth on which the dancers stood had become like a bellows. The corporeal world seemed to have been absorbed by the world of the soul, whose reality now began to break through, just as when the unity of the soul suddenly grips the breath of a dying man, the pulse of a lover, or the body of a butterfly awakening into life.

Above the rhythmical breathing, the song rang out and floated, almost motionlessly, through the air, like a falcon planing, almost motionlessly, above his prey. Now and again a word from the song would pierce one particular heart, and the dancer, whose heart had been struck by the lightning of spiritual realization, fell unconscious to the ground. An old man, who walked amongst the dancers, would cover him with a burnous.

Accompanied by Mulay 'Alî, we went further up the mountainside, and saw, from above, the circle of dancing men. "Do you think these dervishes have lost their reason?" he asked me smiling. "What they do is good," he went on, "for it derives from a saying of the Prophet: 'Whoever does not leap with joy when he hears the name of his friend, does not really have a friend'." Then he added earnestly: "But how easily the senses are misled and the intention deflected. All that you have seen is not yet the way that leads to the Knowledge of God, as the Sufi masters taught it!" "What then is this way?" I asked. He pointed with his hand towards the blinding sun: "It is like that", he said, "and it is also like Christ's injunction to offer the left cheek to him who strikes you on the right."

(from *Fez, City of Islam*)

The Spiritual Life: Hindu

Bathing in the Ganges

For the Hindus, the water of life finds embodiment in the Ganges which, from its source in the Himalayas, the mountains of the Gods, irrigates the largest and most populous plains of India. Its water is held to be pure from beginning to end, and in fact it is preserved from all pollution by the fine sand which it drags along with it. Whoever, with repentant mind, bathes in the Ganges, is freed from all his sins: inner purification here finds its symbolic support in the outward purification that comes from the water of the sacred river. It is as if the purifying water came from Heaven, for its origin in the eternal ice of the roof of the world is like a symbol of the heavenly origin of divine grace which, as "living water", springs from timeless and immutable Peace. Here, as in the similar rites of other religions and peoples, the correspondence of water and soul helps the latter to purify itself or, more exactly, to find anew its own—originally pure—essence. In this process, the symbol prepares the way for grace.

(from "The Symbolism of Water", in *Mirror of the Intellect*)

Woman as the Symbol *par excellence* of Beauty

A central support of spirituality in Hinduism

In its exaltation of feminine beauty, Hindu art far surpasses Greek art, whose spiritual ideal, progressively reduced to a purely human ideal, is *cosmos* as opposed to the indefinity of *chaos*, and therefore the beauty of the male body, with its clearly articulated proportions; the supple and undivided beauty of the female body, its richness both simple and complex, like that of the sea, is absent from Greek art, at least on the intellectual level. Hellenism remains closed to the affirmation of the Infinite, which it confuses with the indefinite. Lacking the conception of the transcendent Infinite, it likewise fails to perceive it at the "prakritic" (i.e. "substantial", as opposed to "essential") level, in other words, as the inexhaustible ocean of forms. It is not until the period of its decadence that Greek art becomes open to the "irrational" beauty of the feminine body, but this removes it from its own *ethos*. In Hindu art, on the other

279

hand, the feminine body appears as a spontaneous and innocent manifestation of universal rhythm, like a wave of the primordial ocean or a flower from the tree of the world.

Something of this innocent beauty also surrounds the images of sexual union (*maithuna*) which adorn Hindu temples.

In their deepest meaning, they express the state of spiritual union, the fusion of subject and object, of inward and outward, in mystical rapture (*samâdhi*). They also symbolize the complementarism of the cosmic poles, active and passive, thus effacing the passional aspect of these images in a universal vision.

In this way Hindu sculpture, effortlessly and without loss of spiritual unity, assimilates means which, in other hands, would lead to naturalism. It transmutes even sensuality, by saturating it with a spiritual awareness that is expressed in the plastic tension of the surfaces; like those of a bell, they seem to be made only to produce a pure sound.

Furthermore, bodily consciousness, which is directly reflected in figural sculpture, is transmuted by the sacred dance.

(from *Sacred Art in East and West*)

The Body as "Temple" of the Holy Spirit: The Temple as "Body" of the Holy Spirit

A symbolic key to Hindu spirituality

The *Vâstu-Purusha-mandala*, the outline of which is derived from the rite of orientation, is subdivided into a number of lesser squares; they form a network within which the foundations of the building are laid out. The analogy between the cosmos and the plan of the temple is carried right through into the plan of the internal arrangements, in which each lesser square corresponds to one of the phases of the great cosmic cycles and to the *deva* who rules over it. Only the central area, consisting of one or several lesser squares, is symbolically situated outside the cosmic order: it is the *Brahmâsthana*, the place where *Brahmâ* dwells. Over this central area the "chamber of the embryo" (*Garbhagriha*) is erected, in the form of a cube; it will hold the symbol of the Divinity to whom the temple is consecrated.

Two types of the *Vâstu-Purusha-mandala* are especially favored for the symbolical plan of the temple, one with 64 lesser squares and one with 81. It should be noted that the numbers 64 and 81 are sub-multiples of the fundamental cyclical number 25920, the number of years comprised in a complete precession of the equinoxes: 64 x 81 x 5 = 25920. The factor 5 corresponds to the cycle of five lunar-solar years (*samvatsara*). The precession of the equinoxes is the ultimate measure of the cosmos, and in itself it is only measurable in terms of lesser cycles. Each of these *mandalas* thus represents an "abbreviation" of the universe conceived as the "sum" of all the cosmic cycles.[11] The rites accompanying the erection of the tree for the Sun Dance show striking analogies with the Hindu rites connected with the erection of the sacrificial post, which is also the axis of the world and the cosmic tree.

The central "field" of the *mandala* represents the *Brahmâsthana,* the "station" of *Brahmâ;* in the *mandala* of 64 squares it occupies four central squares, in the *mandala* of 81 squares, nine. In this field is erected the chamber of the center, which houses the symbol of the titular divinity of the temple and is analogous to the "golden embryo" (*Hiranyagarbha*), the luminous germ of the cosmos.

Regarded as a cosmological diagram, the *Vâstu-Purusha-mandala* fixes and co-ordinates the cycles of the sun and of the moon;[12] the divergent rhythms of these two fundamental cycles could be said to reflect the infinitely varied theme of becoming. In a certain sense, the world endures for as long as the sun and the moon, the "male" and the "female", are not united; that is to say, for as long as their respective cycles do not coincide. The two types of *mandala* are like two complementary figurations of the resolution of the two cycles into a single timeless order. Through this cosmological aspect the *Vâstu-Purusha-mandala* reflects the hierarchy of the divine functions. The various "aspects" of Being, as well as the diverse functions of the Universal Spirit, the cosmic manifestation of Being, can indeed be

---

11. In the solstitial rite of the Sun Dance, the Arapaho Indians build a great lodge, in the middle of which stands the sacred tree, representing the axis of the world. The lodge is constructed of twenty-eight pillars erected in a circle, and sustaining the rafters of the roof which meet the tree in the center. On the other hand the lodge of the Crow Indians is open above, while the space surrounding the central tree is divided into twelve sections in which the dancers take their places. In both cases the form of the sanctuary is related to two cycles, that of the sun, and that of the moon. In the first case the lunar cycle is represented by the twenty-eight pillars of the enclosure, corresponding to the twenty-eight lunar mansions; in the second case it is represented by the twelve months.

12. It is noteworthy that the traditional diagram of the horoscope, representing the ecliptic, is also square.

conceived as so many directions comprised in the totality of space, or as so many "facets" of a regular polygon, their symmetry betraying the unity of their common principle. That is why the *Vâstu-Purusha-mandala* is also the seal of *Virâj*, the cosmic intelligence issuing from the supreme *Purusha*.[13]

An effective transformation of the cosmic cycles, or more precisely of the celestial movements, into crystalline form is also found in the symbolism of the sacred city. The mandala *par excellence* containing 64 squares is compared with the unconquerable city of the gods (*Ayodhyâ*) which is described in the *Râmayâna* as a square with eight compartments on each side. This city holds in its center the abode of God (*Brahmapura*), just as the plan of the temple contains the *Brahmâsthana*. In Christianity also, the changeless and celestial synthesis of the cosmos is symbolized as a city, the Heavenly Jerusalem; its bounds are held up by twelve pillars and are square, and in its center dwells the Divine Lamb.[14] According to the Fathers of the Church, the Heavenly Jerusalem is the prototype of the Christian temple.[15] The *mandala* of 8 x 8 squares corresponds to a chess-board. The game of chess, which comes from India, where it is played by the noble and warrior castes, is an application of the symbolism inherent in the *Vâstu-Purusha-mandala* (see "Chess as the Symbol of Rulership" on p. 168).

We have seen that the construction of a temple is the expression of a cosmology. It carries as well an "alchemical" significance, in so far as it is the support of an inward realization in the artist himself.

---

13. The directions of space correspond very naturally to the Divine Aspects or Qualities, for they are the result of the polarization with respect to a given center of a space that as such is limitless and undifferentiated. The center chosen then corresponds to the "germ" of the world. It may be observed in passing that the "magic square", which serves to "coagulate" subtle forces for the performance of a predetermined operation, is a distant derivative of the *Vâstu-Purusha-mandala*.
14. Attention must be called in passing to the astonishing phonetic and semantic analogy between, on the one hand, *agnus* and *ignis,* and on the other, *ignis* and *Agni*; and in addition, to the analogy between the English word "ram" and the *Ram,* whose name in Hindu symbolism is a sacred word corresponding to fire, and is represented as a ram.
15. The altar then corresponds to the center of the Heavenly Jerusalem, the center occupied by the Lamb. The terrestrial symbol of *Purusha*, the *Vâstu-Purusha-mandala,* is at the same time the plan of the temple, of the city, and of the palace in which a consecrated king lives. It also defines the place of the throne, around which are represented, in certain cases, the 32 gods (*Padadevatâs*), acolytes of *Indra,* who denote the 4 x 8 directions of space.

This "alchemical" significance first becomes apparent in the rite of orientation, which may be compared to a procedure of "crystalliza-tion" or of "coagulation". The indefinite cycle of the heavens is "fixed" or "coagulated" in the fundamental square, with the cross of the cardinal axes as connecting link; the cross thus plays the part of a crystallizing principle. If the world, carried onwards by the indef-inite cyclical movement of the heavens, is in a sense analogous to the soul in its state of passivity and unconscious of its own essential reality, the discriminating cross is then the spirit, or more exactly the spiritual act, and the square is the body "transmuted" by this operation and henceforth the receptacle and the vehicle of a new and superior consciousness. The body is then the alchemical "salt" that unites the active and the passive, the spirit and the soul.

From another point of view the "alchemical" significance of the construction of the temple springs from the symbolism of *Purusha* incorporated in the building and considered in this case in its microcosmic aspect. This aspect is based more particularly on the *mandala* of 81 squares, which corresponds to the subtle body of *Purusha*, represented therein as a man lying face downwards[16] with his head towards the East. In a general way, discounting any anthro-pomorphic figuration, the lines that make up the geometrical dia-gram of the *Vâstu-Purusha-mandala* are identified with the measures of *Prâna*, the vital breath of *Vâstu-Purusha*. The principal axes and diagonals denote the principal subtle currents of his body; their intersections are the sensitive points or vital nodes (*marmas*), which must not be incorporated into the foundations of a wall, a pillar or a doorway. The exact coincidence of the axes of several buildings, such as those of a temple and its dependencies, must be avoided for similar reasons. Any transgression of this rule will be the cause of trouble in the organism of the donor of the temple, who is regarded as its real builder (*kâraka*) and is identified in the rites of founda-tion with *Purusha*, the sacrificial victim incorporated in the building.

(from *Sacred Art in East and West*)

---

16. This position corresponds to the "asuric" aspect of the victim incorporated in the *mandala*.

The Sun Dance and the Sacred Pipe

The following is a description of the author's friendship with Thomas Yellowtail, a Medicine Man of the Crow Indians, and of his attendance at a Sun Dance held on the Reservation of the Crow Indians in Montana.

Meeting with Yellowtail

We met Yellowtail for the first time in the Hôtel des Champs Elysées in Paris. He was there with a group of Indian dancers who were traveling together, not so much to earn money as to see foreign lands. Our friend Frithjof Schuon had told us of the authentic nature of the dances being performed, and the fact of staying in the same hotel as the group of Indians gave us the opportunity of making their acquaintance. Amongst the Indians, Yellowtail, who at that time was not yet a medicine man, stood out by his strong personality. I had never before seen a man who was both so strong and so gentle. He was slow in his movements, with an almost hieratic slowness, and had an expression of serenity and strength. Whenever one spoke of spiritual realities, his face would light up.

We spoke with him about the meaning of the gestures and costumes of certain dances, and he confirmed what we said, with some surprise. Towards midnight of the same evening, he sent a messenger who directed us to his room where he had lit a ritual fire on a copper tray that he had found in the hotel. He explained to us that he was going to celebrate the rite of the full moon, which recapitulated, in brief, the Sun Dance.

Yellowtail opened his medicine bundle and took out several objects that were the vehicles of a subtle force, such as animal skins, birds' feathers, and stones of unusual colors, which he placed around the fire. Then he burnt some sweet grass and said: "With this eagle's feather, which I pass over the sacred fire, I shall purify each one of you; then I shall raise my voice to the Great Spirit, that he may give you an understanding of our religion. You will receive this understanding in the form of a dream." Then he hung an eagle-bone whistle around his neck and, rising up, turned successively to the four directions of space, praying aloud in the language of the Crow Indians. Finally he whistled several times, reproducing the whistling voice of the eagle.

Each of us later had a dream which symbolically revealed one or other aspect of the tradition of the Plains Indians. At that point we had already left Paris; but Yellowtail, with a few members of his family, unexpectedly visited us in Switzerland. The bond of friendship—and more than friendship—remains, and we have subsequently met one another on both continents more often than we would have believed possible.

The Sun Dance

After crossing the immense plain of Wyoming, we reached the reservation of the Crow Indians by the end of the afternoon. It was the second day of the summer solstice, and that very evening the Sun Dance was to begin. We were surrounded by hillsides covered with flowers; no sign of the sacred site could be seen until we crossed the raised edge of a high plateau where the sacred tree of the preceding year—now a leafless skeleton—was outlined against the sky. A little further on stood the newly built Sun Dance lodge. The sacred tree was already in place; there were twelve radially arranged beams, whose upper ends were supported in the fork of the tree, and whose lower ends rested on the surrounding fence of small fir-trees that had been stripped of their bark.

Yellowtail, the Medicine Man, was there with a few other Indians. He had just attached the two great symbols: the bison's head, which was hung from the trunk of the tree, and the eagle, which was placed on one of the radial beams and which swayed gently in the breeze.

The lodge was thus almost entirely complete on our arrival. The first part of the rites, concerning the felling of the tree and its erection in the center of the enclosure, had already taken place. The impression of primordiality that emanated from the lodge was accompanied by an atmosphere of coolness and the fragrance of resin. The sacred enclosure was in the form of a vast circle, the eastern portion of which, facing the rising sun, remained open. I could not prevent myself from embracing Yellowtail, who smiled and said *Ahó* ("it is good").

Hours were spent waiting. At dusk the dancers entered the lodge, after marching round it in two opposed movements. A large drum had been installed and five singers took up their positions round about it. The chants that rose towards the star-filled heavens were melodies without words, apparently imitations of the voices of nature. Each melody, which we could barely differentiate from the one that went before, proceeded like a cascade: it would begin with a high note and then move down until it became low and harsh, like an echo that grows stronger as one gets nearer.

The dance lasted three days and three nights, and during this time the dancers fasted; when they were exhausted, they would rest for a few moments in the shade of the fir-trees and then immediately resume the movement of the dance. This movement took place between a given point on the surrounding fence of fir-trees and the sacred tree in the center, each dancer moving back and forward on his own radial pathway. When he approached the sacred tree, his pace would accelerate; then, having felt the coolness that always surrounded the tree—so it was explained to us—he moved backwards with small steps towards his position on the surrounding fence.

From the second day onwards, certain alleviations are provided for the dancers by members of their families: aquatic plants, rushes and reeds are intertwined from one fir-tree to the next, forming little areas of cover that provide some shade, and sacred sage, which grows profusely in the region, is scattered in the dancers' paths. There were at least sixty dancers, including both men and women, the latter taking up positions alongside each other near the opening at the eastern side of the lodge.

During the night a fire is kept going inside the lodge. It is situated on the axis that links the sacred tree to the point on the horizon at which the sun rises. As soon as it is dawn, the dancers prepare themselves for the most important rite, the greeting of the rising sun. Yellowtail says a long prayer in his native tongue and sings four sacred chants without words. The dancers receive the first ray of sunlight standing in a row, and intensify the sound of their eagle-bone whistles. One might say that their whistling is made visible by the vibration of the eagle-down attached to their whistles. The dancers, the upper parts of whose bodies are bare during the day, cover their shoulders with blankets to shield themselves from the cold wind blowing across the prairie—a sharp contrast to the intense heat of the sun that lasts throughout the whole day and causes considerable suffering to the dancers exposed to it. But the suffering was much greater in olden times when leather thongs, inserted under the skin of the dancers' chest or back, attached them to the trunk of the tree. There is, as it were, a reminder of this custom in the sometimes rapid, sometimes measured movements of the dance. On the movement away from the center, the leather thong would pull on the skin until it broke. But in these inward and outward movements there is also the expression of a spiritual movement which first quickly grasps its object, and then slowly assimilates it by taking up a certain distance from it. Moreover, each participant in the dance has to a certain extent his own particular movement. I remember especially a woman of about forty years of age who accomplished her inward and outward movements with a small number of majestic steps.

On the trunk of the tree are painted three rings which correspond to the three worlds. The eagle dominates all three of these worlds, whereas the bison is associated with the earth; his heavy head can be seen amidst the foliage that faces the sun; sacred sage has been put in his mouth and clay on his cheeks because, as our Indian friends explained to us, the bison in anger causes the earth to tremble. The eagle and the bison are the two symbols that most often appear inwardly to Sun Dance participants when they faint under the heat of the sun or are ravished by an ecstasy. The eagle dominates the tree as the Spirit dominates the Cosmos. "The sacred eagle is called Poor Eagle," Yellowtail told us. This is no doubt because the cosmic Spirit is situated directly beneath the Great Spirit.

As mentioned above, the second day of the Sun Dance is the day of alleviations. It is also the day of supernatural manifestations. It is then that members of the dancers' families ornament the dancers in accord with the Indian art of painting, the purpose of which is to "fix" the presence of certain cosmic powers in the body of their protégé. Since the dancers perform the dance with the upper part of their bodies bare, this lends itself to symbolical painting. Sometimes a simple sign—a ring round about an eye, or a zigzag of lightning along an arm—suffices to associate the one thus ornamented with the vision that he has most often received in dreams.

During all these ceremonies, the drum beating and the monotonous chanting continue unceasingly both day and night. The rhythm is rapid and reminds one of thunder; thunder is also identified with the eagle, which otherwise is manifested in the strident sound of the whistles. The eagle is the spirit, and the spirit is the heart. The wide prairie provides, so to speak, primordial and immediately convincing symbols of all spiritual realities. When, after sunset, one approaches the lodge, still enlivened by the rhythm of the drum and the whistling of the eagle bones and its foliage trembling in the wind, one has the impression of being in the presence of a great living creature endowed with magical strength. From the dance itself there emanates a powerful magic that resonates in the heart for days and days.

The second day is also the culmination of the dance. The third day is the day of cures. From morning onwards, a crowd of people, including entire families of white farmers, come to the Sun Dance site and patiently wait for Yellowtail to let them share in the healing power with which the sacred tree is, as it were, filled as a result of the rite of which it has been the center. Yellowtail heals in the name of the eagle who is his particular protector, and also in the name of the otter. He touches the trunk of the sacred tree with an eagle feather, and then with it he strokes the sick parts of the patient's body; as he does this he holds up an otter's skin. In reality all these gestures are addressed to the archetype of the protecting animal; with the Indians the function of healer is of necessity part of the spiritual rank of the one who is invested with it. Essentially, the Indian seeks the harmony of nature, as well as the harmony of his own people with their cosmic ambience.

The third day ends with the giving of presents to clan relatives who have offered special prayers for the dancers; this exchange is an expression of the harmony between creatures.

A long prayer is said on behalf of the sponsor, who has undertaken to cover the costs of the rite and who, during it, has offered ritual prayers alongside Yellowtail, the Medicine Man. Finally a ritual meal of bison meat is offered to all present.

Yellowtail, in full vigor in spite of his age, could not but be exhausted by the dance and the fast, and we suggested to him that we should camp in a forest in the Bighorn Mountains so that he could rest. He agreed and we left almost immediately. Before choosing our camp-site, we climbed to the ridge of the mountain which, on our side, rose gently; on the other side was a deep gorge. On the ridge is situated the famous "Medicine Wheel", the meaning of which, according to the tradition of his tribe, Yellowtail explained to us: a man who was suffering from a disease of the skin had withdrawn to the solitude of the mountain, there to express in stone the outline of the Sun Dance. Twenty-eight radii joined the rim of the wheel to its axis; these are the twenty-eight mansions of the moon. Four heaps of stones indicated the cardinal directions; they looked like four shrines. According to Yellowtail, the maker of the sacred wheel was able to sleep there by covering himself with fir twigs. The

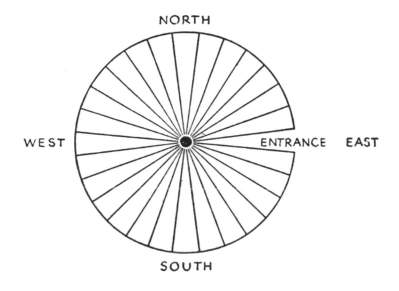

NORTH

WEST
ENTRANCE   EAST

SOUTH

The Sun Dance Lodge
(See p. VI of color section for a photograph,
sketches by Frithjof Schuon.)

construction of the wheel was accompanied by an invocation to the
Great Spirit and when it was completed (it was about the same size
as a Sun Dance lodge) its maker was cured.

On leaving the Medicine Wheel, we went down again to the spot
where the great rivers of the mountains leave the edge of the forest
(in which they have created large swamps) and where deer, as silent
as shadows, move to and fro. We set up our tents near the water, in
a place called Dead Swede. Seated at our camp-fire, we listened to
the Medicine Man: he gave us the history of the transmission of the
powers of healing from one medicine man to another by means of
a "chain" starting with the mysterious "Little People" and ending

with Yellowtail himself. As in many of the Indian traditions, it is lightning that forges the link between the world of men and the world of the spirits. The power of healing is included in the spiritual power, while being vehicled to a greater or lesser extent by natural objects, such as stones or plants. In this connection, Yellowtail told me that no medicine is effective if it does not comprise both herbs and prayer. According to his own experience, the double effect of the medicines prepared in this way sometimes exceeds by far the expectations of the medicine man using them.

He also told us the name of the genius who is the guardian of these powers; he is called "Seven Arrows", a name which is a symbol of the Center: according to tradition, an "arrow" signifies a direction of space. There are firstly the four arrows of the cardinal directions; then there are the Zenith and the Nadir, which make six. The seventh is in reality not a direction, but the Center itself, from which the other directions emanate.

(from *Mirror of the Intellect*)

7

Evocations of Traditional Moroccan Life

Return to Fez

A geode of amethyst, brimful of thousands of tightly packed crystals and surrounded by a silver-green rim: this was Fez, the Old City of Fez, in the twilight. As we came downhill towards it, the hollow in which it lies grew visibly larger; the countless crystals, uniform in themselves, but irregularly grown into one another, now came more clearly into view; one side of them was light, while the other side, the one facing the prevailing wind, had become darkened and weather-beaten. Between them and the silver-green girdle of olive trees, the wall of the Old City with its towers could be seen. Towards the city gate now facing us—Bâb al-Gissa—the small donkey caravans made their way as of old, and from out of the gate into the evening wind and towards the expanse of green, came men and children in Moroccan dress; for it was spring, and the hills round about were covered with yellow and blue flowers.

In the heart of the city, in the lowest point of the hollow, one could make out the tent-shaped roof of green glazed tiles that covers the dome of the tomb of the holy Idrîs, the founder of Fez; nearby was a minaret. Not far away were the equally green roofs of the old Koranic college of al-Qarawiyyîn. The nearer we came to the city, the more minarets rose to Heaven, clear-cut, square, flat-topped towers, similar to the Romanesque city towers of Italy. There must have been hundreds of them. These reveal the position of the larger mosques; even more smaller mosques are hidden from sight in the confusion of the high, grey-white and, at this moment, reddish cubes of houses. A city full of sanctuaries: the European travelers who first visited it at the beginning of the century spoke either of a "citadel of fanaticism", or marveled at it as a place of perpetual prayer.

I asked myself whether the Old City might have inwardly changed during the twenty-five years that I had been away from it. It still looked the same as before: ancient, weather-beaten, withdrawn inside its walls. Only a few groups of white houses outside in the open ground where no one had previously dared to settle, and a few miserable huts which had crept into deserted lime-pits, showed that the army of the poor had now burst outside the protection of the old walls. On our left, towards the East, the hollow in which Fez lies opened up towards the plain of the river Sabû: a wide, flat valley on whose horizon a still snow-covered branch of the Middle Atlas, the Bû Iblân, soared. To the West, on a somewhat higher level, began the plain on which lie the medieval Sultan's city, Fâs Jadîd ("New Fez"), and further away, the modern town built by the French.

The city was getting nearer, and at the same time it loomed up within my own mind, rising out of the darkness of memory, with all of its thousand faces pressing upon me questioningly; for Fez had once been familiar to me, well known and yet full of inexhaustible secrets. In it I had experienced another world and another age, a world of the Middle Ages such as perhaps now no longer existed, an austere and yet enticing world, outwardly poor but inwardly rich. It was a city that had had to yield to foreign rule, and that had accepted in silence the arrival of a new order dominated by the power of machines, yet inwardly it remained true to itself; for at the time I first knew it, men who had spent their youth in an unaltered traditional world were still the heads of families. For many of them, the spirit which had once created the Mosque at Córdoba and the Alhambra at Granada was nearer and more real than all the innovations that European rule had brought with it. Since then, however, a new generation had arisen, one which from its earliest childhood must have been blinded by the glare of European might and which in large measure had attended French schools and thus henceforth bore within it the sting of an almost insuperable contradiction. For how could there be any reconciliation between the inherited traditional life which, despite all its frugalities, carried within it the treasure of an eternal meaning, and the modern European world which, as it so palpably demonstrates, is a force entirely orientated towards *this* world, towards possessions and enjoyments, and in every way contemptuous of the sacred? These splendid men of the now dying generation whom I had once known had indeed been conquered outwardly, but inwardly they had remained free; the younger generation, on the other hand, had won an outward victory when Morocco gained political independence some years ago, but now ran the grave risk of succumbing inwardly. It was thus not without some anxiety that I returned to the familiar city, for nothing could be more painful than the sight of a people robbed of its best inheritance, in exchange for money, haste, and dissipation.

In front of the city gate there was still the neglected cemetery with its irregular crop of graves between mule tracks and flowering thistles, where children were playing on white slabs and, here and there, men sat silently waiting for sunset and the call to prayer.

Just then the last pink glow on the towers disappeared. The sun had completely set and now only the green-gold of the sky shed a mild, non-shadow-forming light, in which everything seemed to float as if weightless and somehow glowing in itself. At that moment the long-drawn-out call to the sunset prayer rang out from the minarets. Lights appeared in the towers. But the city was silent; only a few cries, like suddenly broken-off laments, reached our ears. The wind which had suddenly arisen and which, high above us in the town, blew from mountain to valley, interrupted the sound. But the people who were waiting had heard the call. One could see both individuals and groups spread out their prayer mats and turn towards the south-east, the direction of Mecca. Others hurried through the city gate to reach a mosque, and it was with the latter that we ourselves entered the city.

We were immediately enveloped in the half-light of the narrow streets which descended steeply from the various gates into the hollow where the great sanctuaries lie surrounded by the bazaars or commercial streets (*aswâq:* sing. *sûq*). In the streets all that can be seen of the houses are the high walls, darkened with age, and almost entirely without windows. The only open doors are those of the *fanâdîq* (sing. *funduq*) or caravanserais, where peasants and Bedouins visiting the town leave their steeds and beasts of burden in open spaces surrounding a courtyard, and where, on the upper story, they can hire a room to pass the night or store their wares. Otherwise, the street is like a deep, half-dark ravine which turns unexpectedly, sometimes here, sometimes there, often covered in by bridges from one building to another and only wide enough to allow two mules to squeeze past each other. Everywhere the cry *Bâlek! Bâlek!* ("Take care! Take care!") rings out. Thus do the mule drivers and the porters with heavy loads on their heads make their way through the crowd. Only further down do the shops begin, where the traveler on arrival may find his necessities; there too are the saddlers, the basket-makers, and the cookshop-owners, the latter preparing hearty meals on little charcoal fires. We proceeded past them into the street of the spice-dealers (*Sûq al-'Attârîn*), which runs through the entire town center, and in which one shop lies hard against the next, a row of simple plain boxes, with shuttered doors in front, just as in Europe in the Middle Ages, and with no more space than will allow the merchant to sit down amongst his piled-up wares.

Nothing stirs the memory more than smells; nothing so effectively brings back the past. Here indeed was Fez: the scent of cedar wood and fresh olives, the dry, dusty smell of heaped-up corn, the pungent smell of freshly tanned leather, and finally, in the *Sûq al-'Attârîn*, the medley of all the perfumes of the Orient—for here are on sale all the spices that once were brought by merchants from India to Europe as the most precious of merchandise. And every now and again one would suddenly become aware of the sweet smell of sandalwood incense, wafted from the inside of one of the mosques.

Equally unmistakable are the sounds; I could find my way blind-folded by the clatter of hooves on the steep pavings; by the monot-onous cry of the beggars who squat in the dead corners of the streets; and by the silvery sound of the little bells, with which the water-carriers announce their presence when, wending their way through the *sûqs,* they offer water to the thirsty.

But now I paid attention only to the faces, which here and there loomed up in the glimmer of the newly lit lamps; I thought perhaps to recognize an old friend or acquaintance. But I saw only the fea-tures of familiar racial types: sometimes grave and worthy figures, sometimes the sly and slightly scornful townsman, but no known face. There were also youths, dressed more or less in the European manner, with the mark of a new age on their foreheads, and some-times staring defiantly and inquisitively at the foreigner.

To the right of the spice market, just beside the Sepulchral Mosque of Idrîs II, the holy founder of Fez, there is a cluster of nar-row passages lined with booths. Here all kinds of clothing are on sale: colored leather shoes, ladies' dresses in silk brocade embroi-dered in gold and silver. Near the mosque there are also decorated liturgical candles, frankincense, and perfumed oils; for perfumes belong to the *sunna,* the sacred Tradition, according to the saying of the Prophet: "Three things from your world have been made wor-thy of my love: women, perfumes, and prayer."

Around the Sepulchral Mosque of the holy Idrîs there is a nar-row alley, made inaccessible to horses and mules by means of beams. This constitutes the limits of the *hurm,* the sacratum, within which formerly no one might be pursued. Only a short time before the French withdrawal was this rule broken for the first time—in the revolt against the French-imposed Sultan Ben 'Arafa.

We walked along the arabesque-decorated outer walls of the sanctuary, past the little window, covered with an iron grille, which opens on to the tomb, and reached another brightly lit street which brought us into the vicinity of the great mosque and college of al-Qarawiyyîn. In the streets surrounding it, the advocates and notaries have their little offices and the booksellers and book-binders have their shops—just like their Christian colleagues of old in the shade of the great cathedrals. As we passed by, we stole a glance through several of the many doors of the mosque and gazed into the illuminated forest of pillars, from which the rhythmical chanting of Koranic *sûras* could be heard.

Then through the district of the coppersmiths, where the hammers were already at rest and only here and there a busy craftsman still polished and examined a vessel in the light of his hanging lamp; soon we reached the bridges in the hollow of the town and ascended from there to the gate on the other side, the Bab al-Futûh. As we looked back we saw the Old City lying beneath us like a shimmering seam of quartz. I now knew that the face of Fez, the old once-familiar and yet foreign Fez, was unaltered. But did its soul live on as formerly?

On one of the following evenings we were invited home by a Moroccan friend, to a house which, like all Moorish houses, opened only onto an inner courtyard, entirely white, where roses grew in profusion and an orange tree sparkled festively with blossoms and fruits. The room on the ground floor, where the guests sat in threes and fours on low divans, opened onto this courtyard. Amongst all the men present, there was also a small dark-skinned Arab boy, whose thin face was as if transfigured by an inward fire as well as by a child-like smile. The master of the house told us he was the best singer of spiritual songs in the whole country. After the meal he invited him to sing to us. The boy shut his eyes and began, softly at first, and then gradually more loudly, to render a *qasîda*, a symbolical love-song. And some of the guests who had gathered near him and had drawn back the hoods of their *jellâbas* sang the refrain, which contained the *shahâda* (the attestation of Divine Unity) in a harsh, ancient Andalusian style. The Arabic verses of the poem grew faster and faster, in a quick, intense tempo, while the answering refrain surged forth in widely extending waves. All of a sudden the volume of the chorus, which until then had only "answered" the singer, flowed on without interruption and branched into several parallel rhythms, above which the voice of the leading singer continued at a higher pitch, like a heavenly exultation above a song of war.

It was miraculous how the many strands of the melody never came together in those accords which allow the flow of feeling to rest as if on a broad couch and which promise to human longing an all too easy, all too human consolation; the melody never turned into a worldly "space", its different strands never came together as if reconciled; they continued endlessly, circling incessantly around a silent center, which became ever more clearly audible, as a timeless presence, an other-worldly "space", without yesterday or tomorrow, a crystalline "now", in which all impatience is extinguished.

This was Fez, unalterable, indestructible Fez.

(from *Fez, City of Islam*)

Courtyard of palace (sketch by Titus Burckhardt)

Ito's Cave

I was once a guest in the cave village of the Aït Tserrûsh ("the sons of the jackal"), a Berber tribe of the Middle Atlas. When I woke up in the morning, I did not at first understand why I was surrounded by uneven patches of semi-darkness. But when I turned over on my sheepskin I saw, through the narrow cave mouth, the brilliant light of day. A soft whimpering had awakened me: in one of the large niches that opened out from all around the inside wall of the cave, there lay a small Berber child who was wriggling under some earth-colored blankets. All of a sudden, in the section of sky cut out by the cave mouth, I could see Ito, the child's mother, who had appeared in response to his cry. She put down a jug of water, picked up the child, and laid him on her lap in order to suckle him. Once more in the cave all was silent; one could barely hear, in the distance, the sounds of the day: the cry of an animal or the clattering of hooves. The Berber woman sat in the half-light, motionless as a rock.

When the infant was satisfied, she let it slide to the ground, sat down in front of a mortar, and began to grind wheat. She sieved the flour, mixed it with water in a wooden bowl, and then kneaded the dough with powerful and regular movements. Finally, she divided the dough into six equal-sized balls, which she carefully flattened into circular pieces of bread, having first kept behind in the bowl a piece of dough about the size of an apple, which would be used to leaven the next day's batch.

Ito was too powerful and too solid to be truly beautiful. But her broad face, with its wide-open eyes, looked as if it had been carved out of some bright stone, and shone with a proud and powerful femininity. She carried her dignity with an innocent awareness. Tattoo marks on her forehead and chin both decorated and protected her.

The air in the cave smelled slightly of stone. At this depth one is protected both from the heat of the day and the cold of the night. The world above seemed no longer to be of any concern, and the cave enveloped one maternally; one felt a reluctance to climb up to the hot ground above, rather as if one struggled not to be born.

Once more someone filled the small piece of sky. The child's father, Mohaudris, made his way down. He was a young Berber with regular features and an impenetrable expression, as if he bore on his countenance the reflection of the vast and rocky steppe. He was dressed in a wide, white shirt, and had a narrow turban round his head. Over his shoulders hung a *selham* or burnous (a simple cloak of rough wool), on the back of which a long cross was embroidered—perhaps the sign of the remote Christian origin of his tribe. His name, Mohaudris, is the Berber abbreviation of the double name Mohammed Idrîs.

"Peace be upon thee", came his greeting, "blessed be the morning, may no harm befall thee!" He had brought with him the head of a young goat, and set about preparing it for my breakfast.

I asked him about the life of the community in which I was a guest. A part of the population had gone into the mountains with their tents to pasture their sheep and goats. Those remaining behind attended to the fields of maize which lay further down in the valley.

My horse was tethered in a neighboring cave. When I led him a few yards up into the daylight, he shied at first, as if blinded by the sun. On the surface of the ground, all one could see of the village were the cave openings protected by thorn bushes and a defensive wall that surrounded everything. Looking towards the north, over the edge of the plateau, one could just make out the large yellow hollow in which Fez lay. To the south extended the undulating steppe, a vast plateau where, in the spring, exquisite flowers appear amongst the boulders; but now, in summer, the bare ground was decorated only by tough bushes such as broom and juniper.

On a hill nearby a new mosque had been built. This was the tribes' answer to a French edict promising the Berbers their own legislation independent of that of the Koran. "Why does the Rumi (the European) covet my stony valley?" asks a Berber song, "he who possesses everything that a man can desire? Does he reach out his hand to snatch the faith from my heart?"

The mosque was built of gigantic cedar trunks from the mountains in the south. The outside walls and the flat roof were covered with sun-dried mud. In the inside, trunks with their bark removed stood in rows like high, reddish pillars. The archaic impression made by this building, in its powerful simplicity, was increased even further by the earnest faces of the Berbers, who stood or sat between the cedar pillars. In the faces of several of the older men there was a profound concentration and resignation.

From one end of the village could be heard the haunting sounds of a flute, accompanied by a dull, steady drumbeat. It was the music of a Sufi brotherhood that had its roots amongst the people of the region. The musicians were standing in front of a cave entrance and a Berber woman gyrated in an ecstatic dance. Her hair, held together by a woven ribbon, became undone because of her rapid movements, and swirled through the air like a large black bird.

In the center of the village, beautiful children were playing. And heavily laden beasts of burden entered the village through the gate.

On the horizon of the great plain, down to which I was now riding, there were still some fine strips of morning cloud, light pink in color. The light of dawn sparkled on the dark metallic-looking leaves of the dwarf palms which covered the slopes. Gradually the brown earth flattened out, and seemed to stretch endlessly ahead of me. The caravan track was covered with a network of cracks, and left and right stood desiccated thistles, which looked as if they were made out of blue glass. Further away were low black tents, and half-wild dogs barked at me as I passed.

The Moroccan earth, which from June onwards is almost bare, is everywhere near to man. The Bedouin sleeps on it and rests on it, and his cloak, however often he may wash it, always has in it something of the earth on which he lives. Nothing separates man from the immense and austere body of the earth, which nowhere has an end. But the sunlight filling the sky, the sunlight unobscured by any mist, relieves the earth of its heaviness and unites all things, without suppressing their proper forms, in its infinite crystal.

Towards midday I reached the first wheat fields, already mown, and then the villages of the *fellâhîn* whose white houses of sun-dried mud rested like sarcophagi on the vast plain. A stallion tethered in front of one of the houses raised its head, and neighed loudly. While the flocks crouched down together on top of their own shadows— the sun being now almost vertically above them—I rested awhile beside a well, under an acacia tree. Then I rode on in the direction of Fez, and the nearer I came to the city, the more I overtook small caravans of mules and donkeys making their way there with loads of cedar logs, animal skins, or goatskin bottles full of olive oil. Many had come from afar, having trotted for days over the rocky plateau.

The sun was already sinking before I could see, in the distance, the hills surrounding Fez, with their bright, ocher-colored ridges and silvery green clumps of olive trees. No sooner had the sun set than the scene was transformed into a world of antique gold, jade, and opal, beneath a sky of turquoise.

Slowly the colors were extinguished like a dying brazier. The earth retreated and the sky opened up, a measureless ocean with silvery islands and shimmering shores. Underneath, the caravans, as if drunk with sleep, followed their drovers' song.

(from *Fez, City of Islam*)

Girl skipping (sketch by Titus Burckhardt)

The Fools of God

One must also reckon with the possibility that an apparent madman is in reality a *majdhûb,* one "attracted by God", whose reason has, so to speak, been over-powered by a spiritual drunkenness, so that he forgets his surroundings, and "feels neither hot nor cold".

There are also dervishes who use the mask of madness in order to be able to live alone in the midst of the world and be free from all social fetters. To such a category belonged Mulay as-Siddîq, who died around 1939. He came from a distinguished Fez family and, as a young man, had embarked on a promising career as a lawyer, when he met a Sufi master who wandered through the land as a "fool of God". He became his disciple and adopted the same way of life. When he heard that his brother had spoken of him with rage and disgust, he visited his house at a moment when no one was in, and washed the floors of each room with his own hands. Thereafter, his relatives left him in peace.

Most of the time he traveled. When, however, he visited Fez, he installed himself in a small cemetery that abutted on the house in which I was living at that time. The cemetery was completely full of graves, and surrounded by a wall. A tall, lonely palm-tree grew in one corner, and along one of the sides stood a half-ruined row of pillars, in front of which the strange man had stretched out a mat with which to shelter his wife and children. In these surroundings, which reminded me of the old masters' renderings of the Adoration of the Magi, he would receive his disciples, mostly poor and uneducated people, but occasionally also people from the higher classes. Every morning it was his practice to wander through the market with his most faithful disciples, chanting the profession of faith "there is no god but God", and receiving alms. He wore an enormous rosary, with beads as big as apples, that was wound twice around his neck and hung down over his heavy round body. He supported himself on a staff. His somewhat Mongoloid and impenetrable face was surmounted by a massive blue-green turban. Behind him always walked a herculean, one-eyed son of the desert, who was dressed only in loosely stitched-together pieces of leather that scarcely covered his brown muscles. One might have taken him for a highwayman, had it not been for the child-like look of benevolence in his single eye. It was he who carried the bag for alms.

Sometimes the group would enter a house where a festivity, a wedding or a circumcision, was in progress. The men would sit down in a circle in the courtyard; and when, as was the custom, the host served tea, Mulay as-Siddîq would take the copper tray used to carry the tea-glasses and the hammer used to break the sugar and, beginning to sing a mystical song, he would use these utensils as ear-splitting cymbals. His disciples would then rise, take each other by the hand, and, chanting the Name of God, they would begin to dance. I myself was once witness when aged men suffering from the palsy, who had followed the outlandish master with the greatest of difficulty, suddenly threw away their crutches and, as if transported, threw themselves into the dance. When finally Mulay as-Siddîq stopped the dance and everyone sat down, women who had watched the scene from the flat roof, threw down money and jewel-

Roof-top scene (sketch by Titus Burckhardt)

ry with jubilant cries. When the alms bag was full, couscous, meat, and vegetables would be bought, and, in the cemetery that the group used as a meeting place, a large meal would be prepared on an open fire, to which all the poor of the district were invited.

Mulay as-Siddîq would accept no disciple who did not put at his disposal all that he possessed. Sometimes the master would return a part of this to him, so that he might fulfill his commitments. Everything else was given to the poor.

This "fool of God" was a source of embarrassment to the educated. The middle classes looked on him with a mixture of benevolence and amusement. But many poor people, porters, day laborers, and donkey drivers, as well as not a few craftsmen, and even some educated men and women, venerated him so much that in his presence, they behaved like timid children.

(from *Fez, City of Islam*)

The Comb-maker

I knew a comb-maker who worked in the street of his guild, the *mashshâtîn*. He was called 'Abd al-'Azîz ("slave of the Almighty"), and always wore a black *jellâba*—the loose, hooded garment with sleeves—and a white turban with the *lithâm,* the face veil, which surrounded his somewhat severe features. He obtained the horn for his combs from ox skulls, which he bought from butchers. He dried the horned skulls at a rented place, removed the horns, opened them lengthwise, and straightened them over a fire, a procedure that had to be done with the greatest care, lest they should break. From this raw material he cut combs and turned boxes for antimony (used as an eye decoration) on a simple lathe; this he did by manipulating with his left hand a bow which, wrapped round a spindle, caused the apparatus to rotate. In his right hand he held the knife, and with his foot he pushed against the counter-weight. As he worked he would sing Koranic *sûras* in a humming tone.

I learned that as a result of an eye disease which is common in Africa, he was already half blind and that, in view of long practice, he was able to "feel" his work rather than see it. One day he complained to me that the importation of plastic combs was diminishing his business: "It is not only a pity that today, solely on account of price, poor quality combs from a factory are being preferred to much more durable horn combs," he said; "it is also senseless that people should stand by a machine and mindlessly repeat the same movement, while an old craft like mine falls into oblivion. My work may seem crude to you; but it harbors a subtle meaning which cannot be explained in words. I myself acquired it only after many long years, and even if I wanted to, I could not automatically pass it on to my son, if he himself did not wish to acquire it— and I think he would rather take up another occupation. This craft can be traced back from apprentice to master until one reaches our Lord Seth, the son of Adam. It was he who first taught it to men, and what a Prophet brings—for Seth was a Prophet— must clearly have a special purpose, both outwardly and inwardly. I gradually came to understand that there is nothing fortuitous about this craft, that each movement and each procedure is the bearer of an element of wisdom. But not everyone can understand this. But even if one does not know this, it is still stupid and reprehensible to rob men of the inheritance of Prophets, and to put them in front of a machine where, day in and day out, they must perform a meaningless task."

Consequently, the dire straits in which Moroccan craftsmanship finds itself is not merely an outward predicament, but above all a spiritual threat. Even if not every Arab craftsman has as much understanding of his craft as our comb-maker, nevertheless most professions still have a spiritual content, which will progressively disappear with the innovation of modern industry.

Even the water-carriers, who do nothing else but fill their tarred goatskins at the public fountains in order to offer a cool drink to thirsty people in the market-place, indifferent as to whether they receive a voluntary token or nothing at all, show in their demeanor a human dignity, such as, in European countries, the sower may still have, as he contemplatively scatters his seed. Even the beggars, who squat outside the mosques and on the bridges and who reveal their profession by their much-patched garments, do not make their request with shame, but cry: "Give what is God's!" or intone to themselves in a monotonous voice a pious refrain.

For almost everyone who has not been sucked into the whirlpool of the modern world lives his life here as if it were something provisional which does not definitively engage his soul, but which belongs to the *Divina Commedia* of earthly existence.

(from *Fez, City of Islam*)

The Life of the Nomad

Arab nomadism does not merely have an anti-sedentary aspect; it also possesses a certain nobility, which the famous Emir 'Abd al-Qâdir (1807–1883), that bold and skillful warrior who opposed the French invasion of Algeria in the first half of the 19th century, powerfully evokes in one his poems:

O thou who preferrest the dull life of the town
to wide, free solitude,
dost thou despise nomadic tents,
because they are light, not heavy
like houses of stone and lime?
If only thou knewest the desert's secret!
But ignorance is the root of all evil.
If thou couldst but awake in the dawning Sahara,
and set forth on this carpet of pearls,
where flowers of all colors shower delight
and perfume on our way.
We breathe an air that lengthens life,
because it ne'er blew on the refuse of towns!
If at dawn, after the night's dew,
thou wouldst from a high point look into the distance,
thou wouldst see on the measureless horizon
fallow beasts grazing on scented meadows.
At a moment like this all care would leave thee,
and rest would enter thy restless heart.
On the day of decampment, the camels' *howdahs*
are like anemones weighed down by rain.
They cover virgins, who peep out through peepholes.
Ah peephole that the eye of the *houri* fills!
Behind them sing the drivers in high pitch,
their song more gripping than flutes and cymbals.
But we, on noble horses,
whose decorations cover breast and croup,
stir ourselves into a gallop.
We hunt gazelles and beasts of prey.
None can outrun our rapid coursing!
At night we return to the tribe,
which has already encamped on an unspotted site.
The earth is like musk; even purer it is;

and generous too, moistened at dawn and dusk by rain.
There we put up our tents in rows.
The Earth is dotted with them as the sky with stars.
Those who have passed on truly said
—*and truth undergoeth not change*—
beauty is found in two things,
in a verse, and in a tent of skin.
When our camels graze at night,
their lowing resounds like the thunder of early morning.
They are the ships of the desert; whoso travels on them is saved;
but how dangerous are the ships of the sea!
They are our *mehari*, swift as antelopes,
through them and our horses we achieve fame.
Our horses are always saddled for battle;
whoever seeks our aid, for him we are ready.
For fame we have sold our citizenship forever,
for fame is not won in the town!
We are kings! None can compare himself with us!
Does he then truly live, who lives in shame?

(from *Fez, City of Islam*)

Landscape with flock of sheep and typical Bedouin black tent
(sketch by Titus Burckhardt)

Biographical Notes

About William Stoddart

William Stoddart was born in Carstairs, Scotland, lived most of his life in London, England, and now lives in Windsor, Ontario. He studied modern languages, and later medicine, at the universities of Glasgow, Edinburgh, and Dublin. He was a close associate of both Titus Burckhardt and Frithjof Schuon during the lives of these leading Traditionalists/Perennialists. His books include *Outline of Hinduism* (1993), *Outline of Buddhism* (1998), and *Sufism: the Mystical Doctrines and Methods of Islam* (1986). Stoddart contributed the chapter "Mysticism" to the volume *The Unanimous Tradition* (1998), edited by Ranjit Fernando, and the introductory essay "Meaning Behind the Absurd" to *In Quest of the Sacred* (1994), edited by S.H. Nasr and Katherine O'Brien. He is also the translator of several of the books of Titus Burckhardt and Frithjof Schuon. For many years Dr. Stoddart was assistant editor of the British journal *Studies in Comparative Religion*. Pursuing his interests in comparative religion, he has traveled widely in Europe, North Africa, India, and Ceylon.

About Seyyed Hossein Nasr

Seyyed Hossein Nasr was born in Iran and was educated there and at M.I.T. and Harvard in America. He currently is University Professor of Islamic Studies at the George Washington University in Washington D.C. Professor Nasr is one of the most important and foremost scholars of Islamic, Religious and Comparative Studies in the world today, and is a well known and highly respected intellectual figure both in the West and the Islamic world. He has written over fifty books and five hundred articles which have been translated into several major Islamic, European and Asian languages. He was close to both Titus Burckhardt and Frithjof Schuon, personally and intellectually, and is now one of the most active and influential Traditionalist/Perennialist writers. Professor Nasr is also the president of the Foundation for Traditional Studies, which publishes the journal *Sophia*.

Bibliography
of Titus Burckhardt

Books in German

Land am Rande der Zeit. Basel: Urs Graf Verlag, 1941.

Schweizer Volkskunst/Art Populaire Suisse. Basel: Urs Graf Verlag, 1941.

Tessin (Das Volkserbe der Schweiz, Band I). Basel: Urs Graf Verlag, 1943.

Vom Sufitum–Einführung in die Mystik des Islams. Munich: Otto Wilhelm Barth-Verlag, 1953.

Vom Wessen heiliger Kunst in den Weltreligionen. Zurich: Origo-Verlag, 1958.

Siena, Stadi der Jungfrau. Olten (Switzerland) and Freiburg-im-Breisgau (Germany): Urs Graf Verlag, 1958.

Tessin (Das Volkserbe der Schweiz, Band I [Greatly enlarged edition]). Basel: Urs Graf Verlag, 1959.

Alchemie, Sinn- und Weitbild. Olten and Freiburg-im-Breisgau: Walter-Verlag, 1960.

Fes, Stadt des Islam. Olten and Freiburg-im-Breisgau: Urs Graf Verlag, 1960.

Chartres und die Geburt der Kathedrale. Lausanne: Urs Graf Verlag, 1962.

Von wunderbaren Büchern. Olten and Freiburg: Urs Graf Verlag, 1963.

Lachen und Weinen. Olten and Freiburg: Urs Graf Verlag, 1964.

Die Jagd. Olten and Freiburg: Urs Graf Verlag, 1964.

Der wilde Westen. Olten and Freiburg: Urs Graf Verlag, 1966.

Die maurische Kultur in Spanien. Munich: Callwey, 1970.

Marokko, Westlicher Orient: ein Reiseführer. Olten and Freiburg: Walter-Verlag, 1972.

Spiegel der Weisheit: Texte zu Wissenschaft und Kunst. Munich: Diederichs, 1992.

*

* *

Scipio und Hannibal: Kampf um das Mittelmeer by Friedrich Donauer. Cover design and six illustrations by Titus Burckhardt. Olten and Freiburg: Walter-Verlag, 1939.

Wallis (Das Volkserbe der Schweiz, Band 2) by Charles Ferdinand Ramuz. Translated and edited by Titus Burckhardt. Basel: Urs Graf Verlag, 1956.

Zeus und Eros: Briefe und Aufzeichnungen des Bildhauers Carl Burckhardt (1878–1923), edited by Titus Burckhardt. Basel: Urs Graf Verlag, 1956.

Das Ewige im Vergänglichen by Frithjof Schuon. Translation from the French by Titus Burckhardt of *Regards sur les Mondes anciens*. Weilheim: Otto Wilhelm Barth-Verlag, 1970.

Athos, der Berg des Schweigens by Philip Sherrard. Translation from the English by Titus Burckhardt of *Athos, the Mountain of Silence*. Lausanne and Freiburg: Urs Graf Verlag, 1959.

Articles in German

Foreword to *Der Sinn der Ikonen* by Leonid Ouspensky and Wladimir Lossky. Olten (Switzerland) and Freiburg-im-Breisgau (Germany): Urs Graf Verlag, 1952.

"Die Symbolik des Spiegels in der islamischen Mystik". *Symbolon*, 1960.

"Symbolik des Islams". *Kairos* (Salzburg), 1961.

"Von der Heiligkeit des Wassers". *CIBA-Blätter* (Hauszeitschrift der CIBA Aktiengesellschaft, Basel) Sondernummer: Wasser; Vol. 18, No. 174, July–August 1961.

"Die Lehre vom Symbol in den Grossen Ueberlieferungen des Ostens und des Westens". *Symbolon*, 1962.

"Cosmologia Perennis". *Kairos* (Salzburg), No. I, 1964.

Letter to the Editor. *Kairos* (Salzburg), No. 2, 1964.

"Moderne Psychologie und überlieferte Weisheit". *Kairos* (Salzburg), Nos. 3 & 4, 1964.

"Weil Dante Recht hat". *Antaios* (Stuttgart), May 1965.

"Abstrakte Kunst im alten Fes". *Du* (Zurich), March 1972.

"Die überlieferten Handwerke in Marokko: ihr Wesen und ihr Schicksal". *Zeitschrift für Ganzheitsforschung* (Vienna), No. 2, 1974.

"Betrachtungen zur Alchemie" (translated from the French by Margreth Pietsch). in *Initiative 42: Wissende, Verschwiegene, Eingeweihte,* Freiburg-im-Breisgau, Herder, 1981.

"Die heilige Maske" (translated from the French), in *Initiative 48: Die Macht der Masken,* Freiburg-im-Breisgau, Herder, 1982.

"Betrachtungen über den konservativen Menschen", *Mut* (Asendorf, Germany), no. 261, May 1989.

(*All of the above-listed articles are in the original German of the author, except for the two translations indicated.*)

Books in French

Clef spirituelle de l'astrologie musulmane. Paris: Les Éditions Traditionnelles, 1950; Milan, Archè, 1964.

Du Soufisme. Lyons: Derain, 1951.

Principes et Méthodes de l'art sacré. Lyons: Derain, 1958.

Introduction aux Doctrines ésotériques de l'Islam. Paris: Dervy-Livres, 1969.

Alchimie (translated from the English edition by Madame J. P. Gervy). Basle: Fondation Keimer, 1974; Milan: Archè, 1979.

Symboles: Recueil d'essais. Milan: Archè, 1980; Paris: Dervy-Livres, 1980.

Science moderne et Sagesse traditionnelle. Milan: Archè, 1985; Paris: Dervy-Livres, 1985.

L'Art de l'Islam. Paris: Sindbad, 1985.

Chartres et la Naissance de la Cathédrale (translated from the German by Genia Catalá). Milan: Archè, 1995.

Fès, Ville de l'Islam (translated from the German by Armand Jacoubovitch), in preparation.

(*All of the above-listed books are in the original French of the author, except for the two translations indicated.*)

Articles in French

"Du *Barzakh*". *Études Traditionnelles* (Paris), December 1937.

"De la Thora, de l'Évangile, et du Coran". *Études Traditionnelles*, August–September 1938.

"Le Prototype Unique". *Études Traditionnelles*, August–September 1938.

"Folklore et Art ornemental". *Études Traditionnelles*, August–September–October 1939.

"Une Clef spirituelle de l'Astrologie musulmane". *Études Traditionnelles*, June 1947, July–August 1947, December 1947, January–February 1948.

"Généralités sur l'Art musulman". *Études traditionnelles*, March 1947.

"Principes et Méthodes de l'Art traditionnel". *Études Traditionnelles*, January–February 1947.

"Nature de la Perspective cosmologique". *Études Traditionnelles*, July–August 1948.

"Considérations sur l'Alchimie (I)". *Etudes Traditionnelles*, October–November 1948, April–May 1949.

" 'Nature sait surmonter Nature' ". *Études Traditionnelles*, January–February 1950.

"Le Temple, Corps de l'Homme Divin". *Études Traditionnelles*, June 1951.

"Extraits du Commentaire des Noms Divins par l'Imâm Ghazâli" (Translation and notes by Titus Burckhardt). *Études Traditionnelles*, October–November 1952, December 1954.

" 'Je suis la Porte' ". *Études Traditionnelles*, June 1953, July–August 1953.

"La Genèse du Temple hindou". *Études Traditionnelles*, October–November 1953, December 1953.

"Les Fondements de l'Art chrétien". *Études Traditionnelles*, April–May 1954.

"Les Fondements de l'Art musulman". *Études Traditionnelles*, June 1954.

"Le symbolisme du jeu des Échecs". *Études Traditionnelles*, October–November 1954.

"Le Paysage dans l'Art extrême-oriental". *Études Traditionnelles*, April–May 1955.

"Commentaire succinct de la Table d'Émeraude". *Études Traditionnelles*, November–December 1960.

"Considérations sur l'Alchimie (II)". *Études Traditionnelles*, November–December 1961.

" 'Chevaucher le Tigre' ". *Études Traditionnelles*, July–October 1962.

"Le Masque Sacré". *Études Traditionnelles*, November–December 1963.

"Cosmologie et Science moderne". *Études Traditionnelles*, May–June 1964, July–October 1964, January–February 1965, March–April 1965, May–August 1965.

"La Prière d'Ibn Mashish". *Études Traditionelles*, January–February 1967.

"Mise au point en ce qui concerne l'édition française du livre *Alchemie: Sinn- und Weltbild* ". *Études Traditionnelles*, January–February 1967.

"Le Vide dans l'Art Islamique". *Hermès,* 1970.

"Caractères pérennes de l'art arabe". *Journal of World History,* 1972.

"Fès, une ville humaine" (causerie faite le 21 avril 1973 dans le palais du Pacha devant les membres de l'Association pour la sauvegarde de Fès). *Etudes Traditionnelles,* July–September 1984.

"Note sur le Prophète Mohammed". In *Formes et Substance dans les Religions* by Frithjof Schuon, pp. 86–87. Paris: Dervy-Livres, 1975.

Préface à *Islam, Perspectives et Réalités* by Seyyed Hossein Nasr. Paris: Buchet-Chastel, 1975.

"Les Sciences traditionnelles à Fès". *Études Traditionnelles,* October–December 1977.

"Le Retour d'Ulysse". *Études Traditionnelles,* January–March 1979.

"Fès et l'Art de l'Islam". In *Actes du Séminaire experimental d'Animation culturelle,* 7 mars-28 avril 1978. Fonds international pour la Promotion de la Culture, UNESCO, *Conférences,* volume I, pp. 109–119, 1980.

"La Danse du Soleil", *Connaissance des Religions* (Nancy, France), 1985.

Translations from Arabic into French

De l'Homme Universel (Traduction partielle de "Al-Insân al-Kâmil" de 'Abd al-Karîm al-Jîlî). With an introduction by the translator. Lyons, Derain, 1953; Paris, Dervy-Livres, 1975.

La Sagesse des Prophètes (Traduction partielle des "Fusûs al-Hikam" de Ibn 'Arabî). With an introduction by the translator. Paris, Albin Michel, 1955 and 1974.

Lettres d'un Maître Soufi (Traduction partielle des "Rasâ'il" de Moulay al-'Arabî ad-Darqâwî). With an Introduction by the translator. Milan: Archè, 1978; Paris: Dervy-Livres, 1978.

Books in English

An Introduction to Sufi Doctrine (translated from the French by D. M. Matheson). Lahore: Ashraf, 1959; Wellingborough, England: Thorsons, 1976.

Siena, City of the Virgin (translated from the German by Margaret Brown). Oxford: University Press, 1960.

Famous Illuminated Manuscripts (partial translation of *Von wunderbaren Büchern*). Olten and Lausanne: Urs Graf Verlag, 1964.

Sacred Art in East and West (translated from the French by Lord
    Northbourne). Bedfont, Middlesex, England: Perennial
    Books, 1967; Louisville, Kentucky: Fons Vitae, 2001;
    Bloomington, Indiana: World Wisdom Books, 2001.

Alchemy, Science of the Cosmos, Science of the Soul (translated from the
    German by William Stoddart). London: Stuart and Watkins,
    1967; Baltimore, Maryland: Penguin Books, 1972;
    Longmead, Shaftesbury, Dorset: Element Books, 1986;
    Louisville, Kentucky: Fons Vitae, 2001.

Moorish Culture in Spain (new edition, translated from the German
    by Alisa Jaffa and William Stoddart). Louisville, Kentucky:
    Fons Vitae, 1999.

Art of Islam: Language and Meaning (translated from the French by
    Peter Hobson). London: Islamic Festival Trust Ltd, 1976.

Mystical Astrology according to Ibn 'Arabî (translated from the French
    by Bulent Rauf). Sherbourne, England: Beshara, 1977;
    Louisville, Kentucky: Fons Vitae, 2002.

Fez, City of Islam (translated from the German by William
    Stoddart). Cambridge, England: Islamic Texts Society,
    1992.

Mirror of the Intellect: Essays on Traditional Science and Sacred Art
    (translated by William Stoddart). Cambridge, England:
    Quinta Essentia, 1987; Albany, NY: SUNY, 1987.

Chartres and the Birth of the Cathedral (translated by William
    Stoddart). Ipswich, England: Golgonooza Press, 1995;
    Bloomington, Indiana: World Wisdom Books, 1995.

The Universality of Sacred Art, a précis of *Sacred Art in East and West*
    by Ranjit Fernando, published in *The Unanimous Tradition*,
    Institute of Traditional Studies. Colombo, Sri Lanka: 1999.

Articles in English

"Principles and Methods of Traditional Art". In *Art and Thought*
    (Coomaraswamy Festschrift). London: Luzac, 1947.

"The Spirit of Islamic Art". *Islamic Quarterly* (London), December
    1954.

Foreword to *The Meaning of Icons* by Leonid Ouspensky and
    Vladimir Lossky (translated by E. Kadloubovsky and G. E.
    H. Palmer). Boston: The Boston Book and Art Shop, 1956;
    Crestwood, New York: St. Vladimir's Seminary Press, 1983.

"Insight into Alchemy". *Tomorrow*, Winter 1964; *Studies in Comparative Religion*, Summer–Autumn 1979.

"Cosmology and Modern Science". *Tomorrow*, Summer 1964, Autumn 1964, Winter 1965; also in *Sword of Gnosis* (edited by Jacob Needleman). Baltimore, Maryland: Penguin Books, 1974.

"Because Dante is Right". *Tomorrow*, Summer 1966.

"Perennial Values in Islamic Art". *Al-Abhath*, March 1967; *Studies in Comparative Religion*, Summer 1967; in *God and Man in Contemporary Islamic Thought*. Beirut: Centennial, 1972; in *Sword of Gnosis* (edited by Jacob Needleman). Baltimore, Maryland: Penguin Books, 1974.

"Islamic Surveys: Four Works by Seyyed Hossein Nasr". *Studies in Comparative Religion*, Winter 1968.

"The Symbolism of Chess". *Studies in Comparative Religion*, Spring 1969.

"Teilhard de Chardin (I)". *Studies in Comparative Religion*, Spring 1969.

"The Seven Liberal Arts and the West Door of Chartres Cathedral". *Studies in Comparative Religion*, Summer 1969; also Winter–Spring 1985.

"The Heavenly Jerusalem and the Paradise of Vaikuntha". *Studies in Comparative Religion*, Winter 1970.

"The Void in Islamic Art". *Studies in Comparative Religion*, Spring 1970; also Winter–Spring 1985.

"Note on the Prophet Mohammed". In *Dimensions of Islam* by Frithjof Schuon, pp. 69–70. London: Allen and Unwin, 1970; also in *Form and Substance in the Religions* by Frithjof Schuon, pp. 86-87. Bloomington, Indiana: World Wisdom Book, 2002.

"Arab or Islamic Art?". *Studies in Comparative Religion*, Winter 1971; also in *Sword of Gnosis* (edited by Jacob Needleman). Baltimore, Maryland: Penguin Books, 1974.

"Abstract Art in Ancient Fez". *Du* (Zürich), March 1972.

Foreword to *Geometric Concepts in Islamic Art* by Issam El-Said and Ayse Parman. London: Islamic Festival Trust Ltd, 1976.

"Introduction to Islamic Art" in *The Arts of Islam*, catalog to the special exhibition in the Hayward Gallery. London: The Arts Council of Great Britain, 1976.

"The Prayer of Ibn Mashîsh". *Studies in Comparative Religion*, Winter–Spring 1978; *Islamic Quarterly*, September 1978.

"The Return of Ulysses". *Parabola,* November 1978.

"Concerning the 'Barzakh'". *Studies in Comparative Religion,* Winter–Spring 1979.

"Fez". In *The Islamic City,* UNESCO, Paris, 1980, pp. 166–176.

Preface to R. W. J. Austin's translation of Ibn 'Arabî's *The Bezels of Wisdom* (Fusûs al-Hikam). London: S.P.C.K., 1980; Ramsey, New Jersey: The Paulist Press, 1980.

"The Sacred Mask". *Studies in Comparative Religion,* Winter–Spring 1980.

"Teilhard de Chardin (II)". In *The Destruction of the Christian Tradition* by Rama Coomaraswamy, pp. 211–212. Bedfont, Middlesex, England: Perennial Books, 1981.

"The Role of Fine Arts in Muslim Education". In *Philosophy, Literature and Fine Arts* (edited by Seyyed Hossein Nasr). Sevenoaks, Kent, England: Islamic Education Series, 1982.

"Traditional Science". *Studies in Comparative Religion,* Winter–Spring 1984.

"The Spirituality of Islamic Art". In *The Encyclopedia of World Spirituality,* vol. 20 (edited by Seyyed Hossein Nasr). London: Routledge and Kegan Paul, 1987; also in *Islamic Spirituality: Manifestations* (edited by Seyyed Hossein Nasr). New York: Crossroad, 1991; London: SCM Press, 1991.

"The Universality of Sacred Art" (a précis of *Sacred Art in East and West).* In *The Unanimous Tradition* (edited by Ranjit Fernando). Colombo, Sri Lanka: Institute of Traditional Studies, 1999.

"What is Conservatism?" ("The Conservative Man"). *Avaloka,* vol 5, no's. 1 & 2, Winter 1990; also in *Sacred Web,* no. 3, Summer 1999.

"Degrees of Symbolism in Islamic Art". *Sophia,* vol. 5, no. 2, Winter 1999.

Translations from Arabic into French and then into English

Letters of a Sufi Master (partial translation of the "Rasâ'il" of Mulay al-'Arabî ad-Darqâwî). Bedfont, Middlesex: Perennial Books, 1973; Louisville, Kentucky: Fons Vitae, 2000.

The Wisdom of the Prophets (partial translation of "Fusûs al-Hikam"
by Ibn 'Arabî; translated from the French by Angela
Culmme-Seymour). Sherbourne, England: Beshara, 1975.
Universal Man (partial translation of "Insân al-Kâmil" by 'Abd al-
Karîm al-Jîlî; translated from the French by Angela
Culmme-Seymour). Sherbourne, England: Beshara, 1983.

Books in Italian

L'Alchimia (translated from the German by Angela Terzani
Staude). Turin: Boringhieri, 1961; (translated from the
French by Ferdinando Bruno). Milan: Guanda, 1981.
Scienza moderna e Sagzza tradizionale (translated from the German
by Angela Terzani Staude). Turin: Borla, 1968.
Siena, Città della Vergine (translated from the German by Gisella
Burgisser). Milan: Archè, 1978.
L'Arte sacra in Oriente e Occidente (translated from the French by
Elena Bono). Milan: Rusconi, 1976.
Introduzione alle Dottrine esoteriche dell'Islam (translated from the
French by Barbara Turco). Rome: Edizioni Mediterranee,
1979.
Simboli (translated from the French by Elisabetta Bonfanti Mutti).
Parma: All'Insegna del Veltro, 1983.
Chiave spirituale dell'Astrologia musulmana (translated from the
French). Genoa: Basilisco, 1985.

Articles in Italian

"Una Chiave spirituale dell'Astrologia secondo Muhyiddin ibn
'Arabî". *Rivista di Studii Iniziatici*, Naples, August–October
1947.
Nota sul Profeta Mohamed. In *Forma e Sostanza nelle Religioni* di
Frithjof Schuon. Roma: Edizioni Mediterranee, 1984.

Translations from Arabic into French and then into Italian

L'Uomo Universale (translated from the French by Giorgio
Jannaccone). Rome: Edizioni Mediterranee, 1981.

La Sapienza del Profeti (translated from the French by Giorgio Jannaccone). Rome: Edizioni Mediterranee, 1987.

Lettere d'un Maestro Sufi (translated from the French by Giorgio Jannaccone). Milan: La Queste, 1987.

Books in Spanish

Alquimia (translated by Ana María de la Fuente). Barcelona: Plaza y Janés, 1971.

La Civilización Hispano-Árabe (translated by Rosa Kuhne Brabant). Madrid: Alianza Editorial, 1977.

Esoterismo Islámico (translated by Jesús García Varela). Madrid: Taurus Ediciones, 1980.

Sabiduría Tradicional y Ciencia Moderna (translated by Jordi Quingles and Alejandro Corniero). Madrid: Taurus Ediciones, 1980.

Símbolos (translated by Francesc Gutiérrez). Mallorca: José J. de Olañeta, 1982.

Clave espiritual de la astrología musulmana (translated by Victoria Argimón). Mallorca: José J. de Olañeta, 1982.

Principios y Métodos del Arte sagrado. Buenos Aires: 1984.

El Arte del Islam (translated by Tomás Duplá). Mallorca: José J. de Olañeta, 1988.

Ensallos sobre el conocimiento sagrado (translated by Esteve Serra). Mallorca: José J. de Olañeta, 1999.

Chartres y el nacimiento de la Catedral (translated by Esteve Serra). Mallorca: José J. de Olañeta, 1999.

Fez, ciudad del Islam (translated by Esteve Serra). Mallorca: José J. de Olañeta, 1999.

Espejo del Intelecto (translated by Esteve Serra). Mallorca: José J. de Olañeta, 2000.

Articles in Spanish

"El Simbolismo del Ajedrez". *Cielo y Tierra* (Barcelona), No. I, 1982.

"El Arte sagrado". *Cielo y Tierra* (Barcelona), No. 6, 1983/1984.

Index

The Perennial Philosophy

Series